Penguin Education

Attachment and Loss, Volume II
Separation: Anxiety and Anger

John Bowlby

John Bowlby

Attachment and Loss, Volume II

Separation: Anxiety and Anger

Penguin Books

Penguin Books Ltd,
Harmondsworth, Middlesex, England
Penguin Books, 625 Madison Avenue,
New York, New York 10022, U.S.A.
Penguin Books Australia Ltd,
Ringwood, Victoria, Australia
Penguin Books Canada Ltd, 2801 John Street,
Markham, Ontario, Canada L3R 1B4
Penguin Books (N.Z.) Ltd,
182–190 Wairau Road, Auckland 10, New Zealand

First published by The Hogarth Press and The Institute of Psycho-Analysis 1973
Published in Pelican Books 1975
Reprinted in Penguin Education 1978

This book is Volume 95 in
The International Psycho-Analytical Library

Made and printed in Great Britain by
Hazell Watson & Viney Ltd,
Aylesbury, Bucks
Set in Monotype Times

To Three Friends

Evan Durbin
Eric Trist
Robert Hinde

Contents

Contents

Contents

Contents

Preface

In the preface to the first volume of this work I describe the circumstances in which it was begun. Clinical experience of disturbed children, research into their family backgrounds, and an opportunity, in 1950, to read the literature and to discuss problems of mental health with colleagues in several countries led me, in a report commissioned by the World Health Organization, to formulate a principle: 'What is believed to be essential for mental health is that the infant and young child should experience a warm, intimate and continuous relationship with his mother (or permanent mother-substitute) in which both find satisfaction and enjoyment' (Bowlby 1951). To support this conclusion evidence was presented for believing that many forms of psychoneurosis and character disorder are to be attributed either to deprivation of maternal care or to discontinuities in a child's relationship with his mother figure.

Though the contents of the report proved controversial at the time, most of the conclusions are now accepted. What has plainly been missing, however, is an account of the processes through which the many and varied ill effects attributed to maternal deprivation or to discontinuities in the mother–child bond are brought into being. It is this gap that my colleagues and I have since striven to fill. In doing so we have adopted a research strategy that we believe is still too little exploited in the field of psychopathology.

In their day-to-day work, whether with disturbed children, disturbed adults, or disturbed families, clinicians have of necessity to view causal processes backwards, from the disturbance of today back to the events and conditions of yesterday. Though this method has yielded many valuable insights into possible pathogenic events and into the kinds of pathological process to which they appear to give rise, as a research method it has grave limitations. To complement it, a method regularly adopted in other branches of medical research is, having identified a possible pathogen, to study its effects prospectively. If the pathogen has been correctly identified and the studies of its effects in the short and long term are skilfully executed, it then becomes possible to describe the processes set in train by the pathogenic agent and also the ways by which they lead to the various consequent conditions. In such studies attention must be paid not only to the processes set in train by the pathogen but also to the very many conditions, internal and external to the organism, that affect their course. Only then can some grasp be had of the particular processes, conditions, and sequences that lead from a potentially pathogenic occurrence to the particular types of disturbance with which the clinician was in the first place concerned.

In adopting a prospective research strategy my colleagues and I early became deeply impressed by the observations of our colleague, James Robertson, who had recorded, both on paper and on film, how young children in their second and third years of life respond while away from home and cared for instead in a strange place by a succession of unfamiliar people, and also how they respond during and after return home to mother (Robertson 1952; 1953; Robertson and Bowlby 1952). During the period away, perhaps in residential nursery or hospital ward, a young child is usually acutely distressed for a time and is not easily comforted. After his return home he is likely to be either emotionally detached from his mother or else intensely clinging; as a rule a period of detachment, either brief or long depending mainly on length of separation, precedes a period during which he becomes strongly demanding of his mother's presence. Should a child then come to believe, for any reason, that there is risk of a further separation he is likely to become acutely anxious.

Reflecting on these observations we concluded that 'loss of mother figure, either by itself or in combination with other variables yet to be clearly identified, is capable of generating responses and processes that are of the greatest interest to psychopathology'. Our reason for this belief was that the responses and processes observed seemed to be the same as those found to be active in older individuals who are still disturbed by separations they have suffered in early life. These comprise, on the one hand, a tendency to make intensely strong demands on others and to be anxious and angry when they are not met, a condition common in individuals labelled neurotic; and, on the other, a blockage in the capacity to make deep relationships, such as is present in affectionless and psychopathic personalities.

From the start an important and controversial issue has been the part played in the responses of children to separation from mother by variables other than that of separation *per se*; these include illness, the strange surroundings in which a child finds himself, the kind of substitute care he receives while away, the kind of relations he has both before and after the event. It is plain that these factors can greatly intensify, or in some cases mitigate, a child's responses. Yet evidence is convincing that presence or absence of mother figure is itself a condition of the greatest significance in determining a child's emotional state. The issue is already discussed in Chapter 2 of the first volume, where a description is given of some of the relevant findings, and is taken up again in the first chapter of this one, where attention is given to the results of a foster-care project undertaken in recent years by James and Joyce Robertson in which they 'sought to create a separation situation from which many of the factors that complicate institutional studies were eliminated; and in which the emotional needs of the children would be met as far as possible by a fully available substitute mother' (Robertson and Robertson 1971).[1] Study of the Robertsons' findings has led to some modification of views expressed in earlier publications, in which insufficient weight was given to the influence of skilled care from a familiar substitute.

In parallel with the empirical studies of my colleagues, I have myself been engaged in studying the theoretical and clinical implications of the data. In particular, I have been trying to sketch a schema able to comprehend data derived from a number of distinct sources:

(a) observations of how young children behave during periods when they are away from mother and after they return home to her;

1. In addition to their written report the Robertsons have published a series of films on the children fostered, particulars of which are given in the list of references at the end of this volume.

(b) observations of how older subjects, children and adults, behave during and after a separation from a loved figure, or after a permanent loss;

(c) observations of difficulties found during clinical work with children and adults who, during childhood or adolescence, have either experienced a long separation or a loss or had grounds to fear one; these include various forms of acute or chronic anxiety and depression, and difficulties of every degree in making and maintaining close affectional bonds, whether with parent figures, with members of the opposite sex, or with own children.

First steps towards formulating a theoretical schema were taken in a series of papers published between 1958 and 1963. The present three-volume work[2] is a further attempt at a formulation.

Volume 1, *Attachment*, is devoted to problems originally tackled in the first paper of the series, 'The Nature of the Child's Tie to his Mother' (1958b). In order effectively to discuss the empirical data regarding the development of that tie and to formulate a theory to account for it, it proved necessary to discuss first the whole problem of instinctive behaviour and how best to conceptualize it. In doing so I drew heavily on findings and ideas contributed by ethologists and also on ideas derived from control theory.

This, the second volume, deals mainly with problems of separation anxiety and covers ground originally tackled in two further papers of the original series, 'Separation Anxiety' (1960a) and 'Separation Anxiety: A Critical Review of the Literature' (1961a). Once again, in order to comprehend better the problems before us – the distress occurring during a separation and the anxiety often evident after it – it has proved desirable first to discuss a broad range of related phenomena and theory, notably the various forms of behaviour taken to be indicative of fear and the nature of the situations that commonly elicit fear. This discussion occupies Part II of the volume; it provides a background against

2. In the preface to the first volume I refer only to a second volume. During further work, however, it has become apparent that a third volume will be required.

which are considered, in Part III, the great differences in susceptibility to fear and anxiety that are found when one individual is
compared with another. Since many of the data required for the
completion of this task are missing, much extrapolation is necessary and the resulting picture is patchy. In some places it can be
painted in detail, in others only impressionistically. The aim is to
provide clinicians and others with principles on which they can
base their actions, and research workers with problems to explore
and hypotheses to test.

The third volume, *Loss*, will deal with problems of grief and
mourning and with the defensive processes to which anxiety and
loss can give rise. It will comprise a revision and amplification of
material first published in the remaining papers of the earlier
series – 'Grief and Mourning in Infancy and Early Childhood'
(1960b), 'Processes of Mourning' (1961b), and 'Pathological
Mourning and Childhood Mourning' (1963). Meanwhile two
colleagues, Colin Murray Parkes and Peter Marris, have written
books in which they approach problems of loss in a way close to
my own. The books are *Bereavement* by Parkes (1972) and *Loss
and Change* by Marris (1974).

In the preface to the first volume it was explained that the
frame of reference from which I start is that of psychoanalysis.
The reasons are several. The first is that my early thinking on the
subject was inspired by psychoanalytic work – my own and
others'. A second is that, despite all its limitations, psycho-
analysis and its derivatives remain by far the most used of any
present-day approach to psychopathology and psychotherapy. A
third and most important is that, whereas many of the central
concepts of my schema – object relations (better termed affectional bonds), separation anxiety, mourning, defence, trauma,
sensitive periods in early life – are the stock-in-trade of psychoanalytic thinking, until the last decade or two they have been
given scant attention by other behavioural disciplines.

Nevertheless, although the initial frame of reference is that of
psychoanalysis, there are many ways in which the theory advanced
here differs from the classical theories advanced by Freud and
elaborated by his followers. A number of these differences are

described already in the first chapter of the earlier volume. Others are referred to throughout the present volume, notably in Chapters 2, 5, and 16.

Preface to the Pelican edition

In preparing this edition I have taken the opportunity to correct a few minor inaccuracies and to refer to some recently published work. Brief additions are to be found at the end of Chapter 3 (footnote), in the first section of Chapter 9 (footnote), in the third section of Chapter 15, and in the third section of Chapter 21.

Acknowledgements

In the first volume of this work I listed the many colleagues and friends without whose help over the years these volumes could not have been written; and it is a great pleasure to express to them all once again my very warmest thanks. My debt to them is deep and lasting.

In the preparation of this volume I am indebted especially for help given by Robert Hinde, Mary Salter Ainsworth, and David Hamburg, each of whom read drafts of all or most of the material and offered a great many valuable criticisms and suggestions. James Robertson scrutinized the first chapter and proposed a number of improvements. Others who have contributed in different ways are Christoph Heinicke, Colin Murray Parkes, and Philip Crockatt. To all of them I am deeply grateful for the time and trouble they have given.

To the preparation of the script my secretary, Dorothy Southern, has again brought her customary care and enthusiasm. Library services have again been provided with unfailing efficiency by Ann Sutherland, and editorial assistance, similarly, by Rosamund Robson. The index has been prepared with great care by Lilian Rubin. To each of them my warmest thanks are due.

The many bodies that have supported the research for which I have been responsible at The Tavistock Institute of Human Relations since 1948 are listed in the first volume. Throughout the time that this volume has been in preparation I have been a part-time member of the External Scientific Staff of the Medical Research Council.

For permission to quote from published material, thanks are due to the publishers, authors, and others listed below. Bibliographical details of all the works cited in the text are given in the list of references at the end of the volume.

George Allen & Unwin Ltd, London, and Aldine Publishing Co., Chicago, in respect of *Four Years Old in an Urban Community*

Acknowledgements

by J. and E. Newson; Dr I. C. Kaufman, Dr L. A. Rosenblum, and *Science* in respect of 'Depression in Infant Monkeys Separated from their Mothers' (copyright 1967 by the American Association for the Advancement of Science); Methuen & Co. Ltd, London, in respect of 'Attachment and Exploratory Behaviour of One-year-olds in a Strange Situation' by M. D. S. Ainsworth and B. A. Wittig, in *Determinants of Infant Behaviour*, Vol. 4, edited by B. M. Foss; Dr R. F. Peck and Dr R. J. Havighurst in respect of *The Psychology of Character Development*, published by John Wiley & Sons, Inc., New York; University of Chicago Press, Chicago, in respect of *The Structure of Scientific Revolutions* by T. S. Kuhn; University of London Press Ltd, London, in respect of *Truancy* by M. J. Tyerman.

Acknowledgement is due also to Tavistock Publications Ltd, London, for permission to include, in Chapter 21 of this volume, material that appears in *Support, Innovation, and Autonomy* edited by R. Gosling; and to the *Journal of Child Psychology and Psychiatry* for permission to reproduce, as the basis of Appendix I, a paper that was first published in that journal in 1961.

Part I: Security, Anxiety, and Distress

Chapter 1
Prototypes of Human Sorrow

Unhappiness in a child accumulates because he sees no end to the dark tunnel. The thirteen weeks of a term might just as well be thirteen years.
– GRAHAM GREENE, *A Sort of Life*

Responses of young children to separation from mother[1]

A generation has now passed since Dorothy Burlingham and Anna Freud recorded their experiences of caring for infants and young children in the setting of a residential nursery. In two modest booklets published during the Second World War (Burlingham and Freud 1942; 1944) they describe the immense problem of providing for young children who are out of mother's care. In particular they emphasize how impossible it is in a nursery setting to provide a child with a substitute figure who can mother him as well as his own mother can. When the Hampstead Nurseries were reorganized so that each nurse could care for her own little group of children they tell how the children became strongly possessive of their nurse and acutely jealous whenever she gave attention to another child: 'Tony (3½) . . . would not allow Sister Mary to use "his" hand for handling other children. Jim (2–3) would burst into tears whenever his "own" nurse left the room. Shirley (4) would become intensely depressed and disturbed when "her" Marion was absent for some reason.'

Why, it may be asked, should these children have become so strongly possessive of their nurse and so deeply distressed whenever she was missing? Was it, as some traditionalists might suppose, that they had been spoiled by having been given too much attention and allowed too much their own way? Or was it, by contrast, that since leaving home they had been subjected to too

1. Although throughout this book the text refers usually to 'mother' and not to 'mother figure', it is to be understood that in every case reference is to the person who mothers a child and to whom he becomes attached. For most children, of course, this person is also his natural mother.

many changes of mother figure and/or had too limited access to whoever in the nursery was acting temporarily as their mother figure? On how we answer these questions turn all our practices of child-rearing.

Not only did children in these nurseries become intensely possessive and jealous of their 'own' nurse but they were also unusually prone to become hostile towards her or to reject her, or else to retreat into a state of emotional detachment, as the following records illustrate:

Jim was separated from a very nice and affectionate mother at 17 months and developed well in our nursery. During his stay he formed two strong attachments to two young nurses who successively took care of him. Though he was otherwise a well adjusted, active and companionable child, his behaviour became impossible where these attachments were concerned. He was clinging, over-possessive, unwilling to be left for a minute, and continually demanded something without being able to define in any way what it was he wanted. It was no unusual sight to see Jim lie on the floor sobbing and despairing. These reactions ceased when his favourite nurse was absent even for short periods. He was then quiet and impersonal.

Reggie, who had come to our house as a baby of 5 months, went home to his mother when he was 1 year 8 months, and has been with us ever since his return to the nursery 2 months later. While with us, he formed two passionate relationships to two young nurses who took care of him at different periods. The second attachment was suddenly broken at 2 years 8 months when his 'own' nurse married. He was completely lost and desperate after her departure, and refused to look at her when she visited him a fortnight later. He turned his head to the other side when she spoke to him, but stared at the door, which had closed behind her, after she had left the room. In the evening in bed he sat up and said: 'My very own Mary-Ann! But I don't like her.'

These observations, made in the pressure of wartime and recorded anecdotally with all too little detail, none the less cast a shaft of light on the nature of many forms of psychiatric disturbance. States of anxiety and depression that occur during adult years, and also psychopathic conditions, can, it is held, be linked in a systematic way to the states of anxiety, despair, and detachment described by Burlingham and Freud, and subsequently by others, that are so readily engendered whenever a young child is separated for long from his mother figure, whenever he expects such a separation, and when, as sometimes happens, he loses her altogether. Whereas during later life it is often extremely difficult to trace how a person's disturbed emotional state is related to his experiences, whether they be those of his current life or those of his past, during the early years of childhood the relationship between emotional state and current or recent experience is often crystal clear. In these troubled states of early childhood, it is held, can be discerned the prototype of many a pathological condition of later years.

It is, of course, a commonplace that most children who have had experiences of these kinds recover and resume normal development, or at least they appear to do so. Not infrequently, therefore, doubts are expressed whether the psychological processes described are in reality related so intimately to personality disturbances of later life. Pending much further evidence, these are legitimate doubts. Nevertheless, reasons for holding to the thesis are strong. One is that data from many sources can be arranged and organized into a pattern that is internally consistent and consistent also with current biological theory. Another is that many clinicians and social workers find the resulting schema enables them to understand better the problems with which they are grappling and so to help their patients or clients more effectively.

Why some individuals should recover, largely or completely, from experiences of separation and loss while others seem not to is a central question, but one not easily answered. In living creatures variation of response is the rule and its explanation is often hard to fathom. Of all those who contract poliomyelitis less than 1 per cent develop paralysis, and only a fraction of 1 per cent remain crippled. Why one person should respond one way and another another remains obscure. To argue that, because 99 per cent recover, polio is a harmless infection would obviously be absurd. Similarly, in the field under consideration, to argue that because most individuals recover from the effects of a separation or loss these experiences are of no account would be equally absurd.

Nevertheless the problem of differential response remains important. Conditions likely to be playing a part can be considered under two main heads:

(a) those intrinsic to or closely associated with the separation itself, notably the conditions in which a child is cared for while away from mother;

(b) those present in the child's life over a longer period, notably his relations with parents during the months or years before and after the event.

Here we consider variables in category (a). Those in category (b) are discussed in the later chapters of Part III.

We start by reviewing observations of how children behave when cared for in one of two very different settings. The first is an ordinary residential nursery, in which a child finds himself in a strange place with strange people none of whom is sufficiently available to give him more than very limited mothering. The second is a foster home in which a child receives the full-time and skilled care of a foster mother with whom he has become in some degree familiar beforehand.

Conditions leading to intense responses

In our early studies children were observed during stays in institutional settings and it was on the basis of these observations that the sequence of responses which we term protest, despair, and detachment came first to be delineated (Robertson and Bowlby 1952). Since then two further studies have been conducted by colleagues in the Tavistock Child Development Research Unit, the first by Christoph Heinicke (1956) and the second by Heinicke & Ilse Westheimer (1966). Although in each of these investigations only a handful of children were observed (six in the first and ten in the second), the studies are unique for the care of their design and the amount of systematic observation. Moreover, for each sample of separated children a contrast group was selected and observed: in the first study it was a fairly well-matched group of children observed during their first weeks of attendance at a day nursery; in the second it was a similarly matched group of children observed while living in their own homes. Heinicke & Westheimer treat their data statistically and also describe in some detail the behaviour of individual children.

In the larger investigation (1966), work was conducted in three residential nurseries. Arrangements and facilities were fairly similar. In each, a child belonged to a defined group of children and was cared for mainly by one or two nurses. Ample opportunities were available for free play either in large rooms or outdoors in a garden. Before a child entered the nursery, contact was made with the family by a psychiatric social worker (Ilse Westheimer), who was also responsible either then or later for collecting full information about the family and the child. Arrival at the nursery was observed; and in the course of his stay a child was observed during free play on six occasions each week. Each of the two observers (one male, Christoph Heinicke, and one female, Elizabeth Wolpert) observed for a period of at least half an hour during each of the three sample periods into which the week was broken (Monday and Tuesday; Wednesday and Thursday; Friday, Saturday, and Sunday). The method used, of categorizing behavioural units in terms of agent, object, relation, mode, and intensity, had been used in the earlier study and had been shown to be reliable.

In addition to the categorized observations of free behaviour, similarly categorized observations were made of every child's behaviour in standardized doll-play sessions; and a number of other records of each child's stay in the nursery were kept.

It was originally intended to select the separated children in accordance with the five criteria used in the first study, namely: (i) that the child had had no previous separations of more than three days, (ii) that he fell within the age-limits of fifteen to thirty months, (iii) that he did not enter the nursery with a sibling, (iv) that he was living with both mother and father at the time the separation occurred, and (v) that there was no evidence that being placed in a nursery indicated a rejection by his parents. Because of the difficulty of obtaining cases, however, these criteria had to be modified to allow greater latitude.

Although most of the children had had either no separations or only very brief ones prior to the one being studied, in one case the length of previous separation was four weeks and in two it was three weeks. The age-range was slightly extended and ran from thirteen to thirty-two months, instead of from fifteen to thirty months. But the most marked departure from the previous criteria was that four of the children entered the residential nursery in the company of a sibling: in three cases this was a four-year-old sibling and in one case the sibling was younger. The remaining two criteria remained unmodified: each of the children was living with both mother and father at the time of separation, and there were no indications that he was being rejected by the parents by being placed in the nursery.

The reason that the ten children studied were cared for in a residential nursery was that, in a family emergency, neither relatives nor friends were available to take temporary care of them. In the case of seven families, mother was to be away in hospital having a new baby. In two others mother was to be in hospital for some other form of medical attention. In the tenth case, the family became homeless.

Among much else in their book, *Brief Separations* (1966), Heinicke and Westheimer describe behaviour typical of the ten children during their time in the nursery, and, similarly, behaviour typical of the children after they had returned home. In the paragraphs that follow some of their principal findings are presented. Every one of the patterns reported had also been observed and recorded by Robertson during his earlier, less systematic though more extensive, studies.

Behaviour during Separation

The children arrived at the nursery in the care of one or both parents. Four of them, brought by father, stayed close to him and seemed already subdued and anxious. Some of the others, who had come with mother or both parents, seemed more confident and were ready to explore the new environment. They ventured forth on short or long excursions and then returned.

When the moment came for the parent(s) to depart, crying or screaming was the rule. One child tried to follow her parents, demanding urgently where they were going, and finally had to be pushed back into the room by her mother. Another threw himself on the floor and refused to be comforted. Altogether eight of the children were crying loudly soon after their parents' departure. Bedtime was also an occasion for tears. The two who had not cried earlier screamed when put in a cot and could not be consoled. Some of the others whose initial crying had ceased broke into renewed sobs at bedtime. One little girl, who arrived in the evening and was put straight to bed, insisted on keeping her coat on, clung desperately to her doll, and cried 'at a frightening pitch'. Again and again, having nodded off from sheer fatigue, she awoke screaming for Mummy.

Crying for parents, mainly for mother, was a dominant response especially during the first three days away. Although it decreased thereafter, it was recorded sporadically for each of the children for at least the first nine days. It was particularly common at bedtime and during the night. In the early hours of her second day of separation one child, Katie, aged eighteen months, awoke screaming and shouting for Mummy. She remained awake and continued to cry for mother until noon. During the early days away a visit from father led to renewed crying. Another little girl whose father visited her on the third day cried frantically and continuously for twenty minutes after he left.

Searching for mother occurred also and was particularly evident in Katie. After the first week, Katie stopped crying for mother and, instead, seemed content to sit on the nurse's lap watching television. From time to time, however, she demanded that they go upstairs. When asked what she hoped to find there her unhesitating reply was 'Mummy'.

Oriented as they were to their missing parents, these small children were in no mood either to cooperate with the nurses or to accept comfort from them. Initially the children refused to be dressed or undressed, refused to eat, refused the pot. During the first day all but one child, the youngest, refused to be approached, picked up, or comforted. After a day or two resistance abated, but even at the end of two weeks over one-third of the nurses' requests and demands were still being resisted.

Nevertheless, although resistance to the nurses continued to be frequent, the children also began occasionally to seek some sort of reassuring or affectionate response from them. At first these bids for affection were not discriminating but before the end of the second week a few children were beginning to exhibit preferences. For example, one little girl, Gillian, who had refused any dealings with the nurses during the early days, had by the sixth day singled out one nurse and seemed happy sitting on her lap. When the nurse left the room, moreover, Gillian looked longingly at the door. Even so Gillian's feelings for her nurse were not unmixed: when the nurse returned Gillian walked away.

The children's relations with the two research observers were also not unmixed. During the first day most of the children seemed friendly to at least one of the observers. Subsequently they made a point of avoiding the observers by moving away, turning their back, leaving the room, shutting their eyes, or burying their head in a pillow. Especially dramatic were certain occasions when a child broke into a panic the moment one of the observers entered the room. On seeing him, or her, a child might scream and run to cling to a nurse. Sometimes a child would show marked relief as soon as an observer had left.

Needless to say, the observers were as unobtrusive as possible. In general their role was not to initiate interaction but to respond in a friendly way whenever a child approached them. Nevertheless, part of the plan was that, fairly late during each of the observation periods, the observer 'actively though cautiously approached the child to see how he would react'. In later chapters of this volume (Chapters 7 and 8) it will be seen that, unwittingly, this plan resulted in conditions that, in combination, are likely to be especially frightening. In some degree, at least, the children's fear of the observers must be attributed to these circumstances.

All but one of the ten children brought with them to the nursery a favourite object from home. For the first three days or so they clung closely to their object and became extremely upset if a nurse, trying to be helpful, happened to take hold of it. Subsequently, however, the children's treatment of their favourite object changed: at one moment they would cling to it, at another throw it away. For instance, one little girl alternated between carrying her rag doll about in her mouth, like a mother cat with a kitten, and flinging it away shouting 'All gone'.

Hostile behaviour, though infrequent, tended to increase during the two weeks of observation. It often took the form of biting another child or ill-treating the favourite object brought from home.

A breakdown in sphincter control was usual. Of the eight children who had attained some degree of control before arriving in the nursery, all but one lost it. The exception, Elizabeth, aged two years eight months, was the oldest of the children.

Although certain kinds of behaviour were common to all or almost all the children, in other ways the children differed. For example, four were constantly active whereas two others preferred to stay in a single spot. A few rocked; others, who seemed constantly on the verge of tears, continually rubbed their eyes.

It will be recalled that four of the children entered the nursery with a sibling, in three cases a four-year-old child and in one case a younger one. As had been expected, the frequency and intensity of the responses typical of children staying in a residential nursery were much diminished in these children. They cried less and showed fewer outbursts of marked hostility. During the early days especially, siblings constantly sought each other's company, talked and played together. To outsiders they presented a united front, with exclamations such as 'She's not your sister, she's my sister'.

Behaviour at and after Reunion

Inevitably in a situation of this kind the length of time children remain away from home varies. In this study six children were away from twelve to seventeen days; the other four were away for weeks, the periods being seven, ten, twelve, and twenty-one weeks respectively. The ways in which the individual children responded when they returned home differed in many respects; and part of the difference was related to the length of time they had been away, a finding confidently forecast from the results of Robertson's earlier observations.

In this phase of the study two principal lessons learnt from earlier Tavistock studies were applied. The first was to make continuous first-hand observations of how a child responded on first meeting his mother again and during the next few hours. The second was to pay especial attention to a child's response to the visit to his home of an observer he had seen regularly in the nursery. Accordingly, with three research workers available, the following dispositions were made.

One worker, Ilse Westheimer, who had made contact with each of the families before a child went to the nursery, continued contact while the child was away, e.g. by visiting mother in hospital, and was on the spot to make observations when the child was reunited with his parents. Except for one brief visit, she avoided the children while they were in the nursery. In a complementary role, the two observers, Christoph Heinicke and Elizabeth Wolpert, who were responsible for all the observations made on the children in the nursery, took no part in liaising with the families; and they avoided visiting a child at home after he had returned there until a planned visit was made exactly sixteen weeks after his return.[2] (The only exception to this arrangement occurred because Ilse Westheimer was unavailable on one occasion when a child was returning home, and observation of the return was in this case made by Elizabeth Wolpert.)

In seven cases Ilse Westheimer met mother at the nursery, witnessed the meeting of child and mother, and then drove them home. In three others she met father at the nursery, witnessed the meeting of child and father, and drove the pair home to mother. (In one case they picked mother up on the way, at the hospital in which she had been a patient.)

On meeting mother for the first time after the days or weeks away every one of the ten children showed some degree of detachment. Two seemed not to recognize mother. The other eight turned away or even walked away from her. Most of them either cried or came close to tears; a number alternated between a tearful and an expressionless face.

In contrast to these blank, tearful retreats from mother, all but one of the children responded affectionately when they first met father again. Furthermore, five were friendly to Ilse Westheimer as well.

As regards detachment, two findings of earlier studies were

2. During the intervening sixteen weeks contact with the home was maintained by Ilse Westheimer, who also administered doll-play procedures during the sixth and the sixteenth weeks after reunion, and during the equivalent weeks for the control children.

clearly confirmed in this one. The first is that detachment is especially characteristic of the way in which a separated child behaves when he meets his mother again, and is much less evident with father; the second is that the duration of a child's detachment from mother correlates highly and significantly with the length of his time away.

In nine cases detachment from mother persisted in some degree almost throughout the first three days of reunion. In five children it was so marked that the mother of each complained, characteristically, that her child treated her as though she were a stranger; none of these children showed any tendency to cling to mother. In the other four, detachment was less pronounced: phases during which they turned away from mother alternated with phases during which they clung to her. Only one child, Elizabeth, who was the oldest and whose separation was among the shortest, was affectionate towards her mother by the end of the first day home. Both Elizabeth and the four who alternated soon showed that they were afraid to be left alone and became far more clinging than they had been before they had gone away.

There is reason to believe that after a very prolonged or repeated separation during the first three years of life detachment can persist indefinitely; the problems to which this gives rise will be discussed in Volume III. After briefer separations detachment gives way after a period lasting usually hours or days. It is commonly succeeded by a phase during which a child is markedly ambivalent towards his parents. On the one hand, he is demanding of their presence and cries bitterly if left; on the other, he may become rejecting, hostile, or defiant towards them. Of the ten children studied eight showed a noticeable degree of ambivalence, and in five of them it persisted for not less than twelve weeks. Among determinants of the length of time ambivalence lasts one of the most influential is likely to be the way a mother responds to it.

It will be evident from the descriptions given that when a child returns home after a period away his behaviour presents his parents, especially his mother, with great problems. How a mother responds depends on many factors: for example, the kind of relationship she had with the child before separation and whether she believes that a disturbed and demanding child is better treated with comfort and reassurance or with discipline. A variable to which Westheimer (1970) has drawn attention is the way in which a mother's feelings for her child may change in the course of a long separation from him, lasting many weeks or months, during which she does not see him. Warm feelings are apt to cool and family life to become organized on lines that leave no place into which the returning child can fit.

There is abundant evidence that after a child has been away from home in a strange place and in the care of strangers he is liable to be very frightened lest he be taken away again. This was borne in on Robertson during some of his early studies. Children who had been in hospital tended to panic, he found, at the sight of anyone in a white coat or nurse's uniform, and they indicated clearly their fear of being returned to hospital. Several children were apprehensive when Robertson himself visited them at home. They took care to avoid him and, provided they were not in a detached condition, clung close to mother.

In the Heinicke–Westheimer study one of the two observers who had been present in the nursery visited each child sixteen weeks after his return home. All the children seemed clearly to remember the observer and reacted with strong feeling; all but one made 'a desperate attempt' to avoid the observer. The mothers were much surprised that their child should be so afraid, and affirmed that other strangers who visited the house did not arouse such reactions.

The case of Josephine, who had been aged two years when she was in the nursery for thirteen days and was now aged two years and four months, illustrates the anxious hostile behaviour seen typically on the occasion of these visits.[3]

When CH approached the door of the suburban home, he could hear Josephine making all kinds of excited, joyous noises. As her mother opened the door, however, Josephine at once exclaimed 'No', ran over to the staircase, sat down, ejaculated another 'No', and then picked up the gollywog she had had in the nursery and threw it at the visitor. Mother, observer, and child

3. The case report is adapted and abridged from that given in Heinicke and Westheimer (1966).

then went to sit in the garden. Josephine could not sit still, however, and remained excited throughout. She pulled clothes off the line and began to throw them on the grass. Though this seemed deliberately provocative, her mother at first did nothing.

Josephine became more excited, ran about vigorously and repeatedly threw herself in the air and landed on her bottom, but she seemed to ignore any pain she may have inflicted on herself. Later she became aggressive towards her mother, threw herself at her and began to bite, first her mother's arm and then her necklace. Mother was surprised by this behaviour since nothing like it had occurred for some time, and she now restricted it.

Throughout this time Josephine had been afraid of the observer and had assiduously avoided him. When he walked towards her a very worried look came over her face, she cried 'Mummy' and went over to her. Although Josephine continued to react to any approach of the observer by running away, she would try to sneak up to him and to hit him on his back as long as he remained still. Sometimes she ran away and then turned towards him and hit him suddenly. Finally, while the observer sat quietly in one place, Josephine crept close enough to cover him with a small blanket, whereupon she exclaimed 'All gone'. She then uncovered him again.

Mother remarked that the way Josephine had treated the observer was quite different from the way she had treated other strangers, and she expressed surprise that Josephine should so anxiously avoid someone she had not seen for sixteen weeks.

Support for the view that the children were responding in a specially fearful way to the visitor they had known in the nursery comes from a comparison of their reactions with those of the matched group of children who had not been away. For the control group, a period of weeks was designated that was treated as the equivalent of the separated children's period of separation, and a succeeding period of weeks was treated as the equivalent of the separated children's period of reunion. During the period equivalent to separation, the control children were visited in their homes by either Christoph Heinicke or Elizabeth Wolpert who administered the same doll-play procedures as they had administered to the children in the nursery. In both samples each child was given either two or three such sessions. In the case of the separated children these were on the third and eleventh days of separation, and, when separation lasted more than three weeks, again a few days before return home. (In the case of all the control children sessions were given on the third, eleventh, and twenty-first days.) At the end of the sixteenth week of the period equivalent to reunion each of the control children was visited by one of the two workers who had administered the doll-play procedures, just as the separated children were. The response of the control children was quite different from that of the separated children. In every case the control children seemed to recognize the visitor and then approached.[4]

At one time it was supposed by critics of our thesis concerning separation that distress seen in a child during a period away from mother, and increased ambivalence and anxiety seen after it, must betoken an unfavourable relationship between child and mother before the event, or reflect perhaps a child's anxiety about his mother's pregnancy or illness. Yet observations of healthy children from thoroughly satisfactory homes, who are separated from mother for one of many different reasons, show that, whatever contribution other variables may make, when a young child is in a strange place with strange people and with mother absent, protest, despair, and detachment still occur. The only children so far observed in such conditions who appear undisturbed have been those who have never had any figure to whom they can become attached, or who have experienced repeated and pro-

4. It was not only at the sixteenth-week visit that the control children behaved differently towards the observer when compared with the separated children. When the control children were visited in their homes during the period equivalent to separation they treated CH and EW in a far more friendly way than the separated children had done, and nothing resembling panic was seen. It must be remembered, however, that, compared with the separated children, the control children had a very different experience of the observers during the period equivalent to separation. Whereas the separated children were observed six times each week during play in the nursery as well as given two (or three) doll-play sessions, the control children had only the three doll-play sessions. It is possible, therefore, that some part of the difference in the ways in which the two groups of children treated the observers was due to their different experiences of them.

longed separations and have already become more or less permanently detached.

There can be no doubt that a number of variables when combined with absence of mother figure increase the degree of disturbance seen. For example, the more strange the surroundings and the people, or the more painful any medical procedures, the more frightened a child is likely to be and the greater will be his disturbance, both during and after the separation. Again, however, observations of how very differently young children respond to any or all of these conditions when mother is with them make it clear that these conditions of themselves are not sufficient to cause more than transient distress and that, in determining the sequence of protest, despair, and detachment, a key variable is mother's presence or absence.

Conditions mitigating the intensity of responses

Among conditions known to mitigate the intensity of responses of young children separated from mother the two most effective appear to be:
– a familiar companion and/or familiar possessions
– mothering care from a substitute mother.
As would be expected, when these two conditions are combined, as commonly happens at home when a child is cared for by a grandmother, disturbance is at a minimum.

Heinicke and Westheimer (see p. 29 above) are among several observers who have noted that when a young child is in a residential nursery with a sibling his distress is alleviated, especially during the early days; and Robertson has noted that some comfort is obtained even when the sibling is only two years old and the younger of a pair. Thus the presence of a familiar companion, even when that companion provides a negligible degree of substitute mothering, is found to be a mitigating factor of some significance. Inanimate objects, such as favourite toys and personal clothes, are also known to provide some measure of comfort.

A second and important mitigating condition is the provision of substitute mothering. How effective this can be in reducing disturbance when given by a woman who is a stranger to the child is not systematically recorded. Much evidence of an unsystematic kind shows, however, that initially a young child is afraid of the stranger and rejects her attempts to mother him. Subsequently, he shows intense conflict behaviour: on the one hand he seeks to be comforted by her, on the other he rejects her as being strange. Only after a period of days or weeks may he become accustomed to the new relationship. In the meantime he continues to yearn for his missing mother figure and on occasion to express anger with her for being absent. (Examples of this sequence are given in Chapter 2 of the first volume.)

The period during which disturbance lasts turns partly on the skill of the foster mother in adapting her behaviour to that of a distressed and, at times, frightened and rejecting child, and partly on the age of the child. In one study (as yet reported only briefly) Yarrow (1963) found that every child aged between seven and twelve months was disturbed after being moved from a temporary foster home to a permanent adoptive home. Over this age-span, he found, the 'severity and pervasiveness of disturbance increases with increasing age'.

Thus, while distress is mitigated both by the presence of a familiar companion and by fostering from a motherly but strange woman, each arrangement has serious limitations.

An Experimental Project

In their study already referred to in the preface, James and Joyce Robertson (1971), combining the roles of observers and foster parents, took into their own home four young children who were in need of care while their mothers were in hospital. In doing so they were seeking to discover how young children of previous good experience respond in a separation situation that offers as many ameliorating conditions as are at present known about and possible to arrange, in particular, responsive mothering from a foster mother with whom the child has already become familiar.

For these purposes Joyce Robertson undertook to give each child her full-time care and, in doing so, to adopt so far as she could his mother's own methods of care. Every attention was given to minimizing the strangeness of the situation and to maximizing familiarity. During the month or so prior to the separation, the child was introduced to the foster home and to members of the foster family by means of a series of interchange visits between the families. Meanwhile, the foster mother did all she could to learn about the child's stage of development, his likes and dislikes, and his mother's methods of caring for him, in order to maintain during the fostering period as similar a régime as possible. On coming into care the child brought with him his own bed and blankets, his familiar toys and a photograph of his mother. Moreover, during the child's time away every effort was made to keep alive within him his image of his missing mother. The foster mother made a point of talking about her and showing the child her photograph. Father was encouraged to visit, daily if possible; and both father and foster mother did all they could to assure the child he would soon return home. In these ways everything possible was done to reduce the impact of change, to accept openly the child's concern over loss of his mother, and to assure him that it would not last longer than necessary.

In the event the Robertsons cared for four children, one at a time, in each case while mother was having a new baby. Ages and days in care are set out below:

Kate	2 years 5 months	27 days
Thomas	2 years 4 months	10 days
Lucy	1 year 9 months	19 days
Jane	1 year 5 months	10 days

All four were first children, had been and were living with both parents, and had not previously been separated from mother, except for an occasional few hours in the care of a familiar person.

The degree of disturbance seen in these children was far less than is seen in less favourable circumstances. Nevertheless each child was perceptibly upset. The form of disturbance in the two older children differed from that seen in the two younger. Although for much of the time Kate and Thomas seemed content with the fostering arrangements, both showed plainly that they missed their own mothers. In the brief accounts that follow, derived from Robertson and Robertson (1971), particular attention is given to the episodes when the children expressed discontent.

37

There is therefore some danger of the accounts giving an un-balanced picture.

Thomas, an active and friendly boy who talked well, settled happily with his foster parents. For most of the time he was good-humoured, in friendly contact with his caretakers, and able to enjoy play and activities offered. After two days, however, he began to express both sadness at his parents' absence and also anger about it. He talked much of his mother and sometimes cuddled her photograph. While he seemed to have some grasp of the temporary nature of the separation, as the days passed the situation clearly put increasing strain upon him. On occasion he rejected his foster mother's attentions and indicated that it was his mother's role to look after him: 'Don't cuddle me, my mummy cuddles me.' At the end of a visit from father, Thomas did his best to prevent him leaving, cried bitterly if briefly after he had gone and insisted that no one else should sit on his father's chair. At the end of his visit on the ninth day father summed up the strain of the situation in four words: 'We've both had enough.'

Although in the Robertsons' opinion Thomas came through the experience better than the other three children, and distur-bance after his return home was minimal, he seemed nevertheless to be more aggressive and defiant after it than he had been before. Moreover, when his foster mother visited his home, although he was friendly to her, he was also cautious and throughout made a point of staying close to his mother.

Kate, the other child of nearly two and a half, showed during her first ten days away many of the same features of behaviour as did Thomas. On the one side she ate and slept well, and was cheerful, active, and cooperative with her foster parents. On the other she expressed yearning for her absent parents and occasional anger with them for not taking her home. Owing to mother's obstetric complication, moreover, Kate was away nearly three time as long as Thomas. During the third and fourth weeks her relationship to the foster mother deepened and she seemed to be finding a niche for herself in the foster family. Nevertheless, her yearning for her own mother continued and was 'increasingly intermingled with anger'. Anger, directed at foster mother, was especially strong after Kate's two visits to see mother in hospital.

One other feature of Kate's behaviour during the separation is to be remarked. During the second week she became fearful of getting lost and began to cling. She also cried more easily and at times seemed preoccupied and dreamy. Her query 'What is Kate looking for?', made on one of these occasions, seems to indicate that her yearning and searching for mother, though continuing active in her, were beginning to undergo repression.

When eventually Kate returned home she at once greeted her mother and began to rebuild their relationship. By contrast, she completely ignored her foster mother who had looked after her for nearly four weeks, and who was sitting quietly by.

Although Kate settled back in her family with only slight upset, she was noticeably more demanding of her parents' attention. Moreover, her reaction to an episode that occurred two weeks after her return suggested strongly that she was intensely afraid of another separation. Mother was eager to ensure that, when Kate reached five, she would be able to go to a particular school; so mother took her there to be enrolled, over two years in advance. The following night Kate screamed as though with nightmares and in the morning was acutely breathless. When the doctor, who diagnosed bronchial asthma, inquired about stress, mother realized that, during talk at the school the previous day, the head had agreed to 'take' Kate.

Neither of the two younger children had much language capacity and neither could be helped as much as the two older ones to keep the absent mother clearly in mind. Perhaps because of this, each child seemed to transfer attachment from mother to substitute comparatively easily and to find security in the new arrangement. Neither child showed acute upset. Both continued to function well, learnt new skills, and increased their vocabularies. Yet for both children it was evident that all was not well. By her fourth day away Jane had become restless and demanding of attention and gave the impression of 'a child who was under strain and at times bewildered'. Lucy, similarly, had her bad patches and by the nineteenth day away is described as being 'in a highly sensitive state'.

In these little girls explicit yearning for the missing mother and being angry with her occurred only sporadically, and then only in response to specific reminders of her. Jane, for example, on her sixth day of separation noticed the gate of her own garden, opened it and entered, and tried unsuccessfully to open the door of her parents' apartment. Returning, she spoke the word 'Mama' for the first time and also resisted entering the foster home. Jane's relations with her father deteriorated as the separation progressed. At first she played happily when he visited, then she got angry with him and, finally, she seemed pointedly to ignore him, only to cling and cry when he made to leave. Lucy's relations with her father went through much the same sequence. After one visit when he had taken her to a park near their home, she became very distressed after his departure; at first she refused to be comforted by her foster mother and subsequently clung tearfully to her and refused to be put down.

On reunion each of these younger children recognized mother immediately and responded pleasurably to her. Unlike the two older children, however, they seemed reluctant to relinquish the foster mother. Lucy in particular had difficulty in weaning herself from her and later showed marked conflict in relation to her. For example, during foster mother's visit three days after returning home Lucy 'oscillated between affection and apprehension, smiling and frowning, clinging to her mother yet crying bitterly when foster mother left'. Like Thomas and Kate, both these younger children were more hostile to mother after the separation than they had been before it (though presumably in each case this could have been due in some degree to the presence of a new baby).

Interpretation of Findings

All these children, then, showed far less distress than occurs when young children are separated from mother in less favourable conditions, yet all four showed unmistakable signs of strain and from time to time that they were aware of missing mother. In the interpretation of these responses there is some difference of opinion. The Robertsons, impressed by the fact that care by a responsive substitute mother in a benign environment holds anxiety at a 'manageable level' and permits 'positive development' to continue, believe that the onset of the deteriorative sequence of protest, despair, and detachment can be prevented. This leads them to the view that the responses shown by children fostered in this way are qualitatively different from those of institutionalized children, and cannot be understood as representing a difference of intensity only. An alternative view, however, is that the sequence of protest, despair, and detachment, although greatly reduced in intensity and curtailed, cannot be regarded as absent. In the two older children, for example, the pattern of response, though at low intensity, showed very plainly most of the elements now known to be typical of how young children respond during and after a brief separation in less cushioned conditions – yearning and searching for the missing mother, sadness, increasing protest at her absence and growing anger with her for staying away, increased ambivalence on return home, and evident fear of being separated again. Thanks to the precautions taken despair was admittedly held at bay and with it detachment, though signs suggestive of the latter were seen in Kate. In the two younger children the pattern of response was less clear, but several typical elements were none the less present. This leads to the conclusion that the differences in response between the fostered children and children removed to an institution are properly regarded as differences of intensity.

There are other ways in which the Robertsons contrast their theoretical position with the one I adopt, notably as regards the role of grief and mourning in early childhood. These issues will be discussed in the third volume. Meanwhile it is important to note that, whatever differences there may be between the Robertsons and myself in regard to theory, there are none in practice. For, when the Robertsons come to consider the practical lessons to be derived from their project, they warn that, because these carefully fostered children came through so well, it must not be assumed that the hazards of separation during the early years can be eliminated entirely. On the contrary, they state, their experience has served to reinforce them in the view, which we have long shared, that 'separation is dangerous and whenever possible should be avoided'.

Presence or absence of mother figure: a key variable

From the Robertsons' recent study and the many others now on record two main conclusions can be drawn:

1. The sequence of *intense* protest, followed by despair and detachment, which first caught our attention, is due to a combination of factors, of which the kernel is the conjunction of strange people, strange events, and an absence of mothering either from mother herself or from a capable substitute.

2. Because separation from mother figure even in the absence of these other factors still leads to sadness, anger, and subsequent anxiety in children aged two years and over, and to comparable though less differentiated stress responses in younger ones, separation from mother figure is in itself a key variable in determining a child's emotional state and behaviour.

By 'mother figure' is meant that person to whom a child directs his attachment behaviour by preference; and by 'substitute mother' is meant any other person to whom a child is willing temporarily to direct attachment behaviour. Since, however, an individual as he grows older directs attachment behaviour to others besides mother or someone acting as a substitute mother, it is convenient to have available terms that are less specifically tied to the child–parent relationship. Among terms used here in a generic way to cover anyone towards whom attachment behaviour is directed are 'attachment figure' and 'support figure'.

'Presence' and 'absence' are relative terms and, unless defined, can give rise to misunderstanding. By presence is meant 'ready accessibility', by absence 'inaccessibility'. The words 'separation' and 'loss' as used in this work imply always that the subject's attachment figure is inaccessible, either temporarily (separation) or permanently (loss).[5]

Not only here but elsewhere also, finding suitable language is a

5. The present usage of the word separation should be distinguished from the very different usage of Mahler (1968) who employs it to describe an intrapsychic process which results in 'differentiation of the self from the symbiotic object'. Prior to this development a psychological 'state of undifferentiation, of fusion with mother', termed symbiosis, is postulated.

problem. For example, how long is a temporary separation? Plainly the answer turns on the subject's age. Thus what might seem interminable to a one-year-old might seem insignificant to a schoolchild. What might seem interminable to a schoolchild might seem of no great significance to an adult. Another problem, and one that is more difficult, is to know at what point a separation that started as temporary becomes permanent – or at least becomes conceived by the victim and by others as being so.

Yet a further difficulty turns on the fact that a mother can be physically present but 'emotionally' absent. What this means is that, although present in body, a mother may be unresponsive to her child's desire for mothering. Such unresponsiveness can be due to many conditions – depression, rejection, preoccupation with other matters – but, whatever its cause, so far as her child is concerned she is no better than half-present. Then again a mother can use threats to abandon a child as a means of disciplining him, a tactic that probably has an immeasurably greater pathogenic effect than is yet recognized.

These and other problems are discussed in later chapters. Meanwhile, the thesis can be phrased more precisely. Whether a child or adult is in a state of security, anxiety, or distress is determined in large part by the accessibility and responsiveness of his principal attachment figure.

There have been, and still are, clinicians and others interested in children who have found it difficult to believe that accessibility or inaccessibility of attachment figure can of itself be a crucial variable in determining whether a child (or an adult for that matter) is happy or distressed. One reason for disbelief is the supposition that, when there is nothing 'objective', namely intrinsically painful or dangerous, for a child or adult to be distressed about or afraid of, any distress or anxiety must be irrational and, if irrational, is to be deemed neurotic. Other reasons derive from a faulty theory of the nature of instinctive behaviour, and especially from failure to distinguish causation from function (see Volume I, Chapters 6 and 8). Others again derive from the many confusions and false value judgements to which the concept of dependency gives rise (see Volume I, Chapter 12). Yet another and different sort of reason may be the sheer inconvenience in practical life of the facts of the case as they seem actually to be in comparison with what things would be like were every normal child to be happy and content with any care-taker whatever – provided she were kind. If children were only 'reasonable' in this regard, how much easier would life be!

In order to understand how some of the difficulties have arisen it is useful to consider how separation and loss have been treated in the psychoanalytic literature as situations of relevance to personality development and psychopathology. In particular, it is useful to examine the place given to separation in theories of anxiety, and the kinds of explanation that have been proposed to account for its influence. Some of these ideas are traced in the following chapter, and opportunity is taken to compare the standpoint adopted in these volumes with that adopted in more traditional psychoanalytic works.

Chapter 2
The Place of Separation and Loss in Psychopathology

A new pamphlet of mine, *Inhibitions, Symptoms and Anxiety*, is now being published. It shakes up much that was established and puts things which seemed fixed into a state of flux again. Analysts who above all want peace and certainty will be discontented at having to revise their ideas. But it would be rash to believe that I have now succeeded in finally solving the problem with which the association of anxiety with neurosis confronts us.

— SIGMUND FREUD[1]

Problem and perspective

From Freud's earliest studies of the aetiology of the neuroses until the end of his life, the twin problems of neurotic anxiety and defence were never far from his mind. Again and again he grappled with them, and on the various tentative solutions he offered rest his successive theoretical formulations. Since Freud's death, moreover, theories of anxiety and defence have continued to be the foundation-stones of psychoanalytic psychopathology; and it is through their espousing differing views on the nature and origins of these conditions that the several distinctive schools of psychoanalysis have come into being.

In Freud's earliest formulations there is no hint that anxiety arises from loss or threat of loss, or that defensive processes are evoked in conditions of intense anxiety. Only little by little, and mainly towards the end of his life, did Freud advance such views and, in so doing, bring his ideas on anxiety and defence into relation with his ideas on mourning which, until then, had been a significant but quite distinct strand in his thinking. A principal result of his new formulation was, as he rightly foresaw, to bring everything 'into a state of flux again'.

Although Freud himself at different periods of his life adopted a number of radically different theories in regard to anxiety,

1. Letter to Oskar Pfister, 3 January 1926 (see H. Meng and E. L. Freud 1963).

mourning, and defence, as have the various schools of thought that have grown up subsequently, each theory is based on data obtained by but a single method of inquiry. Data are derived from studying, in the analytic setting, a personality more or less developed and already functioning more or less well; and from these data an attempt is made to reconstruct the phases of personality that have preceded what is now seen. To many the resulting literature is as frustrating as it is stimulating. On the one hand, it is plainly dealing with problems that every sensitive clinician recognizes to be of central consequence for understanding and helping his patients; on the other, it presents a complex web of competing and often inconsistent theorizing without providing methods by which to sort grain from chaff.

What is attempted in these volumes is to approach the classic problems of psychoanalysis prospectively. The primary data are observations of how young children behave in defined situations; in the light of these data an attempt is made to describe certain early phases of personality functioning and, from them, to extrapolate forwards. In particular the aim is to describe certain patterns of response that occur regularly in early childhood and, thence, to trace out how similar patterns of response are to be discerned in the later functioning of the personality.[2]

Some of the essential data, as described in the previous chapter, can be summarized as follows. Whenever a young child who has had an opportunity to develop an attachment to a mother figure is separated from her unwillingly he shows distress; and should he also be placed in a strange environment and cared for by a succession of strange people such distress is likely to be intense. The way he behaves follows a typical sequence. At first he *protests* vigorously and tries by all the means available to him to recover his mother. Later he seems to *despair* of recovering her but none the less remains preoccupied with her and vigilant for her return. Later still he seems to lose his interest in his mother and to become emotionally *detached* from her. Nevertheless, provided the period of separation is not too prolonged, a child does not remain detached indefinitely. Sooner or later after being reunited

2. The point of view adopted is described at greater length in the first chapter of Volume I.

with his mother his attachment to her emerges afresh. Thenceforward, for days or weeks, and sometimes for much longer, he insists on staying close to her. Furthermore, whenever he suspects he will lose her again he exhibits acute anxiety.

When I came to examine the theoretical problems raised by these observations it was evident that the first step must be to gain a clearer understanding of the bond that ties child to mother. Next, it gradually became apparent that each of the three main phases of the response of a young child to separation is related to one or another of the central issues of psychoanalytic theory. Thus the phase of *protest* is found to raise the problem of separation anxiety; *despair* that of grief and mourning; *detachment* that of defence. The thesis that was then advanced (Bowlby 1960a) was that the three types of response – separation anxiety, grief and mourning, and defence – are phases of a single process and that only when they are treated as such is their true significance grasped.

A reading of the psychoanalytic literature shows that, as a rule, separation anxiety, mourning, and defence have been considered piecemeal. The reason for this is the inverted order in which their psychopathological significance was discovered: for it was the last phase that was recognized first, and the first last. Thus the significance of defence, particularly repression, was realized by Freud in the earliest days of his psychoanalytic work and provides the basis of his original theorizing: his first paper on the subject is dated 1894 ('The Neuro-psychoses of Defence', *SE* 3).[3] His grasp of the roles of grief and of separation anxiety, on the other hand, was at that time still fragmentary. Although he was early alive to the place of mourning in hysteria and melancholia (see note of 1897 to Fliess, *SE* 14: 240), twenty years were to elapse before, in 'Mourning and Melancholia' (1917a, *SE* 14), he gave it systematic attention. Similarly in the case of separation anxiety: although in the *Three Essays on the Theory of Sexuality* (1905b) he gave it a paragraph (*SE* 7: 224) and in the *Introductory Lectures*

3. The abbreviation *SE* denotes the Standard Edition of *The Complete Psychological Works of Sigmund Freud*, published in 24 volumes by the Hogarth Press Ltd, London. All quotations from Freud in the present work are taken from this edition.

(1917b) three pages (*SE* **16**: 405–8), it is not until 1926 that in his revolutionary late work *Inhibitions, Symptoms and Anxiety* he accorded it the central place in what was to be his final theory of anxiety. 'Missing someone who is loved and longed for', he there affirms, is 'the key to an understanding of anxiety' (*SE* **20**: 136–7).[4]

The reason for this inverse recognition of the three phases is clear: always in the history of medicine it is the end-result of a pathological sequence that is noted first. Only gradually are the earlier phases identified, and it may be many years before the exact sequence of the whole process is understood. Indeed it was understanding the sequence that baffled Freud longest. Does defence precede anxiety, or anxiety defence? If the response to separation is pain and mourning, how can it also be anxiety? (*SE* **20**: 108–9 and 130–1.) During the thirty years of his main psychoanalytic explorations, it can now be seen, Freud traversed the sequence backwards, from end-result to initial stage. Not until his seventieth year did he clearly perceive separation and loss as a principal source of the processes to which he had devoted half a lifetime of study. But by then others of his ideas were already firmly established.

By 1926 a substantial corpus of psychoanalytic theory was already being taught. As regards anxiety, castration anxiety and superego anxiety were corner-stones of thought and practice in Vienna and elsewhere; also, Melanie Klein's hypothesis relating anxiety to aggression had recently been formulated and, linked to the concept of the death instinct, was soon to become a key concept in a significant new system. The full weight of Freud's ideas on separation anxiety and its relation to mourning came too late to influence the development of either of these two schools of thought.

Apart from an early reference by Hug-Hellmuth (1913) and a brief word by Bernfeld (1925), moreover, some years were to pass before the clinical papers drawing attention to the pathogenic significance of separation experiences were published. Some of

4. For an account of the development of Freud's theories of anxiety, see Strachey's introduction to the Standard Edition of *Inhibitions, Symptoms and Anxiety* (1959, *SE* **20**: 77–86); see also Appendix I to this volume.

the earliest, by Levy (1937), Bowlby (1940; 1944), and Bender and Yarnell (1941), presented empirical evidence suggesting an aetiological relationship between certain forms of psychopathic personality and severely disrupted mother–child relationships. At about the same time, Fairbairn (1941; 1943) was basing his revised psychopathology on separation anxiety, having been preceded by Suttie (1935) and to be followed a few years later by Odier (1948); Therese Benedek (1946) was describing responses to separation, reunion, and bereavement as observed in adults during the Second World War; and Dorothy Burlingham and Anna Freud (1942; 1944) were recording their first-hand observations (cited in Chapter 1 above) of how young children respond to separation. In addition, studies of a different though related kind, concerned with the effects on infants of being raised without any mother figure, were being conducted by Goldfarb (1943 and later) and by Spitz (1946).

Nevertheless, despite all this work, separation anxiety has been extremely slow to gain a central place in psychoanalytic theorizing. Indeed Kris, writing as a participant in the Viennese scene, remarked in later years how, when in 1926 Freud advanced his views regarding separation anxiety, 'there was no awareness among analysts . . . to what typical concrete situations this would apply. Nobody realized that the fear of losing the object and the object's love were formulae to be implemented by material which now seems to us self-evident beyond any discussion' (Kris 1956). He acknowledged that only in the preceding decade had he himself recognized the significance of such fears, and could have added that even when he wrote there were schools of analytic thought that failed to recognize their importance. The long-continued neglect of separation anxiety is well illustrated by an authoritative survey of 'the concept of anxiety in relation to the development of psychoanalysis' (Zetzel 1955) in which it is not once mentioned; and even in a recent book by Rycroft (1968a) it is given scant attention.

In the event, it is clear, some of the ideas Freud advanced in *Inhibitions, Symptoms and Anxiety* fell on stony ground. This was a pity, since in that book, written at the end of his professional life, he was struggling to free himself of the perspective of his

S.A.A. – 3

travels – defence, mourning, separation anxiety – and instead to view the sequence from his new vantage-point: the priority of separation anxiety. In his concluding pages he sketches out a new route: anxiety is the reaction to the danger of losing the object, the pain of mourning the reaction to the actual loss of object, and defence a mode of dealing with anxiety and pain.

The route finally taken by Freud is also the route followed in this work. Yet, for reasons that emerge more clearly in Chapter 5, the perspective in which the route is viewed is in many respects very different from the perspective adopted by Freud and adopted too by most of his followers. A principal reason for this difference is that, whereas the perspective adopted here is based on a Darwinian-type theory of evolution, that of Freud is not.

Separation anxiety and other forms of anxiety

The fact that in his later years Freud came to see separation anxiety as the key to the whole problem of neurotic anxiety does not mean that he was right. The term 'anxiety' has been used in very many ways to cover what may well prove to be a range of widely heterogeneous states. The term 'neurotic anxiety' is also ill defined and may also cover a range of heterogeneous states, perhaps of very diverse origin. In this complex scene the place of separation anxiety is still unclear. In particular, it remains uncertain how large a contributor it is to sources of neurosis in comparison with anxieties and fears of different origin.

Eager though every clinician must be to have these matters clarified, the task is outside the compass of this work. No attempt is made to present a general theory of anxiety. Nor is any attempt made to judge how a better understanding of separation anxiety can aid such a project. Those are tasks for the future.

What is attempted here is more limited. Young children are upset by even brief separations. Older children are upset by longer ones. Adults are upset whenever a separation is prolonged or permanent, as in bereavement. A pile of clinical reports, moreover, starting with Freud's early studies of hysteria and swelling to increasing volume in recent years, shows that experiences of separation and loss, occurring recently or years before, play a weighty role in the origin of many clinical conditions. These are grounds enough for concentrating attention on our problem.

Study of the problem suggests, indeed, that Freud was probably mistaken in claiming that missing someone who is loved and longed for is *the* key to an understanding of anxiety. As likely as not there is no single key: fear and anxiety are aroused in situations of many kinds. What seems certain, nevertheless, is that missing someone who is loved and longed for is *one* of the keys we need, and that the particular form of anxiety to which separation and loss give rise is not only common but leads to great and widespread suffering. That being so, let us grasp the key at hand and see what doors it opens.

A challenge for theory

Once we are aware of the form and sequence of the very intense responses that can result from a separation lasting a few days or longer, we become alert also to the form and sequence of the comparable but far less intense responses that are to be seen in young children during the course of everyday living. For example, we notice that in the presence of a responsive mother figure an infant or young child is commonly content; and, once mobile, is likely to explore his world with confidence and courage. In her absence, by contrast, an infant is likely, sooner or later, to become distressed; and he then responds to all sorts of slightly strange and unexpected situations with acute alarm. Furthermore, when his mother figure is departing or cannot be found, he is likely to take action aimed at detaining her or finding her; and he is anxious until he has achieved his goal.

Elemental though these data are, and well known to every perceptive mother, it yet remains true that within this bare catalogue of routine sequences of behaviour there lies a cauldron of controversy. Why should a child be distressed in his mother's absence? What is he afraid of? Why should he be anxious when she is missing and cannot be found? Why is he apprehensive lest she leave him again?

The psychoanalytic literature is strewn with attempts to answer these questions and no fewer than six types of theory can be discerned. Two theories, namely Rank's birth-trauma theory (1924) and Freud's signal theory (1926a), were developed explicitly to account for the observation that a young child is anxious when his mother leaves him. Another three, namely Freud's earlier theory of transformed libido (1905b) and both of Klein's theories, of persecutory and depressive anxiety (1934; 1935), had different origins and came only later to be applied to the problem of separation anxiety. All these five theories, however, are distinctly complex since in each case the author rules out of court the idea that absence of mother could, in and of itself, be the real cause of the distress and anxiety seen. Consequently each author feels constrained to search for a reason of some other kind or else applies a theory developed in another context. Only occasionally has a student of the problem accepted the data at their face value and presented a theory of a sixth type, one that regards the distress and subsequent anxiety as primary responses not reducible to other terms and due simply to the nature of a child's attachment to his mother. Among those who have advanced this view are Suttie (1935), Hermann (1936), and, with some qualifications, Fairbairn (1943; 1963) and Winnicott (e.g. 1952). Half a century earlier, it is interesting to note, William James (1890) had recorded his view that 'The great source of terror in infancy is solitude'.

The very similar generalization made by Freud in 1905, and quoted at the head of the next chapter, shows that he was early aware of the data. Indeed, as Strachey makes apparent in his introduction to the Standard Edition of *Inhibitions, Symptoms and Anxiety* (*SE* 20: 77–86), from that time onwards the anxiety manifested by a young child when separated from his mother is constantly in Freud's mind and he returns to it repeatedly whenever he makes a further attempt to solve the problem of anxiety. Nevertheless, because the basic postulates from which he began his theorizing biased him in other directions, Freud himself never adopted a theory of the sixth type.

These varied attempts to account for the phenomena of separation anxiety are not only of historical interest but of great practical importance, because each theory gives rise to a different model of personality functioning and psychopathology and, in consequence, to significantly different ways of practising psycho-therapy and preventive psychiatry. Because of their continuing and living influence, a detailed review of psychoanalytic theories of separation anxiety is presented in Appendix I. Some of the assumptions on which they rest are evaluated in Chapter 5 in the light of present knowledge of biology and ethology.

Before discussing theory further, however, it is useful to con-sider additional observations of behaviour during and after separation, starting with the behaviour of human children and proceeding thence to a comparison with the behaviour of young of other species. In all the studies to be described, it must be emphasized, either mother leaves child or child is removed more or less unwillingly from mother. The very different behaviour seen in the reverse situation, in which mother remains in a known place while child explores, is described already in the first volume (Chapter 13) and is the subject of papers by Anderson (1972a, b, c) and Rheingold and Eckerman (1970). Provided a child initiates the movement himself, in the certain knowledge of where mother can be found, he is not only content but often adventurous. In what follows the word 'separation' always implies that the initiative is taken either by mother or by some third party.

Chapter 3
Behaviour with and without Mother: Humans

Anxiety in children is originally nothing other than an expression of the fact that they are feeling the loss of the person they love.
– SIGMUND FREUD (1905b)

Naturalistic observations

Chapter 1 presented data concerning the behaviour of young children when they are away from home and placed for days or weeks either in a residential nursery or in a foster home. Here, by contrast, we are concerned with separation situations of much shorter duration. We begin with separations lasting from a day to a few hours, all requiring a child to be in a strange place with strange people and without substitute mothering.

A number of psychologists have made records of the behaviour of young children when they first enter nursery school or go to a research centre for examination. In so doing the psychologists have, usually without intending it, amassed evidence that to start nursery school much before the third birthday is for most children an undesirably stressful experience. The records, indeed, make it apparent that ignorance of the natural history of attachment behaviour, coupled with a misguided enthusiasm that small children should quickly become independent and 'mature', has resulted in practices that expose children, and their parents, to a great deal of unnecessary anxiety and distress. Nevertheless, for scientific purposes the resulting records have the great advantage that there is no danger that the degree of upset has been exaggerated; indeed the reverse is probably the case.

The first and largest study of this kind seems to have been undertaken by Shirley at the Harvard School of Public Health (Shirley and Poyntz 1941; Shirley 1942). In this study, 199 children (101 boys and 98 girls) between the ages of two and eight years were observed in the course of an all-day visit to a research centre, during which they were subjected to a variety of psychological and medical examinations, interspersed with periods for play, meals, and rest. The children were without mother throughout the day. The authors express the belief that 'the responses of these children to separation from their mothers were fairly typical for children who are cared for predominantly by their mothers during their pre-school period'.

All children visited the centre at six-monthly intervals; and any one child attended over a period of about three years. Age at starting varied: twenty-five paid their first visit at two years, a further twenty-eight at two and a half, and other batches at each half-year of age up to about five. As a result the number of children observed at each age-level varied from twenty-five at the age of two years to a maximum of 127 at the age of five and a half years. Results are given in terms of the percentage of children of each age-level and sex who were upset in each of three situations met with during the day – leaving mother, play period at centre, and meeting mother at end of day. Published data do not distinguish between the responses of children on their first visit to the centre and those of children who had paid one or more previous visits.

Of the children aged from two to four years, about half[1] are reported as upset on leaving mother at the day's start and half also on meeting mother again at the end of the day. The proportion upset diminishes in the older age-groups, though at the day's end it never falls below 30 per cent in the case of the boys. Even during the free play period with a congenial though strange mother-surrogate the percentage of children upset is substantial, varying from about 40 per cent of the youngest children (two to three years old) to about 20 per cent at four years and 15 per cent of the older ones (five- to seven-year-olds):

... emotional upsets during the play period were by no means uncommon. The children manifested their uneasiness in the playroom in a variety of ways in addition to crying and calling for mother. Some merely stood disconsolately killing time; some shifted uneasily from one foot to the other; some peered out the window disappointedly

1. Because results are expressed in percentages and the N varies for each age-group and sex, it is not possible to calculate an exact percentage for larger categories of children.

searching for father's familiar car in the stream of traffic. . . . Such children ignored the proffered toys and resisted the play suggestions that were offered.

Some sat distracted, aimlessly fiddling with a toy or sifting sand. Of the younger children, half were explicit in expressing a desire for mother; of those between four and a half and six years of age, the proportion asking for mother dropped to about one-quarter.

A number of children who had not expressed upset during the day's proceedings showed it on reunion with mother:

Usually it was the child who had bravely winked back the tears and made a determined effort to surmount his feelings of insecurity earlier in the day that gave way to his pent-up emotion in tears. At the sight of mother his needs for autonomy and independence vanished, and he reverted to the degree of babyishness he had overcome early in the morning.

At each age-level, proportionally fewer girls than boys were overtly upset. Moreover, when girls were upset, the intensity and duration of upset were less than in boys. It is evident that the authors of the study approve the girls for their greater 'maturity' and regret the 'babyishness' of the boys.

The authors note that the three-year-olds tended to be more upset than both the younger children and those older: 'Children of two and two and a half years were little aware of what the day would bring forth; they had little anticipatory dread.' By three years they were 'more aware of the demands of the day, and more reluctant to leave home'. This was true especially of those who had paid one or two previous visits to the centre. Naturally, both the physical examination and the psychological testing were carried out as kindly as possible. Nevertheless, in mother's absence, so far from becoming used to the six-monthly examinations, the children became more apprehensive about them: 'Familiarity with the situation from one or two previous experiences seemed to make the children grow more apprehensive' and they tended to be more upset when the day began (Shirley 1942). By contrast, children aged five years and upwards were more likely to settle down, and some are reported to have enjoyed the day.

A study that derives from Shirley's but is confined to a very small part of the area covered by the earlier investigation is described by Heathers (1954). Not only is the age-range restricted to the youngest children but the behaviour reported is confined to the way in which they respond to being removed from home to go to a nursery school.

Thirty-one children between the ages of twenty-three and thirty-seven months, from middle-class homes and of above average intelligence, were observed during their first five days of starting nursery school. On each of those days each child was called for by a student he had not previously met and taken off to school by car. To meet the researcher's requirements, each 'child's mother was asked to part with him at the door and to let the observer take him out to the car'. Although each mother had attempted to explain to her child what was in store for him, it is very doubtful whether explanation could have conveyed much to such young children.

Observed behaviour was checked against a list of eighteen items, which conveys a vivid picture of the kinds of response likely to occur. It runs as follows:

When taken from home to car
1 Cries
2 Hides, tries to hide, etc.
3 Resists getting dressed to go
4 Clings to mother
5 Calls for mother
6 Tries to go back to house
7 Must be carried to car
8 Resists being carried to car

During first five minutes in car
9 Cries
10 Calls for mother
11 Seeks reassurance or comforting
12 Resists reassurance or comforting
13 Tense, withdrawn or unresponsive

When arrives at school and enters building
14 Cries
15 Resists leaving car
16 Must be lifted out, carried
17 Clings to trip observer
18 Holds back, reluctant to enter.

The daily scores of the thirty-one children on the above eighteen items ranged during the five days from zero to 13, and thus show great individual variation. On the first day the mean score was 4·4. Although by the fifth day the upset score of twenty-one children was lower than it had been on the first day, in the case of four children it was higher.

It is of interest to note that, on the first day, the older children (aged from thirty to thirty-seven months) were significantly more upset than the younger ones (twenty-three to twenty-nine months); on succeeding days, however, there was no difference between children of the two age-groups. Heathers follows Shirley in noting the possibility that the slightly older children were more upset at first because, having experienced more previous visits to the research centre for purposes of testing, they were more apt to foresee what was going to happen.

A third study in the same tradition as those of Shirley and Heathers is already referred to in the first volume of this work (Chapter 11) where a brief account is given of observations made by Murphy (1962) of children visiting a research centre for a planned play session. In this later study the arrangements for collecting the children by car resembled those adopted by Heathers, but parting from mother was handled very differently. Though the children were encouraged to go off in the car on their own with an escort, the escort was not entirely strange. Furthermore, no obstacle was put in the way of mother going too, should child protest or mother prefer to accompany him. It is no surprise that only a small minority of the fifteen children aged between two and a half and four years agreed to go without mother. On arriving at the centre, however, mother departed leaving the child alone.

Murphy's findings are consistent with those of the earlier studies. Her records of individual children include some that give a clear account of a child's determination to have his mother accompany him. There is good reason to believe that such a reaction is entirely healthy and natural for a young child in a situation in which he is being invited to accompany two ladies he hardly knows to an unknown destination.

A detailed descriptive study by Janis (1964) of one little girl, who began attending nursery school for two half-days a week when she was no more than two years and three months old, illustrates well both how anxious a child of this age is made by the experience and how such anxiety can be hidden, at least for a time.

Lottie is described as 'a normal, highly verbal child', the youngest of three girls in a professional family. Her parents are described as 'sensitive to the needs of their children [and] aware of the possibility of separation difficulties'. The nursery school itself had a policy whereby a child's mother stayed with him at school until he seemed ready to be there alone.

During the first two occasions that Lottie attended, mother stayed with her. On the third occasion, when mother left her briefly, Lottie, laughing, called out repeatedly 'Mommy! Daddy! Dorrie! Heidi!' (the names of her two sisters, aged respectively five and three-quarters and ten and a half). A week later, on the fifth visit, Lottie insisted on wearing a skirt like one worn by Dorrie, to whom she was strongly attached. By the fourteenth session Lottie was claiming to be Dorrie: 'I'm Dorrie. Call me Dorrie.'

During the next few sessions, however, Lottie began objecting more strongly than she had done earlier to her mother leaving, and she occasionally cried for her. On the day before the eighteenth session Lottie (at home) insisted on following her mother around the house and holding on to her. On the next day, at nursery school, 'Lottie bursts into tears when her mother says good-bye. She cried hard . . . her face hot and flushed.' Thenceforward, Lottie ceased to call herself Dorrie.

Instead of the steady improvement that her mother anticipated with Lottie's acknowledgement of nursery school as her own, Lottie's behaviour deteriorates. She cannot let her mother leave at all; she cries bitterly when her mother does go; she clings more and more to her mother in school, less able to play independently than before; her play is limited, regressed, uncontrolled and violent at times; she loses urinary control at home, in token fashion (a few minor accidents), for the first time after being completely dry for half a year.

Furthermore, during these weeks, whenever Lottie was left at home with a familiar person while her mother went out, she showed increasingly intense longing for her mother. She also became increasingly obstinate and disobedient.

During the early sessions of the next school term, which started when Lottie was two years and six months, Lottie insisted on her mother staying with her. Later, though she accepted that her mother should leave, she was listless and half-hearted in her play; and on mother's return Lottie's first remark was: 'I didn't cry.' By the end of four weeks, however, she was once again crying when her mother left, and this continued on and off for the rest of the term. In the upshot, it was not until the third term, which started when Lottie was two years and nine months, that she began to settle happily at school without her mother.[2]

Although Lottie's parents are described as sensitive to their children's needs and the nursery school régime as benign, it is evident from the account that both of Lottie's parents and the teacher were expecting far too much of so young a child. Much pressure, it is clear, was put on her not to cry. Although often she succeeded in controlling herself, her constant preoccupation with not crying, which runs through the report, is evidence of the strain she was under.

Had there not been so many misconceptions about the norms of behaviour to be expected of young children when left, even briefly, in a strange place with strange people, it would have been unnecessary to present these data so fully. Yet misconceptions persist, especially among professional people. Again and again it is implied that a healthy normal child should not make a fuss when mother leaves, and that if he does so it is an indication either that mother spoils him or that he is suffering from some pathological anxiety. It is hoped that such reactions will be seen in a new and more realistic light when the natural history and function of attachment behaviour are understood.

Experimental studies

Because subjecting a child to a very brief separation, lasting only a few minutes, is ethically permissible, the behaviour to which it

2. Lottie's methods of coping in mother's absence, for example by claiming to be a big girl like her sister, will be discussed in Volume III.

gives rise can be examined in experimental conditions; variables can therefore be controlled and detailed systematic observation is relatively easy. Moreover, the behaviour of a child when his mother is absent can be compared with his behaviour when she is present, with other conditions remaining unchanged.

The first to undertake such studies was Arsenian (1943). In recent years a number of other workers have followed suit, for example Ainsworth (Ainsworth and Wittig 1969; Ainsworth and Bell 1970), Rheingold (1969), Cox and Campbell (1968), Maccoby and Feldman (1972), Lee, Wright and Herbert (in preparation), and Marvin (1972). The overall picture that emerges of the behaviour of children as it develops from the first birthday through to the third is a consistent one.

Ainsworth's study is alluded to briefly in the first volume of this work (Chapter 16) when patterns of attachment are under consideration. Since that volume was written, she and her colleagues have published observations in more detail and on a much larger sample of children (for a recent review of findings see Ainsworth, Bell and Stayton, 1974).

The subjects of Ainsworth's study are fifty-six infants, aged one year, of white American middle-class families, reared within their family in ways typical of the 1960s. In respect of a sub-sample of twenty-three infants, detailed observations were made throughout the first year of life of the development of their social behaviour, with particular reference to attachment behaviour. In respect of the other thirty-three infants, limited observations of development were begun during their ninth month (Bell 1970). Then the behaviour of all fifty-six babies was observed around the time of the first birthday. When a baby neared his birthday,[3] his mother was invited to participate with him in a brief series of experimental episodes, the purpose of which was to learn how the infant would behave in a congenial though slightly strange setting, first in the presence of mother and later in her absence.

To this end Ainsworth furnished a small room with three chairs and an open space in the middle. A chair near one end of the room was for mother, another, at the same end and opposite, was

3. Thirty-three of the babies were aged forty-nine and fifty weeks, twenty-three were fifty-one weeks old.

for a stranger, and a small chair at the other end had toys heaped upon it. The situation was designed to be novel enough to excite a child's interest but not so strange that he would be frightened. The entry of the stranger (female) was intended to be so gradual that any fear it evoked could be attributed to her unfamiliarity and not to any abrupt or alarming behaviour. There were eight experimental episodes, arranged so that the least disturbing ones came first; moreover, the series as a whole was similar in kind to many that an infant might be expected to encounter in his ordinary life. Both mother and stranger were instructed in advance regarding the roles they were to play. The episodes were arranged as follows.

In a *preliminary episode* a mother, accompanied by one of the observers, carried her infant into the room; the observer then left.

During *episode 2*, which lasted three minutes, mother put her infant down between the two chairs meant for the adults and then sat quietly in her own chair. She was not to participate in her infant's play unless he sought her attention, and then to do so only a little.

At the start of *episode 3*, which also lasted three minutes, the stranger entered. For one minute she sat quietly in her chair; then, for a second minute, she conversed with mother; finally, for a third minute, she gently approached the infant showing him a toy. Meanwhile mother sat quietly.

Episode 4 began with mother leaving the room unobtrusively, leaving her handbag on the chair. If the infant was playing happily the stranger stayed quiet; but if he was inactive she tried to interest him in a toy. Should an infant become distressed she did what she could to distract him or comfort him. Like the previous two episodes, this one lasted three minutes; but if an infant was much distressed and could not be comforted the episode was curtailed.

Episode 5 began with mother's return, after which the stranger departed. On entering, mother was to pause in the doorway in order to see what her infant's spontaneous response to her return would be. Thenceforward she was free to do whatever suited – to comfort him if required and to settle him afresh in play with the toys. Once he was settled she was to leave the room again, pausing briefly as she went to say 'bye-bye'.

During *episode 6*, in consequence, the infant was left all alone. Unless curtailed because of distress, this episode lasted the usual three minutes.

Thereafter first stranger and then mother returned to make *episodes 7* and *8*.

Throughout the series of episodes the behaviour of infant, mother, and stranger was recorded by observers from behind a one-way vision window. From the narrative record two measures of behaviour could be obtained for each infant: (a) the frequency with which different sorts of behaviour were shown during each episode, the frequency in every case being measured by scoring 1 for each period of fifteen seconds during which that behaviour was seen (thus, for a three-minute episode a score could range from zero to 12); (b) the intensity of certain kinds of behaviour shown during each episode; in making ratings of intensity it was often necessary to take account of how mother or stranger was behaving to the infant.

The finding to which attention is specially drawn in this chapter is that the behaviour of these fifty-six one-year-old infants during the episodes when mother was absent (nos. 4 and 6) was in all cases much changed from what it had been during the earlier episode (no. 2) when mother was sitting quietly in the room with them. Every infant showed behaviour of a kind that everyone would describe as anxious or distressed, and as being due to his missing his mother.

During episode 2 while his mother was present, the typical picture of an infant was one of active interest in the scene. As a rule he moved around freely and played with the toys, giving only an occasional glance towards his mother; a small minority (seven infants), however, were inactive and tended to stay where they had been put. During this episode crying was conspicuous by its absence, though an occasional child whimpered for a few moments to begin with.

During episode 3, in which the stranger joined mother and infant, the behaviour of most of the children changed substantially. Staring at the stranger was almost universal; many infants moved rather closer to mother; and exploration and play diminished, on average to about half what they had been. Some infants showed a tendency to cry or grizzle; but in only five cases was crying of any intensity. As a rule the stranger was treated with interest and, fairly soon, with cautious friendliness.

During episode 4 mother had departed and infant found himself alone with stranger. Half the infants showed a strong tendency to seek mother, starting usually as soon as they realized she had gone. Eleven followed mother to the door or struggled to do so; the others either looked at the door frequently or for long periods, or else searched for mother in the chair on which she had been sitting. There was also much crying and other signs of distress. For the group as a whole there was four times as much crying during mother's absence as there had been during episode 3. A dozen infants cried practically the whole time and another thirteen for a part of it. In all, thirty-nine infants either cried or searched, or did both (thirteen cases). This leaves seventeen, a fairly substantial minority, who did neither.

During episode 5, which began with mother's return, half of the infants actively approached mother and showed a clear desire to be close to her, while another six either signalled or approached in a less purposeful way. Thirteen of the more active ones, having achieved close physical contact with mother, maintained it both by clinging to her and by resisting her attempts to put them down. All who had been crying stopped doing so although some infants who had been acutely distressed were not comforted quickly. The behaviour, on mother's return, of the twenty-three sub-sample infants, is discussed further in Chapter 21.

During episode 6, after mother had departed again, this time leaving her infant all alone, searching and crying were seen in more infants and were also more intense than they had been during episode 4. On this occasion forty-four infants searched for mother, of whom thirty-one followed her to the door. Of the thirty-one, fourteen banged on the door or tried to open it: they either reached vainly for the knob or tried to insert their fingers into the crack. Among the dozen infants who did not search for mother, there were a few who had searched for her during the first separation episode but who on the second occasion showed only distress. During episode 6 there was also a great deal of crying. Forty infants cried more or less strongly; these included all those who had been distressed during the earlier episode as well as many others. Some rocked, or kicked their heels on the floor, or moved at random 'like a little trapped animal'. Only two infants neither searched nor cried; thirty did both.

Episode 6 was ended by stranger's return and the start of episode 7. After three minutes, during which infant was with stranger, mother returned and episode 8 began.

During episode 8, the tendencies to approach mother, to cling to her, and to resist being put down were much stronger and were seen in more of the infants than had been the case during the previous reunion episode. This time thirty-five of the fifty-six infants actively approached mother and showed an evident desire for physical contact; a further nine either signalled their desire for contact or else approached mother in a less purposeful way. Two other infants, though they did not approach mother, engaged in lively interchange with her across a distance. Most striking was the large number of infants (forty-two) who both actively clung to mother and resisted being put down by her; another three, though they did not cling, resisted being put down.

A minority of infants included in the above figures showed signs of ambivalence towards mother of greater or less degree. Thus a few were seen to ignore mother briefly before approaching her, and others alternated between approaching and turning away. There were a few others who were so ambivalent that they mingled active attempts to seek and maintain contact with mother with attempts to get away from her.

A further small minority of infants (seven) behaved quite differently: they neither approached mother nor showed any desire to do so. Instead, they persistently ignored her and refused to respond when she invited them to come. Some even avoided looking at her.

To return to episodes 4 and 6: when behaviour shown during these two episodes, when mother was absent, is examined it is found that an infant was extremely likely either to search or to cry or to do both together. The table overleaf shows the number of children who responded in one of these three ways for each episode.

When the behaviour of any one infant in episode 6 is compared

Behaviour	Episode 4	6
Cry only	12	10
Search only	14	14
Search and cry	13	30
Total ($N = 56$)	39	54

with what he showed in episode 4 the following sequences are found:
- those who cried only in episode 4 were likely to do the same in episode 6
- those who searched only in episode 4 were likely to search and cry in episode 6
- those who searched and cried in episode 4 were likely to do the same in episode 6, though a few cried only.

The individual differences in the responses of these children are of great interest and (as is discussed in Chapter 21) are correlated with the different patterns of mother–child interaction observed in the preceding year. Here, however, our concern is with the features that the infants' responses had in common. On each occasion when mother left the room, first leaving infant with stranger and then leaving him all alone, the behaviour of every infant changed. Play and exploratory behaviour either slowed down or ceased altogether. On the second occasion especially, all but two of the infants showed marked dislike of the situation and expressed it by seeking mother, by crying unhappily, or by doing both together. The extent of distress and anxiety during mother's absence was considerable, even though the room and the toys remained exactly as they had been.

While to describe the broad features of behaviour for the sample as a whole enables generalizations to be framed with confidence, it tends also to be a little impersonal. To illustrate something of what the series of episodes meant to one small boy and his mother, a description is given of one case, selected to be as representative as any one case can be:[4]

4. This description is taken from Ainsworth and Wittig (1969).

Behaviour with and without Mother: Humans

1. *Mother, Baby, Observer*. Brian had one arm hooked over his mother's shoulder as they came into the room; he was holding on to her, grasping a fold of her blouse. He looked around soberly, but with interest, at the toys and at the observer.

2. *Mother, Baby*. After being put down, Brian immediately crept towards the toys and began to explore them. He was very active, picking toys up, then dropping them or moving them about, with vigorous movements. He crept around quite a bit, mostly on his mother's side of the room. Although his attention was fixed on the playthings, he glanced up at his mother six times, and smiled at her twice. She glanced at him covertly, from time to time, but their glances did not seem to meet. Once he threw a toy with a clatter at her feet; she moved it back towards him. Otherwise there was no interaction between them. Towards the end of the three minutes he blew into a long cardboard tube, vocalizing as though pretending it were a horn, and then he looked up at his mother with a smile, seeming to expect her to acknowledge his accomplishment.

3. *Stranger, Mother, Baby*. He turned to look at the stranger when she entered, with a pleasant expression on his face. He played with the tube again, vocalized, smiled, and turned to glance at his mother. He continued to play, glancing at the stranger twice. When the stranger and his mother began to converse, he continued to explore actively at the end of the room, and looked up only once – at the stranger. Towards the end of this minute of conversation he crept over to his mother, pulled himself up, and stood briefly, holding on to her knee with one hand, and clutching her blouse with the other. Then he turned back to play. When the stranger began her approach by leaning forward to offer him a toy, he smiled, crept towards her, and reached for it. He put the toy in his mouth. She offered him the tube and he blew into it again. He looked back and forth from the toys to the stranger and did not look at his mother at all.

4. *Stranger, Baby*. He did not notice his mother leave. He continued to watch the stranger and the toys she was manipulating. Suddenly, he crept to his mother's chair, pulled himself up into a standing position, and looked at the stranger. She tried to distract him with a pull-toy. He approached the toy, and began to roll it back and forth; but he glanced again at his mother's empty chair. He was less active than he had been when alone with his mother, and after two minutes his activity ceased. He sat chewing the string of the pull-toy, and glancing from the stranger to his mother's chair. He made an unhappy noise, then a cry-face, and then he cried. The stranger tried to distract him by offering him a block; he took it but then threw it away with a petulant gesture. He gave several more little protesting cries, but he did not cry hard.

5. *Mother, Baby.* When his mother opened the door and paused in the doorway, Brian looked at her immediately and vocalized loudly, with a quality that could have been either a laugh or a cry; then he crept to her quickly, and pulled himself up, with her help, to hold on to her knees. Then she picked him up, and he immediately put his arms around her neck, his face against her shoulder, and hugged her hard. He then gave her another big hug before she put him down. He resisted being put down; he tried to cling to her and protested loudly. Once on the floor, he threw himself down, hid his face in the rug, and cried angrily. His mother knelt beside him and tried to interest him in the toys again. He stopped crying and watched. After a moment she disengaged herself and got up to sit on her chair. He immediately threw himself down and cried again. She helped him to stand, and cuddled him. For a moment he reciprocated in the cuddle, but then he threw himself down on the floor again, crying. She again picked him up, and tried to direct his attention to a squeaky ball. He looked at it, still holding on to his mother, with one arm hooked over her shoulder. He began to play, but quickly turned back to his mother with a brief cry, and clung to her. This alternation of play and clinging continued. After four and a half minutes, his mother, apparently not wishing to delay us, picked a moment when he was interested in a ball, and moved to the door.

6. *Baby Alone.* As she said 'bye-bye' and waved, Brian looked up with a little smile, but he shifted into a cry before she had quite closed the door. He sat crying, rocking himself back and forth. He cried hard, but occasionally lulled a little and looked around. After a minute and a half the episode was curtailed and stranger instructed to enter.

7. *Stranger, Baby.* Brian lulled slightly when he saw the stranger enter, but he continued to cry. She first tried to distract him, then offered her arms to him. Brian responded by raising his arms; she picked him up, and he stopped crying immediately. She held him in her arms, and showed him the pictures tacked up around the edges of the mirror-window. He looked with apparent interest; he held on to her tightly, grasping a fold of her clothing. Occasionally he gave a little sob, but for the most part he did not cry. But when she put him down, he screamed. She picked him up again, and he lulled.

8. *Mother, Baby.* At the moment that his mother returned Brian was crying listlessly. He did not notice his mother. The stranger half-turned and pointed her out. Brian looked towards her, still crying, and then turned away. But he soon 'did a double take'. He looked back and vocalized a little protest. His mother offered her arms to him. He reached towards her, smiling, and leaned way out of the stranger's arms and his mother took him. He threw his arms around her neck, hugging her

hard, and wiggling with excitement. Then the stranger tried to attract his attention. Brian did not notice her advance until she touched him; he immediately clung to his mother and buried his face in her shoulder. His mother continued to hold him, and he cuddled and clung to her, as the episode ended.

Since Ainsworth first reported her findings the results of several other studies have come to hand. In three of them (Maccoby and Feldman 1972; Marvin 1972) the series of experimental situations used was planned to be as similar to Ainsworth's as possible, but in each the children were older. In a further two studies (Cox and Campbell 1968; Lee *et al.*, in preparation) the situations differ from those used by Ainsworth, but in each there is opportunity to study children in an experimental setting first with mother present and later with mother absent. Details are given in the table below.

Because the last two studies listed give data comparing behaviour at one year with that to be seen at two years and onwards it is convenient to present findings from one of them first.

Preliminary findings reported by Lee and his colleagues show that, while attachment behaviour continues to be extremely active at the time of the second birthday, the behavioural system governing it has altered in many respects since the first birthday. A

Authors	Samples	Ages at which children studied
Maccoby and Feldman	White American 30–60, longitudinal	2, 2½, 3 years
Maccoby and Feldman	From Israeli kibbutzim 20, cross-sectional	2½ years
Marvin	White American 3×16, cross-sectional	2, 3, 4 years
Cox and Campbell	White Canadian 2×20, cross-sectional	14 months 24–37 months
Lee *et al.*	Middle-class English 27, longitudinal	1, 2, 3 years

comparison of the behaviour of the same children placed in the same situation at one year and two years of age shows that, at two years of age, children are likely:

- to maintain *greater* proximity to mother – a finding already reported from observations made out of doors by Anderson (1972a)
- to be more hesitant in approaching a stranger.

On the other hand, merely to be close to mother and to be able to see her seem sufficient to give a child of two years a sense of security, whereas a one-year-old is likely to insist on physical contact. Two-year-olds, moreover, protest less than do one-year-olds during a brief period when mother leaves them alone. Lee concludes that, compared with one-year-olds, two-year-olds have available more sophisticated cognitive strategies for maintaining contact with mother. They make much more use of looking and verbal communication, and are probably also using mental imagery in ways hardly possible for a one-year-old. As a result their attachment behaviour is better organized and their proximity-keeping is more proficient than it was when they were a year younger.

During the third year of life changes in the behaviour seen in the experimental situations are probably also in large part a result of the developments occurring in a child's cognitive competence. In their longitudinal study of children between their second and third birthdays, Maccoby and Feldman (1972) note the much greater ability of three-year-olds to communicate with mother over a distance and also their increased ability to understand, when mother leaves the room, that she will soon be returning. As a result, when the reaction of three-year-olds to mother's brief absence is compared with that of two-year-olds, both crying and going to the closed door show a marked decrease. In addition, three-year-olds who have been left alone recover their equanimity when they are rejoined even by a stranger, whereas two-year-olds remain as upset when the stranger returns as they were when left entirely alone.

The responses of the children observed by Maccoby and Feldman when tested at the intermediate age of two and a half years in the same series of situations were roughly intermediate between the responses seen at two years and those seen at three years. Interestingly enough, the behaviour shown in the same situations by kibbutzim children at the age of two and a half differed very little from that of the American children at that age. Similarities between the groups were found in regard both to the means for the groups and to the range of individual variation within them. These findings are in keeping with other observations that suggest that the development of attachment behaviour in children brought up in kibbutzim is in most cases very similar to that of children brought up in traditional families (see Volume I, Chapter 15).

Although attachment behaviour develops in important ways during the second and third years of life, a child's behaviour in these experimental situations when mother is absent continues to be very different from what it is when she is present. For example, Maccoby and Feldman found that the manipulative play of two-year-olds decreased by about one-quarter when they were left with a stranger and by about half when they were left alone. Conversely, the proportion of children who cried increased enormously, from 5 per cent when mother was present to 30 per cent when the children were left with a stranger and to 53 per cent when they were left alone. Changes in the behaviour of three-year-olds when mother was absent were less striking than in two-year-olds but in the same direction. Their manipulative play decreased by one-sixth when they were left with a stranger and by one-third when they were left alone. The proportion of children who cried rose from zero to 5 per cent and 20 per cent respectively in the two situations in which mother was absent.

In addition to crying after mother had departed, there were many children at each age-level who showed a desire to follow her. Of the two-year-olds, 30 per cent not only went to the door but made efforts to open it; and a further 21 per cent stood near the door or leaned against it. Of the three-year-olds, 34 per cent attempted to open the door, and nearly half of them banged on it vigorously. At each age-level, again, a substantial minority of children expressed anger at mother's absence: 19 per cent at two years, 31 per cent at two and a half years, and 14 per cent at three years.

In noting the increased activity observed when children were left alone, especially evident at the ages of two and two and a half, Maccoby and Feldman write:

This increased activity frequently took the form of anxious searching or agitated movement. There was occasionally a quite opposite kind of reaction to the stress of being alone: a kind of frozen immobility. . . . some children stood very still. This might occur near the door, when the child appeared to be waiting for his mother's return, or it might occur elsewhere in the room. In a few instances the child played with the toys, but each movement occurred at a markedly reduced speed, much as though the action had been rendered on a slow-motion film. Also, it occasionally happened that a child who was upset over separation would alternate between an unfocused running activity and immobility.

As regards the evaluation of these observations it is perhaps necessary to remind readers that on each occasion when mother departed she was absent for no more than three minutes, and for an even shorter time if the child was distressed, and that on the first of the two occasions the child was left with a friendly female stranger whom he had first met in the presence of mother. Further-more, the toys he had been playing with were still there.

The findings of a cross-sectional study of samples of eight boys and eight girls at each of three age-levels by Marvin (1972) are in broad agreement with those of Maccoby and Feldman and here observations are extended to the fourth birthday. In Marvin's study the behaviour of boys and girls tended to differ. The two-year-old boys were as much upset as were Ainsworth's one-year-olds. Three-year-old boys were less upset than two-year-olds; and four-year-old boys were comparatively little affected by any of the situations. By contrast, the two- and three-year-old girls were appreciably less affected by events than were one-year-olds, whereas the four-year-old girls were much more upset, especially by being left alone. An explanation suggested by Marvin of this last result, which is unexpected, is that a four-year-old girl may be especially disturbed by mother's apparently arbitrary behaviour in the test situation and by her unwillingness to cooperate when the child asks her not to leave her alone.

Although in broad outline the findings of these different studies are consistent, there are many differences of detail. For example, neither Ainsworth with her one-year-olds nor Maccoby and Feldman with their two- and three-year-olds found sex differences of any magnitude; whereas Lee and his colleagues with their one- and two-year-olds and also Marvin with his twos, threes, and fours were struck by the differences between boys and girls. This and other discrepancies in the results reported in different studies are not easy to interpret. It seems not unlikely that relatively small differences in the arrangements for the testing, for example, in the behaviour of the stranger, can affect considerably the intensity, though not the form, of any behaviour exhibited.

From these and other miniature separation experiments certain conclusions can be drawn:

(a) In a benign but slightly strange situation, young children aged between eleven and thirty-six months, and brought up in families, are quick to notice mother's absence and commonly show some measure of concern, varying considerably but amounting very often to obvious, and in some cases to intense, anxiety and distress. Play activity decreases abruptly and may cease. Efforts to reach mother are common.

(b) A child of two years is likely to be almost as upset in these situations as a child of one, and at neither age is he likely to make a quick recovery when rejoined either by mother or by a stranger.

(c) A child of three is less likely to be upset in these situations and is more able to understand that mother will soon return. On being rejoined by mother or a stranger he is relatively quick to recover.

(d) A child of four may either be little affected by the situations or else be much distressed by mother's apparently arbitrary behaviour.

(e) As children get older they are able to use vision and verbal communication as means for keeping in contact with mother; should they become upset when mother leaves the room older children will make more determined attempts to open the door in order to find her.

(f) Up to 30 per cent of children are made angry by mother's leaving them alone in these circumstances.

(g) In some studies and at some ages no differences are observed in the behaviour of boys and girls. In so far as any differences are observed, boys tend to explore more in mother's presence and to be more vigorous in their attempts to reach her when she has gone; girls tend to keep closer to mother and also to make friends more readily with the stranger.

A further finding from these miniature separation experiments, and one that links with the findings of Shirley (1942) and Heathers (1954) (see pp. 56 and 58 above), is only very recently reported, This is that when a child of about one year is tested in Ainsworth's series of episodes for a second time, a few weeks after the first testing, he is more upset and anxious than he was on the first occasion. When mother is present he keeps closer to her and clings more tightly. When she is absent he cries more (Ainsworth, Blehar, Waters and Wall, in preparation). These findings emerge from a test–retest study of twenty-three babies tested first at fifty weeks of age and a second time two weeks later. On the assumption that increased sensitivity is not due simply to maturation, which is unlikely, these findings provide the first experimental evidence that at one year of age a separation lasting only a few minutes, in what would ordinarily be regarded as a bland situation, is apt to leave a child more sensitive than he was before to a repetition of the experience.

Ontogeny of responses to separation

The First Year

Since the responses to separation that are so unmistakable in infants of twelve months and older are not present at birth, it is clear that they must develop at some time during the first year of life. Unfortunately, studies designed to throw light on this development are few, and are confined to infants admitted to hospital. Nevertheless such evidence as is available is unambiguous. It is in keeping, moreover, with what is known about the development of attachment behaviour and about cognitive development generally.

In Chapter 15 of the earlier volume the steps by which, during the early months of life, an infant's attachment behaviour gradually becomes focused on a discriminated and preferred attachment figure are described. Development can be summarized as follows: before sixteen weeks differentially directed responses are few in number and are seen only when methods of observation are sensitive; between sixteen and twenty-six weeks differentially directed responses are both more numerous and more apparent; and in the great majority of family infants of six months and over they are plain for all to see. It comes as no surprise, therefore, that the full range of responses to separation described in earlier sections of this chapter is not seen before six or seven months of age.

Schaffer studied seventy-six infants of various ages under twelve months admitted to hospital: none was marasmic, deformed, or thought to be brain-damaged. Of the total, twenty-five were healthy infants admitted for elective surgery. While in hospital each child was observed during a two-hour session on each of the first three days (see Schaffer 1958; Schaffer and Callender 1959). Infants were not only without mother but had very little social interaction with nurses.

The responses observed in these twenty-five healthy infants differed greatly according to the child's age. The dividing-point was twenty-eight weeks. Of the sixteen aged twenty-nine weeks and over, all but one fretted piteously, exhibiting all the struggling, restlessness, and crying so typical of two- and three-year-olds. Of the nine aged twenty-eight weeks and under, by contrast, all but two[5] are reported to have accepted the situation without protest or fretting: only an unwonted and bewildered silence indicated their awareness of change.

Schaffer emphasizes that the shift from a bewildered response to active protest and fretting occurs suddenly and at full intensity at about twenty-eight weeks of age. Thus, of the sixteen infants aged between twenty-nine and fifty-one weeks, both the length of the period of fretting and the intensity of it were as great in those of seven and eight months as in those of eleven and twelve months.

Furthermore, responses both to the observers and to mother when she visited changed equally suddenly at about thirty weeks:

In the younger infants [twenty-eight weeks and less] most observation sessions showed these infants to be normally responsive, although the people confronting them were complete strangers. This held as much for the nurses who fed and bathed them as for the observers. . . . In the older group, on the other hand, normal [i.e. friendly] responsiveness

5. One of the exceptions was an infant already twenty-eight weeks of age.

was almost completely lacking, and the majority of observation sessions showed these infants to be negative and frightened when approached by a stranger – a type of behaviour not seen at all in the younger group (Schaffer and Callender 1959).

Although there were too few observations for statistical comparisons to be made of how infants of different ages responded to mother's visit, such observations as could be made support the thesis of a sharp change around twenty-eight to thirty weeks. Infants older than that mostly clung rather desperately to mother, behaviour that was in striking contrast to their negative responses to the observers. The younger infants, by contrast, tended to respond to mother and to observers without showing marked discrimination between them. Similarly, when mother departed, whereas older infants cried loudly and for a long time, even desperately, the younger ones showed no sign of protest.

Finally, the behaviour of the infants on their return home from hospital differed greatly according to age-group. Most of the infants aged seven months and over showed intense attachment behaviour. They clung almost continuously to mother, cried loud and long when left alone by her, and were notably afraid of strangers. Even figures formerly familiar, such as father and siblings, were sometimes regarded with suspicion. Infants aged under seven months, by contrast, showed little or no attachment behaviour during their early days at home. Their mothers described them as 'strange'. On the one hand, these infants seemed utterly preoccupied in scanning the environment; on the other, they seemed unheedful of adults or perhaps averted their head when approached:

For hours on end sometimes the infant would crane his neck, scanning his surroundings without apparently focusing on any particular feature and letting his eyes sweep over all objects without attending to any particular one. A completely blank expression was usually observed on his face, though sometimes a bewildered or frightened look was reported. In the extreme form of this syndrome the infants were quite inactive throughout, apart from the scanning behaviour, and no vocalization was heard though one or two were reported to have cried or whimpered. When confronted with a toy the infant disregarded it.

To attempts by adults to make contact with them some of these younger infants seemed altogether oblivious. Others seemed to avoid the adults, and others again to gaze 'through' them with the same blank look that they used for the rest of the environment.

The only way in which the responses of the infants of the two age-groups were similar was in regard to sleep: in infants of both groups disturbed sleep and night-crying were common.

How the responses of infants of under seven months are best understood, and what their significance for an infant's future development may be, is difficult to know. It is plain, however, that the responses of these younger infants to separation are very different at every phase from those of older ones, and that it is only after about seven months of age that the patterns that are the subject of this work are to be seen.

In discussion of his findings Schaffer (1958) draws on Piaget's work on the development of an infant's concept of an object (Piaget 1937). Only during the second half of the first year, Piaget finds, is there evidence that an infant is beginning to be able to conceive of an object as something that exists independently of himself, in a context of spatial and causal relations, even when it is not present to his perception, and so to search for it when it is missing. Bell (1970) confirms Piaget's findings and, in addition, reports the results of an experiment designed to test whether or not an infant develops a capacity to conceive of a person as a persisting object earlier than he develops the capacity in regard to inanimate things. Although her results show that a majority of infants develop the capacity in regard to a person earlier than in regard to things, it is not until about the ninth month that the capacity in regard to persons is reasonably well developed, and in a minority it lags some weeks behind that. For reasons to do with cognitive development, therefore, the types of response to separation with which we are concerned could hardly be expected in infants younger than those in whom they are seen.

Change after the First Birthday

All the evidence suggests that, once established, the typical patterns of response to being placed in strange surroundings with strange people do not undergo marked change, either in form or in intensity, much before the third birthday. Thenceforward their intensity begins to diminish, but only slowly. As an example, the change in Lottie's feelings about going to nursery school that appeared at the beginning of the third term, when she was aged two years and nine months (see above, p. 60), is characteristic of many children. Provided he knows where his mother is and has good reason to expect her to return soon, a child begins to accept another fairly familiar person, even when he is in a fairly unfamiliar place.

The only conditions at present known that reduce appreciably the effects of separation from mother are familiar possessions, the companionship of another and familiar child and, as Robertson and Robertson (1971) have shown, especially mothering from a skilled and familiar foster mother. By contrast, strange people, strange places, and strange proceedings are always alarming; and they are especially alarming when encountered alone (see Chapters 7 and 8).[6]

Since distress at being separated unwillingly from an attachment figure is an indissoluble part of being attached to someone, changes occurring with age in the form of response to separation accompany, step by step, changes in the form that attachment behaviour takes. These changes are sketched in the first volume (Chapters 11 and 17) and need not be described further here. In so far as attachments to loved figures are an integral part of our lives, a potential to feel distress on separation from them and

6. The ways in which young children and their mothers behave in sessions before and after the children start part-time nursery school (at ages ranging from two years eleven months to four years three months) are well described in a recent paper by van Leeuwen and Tuma (1972). The authors, using measures derived from attachment theory, report that children who started school at or before the age of three years two months became noticeably more clinging fifteen days after starting than they had been before, and that when mother was absent some showed a marked decrease in their concentration on and enjoyment in play. Three boys who had spent from five to seven months in a previous nursery school, two of them starting at two years eight months and one at two years ten months, were especially disturbed during early weeks at their new school. Reviewing their findings the authors conclude that 'we should approach nursery school entry with much greater caution [than is commonly given] and possibly delay it until the child is older'.

anxiety at the prospect of separation is so also. That is a theme running through the rest of this volume.

Meanwhile, in order that we may view the responses to separation seen in humans in a perspective broader than has been traditional, it is useful to compare the responses of young human children with those of the young of other species. When that is done it becomes evident that, just as attachment behaviour occurs in rather similar forms across a number of mammalian and avian species, so also do responses to separation. Here again man is no isolated case.

Chapter 4
Behaviour with and without Mother: Non-human Primates

Man with all his noble qualities, with sympathy that feels for the most debased, with benevolence which extends not only to other men but to the humblest living creature, with his god-like intellect which has penetrated into the movements and constitution of the solar system – with all these exalted powers – still bears in his bodily frame the indelible stamp of his lowly origin.
– CHARLES DARWIN (1871)

Naturalistic observations

It has long been known that isolation and separation from a mother figure can cause distress, expressed in calling and searching, in the young of many species of bird and mammal. The 'lost piping' of young ducklings who have become attached to and have temporarily lost a mother figure is a familiar example. Others are the bleating of lambs and the yelping of puppies. Coming nearer man, there are numerous examples in the accounts of monkey and ape infants brought up by human caretakers. All accounts agree on the intensity of protest exhibited whenever a baby primate loses its mother figure, and the intensity of distress that follows when she cannot be found. All agree, too, on the intensity of clinging that occurs after the two are reunited.

For example, Bolwig (1963), in his account of the little patas monkey he reared from a few days old,[1] describes how from the first the little monkey 'showed no fear of man, cried much, and panicked when left alone ... The screaming, with wide open mouth and distorted face, was only heard when the observer moved out of the monkey's immediate reach or sight. On such occasions he would more often than not run staggering to the nearest person in sight.' Soon the monkey's attachment had become focused on Bolwig himself and then, until three and a

[1]. See Volume I, Chapter 11.

half months of age, the monkey could be very troublesome unless perpetually with his caretaker.

By the age of four months, however, the little monkey was exploring increasingly far afield and his master decided

to leave him for some hours every day in a cage with other monkeys of his own kind. This attempt was, however, not very successful. Although he knew the other monkeys well and was accustomed to play with them he panicked as soon as he knew I wanted to leave him behind, screamed, clung desperately to me and then tried to tear the door open. He would sit and cry until I finally let him out. Afterwards he would cling to me and refuse to leave me out of sight for the rest of the day. In the evening when asleep he would wake up with small shrieks and cling to me, showing all signs of terror when I tried to release his grip.

Accounts of similar behaviour are given of infant chimpanzees. Cathy Hayes (1951) recounts how Viki, a female she adopted at three days, would, when aged four months, cling to her foster mother

from the moment she left her crib until she was tucked in at night. . . . She sat on my lap while I ate or studied. She straddled my hip as I cooked. If she were on the floor, and I started to get away, she screamed and clung to my leg until I picked her up. . . . If some rare lack of vigilance on her part let a room's length separate us, she came charging across the abyss, screaming at the height of her considerable ability.

The Kelloggs, who did not adopt their female chimp, Gua, until she was seven months old and who kept her for nine months, report identical behaviour (Kellogg and Kellogg 1933). They describe

an intensive and tenacious impulse to remain within sight and call of some friend, guardian, or protector. Throughout the entire nine months . . . whether indoors or out, she almost never roamed very far from someone she knew. To shut her up in a room by herself, or to walk away faster than she could run, and to leave her behind, proved, as well as we could judge, to be the most awful punishment that could possibly be inflicted. She could not be alone apparently without suffering.

Comparing Gua with their son, who was two and a half months older than she, the Kelloggs report:

Security, Anxiety, and Distress

Both subjects displayed what might be called anxious behaviour (i.e. fretting and crying) if obvious preparations were being made by the grown-ups to leave the house. This led (in Gua) to an early understanding of the mechanism of door closing and a keen and continual observation of the doors in her vicinity. If she happened to be on one side of a doorway, and her friends on the other, the slightest movement of the door toward closing, whether produced by human hands or by the wind, would bring Gua rushing through the narrowing aperture, crying as she came.

The very detailed observations made by van Lawick-Goodall (1968) of chimpanzees in the Gombe Stream Reserve in central Africa show not only that anxious and distressed behaviour on being separated, as reported of animals in captivity, occurs also in the wild but that distress at separation continues throughout chimpanzee childhood. During the first year an infant is rarely out of actual contact with mother and, although from its first birthday onwards it spends more time out of contact, it none the less remains in proximity to her. Not until young are four and a half years of age are any of them seen travelling not in the company of mother, and then only rarely.[2]

Once an infant begins to spend time out of contact with mother, proximity is maintained largely by auditory signals. Either mother or infant emits a 'hoo' whimper to which the other promptly responds:

When the infant ... begins to move from its mother, it invariably utters this sound if it gets into any difficulty and cannot quickly return to her. Until the infant's locomotor patterns are fairly well developed the mother normally responds by going to fetch it at once. The same sound is used by the mother when she reaches to remove her infant from some potentially dangerous situation or even, on occasion, as she gestures it to cling on when she is ready to go. The 'hoo' whimper therefore serves as a fairly specific signal in re-establishing mother–infant contact.

Another signal used by infants is a scream; it is elicited whenever an infant falls or nearly falls from its mother or is frightened by a sudden loud noise. When her infant screams a mother almost

2. For a brief description of the developmental course of attachment behaviour in chimpanzees see Volume I, Chapter 11.

unfailingly retrieves it and cradles it: 'On several occasions infants screamed loudly when their mothers started to move away without them. Each time the mothers immediately turned back and retrieved them. Indeed, throughout infancy, screaming normally results in the mother hurrying to rescue her child.'

Juveniles up to five or six years old also scream when lost or in trouble, and again mother usually hurries to the rescue:

On several occasions juveniles were observed who had accidentally lost their mothers. In each instance, after peering round from various trees, whimpering and screaming as they did so, they hurried off – often in the wrong direction. On three occasions I was able to observe the reaction of the mother and every time, although she set off in the direction of her offspring's screaming, she herself made no sound to indicate her whereabouts.

In one case a juvenile female aged five years lost her mother in the evening and was still whimpering and crying the following morning. In another case, a juvenile stopped screaming before her mother found her, which resulted in a separation lasting several hours. (No information is available regarding behaviour of the young after reunion.)

Thus in these wild-living chimpanzees proximity of young to mother is maintained until pre-adolescence. Separations are rare, and usually quickly rectified by vocal signals and mutual search.

Early experimental studies

These naturalistic accounts show plainly not only that the attachment behaviour of young non-human primates is very similar to the attachment behaviour of young children but that their responses to separation are very similar also. Because of this, and because experimental separations lasting longer than minutes are inadmissible in the case of human young, more than one scientist has turned to monkey young for experimental subjects. A number of studies from at least four different centres are now published. Animals used include infants aged between two and eight months, of five different species, namely four species of macaque (the rhesus, the pigtail, the bonnet, and the Java) and the patas monkey. All five are species of semi-terrestrial and group-living old-world monkeys.[3]

Responses to separation differ as between species, though differences are more of intensity than of kind. In the case of rhesus, pigtail, and Java macaques great distress is observed throughout the period of separation itself and, afterwards, there is a very marked tendency to cling to mother and to resist any attempt at a further separation, however brief. In the case of both bonnet macaques and patas monkeys, intense distress is again seen during the first hours after separation, but then it wanes; thereafter activity is less depressed than in the other species of macaque and there is much less disturbance after reunion with mother. The reduction of distress in the bonnet macaques appears to come about in great part because the separated infant receives continuous substitute care from one of the other familiar females in the group.

In what follows attention is given to the studies using rhesus and pigtail infants both because their responses appear to resemble more closely those of human infants and because the studies of these species are more numerous and extensive, especially in the case of the rhesus. Those wishing to compare the behaviour of bonnet macaques are referred to the study by Rosenblum and Kaufman (1968; see also Kaufman and Rosenblum 1969); and of patas monkeys to the study by Preston, Baker and Seay (1970). A useful review of separation studies is given by Mitchell (1970).

An early experimental study was carried out by Jensen and Tolman (1962). When two infant pigtail monkeys, each reared in a cage alone with mother, were aged respectively five and seven months, the infants and mothers were exchanged on several occasions for periods of no longer than five minutes. Observation was through a one-way vision screen.

Because mother and infant cling tightly to one another separation cannot be achieved with monkeys except by deception or by

3. The nearest experiments so far reported with chimpanzees are those by Mason (1965), but in this case the separations were from a cage-mate of the same age and not from mother.

the exercise of a good deal of force. The protests of both parties are intense. Jensen and Tolman give a vivid account:

Separation of mother and infant monkeys is an extremely stressful event for both mother and infant as well as for the attendants and for all other monkeys within sight or earshot of the experience. The mother becomes ferocious toward attendants and extremely protective of her infant. The infant's screams can be heard over almost the entire building. The mother struggles and attacks the separators. The baby clings tightly to the mother and to any object which it can grasp to avoid being held or removed by the attendant. With the baby gone, the mother paces the cage almost constantly, charges the cage occasionally, bites at it, and makes continual attempts to escape. She also lets out occasional mooing-like sounds. The infant emits high pitched shrill screams intermittently and almost continuously for the period of separation.

As soon as the five minutes had elapsed and mother and infant were reunited each immediately went to the other and the two remained in the closest possible contact: 'The mother sits quietly holding her baby, and if no attendants are present she very quickly seems content and relaxed. All is quiet in the room. No more piercing screeches of the baby or sounds from the mother are heard.' The duration of this unbroken period of intense mutual clinging following a separation that had lasted a mere five minutes was never less than fifteen minutes and in some cases as long as forty.

Other workers have subjected their monkey infants to much longer separations, the periods ranging from six days to as long as four weeks. In the case of pigtail and rhesus infants all observers report extreme and noisy distress during the twenty-four hours or so immediately after separation followed by a quieter period of a week or more during which the infants show little activity or play and, instead, sit hunched up and depressed.

Harlow has been responsible for two such studies. In one (Seay, Hansen and Harlow 1962), four rhesus infants, ages ranging from twenty-four to thirty weeks, were kept apart from mother for a period of three weeks.[4] Since mother was in an adjacent cage and

4. For an account of attachment behaviour in rhesus monkeys see Volume I, Chapter 11. Until it is about three years of age a young rhesus monkey in the wild remains close to mother.

Security, Anxiety, and Distress

only a transparent screen separated the two, each could see and hear the other. Observations were made at regular intervals during the three weeks prior to separation, during the three weeks of separation, and for three weeks following separation. On each occasion two infants, already familiar with each other, were separated simultaneously and, during the period of separation, each infant had free access to the other. Thus throughout the period of separation all four infants had companionship, access to food and water, and also visual and auditory contact with mother. Only physical contact with mother was missing.

As soon as the transparent screen had been lowered all four infants engaged in 'violent and prolonged protest'. There was much high-pitched screeching and crying, they made numerous attempts to reach mother, including hurling themselves against the screen, and they also scampered in a disoriented way around the cage. Later, when quiet, the infants huddled against the screen in as close proximity to mother as they could get. Initially mothers barked and threatened the experimenter, but their responses were less intense and persistent than the infants'. Throughout the separation period the pairs of separated infants showed little interest in one another and little play, in contrast to the active play between them seen in the three weeks prior to separation and after it was over. In the days after mother and infant had been reunited there was a very marked increase in the incidence of infant clinging to mother and keeping in contact with her compared with what had occurred during the days before separation.

In a second and similar experiment Seay and Harlow (1965) separated a further eight rhesus infants from mother when the infants were aged thirty weeks. On this occasion the separation lasted only two weeks and mother was removed completely; a second separated infant was again available for play, but this time for only half an hour each day. Results were as before, including on the first day 'disoriented running about, climbing, screeching and crying'; relatively little interest was shown in the companion infant. After the phase of protest (duration of which is not reported) the infants 'passed into a stage characterized by low activity, little or no play and occasional crying'. The writers express the belief that 'this second stage is behaviorally similar to that described as despair of children separated from their mothers'. Immediately after reunion once again there was a phase of strong mutual clinging by mother and infant.

In 1966 and 1967 reports were published of closely similar findings by two other groups of workers, Spencer-Booth and Hinde using rhesus macaques in Cambridge, Kaufman and Rosenblum using pigtail macaques in New York. These two studies have much in common and are more informative than the earlier ones. Whereas in both Jensen's and Harlow's laboratories the infants had been brought up with mother alone, each pair in a small cage, in the laboratories of Hinde and of Kaufman infant and mother lived as part of a stable social group in a fairly large cage. Present with them were an adult male, two or three other adult females, and often other young. In both laboratories separation was effected by removing mother from the cage. This meant that the infant remained behind in a completely familiar environment with a number of other familiar animals: the only change in its life was the absence of mother.

A second advantage of the Hinde and the Kaufman studies is that results are reported in much greater detail, both in regard to the course of behaviour during the week or more of separation and in regard to the behaviour of both partners during the period of months, and in the Hinde study of nearly two years, after the separation was over. These observations are especially valuable in giving information about subsequent effects of the experimental separation.

In the experiment of Kaufman and Rosenblum (1967) the subjects were four infant pigtail monkeys ranging in age from twenty-one to twenty-six weeks. In each case mother was removed from the cage for a period of four weeks. The behaviour seen during the separation is reported to have fallen into three phases, described as 'agitation, depression and recovery'. Whereas three infants went through all three phases, the fourth, the daughter of the dominant female of the group, showed comparatively little depression and spent much of her time with the other adult females of her group. The behaviour of the remaining three infants is described as follows:

During the first phase pacing, searching head movements, frequent trips to the door and windows, sporadic and short-lived bursts of erratic play, and brief movements toward other members of the group seemed constant. Cooing, the rather plaintive distress call of the young macaque, was frequent. There was an increased amount of self-directed behaviour, such as sucking of digits, and mouthing and handling of other parts of the body, including the genitals. The reaction persisted throughout the first day, during which time the infant did not sleep.

After 24 to 36 hours the pattern in three infants changed strikingly. Each infant sat hunched over, almost rolled into a ball, with his head often down between his legs. Movement was rare except when the infant was actively displaced. The movement that did occur appeared to be in slow motion, except at feeding time or in response to aggression. The infant rarely responded to social invitation or made a social gesture, and play behaviour virtually ceased. The infant appeared disinterested in and disengaged from the environment. Occasionally he would look up and coo.

After persisting unchanged for 5 or 6 days the depression gradually began to lift. The recovery started with a resumption of a more upright posture and a resurgence of interest in the inanimate environment. Slow tentative exploration appeared with increasing frequency. Gradually, the motherless infant also began to interact with his social environment primarily with his peers, and then be began to play once again. The depression continued, but in an abated form. Periods of depression alternated with periods of inanimate-object exploration and play. Movement increased in amount and tempo. Toward the end of the month the infant appeared alert and active a great deal of the time, yet he still did not behave like a typical infant of that age.

Throughout the three months following mother's return the behaviour of mother and infant was recorded. In all four cases significant changes were observed, similar in direction to those observed in earlier studies:

When the mother was reintroduced to the group another dramatic change occurred. There was a tremendous reassertion of the dyadic relationship with marked increases in various measures of closeness in all four pairs. Clinging by the infant, protective enclosure by the mother, and nipple contact all rose significantly in the month after the reunion as compared to the frequency of these actions in the month before separation. Even in the third month after the reunion this trend was evident. This significant rise in measures of dyadic closeness is particularly striking in view of the fact that ordinarily for the age periods involved these particular behaviours fall considerably.

The increased closeness was manifest in other ways as well. A measure of mother–infant physical separation that we have found valuable in our normative studies concerns departures (usually by the infant) to another level of the pen. The frequency of such departures during the month after the reunion fell to 20 per cent of the departures in the month before the separation. Furthermore, the mean duration of these departures fell from 60·5 seconds to 34·4 seconds.

Not only did infants depart less frequently and for shorter periods than before the separation had occurred but mothers were more tolerant than before of their infant's persistent proximity, only rarely discouraging it by rejection or withdrawal.

Compared with the four subjects of Kaufman's experiment, the four subjects described initially by Spencer-Booth and Hinde were not only of a different species (rhesus instead of pigtail infants) but were rather older (thirty to thirty-two weeks of age instead of twenty-one to twenty-six weeks); and the length of time for which mother was removed was much shorter – only six days in place of four weeks. Nevertheless, the behaviour observed both during the separation and during the months afterwards closely resembled what Kaufman and his colleagues were seeing (see Hinde, Spencer-Booth and Bruce 1966; Spencer-Booth and Hinde 1967).

Since their first reports Spencer-Booth and Hinde have published findings from a series of further studies in which the initial sample of four infants was increased to twenty-one, infants in certain sub-samples were exposed to a second separation, and another six infants were exposed to a longer separation (thirteen days). Almost all these infants were then studied for a further two years, namely until they were aged two and a half years, and their development was compared with that of a control sample of eight infants who had remained with mother throughout. A useful summary of findings from all these studies is given in Hinde and Spencer-Booth (1971).

Since findings on the initial four infants in regard to behaviour both during the separation and during the months after it are amply confirmed in the larger study, and since in the early publication by Spencer-Booth and Hinde (1967) behaviour is described in considerable detail, the account following is taken from that paper. Although, as in Kaufman's study, there was some variation in the reactions of the infants, they showed an overall pattern in common.

During the first day of separation all four infants screamed and geckered persistently. Although they did so less on subsequent days the amount continued much above what it had been before separation (and it continued so also for some weeks after mother's return). In contrast to Kaufman's pigtail infants, however, the rhesus infants were notably inactive immediately after mother's removal. This state of relative inactivity persisted throughout the remaining days of separation for all four infants: 'In general, the infants' behaviour during the mother's absence can only be described as depressed. They sat in the hunched, passive attitude of a subordinate animal.' On the first day of separation both manipulative play and social play decreased dramatically. Although on subsequent days there was some recovery in manipulative play, social play remained low and tended to get progressively less during the six days.

Interaction of the infant with the adult male or one of the adult females of its group was greater during separation than either before or after it, but none the less was only a fraction of what the infant had been used to with its mother before separation. Here again there was much variation between infants. Whereas one separated infant was never observed being cradled by or clinging to an adult, each of the others was observed so for up to 20 per cent of the observation units. Nevertheless, such episodes were usually extremely brief in comparison with the long spells spent on mother before separation. Instead of a close cuddling the more normal picture was of a separated infant sitting touching or nearly touching aunts or the male; when adult moved away the infant would often whoo or gecker. Two of the infants, especially, often sat with the adult male of their group, running to him for protection. Thus the separated infants received some substitute care from the other adults, but it was only a small proportion of what they had been receiving from their own mother.

The eating behaviour of the separated infants changed, too, in ways frequently seen in separated human children. On the first day of separation one infant ate hardly at all. Subsequently all four showed a tendency to eat more.

Although the acute disturbance of the first day subsided, then, the behaviour of all four infants remained far from normal throughout the subsequent five days of separation.

Disturbed behaviour was also much in evidence during the weeks after mother's return. After mother was returned to the cage all four infants 'were more clinging than they had been before the separation. They showed exceptionally intense tantrums when rejected by their mothers, and often flung themselves violently on to their mothers, or sometimes, when the mother had rejected them, on to aunts.' With two of the infants 'the effect was dramatic and long-lasting': they hardly came off their mothers during the first day of reunion.

A particularly striking feature during the first week or two of reunion was the way in which an infant might 'change from being relaxed to being very upset and clinging without apparent cause'. On the second and third days after reunion one infant 'was recorded as coming off his mother in an apparently calm fashion, then suddenly panicking and going on her geckering'. Another infant (female) on the sixth day of reunion was observed to play in a relaxed way for half an hour and then to sleep on mother for a time: 'When she awoke she seemed very upset and terrified, cringed and would hardly leave her mother.' Subsequently, however, she again seemed relaxed and began to play.

The behaviour of the four mother–infant pairs during the four months after reunion, up to the first birthday, varied much from pair to pair. Nevertheless, when the behaviour of the four infants was compared with that of a control group of eight infants who had had no separation experience, all four were found to have been affected, 'all taking the initiative in being close to their mothers more, relative to the controls, than before separation'. The tendency to cling and to stay close to mother was very marked; in one infant it persisted for the whole of the four months to the first birthday and in another for half that time.

Even more striking were the differences in behaviour shown by the four separated infants as compared with the eight controls when they were tested in slightly strange situations, first at twelve months of age and later at thirty months. The four who had been separated tended, in comparison with the controls, to be less willing to approach an experimenter offering food, to stay closer to mother when moved to a strange cage, to make shorter visits to a cage containing strange objects, and to be less active after having been frightened by a minor happening (Hinde and Spencer-Booth 1968).

The results of these experiments, conducted almost two years after a separation lasting only six days, are impressive evidence that separation from mother can be traumatic. Whereas the behaviour of these young monkeys during the course of an uneventful day might show no differences from that of control monkeys, once the environment becomes a little unusual differences show up: the behaviour of those who have been separated is more timid and anxious than is that of the controls. That this is true also of human infants has been noted on a number of occasions by Robertson (1953; 1958b) and the present writer (Bowlby 1951; 1960a).

As remarked above, since their pioneer study of four rhesus infants separated for six days Hinde and Spencer-Booth have done much further work and greatly amplified their findings. For those interested a description of some of the principal ones follows.

Further studies by Hinde and Spencer-Booth

From their extensive further studies Hinde and Spencer-Booth are able not only to confirm and amplify their data on the effects on young rhesus monkeys of a single six-day separation from mother but also to compare them with (a) the effects of a second short separation of six days and (b) the effects of a single, rather longer, separation of thirteen days. In addition, they are able to cast light on the factors responsible for the considerable degree of individual variation seen in the responses.

We consider, first, the short-term effects on the twice-separated infants; next, the long-term effects on infants who had been subjected to either one or two six-day separations; and, third, the short-term effects of a thirteen-day separation. (Long-term findings in respect of the last group of infants are not yet available.)

Short-term Effects of a Second Six-day Separation

When aged thirty to thirty-two weeks a total of eleven infants were separated from mother for six days for their first and only time and a total of ten for their second time. (Of the latter, five had had a first separation ten weeks earlier and five had had one five weeks earlier.) When the behaviour of the infants separated for their second time was compared with that of infants of the same age separated for their first time no differences were apparent, on the measures used, either during the separation itself or during the subsequent month (Spencer-Booth and Hinde 1971a). Evidence from the follow-up shows, however, that it would be a mistake to conclude that the effects of two separations are no different from the effects of one.

Long-term Effects of One and Two Six-day Separations

In their report on the long-term effects of six-day separations Spencer-Booth and Hinde (1971c) compare observations of infants from three samples: control infants, $N = 8$; infants that underwent a single six-day separation, $N = 5$; and infants that underwent two six-day separations, $N = 8$.[5] For some comparisons numbers are reduced; and on occasion it is necessary to pool data for the once- and the twice-separated infants.

Stated briefly, findings are as follows:

1. When tested at twelve and again at thirty months of age and compared with the controls, the previously separated infants of both groups still showed 'some persistence of those symptoms of depression and of disturbed mother–infant relations which had been conspicuous in the month immediately following the mother's return'.

5. Two infants first separated at twenty-one weeks of age, and one first separated at twenty-six weeks, died before they were a year old, and a second of the twenty-six-week group died soon after its second birthday. One of the long-separated group, together with three infants separated at eighteen weeks and omitted from consideration, also died before their first birthday. It is not clear how far the deprivation experience may have contributed to the death of these infants.

2. The differences in behaviour between the previously separated infants and the controls were far more evident when the infant was tested in a strange environment than when it was in its home run.

3. Differences were much less marked at thirty months than at twelve months, but all the differences that were significant were in the direction that the previously separated animals showed poorer or more disturbed behaviour than the controls.

4. Most of the significant differences were between the controls and the twice-separated infants, with the once-separated infants generally occupying an intermediate position.

Let us consider these findings one by one.

In the home run at twelve months of age the previously separated animals of both groups tended to spend less time at a distance from mother, and to play a greater relative role in maintaining proximity to her, than did the control infants. Few of these differences were significant, however, and they were no longer observable either at eighteen or at thirty months. At all three ages, however, there was a significant tendency for the previously separated infants to show less locomotor activity and less social play than the controls.

Whereas the differences found in the behaviour of the previously separated animals and the controls while they were still in their home runs were not very conspicuous, when the animals were *in a strange environment* and tested there, differences were marked. The importance of this finding in its clinical implications can hardly be exaggerated.

At the age of twelve months each infant with its mother was brought to a strange laboratory cage which communicated with a similar cage (the filter cage) by means of a passage large enough for the infant but not for the mother. Testing was conducted over a period of nine days and consisted of placing food or a strange object in the filter cage and seeing how the infant responded. Objects included a mirror, pieces of banana, and a yellow ball. On almost every test there was a significant tendency for the previously separated infants, in comparison with the controls, to wait longer before venturing to go alone into the filter cage, to pay shorter visits there, and to spend less total time in it. Furthermore, whenever scores of the twice-separated infants differed from scores of the once-separated, divergence from the controls' scores was consistently greater in the case of the twice-separated infants. The table below, giving results for a test on the sixth day, when a yellow ball was placed in the filter cage, shows a typical pattern of differences.

| Measure | Median score in minutes | | |
	Controls N = 6	Once-separated N = 5	Twice-separated N = 8
Latency to entering cage	0·1	0·1	0·7
Total time in cage	7·0	3·9	3·0
Median length of visit	0·5	0·3	0·2
Time spent playing	2·3	0	0

Another test given at twelve months which showed significant differences between the previously separated infants and the controls was one in which an infant was offered vitamins by an experimenter. The previously separated animals were much less willing to approach to obtain the vitamin than were the controls, and this was so even when the test was carried out in the home run. A probable explanation of that is that one of the experimenters had taken part in catching and removing the infants' mothers at the time of the separation.

Eighteen months later when aged thirty months each animal was given a series of comparable tests. On this occasion it was tested over a period of sixteen days when by itself in a screened laboratory cage. Out of many tests only a few showed significant differences between groups. One was when the experimenter offered the vitamins. Another was when, on the second and sixth days, a piece of date was hung outside the cage just out of reach: the previously separated animals were much longer than the controls before making an attempt to get it, made fewer attempts, and persisted in making attempts for less long. (The number of animals available for this test made differentiation between once- and twice-separated animals impossible.)

Short-term Effects of a Thirteen-day Separation

At the age of thirty to thirty-two weeks a further six infants were separated for a single period lasting thirteen days (see Spencer-Booth and Hinde 1971b). During the whole of the second week they remained about as depressed and inactive as they were at the end of the first week. (This is in contrast to the moderate degree of recovery seen after the first week of separation in pigtail infants by Kaufman & Rosenblum.)

During the month following the separation it was found that the infants separated for thirteen days were significantly more affected than were infants in either of the other two separated groups. For at least the first week after reunion they emitted more distress calls; and throughout the month they were more depressed. During the time they spent out of contact with mother they spent more time sitting about inactive than did the other separated infants, and when they were active they were less so. Whereas by the end of the first month of reunion infants separated once and for only six days were showing at least as much activity as they had done before the separation, the activity level of those separated for thirteen days was still significantly reduced. At this time the activity level of the twice-separated infants was intermediate between that of infants separated for a single six-day period and that of those separated for thirteen days.

From all these findings we can conclude with confidence not only that a single separation of no longer than six days at six months of age has perceptible effects two years later on rhesus infants, but that the effects of a separation are proportionate to its length. A thirteen-day separation is worse than a six-day; two six-day separations are worse than a single six-day separation. In these regards the effects of separation from mother can be likened to the effects of smoking or of radiation. Although the effects of small doses appear negligible, they are cumulative. The safest dose is a zero dose.

Individual Variations of Response

There is much individual variation in the responses of rhesus infants to separation. Within the age-range studied age had little effect: whether a six-day separation was at twenty-one to twenty-two weeks, at twenty-five to twenty-six weeks, or at thirty to thirty-two weeks seemed to make little difference. Sex played some part: both during separation and after it males were more affected than females. Whether or not an infant was able to cling to another animal during separation had no effect on behaviour after reunion though such clinging did reduce the amount of distress calling at the time.

The most striking results to emerge from the analysis of the data on individual variation are the significant correlations between degree of distress shown by an infant and certain features of the mother–infant relationship (Hinde and Spencer-Booth 1970). The infants that are most distressed during the first month after separation tend to be those that are most frequently rejected by mother and that play the greatest relative role in maintaining proximity to her. Since in regard to these features there is consistency for each mother–infant pair over time (as measured by rank-order correlations), it is not surprising to find that the degree of distress shown after separation is correlated both with the frequency with which a mother rejects her infant during the period before separation and with the frequency with which she rejects it during the period after reunion. In fact, it is found that, soon after mother returns, correlation of infant distress is higher with frequency of maternal rejection before separation than with frequency of rejection contemporaneously. Subsequently the balance changes and degree of distress becomes more highly correlated with the frequency with which she is rejecting her infant at the time.

Hinde and Spencer-Booth (1971) emphasize that these correlations do not justify the conclusion that differences in the mother–infant relation necessarily cause the differences in infants' responses to separations; nevertheless they believe that to be likely.

In a recent experiment Hinde and Davies (1972) altered the conditions in which separation occurs: instead of mothers being removed from the home cage and placed in a strange one, the infants were removed and mothers remained behind. During their thirteen days of separation the behaviour of the five infants conformed to expectations. Although large individual differences made comparisons difficult, the infants separated in a strange cage seemed even more disturbed than did infants that remained in the home cage while mother was removed. After reunion with mother, however, the infants that had been separated in the strange cage were *less* disturbed than were infants whose mothers had been removed.

Certain observations of the behaviour of the mothers suggest an explanation of this unexpected finding. Compared with mothers that had been removed to the strange cage, mothers that remained behind were less distressed during their infant's absence and, after reunion, were more maternal and less rejecting of it; and harmonious interaction between the two was restored more quickly. These findings tend to support the view that a major determinant of the effect of a separation on a rhesus infant is how mother behaves towards it after reunion.

One form of behaviour that is extremely common in young children after a separation lasting a week or longer in strange surroundings and without substitute mothering, but that has only once been reported for monkey young, is detachment, namely a failure to recognize or respond to mother on reunion. In a study by Abrams (described by Mitchell 1970) twenty-four rhesus infants underwent a two-day separation from mother when aged between eight and twenty weeks. At the time of reunion one-quarter of the infants observed ran away from mother as she approached; and after a second two-day separation a few weeks later, the proportion that ran away doubled. Since, although on the lookout for detachment, Hinde & Spencer-Booth never observed it, the response may prove to be confined to infants in the very young age-range studied by Abrams. It is not yet clear, however, whether the response observed by Abrams can be regarded as homologous with that seen in young children.

The findings of the primate experiments have been described at length because they leave no serious doubt that most of what is to be seen during and after a brief separation in human infants is to be seen also in infants of other species. Explanations of human responses that presume cognitive processes at a specifically human level are thus called in question.

Part II: An Ethological Approach to Human Fear

Chapter 5
Basic Postulates in Theories of Anxiety and Fear

> Paradigms provide scientists not only with a map but also with some of the directions essential for map-making. In learning a paradigm the scientist acquires theory, methods and standards together, usually in an inextricable mixture. ... That is [a] reason why schools guided by different paradigms are always slightly at cross-purposes.
> — THOMAS S. KUHN (1962)

Anxiety allied to fear

Though at intervals down the years one student of the problem after another has been struck that a principal source of anxiety and distress is separation from loved figures, or the threat of separation, there has been great reluctance to accept that simple formula. Objections to it are extremely deep-seated and based on one or more of several common assumptions each of which, it is argued here, is tenable no longer.

In this and the following chapters the simple view is once again advanced. And because there has been so much incredulity and therefore reasoned opposition to it, it is presented in some detail. We begin by considering some of the common assumptions that underlie the traditional incredulity and opposition, with special reference to the influence of Freud's early formulated theory of motivation.

In all psychoanalytic and psychiatric discussion of anxiety it is taken for granted that the emotional states referred to respectively as 'anxiety' and 'fear' are closely related. In just what way they are related is the puzzle. Freud is concerned repeatedly both to compare and to contrast the two: see, for example, Addendum B to *Inhibitions, Symptoms and Anxiety* (*SE* **20**: 164–8). Others have followed in his steps. Reviewing the whole confused scene in a recent article, Lewis (1967) emphasizes that, throughout the broad field of psychopathology, the word 'anxiety' is used habitually to refer to 'an emotional state with the subjectively experienced quality of fear or a closely related emotion'. Often, we know, the two words are used interchangeably. In view of the close relatedness of the emotional states concerned and also of the meanings of the two words, it is hardly surprising that ideas about the conditions that give rise to the one state should influence ideas about the conditions that give rise to the other.

Nevertheless, in all this diverse, confusing, and contradictory theorizing there is one matter on which all seem agreed: whereas the nature and origin of anxiety are obscure, the nature and origin of fear are simple and readily intelligible.

In the theories advanced in this work there is only one break with that tradition. As hitherto, the states referred to by the words 'anxiety' and 'fear' are seen as closely related. Furthermore, ideas about what arouses states of the one kind are, also as hitherto, closely linked to ideas about what arouses states of the other. Where thinking diverges is on an altogether different issue, namely on the nature of the conditions that are apt to arouse what is allegedly the more easily understood of the two states, that of fear itself.

In psychoanalytic and psychiatric circles, it is argued, there still flourish seriously misconceived assumptions about fear and the conditions that arouse it. These mistaken assumptions have long had, and continue to have, a most adverse effect on our ability to understand the distressing anxieties and fears from which our patients suffer.

Perhaps the most basic and pervasive of these traditional assumptions is that the only situation that properly arouses fear is the presence of something likely to hurt or damage us; with the corollary that fear arising in any other situation must be in some way abnormal, or at least requires special explanation. While this assumption may appear plausible at first sight, there are two distinct ways in which it proves to be mistaken.

One type of mistake concerns the nature of the stimuli and objects that frighten us and lead us to retreat. Not infrequently, it is found, they bear only an *indirect* relationship to what is in fact dangerous. The second type of mistake is just as basic. We are frightened not only by the *presence*, or expected presence, of situations of certain sorts, but by the *absence*, or expected absence, of situations of other sorts.

In what follows some of the origins and effects of these two types of mistake are considered. When examined, they are found to be intimately linked with assumptions made early in Freud's thinking, and especially with the model of motivation he adopted. When a different model of motivation is applied, as it is in this work, the perspective changes.

Models of motivation and their effects on theory

The long tradition of psychoanalytic theorizing about fear and anxiety has been influenced profoundly by the model of motivation that Freud adopted in his very earliest formulations, long before he realized that problems of separation and loss are central to psychopathology, and that he retained thereafter in all his metapsychological theorizing. This is the model that assumes that stimuli of every kind are responded to by the organism simply as things to be got rid of, whenever possible by means of escape and, when this is not possible, by some other kind of action.

Since it is not always recognized how deep and long-lasting an influence this model has had on psychoanalytic theories of anxiety, including separation anxiety, it may be useful to quote Freud's own words. In 'Instincts and their Vicissitudes' (1915a), one of a succession of publications in which he discusses his basic ideas, Freud once again states it as a basic postulate, which he assumes and never argues, that 'the nervous system is an apparatus which has the function of getting rid of the stimuli that reach it, or of reducing them to the lowest possible level; or which, if it were feasible, would maintain itself in an altogether unstimulated condition'. External stimuli, Freud maintains, are easily dealt with by withdrawal. 'Instinctual stimuli', on the other hand, by maintaining 'an incessant and unavoidable afflux of stimulation' present a far greater problem since, being of internal origin, to withdraw from them is impossible. In order to deal with their incessant welling up, Freud continues, the nervous system undertakes 'involved and interconnected activities by which the external world is so changed as to afford satisfaction'; and satisfaction, he holds, 'can only be obtained by removing the state of stimulation at the source of the instinct' (*SE* **14**: 120, 122).

No biological function, in terms of the survival of the population of which the individual is a member, is attributed to the activities in question. The reason for this omission is that, when the theory was advanced, the distinction between causation and function was not appreciated.

The basic postulate, or model, referred to by Freud in his every discussion of metapsychology, and the one that underlies his 'economic viewpoint' (*SE* 14: 181), has as one of its corollaries that no external object is ever sought in and of itself, but only in so far as it aids in the elimination of the 'incessant afflux' of instinctual stimulation. Thus a mother is sought only in so far as she helps to reduce a build-up of tension arising from unmet physiological drives, and is missed only because it is feared such tension may go unrelieved.

This postulate still has a deep influence on clinical thinking. For example, it is this assumption that led Freud (1926a) confidently to conclude that 'the reason why the infant in arms wants to perceive the presence of its mother is only because it already knows by experience that she satisfies all its needs without delay'; and that led him, further, to the idea that the ultimate 'danger-situation is a recognized, remembered, expected situation of helplessness', a situation that he refers to also as 'traumatic' (*SE* 20: 166).

That conclusion, it is argued here, a conclusion consistent with a theory of secondary drive to account for the child's tie to his mother, has had certain adverse effects. A principal one is the still commonly held belief that a key source of fear is helplessness, and consequently that it is childish, even babyish, to yearn for the presence of a loved figure and to be anxious or distressed during her (or his) absence. Such beliefs, it is held, are not only mistaken but are far from being favourable for the way we treat our patients.

Now there is nothing self-evident about Freud's basic postulate; nor, it must be remembered, did it derive from clinical practice.[1] On the contrary, the status of that postulate, as of all

1. For a sketch of the historical origins of Freud's basic model and the influence especially of Fechner, see Volume I, Chapter 1. For an account of the variants of theory derived by Freud from his basic postulate and their relation to his concepts of pleasure and unpleasure, see Schur (1967). For a critique of Freud's basic postulate, see Walker (1956).

similar ones in science, is that it is advanced only in order that scientists may try it out to discover what its explanatory value may be. In the words of Thomas Kuhn (1962), a postulate of this kind provides a paradigm in terms of which a body of theory is formulated and research conducted. Whenever workers in a single field adopt different paradigms, as occurs from time to time, great difficulties of communication ensue.

In Chapter 1 of the first volume of this work reasons are given for not adopting Freud's model of motivation and in later chapters (3 to 8 inclusive) an account is given of what appears to be a more promising model derived from ethology and control theory. Within the field of psychoanalysis, the model advanced constitutes a new paradigm, different from Freud's and different also from others advanced by analysts, for example that of Klein. As a result difficulties of communication are inevitable.

A principal way in which the old and the new paradigms differ is in their relation to evolution theory. When Freud advanced his paradigm during the 1890s, although biological evolution was much discussed and its historical reality widely accepted, no agreement had yet been reached regarding the processes likely to be responsible for its occurrence. Darwin's theory, that evolution occurs as a result of the differential breeding success of certain variants in comparison with others, was still hotly debated by scientists, many of whom supported alternative theories. As it happens, Darwin's theory, which, in developed form, has come to provide the paradigm for twentieth-century biology, did not appeal to Freud. Instead, he came to prefer the vitalism of Lamarck.[2] For psychoanalysis the effects of Freud's choice have been very serious, because the paradigm he adopted has led psychoanalysis to be increasingly estranged from its sister sciences.

The paradigm adopted in the present work is based on current evolution theory and is thereby the same as that of modern biology. Its main features are inherent in the model of motivation sketched in the earlier volume They can be summarized as follows:

2. In Appendix II to this volume an account is given of Freud's views on evolution in the context of ideas on the subject current at the time he wrote.

- behaviour results from the activation, and later the termination, of *behavioural systems* that develop and exist within the organism, and are of very varying degrees of organizational complexity;
- the behaviour that results from the activation and termination of certain types of behavioural system is traditionally termed *instinctive* because it follows a recognizably similar pattern in almost all members of a species, has consequences that are usually of obvious value in contributing to species survival, and in many cases develops when all the ordinary opportunities for learning it are exiguous or absent;
- the *causal factors* that either activate or terminate systems responsible for instinctive behaviour include hormonal levels, the organization and autonomous action of the central nervous system, environmental stimuli of particular sorts, and proprioceptive stimuli arising within the organism;
- the *biological function* of a system responsible for instinctive behaviour is that consequence of its activity that promotes the survival of the species (or population) of which the organism is a member, and does so in such degree that individuals endowed with the system leave behind them more progeny than those not endowed with it;
- the *environment of evolutionary adaptedness* is the environment in which a species lived while its existing characteristics, including behavioural systems, were being evolved, and is the only environment in which there can be any assurance that activation of a system will be likely to result in the achievement of its biological function;
- behavioural systems develop within an individual through the interaction during ontogeny of genetically determined biases and the environment in which the individual is reared; the further the *rearing environment* departs from that of evolutionary adaptedness the more likely are that individual's behavioural systems to develop atypically.

It will be seen that in this model a sharp distinction is drawn between, on the one hand, the causal factors that result first in the activation and later in the termination of a behavioural system and, on the other, the biological function served by the behaviour. Causal factors, listed above, include hormonal levels, actions of the central nervous system, environmental stimuli of special sorts, and proprioceptive feedback from within the organism. Functions, by contrast, are certain special consequences that arise when a system is active in the organism's environment of evolutionary adaptedness, and are a result of the way in which the system is constructed. In the case of sexual behaviour, as an example, the distinction runs as follows. Hormonal states of the organism and certain characteristics of the partner, together, lead to sexual interest and play causal roles in eliciting sexual behaviour; and the feedback of stimuli arising in the consummatory situation terminate it. These are all causal factors. The biological function of that behaviour is another matter and derives from certain consequences of the activity: those consequences are fertilization and reproduction. It is only because causation and function are distinct that it is possible, by means of contraception, to intervene between the behaviour and the function it was evolved to serve.

Once a model of motivation that distinguishes causation from function, and is set within an evolutionary framework, is applied to problems to do with anxiety and fear new solutions become possible. A comparison follows between solutions that derive, on the one hand, from Freud's model of motivation and, on the other, from a model compatible with current evolution theory.

Puzzling phobia or natural fear

When in 1926 Freud came to reconsider his ideas about anxiety, he did so still adhering to his original model of motivation and also holding to the assumption (never completely explicit but repeatedly apparent) that the only situation that should properly arouse fear in a human being is the presence of something likely to hurt or damage him. Principal consequences of that assumption are: first, Freud's extreme perplexity in understanding why fear should be aroused, and be aroused so commonly and strongly, in situations of quite other kinds; second, the far from simple theories to which he and his successors resort in order to account for such fear; and, finally, a mistaken yardstick with which to measure what is healthy and what pathological.

The argument Freud advances in *Inhibitions, Symptoms and Anxiety* can be put in a nutshell, using his own words: 'A real danger is a danger which threatens a person from an external object.' Whenever anxiety is 'about a known danger', therefore, it can be regarded as 'realistic anxiety'; whereas whenever it is 'about an unknown danger' it is to be regarded as 'neurotic anxiety'. Since fear of certain situations, for example of *being alone* or *in the dark* or *with strangers*, is, in Freud's view, fear of unknown dangers, it is to be judged neurotic (*SE* **20**: 165–7). Because all children are afraid of such situations, moreover, all children are held to suffer from neurosis (pp. 147–8).

Readers of that work can trace Freud's persistent efforts to solve the problem of what he terms the 'puzzling phobias' of young children, among which he includes 'fear of being alone or in the dark or with strangers' (*SE* **20**: 168), none of which examples, in terms of his assumptions, is at all easily intelligible. The conclusion to which he is driven, in keeping with his basic postulate, is that fear of each of these commonplace situations is to be equated initially with fear of losing the object and ultimately with fear of psychical helplessness in the face of mounting instinctual stimulation (p. 166). Viewed in this light, fear of such situations is held by Freud to be not only childish but on the borderland of pathology. Provided development is healthy, Freud believes, fear of all these situations is left well behind: 'The phobias of very young children, fear of being alone or in the dark or with strangers – phobias which can almost be called normal – usually pass off later on: the child "grows out of them" . . .' (p. 147). When, however, development is unhealthy it is fear of just these types of situation that persists: 'a great many people remain infantile in their behaviour in regard to danger and do not overcome determinants of anxiety which have grown out of date . . . it is precisely such people whom we call neurotics' (p. 148).

Klein, like almost all other psychoanalysts, accepts Freud's view that what a child fears cannot be understood as in any sense 'realistic', and that it is therefore necessary to explain such fear in other ways. Impressed by the prevalence of aggressive behaviour in disturbed children aged two years and upwards, she advances a novel theory: 'I hold that anxiety arises from the operation of the death instinct within the organism, is felt as fear of annihilation (death) and takes the form of fear of persecution' (Klein 1946). This theory is the heart of the Kleinian system.

In all these matters the position adopted in this work is radically different from those of Freud, Klein, and most other psychoanalysts. So far from being either phobic or infantile, it is argued, the tendency to fear all these common situations is to be regarded as a natural disposition of man, a natural disposition, moreover, that stays with him in some degree from infancy to old age, and is shared with animals of many other species. Thus it is not the presence of this tendency in childhood or later life that is pathological; pathology is indicated either when the tendency is apparently absent or when fear is aroused with unusual readiness and intensity. When considered in the light of a different theory of motivation and a modern evolutionary perspective, the argument continues, the existence and prevalence of a tendency to fear any and all of these common situations are readily intelligible in terms of survival value.

An Evolutionary Perspective

Comparative studies of the behaviour of man and other mammals present a picture of the conditions that lead to fear and retreat very different from the one that stems from Freud's assumptions. Not infrequently, it is found, the conditions that give rise to fear bear a regular but only *indirect* relation to what is in fact liable to hurt or damage us. This issue is already touched on in the earlier volume (Chapter 15) in which evidence is presented that, in a wide array of animal species including man, a principal condition that elicits alarm and retreat is mere strangeness. Others are noise, and objects that rapidly expand or approach; and also, for animals of some species though not for others, darkness. Yet another is isolation.

Now it is obvious that none of these stimulus situations is in itself dangerous. Yet, when looked at through evolutionary spectacles, their role in promoting survival is not difficult to see.

Noise, strangeness, rapid approach, isolation, and for many species darkness too – all are conditions statistically associated with an increased risk of danger. Noise may presage a natural disaster: fire, flood, or landslide. To a young animal a predator is strange, it approaches fast and perhaps noisily, and often strikes at night; and it is far more likely to do so when the potential victim is alone. Because of their association with increased risk of danger, therefore, each of these conditions acts as a *naturally occurring clue* to the likelihood of danger threatening and as such can be utilized by animals. In the long run, moreover, sensitivity to such clues can affect the way in which animals evolve. Because to behave so promotes both survival and breeding success, the theory runs, the young of species that have survived, including man, are found to be genetically biased so to develop that they respond to the properties of noise, strangeness, sudden approach, and darkness by taking avoiding action or running away – they behave in fact as though danger were actually present. In a comparable way they respond to isolation by seeking company. Fear responses elicited by such naturally occurring clues to danger are a part of man's basic behavioural equipment.

It is not without interest that, in an afterthought to his essay, Freud toyed with the idea that some of the 'phobias' he found so puzzling may conceivably have a biological function: '. . . the fear of small animals, thunderstorms, etc. might perhaps be accounted for as vestigial traces of the congenital preparedness to meet real dangers which is so strongly developed in other animals'. Nevertheless, he quickly dismisses that possibility and concludes by expressing the view that 'In man, only that part of this archaic heritage is appropriate which has reference to the loss of the object' (*SE* **20**: 168); and, as we have already seen, even that part Freud interprets in a non-evolutionary way, namely as a safeguard against the individual's being exposed to excessive stimulation from within.

In the theory here advanced it is, of course, that very archaic heritage that is placed at the centre of the stage. A tendency to react with fear to each of these common situations – presence of strangers or animals, rapid approach, darkness, loud noises, and being alone – is regarded as developing as a result of genetically determined biases that indeed result in a 'preparedness to meet real dangers'. Furthermore, it is held, such tendencies occur not only in animals but in man himself and are present not only during childhood but throughout the whole span of life. Approached in this way, fear of being separated unwillingly from an attachment figure at any phase of the life-cycle ceases to be a puzzle and, instead, becomes classifiable as an instinctive response to one of the naturally occurring clues to an increased risk of danger.

Chapter 6
Forms of Behaviour Indicative of Fear

Thus, while some animals capable of rapid movement will take to flight under the influence of fear, others, who can move but slowly, will under the same influence remain immobile, or, like the hedgehog or a caterpillar, curl up. But man, where a too urgent fear does not deprive him of his power of forecasting different results, or of judging between them, may choose either to take to flight, or to conceal himself where he is, or to adopt some other means of safety.
— ALEXANDER F. SHAND (1920)

An empirical approach

The theme of this chapter and the next is that, if we are to understand the stimulus situations that cause human beings to feel fearful and anxious, or by contrast to feel secure, it is necessary to eschew all preconceived notions of what it might be 'realistic' or 'reasonable' or 'appropriate' to fear. Instead, our task must be an empirical one, to examine what is known of the actual situations in which fear and anxiety, or alternatively a sense of security, tend to be felt – by children, by women, and by men. Only when the natural conditions that arouse fear in man are chronicled and understood shall we be in a position to consider afresh the nature and origin of those heightened and persistent fears and anxieties that affect our patients and are deemed neurotic.

Terminological problems abound, not least in the numerous and varied attempts to distinguish anxiety from fear. Since at this point in the discussion some agreement on terminology is essential, the usage adopted here in respect of certain terms is explained briefly below; more detailed consideration of this topic is, however, postponed to Chapter 12, after the empirical evidence has been displayed and its theoretical implications studied.

Following everyday practice the word 'fear' is used here in a broad, general-purpose way. Like every word denoting emotion, fear has as referent both how we suppose a person to be feeling and how we predict he is likely to behave (see Volume I, Chapter 7). Since there is reason to think that fear behaviour has hitherto been given far too little attention, that is where we start.

Fear Behaviour

Let us examine the various forms of behaviour that are commonly held to be indicative of fear. They include, of course, the initial forms of behaviour, such as posture, expression, and incipient action, that lead us to infer that a person or animal is feeling afraid, and also the less subtle and more active forms of behaviour that often, but not always, follow.

Both in ordinary life and in systematic field observation there is a large array of distinct forms of behaviour that it is common practice to group together as being indicative of fear. They include wary watching combined with inhibition of action, a frightened facial expression accompanied perhaps by trembling or crying, cowering, hiding, running away, and also seeking contact with someone and perhaps clinging to him or her. When we ask why all these diverse forms of behaviour should be grouped together, we find the following four reasons:

(a) many of these forms of behaviour, though not all, tend to occur either simultaneously or sequentially;

(b) events that elicit one of these forms tend to elicit others also (though not necessarily all the others);

(c) most of them seem plainly to serve a single biological function, namely protection;

(d) when asked how they are feeling, persons behaving in these ways commonly describe themselves as feeling afraid or anxious or alarmed.

Although these are good reasons for grouping such diverse forms of behaviour together, there are nevertheless risks in doing so. In particular, the conditions that elicit one form of fear behaviour may differ in certain respects from those that elicit another form; and the autonomic responses that accompany one form may well differ from those that accompany another. In animals the distinctiveness of the forms is attested by experiment. Hinde (1970) discusses work by Hogan that suggests that, at least in young animals, not only may freezing and withdrawal be separate systems of behaviour, elicited by different types of external stimulation, but they may even be mutually inhibiting. Further evidence on this issue is given in Chapter 8.

A point to be especially noted, and a corner-stone of the present argument, is that, in ordinary usage, grouped under this single heading of behaviour indicative of fear are to be found forms of behaviour that have at least three distinct kinds of predictable outcome: (a) immobility, (b) increased distance from one type of object, and (c) increased proximity to another type of object. The contrast between the last two outcomes is especially important. For, on the one hand, is behaviour that *increases* distance from persons and objects that are treated as though they were threatening; on the other is behaviour that *reduces* distance from persons and objects that are treated as though they provided protection. Naturally, both these types of behaviour do not always occur. Yet they occur together with sufficient frequency to enable us to take the combination for granted. When we flush a rabbit we expect it not only to run *from* us but to run *to* cover. When a child is afraid of a barking dog we expect him not only to withdraw *from* the dog but to retreat *towards* a parent figure.

Now the usual practice of including under a single heading, that of behaviour indicative of fear, forms of behaviour that have such different predictable outcomes is of great significance. Yet it can very easily make for confusion. In particular it has often tempted psychologists, for example McDougall (1923), and also others, to postulate a single all-embracing 'instinct of fear'. An alternative theory and one that keeps far closer to observed data is that we are dealing, not with some single comprehensive form of behaviour, but with a heterogeneous collection of interrelated forms, each elicited by a slightly different set of causal conditions and each having a distinctive outcome. In the sense defined in Part II of the first volume, each such form can be regarded as an example of instinctive behaviour.

In order to sort out these different forms of behaviour a first step is to examine how attachment behaviour and fear behaviour are related to one another.

Withdrawal behaviour and attachment behaviour

It may already have been noticed that, of the three forms of behaviour with such different predictable outcomes that are habitually treated as indicative of fear, one is already familiar. The behaviour that reduces distance from persons or objects that are treated as though they provided protection is nothing other than attachment behaviour. Viewed in this perspective, therefore, though not in others, attachment behaviour appears as one component among the heterogeneous forms of behaviour commonly grouped together as fear behaviour.

It is evident that, if confusion is to be avoided, distinctive names are required also for any other components of fear behaviour that can be clearly identified. For behaviour that tends to increase distance from persons and objects that are treated as though they were threatening, the terms 'withdrawal', 'escape', and 'avoidance' are all convenient. For another principal and well-organized component, namely behaviour that results in immobility, the usual term is 'freezing'. Since, in humans, freezing has been little studied, most of the coming discussion hinges on the relations between attachment behaviour and withdrawal behaviour.

There need, of course, be no surprise that attachment behaviour and withdrawal behaviour are so frequently found together. For, as already argued in the first volume, both serve the same function, namely protection; and, because of that, both show many of the same eliciting conditions. Furthermore, when they are active together, as so frequently they are, the two forms of behaviour are usually compatible: more often than not it is easy to combine in a single action withdrawing from one zone and approaching another. It is in fact for these very reasons that the two are so habitually paired together, without distinction or thought, under the general rubric of fear behaviour.

Nevertheless, although attachment behaviour and withdrawal behaviour have so much in common, there are strong reasons for keeping them distinct. One is that, although they share many eliciting conditions, they do not share all. For example, attachment behaviour may be activated by fatigue or illness as well as by a situation that arouses fear. Another is that when the two forms of behaviour are active together, though they are usually compatible, they may not be. Conflict can easily occur, for example, whenever a stimulus situation that elicits both escape and attachment behaviour in an individual happens to be situated between that individual and his attachment figure; a familiar instance is when a barking dog comes between a child and his mother.

In a conflict situation of that sort there are at least four ways in which the frightened individual may behave, depending on whether escape behaviour or attachment behaviour takes precedence or whether they are evenly balanced. Examples of balance are when the frightened individual stays stationary, and also when he gets to his attachment figure by making a detour to avoid whatever is frightening him. Examples of one or other form of behaviour taking precedence are when the frightened individual goes more or less directly to his attachment figure despite having to pass close to the frightening object in order to do so, and also when he runs away from the frightening object even though by doing so he increases the distance from his attachment figure.

Although there is a large literature on approach/avoidance conflict, it is doubtful whether any experiments have been undertaken to determine, in the case of this version of the conflict, which of these different solutions is favoured by creatures of different age and species, and in different conditions. Any assumption that escape behaviour commonly takes precedence over attachment would, however, certainly be wrong. Much everyday experience shows that, in young animals of many species, attachment behaviour frequently takes precedence over escape. An example is the behaviour of lambs on a hill road when a car approaches. Caught on the side of the road opposite to its mother and frightened by the approaching car, a lamb will as often as not rush across the road in front of the car. Small children are apt to do the same.

Studies of human behaviour during and after a disaster contain countless vivid accounts of how no member of a family is content, or indeed able to attend to anything else, until all members of the family are gathered together. The studies describe also the tremendous comfort that the presence of another familiar person can bring and how, during the weeks after a disaster, the rule is for people to remain in close contact with attachment figures. Again and again attachment behaviour takes precedence over withdrawal. The findings of some of these studies are referred to again at the end of Chapter 10.

A special but not unusual situation in which there is conflict between attachment behaviour and withdrawal is when the attachment figure is also the one who elicits fear, perhaps by threats or violence. In such conditions young creatures, whether human or non-human, are likely to cling to the threatening or hostile figure rather than run away from him or her (for references, see Volume I, Chapter 12). This propensity may be playing a part in so-called phobic patients, whose inability to leave home is found often to be a response to alarming threats made by their parents (see Chapters 18 and 19).

This analysis shows that attachment behaviour and withdrawal behaviour are distinct behavioural systems that (a) have the same function, (b) may be elicited by many of the same conditions, (c) are frequently compatible with each other, but (d) can easily be in conflict. In cases of conflict it is a matter for inquiry to discover which, if either, takes precedence.

Fear and Attack

Stimulus situations that are likely to arouse fear in humans can also, when circumstances are a little changed, evoke attack. The close link between the two very different forms of behaviour is considered in Chapter 8 in so far as it is seen and studied in animals and in Chapter 17 in so far as it occurs in humans.

Feeling afraid and its variants: feeling alarmed and feeling anxious

Whether compatible or in conflict with one another, attachment behaviour and escape behaviour are commonly elicited by many of the same stimulus situations and are, it is held, always serving the same function, that of protection. It is not surprising, therefore, that in at least some circumstances the two forms of behaviour are accompanied by rather similar subjective experience.

An Ethological Approach to Human Fear

When confronted by a stimulus situation that makes us want to withdraw or escape from it, we are likely to describe ourselves as feeling afraid, or frightened, or alarmed, or perhaps anxious. Equally, whenever our attachment behaviour is aroused, perhaps by a similar sort of situation, but for some reason we are unable to find or reach our attachment figure, we are likely to describe how we feel in much the same words. For example, we might say, 'I was afraid you were gone', or 'I was frightened when I could not find you', or 'Your long absence made me anxious'.

This rather promiscuous use of language is both revealing and confusing. On the one hand, it strongly suggests that escape behaviour and attachment behaviour may share certain basic features in common. On the other, it becomes easy for the unwary to assume that, because in common speech words are used without discrimination, whatever is referred to can be treated as though it were undifferentiated. In addition, promiscuous usage makes it extremely difficult to tie any specialized meaning to any particular word.

It has already been emphasized how, despite Freud's increasing insistence on the key role of separation anxiety in neurosis, there has been marked reluctance to adopt his ideas, partly because of the influence of his earlier theories and partly because of the difficulty that both he and others have had in understanding why separation should in and of itself engender fear or anxiety. This long-lasting difficulty is well illustrated in a passage in a recent book on anxiety by Rycroft (1968a), comment on which serves to further the argument.

After referring briefly to evidence of the kind set out fully in Chapters 3 and 4 of this volume, Rycroft proceeds:

Observations of this kind, made on both animals and human infants, have given rise to the idea that all anxiety – or at least all neurotic anxiety – is in the last resort separation-anxiety, a response to separation from a protecting, parental object rather than a reaction to unidentified danger. There are, however, objections to this idea. In the first place it is surely illogical to regard the absence of a known, protective figure rather than the presence of an unknown, threatening situation as the cause of anxiety. To do so is like attributing . . . frostbite to inadequate clothing and not to exposure to extreme cold.

Reflection shows that there is in fact nothing illogical in making the attributions to which Rycroft objects. The causal conditions producing frostbite include *both* extreme cold *and* inadequate clothing. It is, therefore, just as reasonable to inculpate the one as the other.[1]

For our purpose, however, another analogy in which two conditions are equally relevant for safety is more apt. The safety of an army in the field is dependent not only on its defending itself against direct attack but also on its maintaining open communications with its base. Any military commander who fails to give as much attention to his base and lines of communication as to his main front soon finds himself defeated. The thesis advanced here, then, is that it is no less natural to feel afraid when lines of communication with base are in jeopardy than when something occurs in front of us that alarms us and leads us to retreat.

Though a military analogy is useful, it requires amplification. As a rule a commander-in-chief in charge of front-line forces is also in command of his base. Therefore any threat to his base or to his lines of communication is likely to come only from a single source, the enemy. Let us suppose, by contrast, that the general commanding the front-line forces is not in command of the base, and that another general of equal or superior status is in charge there. In such a situation the general commanding at the front could well have two sources of anxiety, one regarding possible enemy attack and the other regarding possible defection by his colleague at base. Only if there were complete confidence between the two generals could the arrangement be expected to work.

A situation of that kind, it is suggested, holds between an individual and his attachment figure. Each party is inherently

1. Rycroft puts forward two other arguments to support his case. One is that 'the young of both animals and man do not invariably become anxious when left alone; they may remain quiet and contented unless some other disturbing element is present'. This argument has substance and is discussed in Chapter 12. The other is that 'the exposure of infants and young animals to simultaneous stress and isolation is an unnatural artefact'. This is certainly not so. There is ample evidence that exposure of infants and young animals to simultaneous stress and isolation occurs in the wild, even if infrequently (see, for example, van Lawick-Goodall's observations on young chimpanzees, described briefly in Chapter 4, pp. 82–3 above).

autonomous. Given basic trust the arrangement can work well. But any possibility of defection by the attachment figure can give rise to acute anxiety in the attached. And should he be experiencing alarm from another source at the same time, it is evident that he is likely to feel the most intense fear.

In clinical work, it is held, we should be as much concerned with threats to rear as with threats to front. In Part III of this volume evidence is presented that suggests that the acute and chronic anxieties of patients stem as often from breakdown in relations with base as from all other hazards put together. It is, indeed, a special merit of some psychoanalytic traditions that, in their concern with object relations, they have focused attention especially on relations with base.

It is necessary to emphasize that at one important point the military analogy breaks down. Whereas generals are concerned to assess real dangers, animals and children, and in great degree human adults also, are attuned to respond mainly to rather simple stimulus situations that act as natural clues either to an increased risk of danger or to potential safety, clues that are only roughly correlated with actual danger or actual safety. This much neglected fact was touched on at the end of the previous chapter and is explored systematically in Chapters 8, 9, and 10.

Terminology

The fact that the same vocabulary is in everyday use to describe how we feel both when threatened with attack and when our base is threatened suggests a similarity of feeling in the two situations. Yet it seems probable that feeling experience in the two situations is not identical. For this reason there would be advantages in having distinctive words.

In discussion of the problem in earlier papers (Bowlby 1960a; 1961a) and again very briefly in the first volume (end of Chapter 15) a usage is proposed not dissimilar to that adopted by Freud in his later work. In so far as we may try at times to withdraw or escape from a situation, the word 'alarmed' is in many ways a suitable one to describe how we feel. In so far as we may at times be seeking an attachment figure but be unable to find or reach him (or her), the word 'anxious' is in many ways a suitable one to describe how we feel. This usage can be supported by reference both to the etymological roots of the respective words and to psychoanalytic tradition. Supporting arguments are presented in Appendix III to this volume.

In the terminology adopted, therefore, fear behaviour and feeling afraid are used as general-purpose terms, terms that encompass all forms of behaviour and, for humans, all shades of feeling also. When greater discrimination is required, the terms used are freezing and withdrawal or escape behaviour, which go with feeling alarmed, and attachment behaviour, which, when not terminated, goes with feeling anxious. Not infrequently, of course, a person is trying simultaneously to escape from one situation and, without success, to gain proximity to another. In such a case he would be described in this terminology as feeling both alarmed and anxious.

Chapter 7
Situations that Arouse Fear in Humans

... certain *ideas* of supernatural agency, associated with real circumstances, produce a peculiar kind of horror. This horror is probably explicable as the result of a combination of simpler horrors. To bring the ghostly terror to its maximum, many usual elements of the dreadful must combine, such as loneliness, darkness, inexplicable sounds, especially of a dismal character, moving figures half-discerned ... , and a vertiginous baffling of the expectation. This last element, which is *intellectual*, is very important.
– WILLIAM JAMES (1890)

A difficult field of study

Evidence is given (Chapters 3 and 4) of the distress and anxiety that are aroused when young creatures, human and other, are removed from a figure to whom they are attached and placed with strangers. In such circumstances, we know, behaviour is directed as least as much to regaining the familiar figure as it is to escaping from the strange people and situation. In those chapters attention is concentrated on the effects on behaviour of a single variable, presence or absence of mother; and thereby light is thrown on one-half of our problem, a half hitherto much neglected. It is time now to give attention to the other and more familiar half, the nature of some of the other variables that are likely to elicit one or another form of fear behaviour.

Not only are the forms of behaviour usually classified as fear behaviour heterogeneous, but so also, as we have seen, are the immediate situations and events that commonly elicit them. They include, besides being lost or alone, sudden noises and movements, strange objects and persons, animals, height, rapid approach, darkness, and anything we have learnt can cause pain. It is a motley list. And not only motley but the power of each situation or event to elicit fear is most uncertain. Where one person is afraid another is not. Where someone is unafraid today he is afraid tomorrow, or the other way round.

To all these immediate and concrete situations that are apt to arouse fear must then be added all those potential situations that, on good or less good grounds, a person may foresee as disagreeable or dangerous, including all the so-called imaginary fears.

The resulting scene is undoubtedly confusing; and perhaps it is no wonder that, in the attempt to understand it, many theories have been advanced, some empirically based, some more speculative, some testable and others not. At one extreme is J. B. Watson's simplistic theory that stimulus situations of any kind that later elicit fear can be traced to primal fear of two basic stimulus situations, one a loud sound and the other loss of support; at another is the type of theory first put forward by Freud, and carried further by some of his followers, that regards the situations a man fears in the external world as being reflections mainly of the danger situations he encounters in his internal one.

But we need not be tossed hither and yon. When the empirical evidence is arrayed, derived from studies both of men and of animal species, not only do the characteristics of fear-arousing situations become clear but the contribution made to species survival by response to them is usually not difficult to see. A finding of central importance to the argument is that two stimulus situations that, when present singly, might arouse fear at only low intensity may, when present together, arouse it at high intensity. Another and related one is that the presence or absence of an attachment figure, or other companion, makes an immense difference to the intensity of fear aroused. Only if these two findings are borne constantly in mind can the conditions that elicit intense fear be understood.

In this chapter an account is given of the situations that commonly arouse fear in humans, and in the next a comparable account of the situations that commonly arouse fear in animals. In each chapter the earlier part is concerned with stimulus situations that seem to have an inherent potential for arousing fear and eliciting one or another form of fear behaviour, and the later part with the greatly intensified effects seen when an individual is confronted by a situation compounded of two or more of such fear-inducing conditions, including being alone.

Considering the immense importance of fear in human life, and especially in psychiatric illness, it is surprising how few researchers have made systematic attempts to study the situations that commonly arouse fear in humans. Very recently, it is true, a fresh start has been made with the empirical investigation of situations that arouse fear during the first year or so of life. During that phase experiment is not too difficult because both mobility and cognitive development are limited. Once a child is beyond that phase, however, conditions for studying fear grow harder. Very few first-hand studies have been reported and, instead, there has been a tendency to rely on reports given by mothers during interview. Though such reports are of some value, there are several reasons why their value is limited.

Inadequacy of Mothers' Reports

Mothers are not expert observers nor are they disinterested. As will appear, the study of situations that give rise to fear is technically very difficult. First, it must be agreed what forms of behaviour are, and what are not, to count as indicative of fear. Next, it becomes evident that whether fear behaviour is shown is enormously influenced both by particular environmental conditions and by the state of the child: unless these details are reported, interpretation of results is difficult or impossible.

Apart from the technical difficulties in reporting, no mother is disinterested, and some may be heavily biased. A mother may exaggerate or minimize the intensity of her child's fear responses, or overlook or invent situations that elicit fear in him. In such matters the possibility of wishful thinking or of attributing to her child fears that belong only to herself is obvious. Another difficulty is that inevitably a mother is often ignorant of what does and what does not make her child afraid.

Marked discrepancies in reports made independently by mothers and their children were found in a study by Lapouse and Monk (1959). A sample of 193 children aged between eight and twelve years were interviewed and asked about what situations made them afraid; the mothers were also interviewed, separately, and asked the same questions. Disagreement between informants varied from a mere 7 per cent in regard to certain situations to as high as 59 per cent in regard to others. When mother and child gave different answers the reason was very frequently that a child described himself as being afraid of a situation of which his mother said he was not afraid. Among situations notably under-reported by mothers were the following: fear of getting lost or kidnapped; fear of strangers; fear of calamities such as fire, wars, floods, and murders; fear of a member of the family falling sick, having an accident, or dying; fear of falling sick oneself.[1] For each of these situations there were between 42 and 57 per cent of families in which mother reported her child as unafraid and the child reported otherwise. By contrast, in respect of these situations there were never more than 10 per cent of families in which the child claimed he was not afraid when his mother reported he was.

For all these reasons it is necessary to be very cautious in accepting the reports of mothers. In regard to the classes of situation likely to be feared their answers are of use. For calculating the proportion of a particular sample of children who are in fact prone to be afraid of a particular situation, their answers are insufficiently reliable. In what follows, therefore, we are guided mainly by results obtained from direct observation of children or from interviews with them.

Psychoanalysts and ethologists are agreed that a principal key to the understanding of any sort of behaviour is to study it developmentally. Nowhere is this perspective more necessary than in the study of fear behaviour in man. We start, therefore, with fear in infancy.

Fear-arousing situations: the first year

Initially during infancy the responses in which we are interested consist of little more than startle, crying, and diffuse movements. Whether it is useful to term them fear is almost a matter of taste. Because during the first three months both discriminated perception and organized movement are limited, Bronson (1968)

1. The incidence of fear of sickness etc. (either in a family member or in the self) reported in this study is much higher than it is in others. The probable reason for this is that the special sample from which these findings come was drawn 'from the outpatient clinics of two hospitals and the offices of several pediatricians'.

suggests they are better termed 'distress'. A little later, between the fourth and sixth months, a time when perceptual ability is developing, Bronson (1972) suggests it is useful to speak of an infant's being 'wary'.

During the second half of the first year, when perception becomes more discriminating and responses are better organized, the term fear is clearly appropriate. With greater or less efficiency an infant is effecting movement away from certain types of object or event, and towards others. By the end of the year, moreover, a baby can predict unpleasant happenings from the presence of simple clues that he has learnt. And during the second and, more especially, later years the capacity to foresee disagreeable situations and to take precautionary measures is greatly extended.

Early Situations and Responses

Bronson (1968) has reviewed studies of the types of stimulus situation that evoke distress responses during the early months of life.

Initially, discomfort, pain, and sudden sharp sounds upset a baby and may lead to crying, muscle tension, and diffuse movement. By contrast, a baby is quieted by being rocked or patted and by engaging in non-nutritive sucking (see Volume I, Chapter 14). Although it has been thought that during the earliest months vision plays only a small part in arousing fear, a recent experiment (Bower, Broughton and Moore 1970) shows that a baby of a few weeks flinches and cries whenever he sees an object approaching close to him. From about four months onwards, moreover, an infant is beginning to distinguish the strange from the familiar and to become wary of whatever is not familiar. Then, in a few children from about seven months, and in most by nine or ten, the sight of a stranger may be seen to arouse an unmistakable fear response. Some discussion of this response is already given in Volume I (Chapter 15). Since then further study of the genesis of the response has been undertaken by Bronson and by Scarr and Salapatek in the United States and by Schaffer in the United Kingdom. When account is taken of the different experimental situations and different methods of scoring responses, findings are highly compatible.

Fear of Strangers

Using videotape-recording and sensitive measures of response, Bronson (1972) has studied reactions to strange persons in thirty-two infants in their familiar home surroundings, during their development from the age of three to nine months. He reports that, usually starting at about four months, most infants will *occasionally* respond to a strange person with a cry, a whimper, or a frown, and that these wary responses start to appear at the age when undiscriminating smiling at strangers begins to wane. Throughout the fourth and fifth months, however, visual discrimination of strangers remains slow and uncertain. An infant of this age may spend long periods staring intently at a nearby stranger and may delay a long time before responding; and, on occasion, his response may change from a smile to a frown. Whether wariness is shown is determined by such variables as the visual characteristics of the stranger, his proximity and manner of approach; but before six months, in contrast to later (see below, pp. 148–51), it makes little difference whether or not an infant is held by, or can see, mother. At this age, moreover, the response in any one infant is far from stable.

Once infants are past six months, these responses usually become more differentiated and, for any one infant, more predictable. In the first place the response is more clearly aversive, so that the term fear becomes more applicable. In the second, perceptual identification of a stranger is posing fewer difficulties. Even so, as Schaffer (1971) points out, the earliest occasions on which an infant shows fear of strangers are when mother is herself present and the infant, by looking to and fro, can compare the two figures. Only later is an infant able readily to make the comparison, from memory, when his mother is absent.

As an infant reaches the end of his first year, his responses become still more predictable, and he may show unease either towards a particular person or towards members of a particular sex.

A point emphasized in the first volume is that, in any one infant, fear of strangers varies greatly according to conditions. How far distant from the infant a stranger is, whether he approaches, and whether he touches the infant are all extremely important; so also is the distance the child is from his mother. The significance of these variables for an understanding of fear is discussed later in this chapter and in those that follow.

Fear of Strange Objects

At about the same age as a child is becoming afraid of strangers he is apt also to become afraid of the sight of novel situations and strange objects. For example, Meili (1959) found, during a longitudinal study, that many infants become afraid of a jack-in-the-box at about ten months. Support for this finding comes from Scarr and Salapatek (1970) who undertook a cross-sectional study of fear responses as they occur in children between the ages of about five and eighteen months. At every age between nine and fourteen months rather more than a third of the children were frightened both by the jack-in-the-box test and by the approach of a mechanical dog. Fewer of the younger and of the older children were afraid of these situations.

Schaffer has investigated the development of responses to unfamiliar objects. In a series of experiments, Schaffer and Parry (1969; 1970) have shown that at the age of six months, although infants are fully capable of perceiving differences between a familiar object and an unfamiliar one, they none the less approach both kinds of object without any discrimination. From about eight months of age onwards, however, infants begin to show sharp discrimination. Thenceforward, whereas a familiar object is approached with confidence, an unfamiliar one is treated with caution: in the experiments some children merely stared at the unfamiliar object, others appeared as if frozen, while yet others were distressed and withdrew. Even when, after they had become familiar with the object, they began to touch it, they still did so only briefly and tentatively.

A particularly interesting observation reported by Schaffer (1971) is the way in which a one-year-old infant habitually turns to his mother when uncertain, whereas an infant aged six months does not. Two groups of infants, one aged six months and the other twelve months, were presented with an array of stimulus objects. Behind each infant sat his mother, with instructions to say and do nothing unless her infant became upset. Whereas the younger infants seemed to be spellbound by the objects in front of them and unaware that mother was immediately behind, the older infants turned frequently from the objects to mother and back again, apparently well able to keep mother in mind despite her being perceptually absent. Thus by twelve months of age an infant is capable of organized fear behaviour characterized typically by movement *away* from objects of one class and *towards* objects of another. The development in an infant, during the second half of the first year, of the capacity to turn to mother when he is frightened and to find comfort in her presence is described in greater detail in the final section of this chapter.

Certain other conditions that regularly arouse fear behaviour in human infants during the second half of the first year are constellations of visual stimuli that act as naturally occurring clues to the imminence of two dangers common in the wild: the danger of falling, and the danger of being attacked or overwhelmed by an object rapidly approaching.

Fear of the Visual Cliff

Walk and Gibson (1961) have described the behaviour of thirty-six infants, aged from six to fourteen months, all of whom could crawl, when tested on an apparatus known as the 'visual cliff'. This consists of a board laid across a sheet of heavy glass, with a patterned material that is directly beneath the glass on one side and, by dropping vertically, is several feet below it on the other. The infant is placed on the centre of the board while his mother stands at one or other side, calling her child to come to her across the glass-covered table which, according to the side at which she is standing, appears to be either solid table or deep chasm. Since each mother alternated her position it was easy to determine whether or not an infant was afraid to venture across the glass-covered 'chasm'.

Of the thirty-six infants tested only three, all boys, crossed the chasm to get to mother. All the others refused: some cried, others backed away to avoid the chasm, others peered through the glass or patted it. Yet, when mother was on the 'solid' side, most of the infants crawled quickly towards her. In the majority, then, discrimination was very evident.

Scarr and Salapatek (1970) repeated the experiment with their sample and found that the older the child the more likely was he to refuse to cross the chasm. Whereas of the children aged between seven and eleven months nearly half were willing to cross to get to mother, all those aged thirteen months and over refused to do so.

Since Walk and Gibson tested the young of many animal species on the visual cliff, it was possible for them to draw broad conclusions. Certainly in other species, and probably in humans as well, it is clear that fear on perception of clues indicative of height develops very early, and even when an infant has had no experience of falling. The perceptual cue that appears to trigger off avoidance behaviour is 'motion perspective', namely the differential motion of foreground and background produced by the infant's own actions. Compared with lambs and kids, all of which show reliable discrimination and accurate avoiding movements from the beginning, human infants are both less reliable in discriminating and more clumsy in movement. Nevertheless, a strong bias to avoid the chasm was evident in all but a small minority.

Fear of an Approaching Object (Looming)

Another stimulus condition that seems to elicit a natural fear reaction in human infants and to do so very early in life is a visual stimulus that expands rapidly, which is habitually interpreted by adults as indicating something rapidly approaching.

Many years ago Valentine (1930) noted that approach elicits fear in young children. A small girl of fourteen months, he reported, showed great fear of a teddy bear whenever it was moved towards her but would pick it up and kiss it whenever it was still.

In recent times Bower *et al.* (1970) have shown that a defensive response to an approaching object occurs in infants as young as two weeks (provided they are alert in an upright or near upright position). In a study of over forty infants they report that, each time a soft object (foam-rubber cube 20 cm per side) approaches to within about eight inches of a baby's face, without touching him, the infant pulls his head backwards, puts his hands between his face and the object, and cries loudly. The closer the object comes, the louder the cry. Further tests show that, when the stimulus consists merely of a shadow rapidly expanding on a screen, the response is similar though less intense. By contrast, when an object moves away there is no response. In the next chapter it is seen that young rhesus monkeys behave in very similar ways.

The fear eliciting properties of an approaching or looming object have probably been underestimated in the past; and it seems likely that, in some of the experiments on an infant's response to strangers and to novel objects, approach of the stranger or object has played a larger part in determining a fear response than the experimenters realized.

A stimulus condition related to looming and approach is darkness. During the first year of life, fear of darkness, which is common in later years, is not very evident. Even so, by the age of ten months, infants are more likely to leave mother to enter and explore a brightly illuminated room than a dimly lit one (Rheingold and Eckerman 1970).

Fear of an Anticipated Situation

Yet another situation that arouses fear, observable towards the end of the first year but not earlier, is when a baby uses current clues to anticipate something unpleasant. Levy (1951) describes the behaviour of babies of different ages when they catch sight of a doctor preparing to repeat an injection first given a few weeks earlier. Before eleven months of age only a very occasional infant was observed to react with fear. At ages eleven and twelve months, however, one-quarter of the sample did so. In such cases, it seems probable, learning from experience has occurred.

Thus by the end of the first year an infant is withdrawing in an organized way when he perceives any of a number of stimulus situations that can be regarded as naturally occurring clues to potentially dangerous situations. Further, he has learnt a good deal about his perceptual world. Towards the familiar and the strange, and towards what he has learnt is agreeable and what disagreeable, he is behaving with a rough-and-ready discrimination. He moves towards the one and away from the other.

Fear-arousing situations: the second and later years

Sources of Data

It has already been noted how few researchers have made systematic attempts to study the situations that commonly arouse fear in humans. Most of the few data published during recent decades come from various longitudinal studies of children developing. Examples are a study by Macfarlane, Allen and Honzik (1954) of about one hundred children in California and another by Newson and Newson (1968) of 700 children and their parents in an English urban community. In none of these studies, however, was the nature of the situations that arouse fear at the centre of interest, nor was the information reported obtained either from direct observation or from interview of the children themselves. The latter limitation applies also to the findings of a cross-sectional study of nearly 500 children undertaken by Lapouse and Monk (1959) in New York State.[2] In all these projects information came only from mothers.

Because of the paucity of recently gathered data it is necessary to turn to the results of work done during the early years of child development research.

Some forty years ago an American psychologist, A. T. Jersild, began a series of studies in which he set out to describe the kinds of situation in which children exhibit fear, and how these change as a child grows older.[3] Different methods of obtaining information were employed in different studies. The four main methods were: day-to-day recording by parents; simple experiments;

2. A representative sample, distinct from the smaller sample referred to on p. 124 above.

3. Jersild's principal studies are published as monographs: Jersild, Markey and Jersild (1933) and Jersild and Holmes (1935a). Abstracts of these and other studies with full references are in the symposium on *Child Behavior and Development* edited by Barker, Kounin and Wright (1943), and also in Jersild (1947).

interviewing children about situations of which they were currently afraid; giving questionnaires to adults about what they recalled of the situations that made them afraid as children. The subjects of each study were different and were drawn from different age-ranges. Despite a number of shortcomings, these studies are still much the most extensive yet attempted and therefore remain principal sources. Not only do the findings conform with ordinary experience, but at a number of points they are supported and amplified both by earlier (e.g. Hagman 1932) and by more recent work.

Findings from Parents' Records and Naturalistic Observations

The aim of one of Jersild's studies was to obtain a detailed record of the occasions and situations in which ordinary children exhibit fear during the course of their everyday lives. To this end the parents of over one hundred young children were enlisted, all of whom were prepared to keep detailed records of every occasion on which their child showed fear during a period lasting twenty-one days. Mimeographed forms and instructions were issued. On each occasion that a child showed fear parents were asked to record: (a) the actual behaviour exhibited (e.g. startle, withdrawing, turning to an adult, cries or other vocalizations, and words spoken); (b) the situation in which the behaviour occurred, in terms not only of its apparent cause (specific stimulus) but of the setting (place, time, what child was doing, persons present); and (c) the child's current condition (well or ill, fresh or tired).

In all, 136 records were obtained of children between twelve and fifty-nine months of age (the records of a few younger and older children were too few to give useful results). The sample was biased towards the higher end of the socio-economic scale. A majority lived in a large city, but there were also children living in suburbs, small towns, and rural areas. Distribution by age was as follows: second year, twenty-three children; third year, forty-five; fourth year, forty-six; and fifth year, twenty-two children.

The authors were struck by how few were the occurrences of fear recorded by the parents of children in these age-groups, a finding confirmed when observations were made of some of the same children in a nursery school. The occurrences recorded during the three weeks for children in the two younger age-groups averaged only six per child, or two a week. For children in the two older age-groups the average was three and a half per child, or barely more than one a week. For about one in ten of the children at each age-level no occurrence of fear was recorded throughout the three-week period.

Although these figures suggest that some occurrences of slight or transient fear may have gone unrecorded, there is independent evidence that at least some children during their second year show fear very infrequently. For example, Valentine (1930), who kept daily notes on his children, was impressed by the infrequency with which he saw fear responses in them and describes how surprised he was when a child who had fallen and hurt himself would none the less immediately go climbing again. Anderson (1972a), who observed fifty-two children between the ages of twelve months and three years two months in a London park, also remarks how infrequently the children exhibited fear. Occurrences, he reports, were 'uncommon and short-lived'. It should, however, be noted that in both these studies and also in Jersild's the children observed were *not alone*. The difference made by presence or absence of a trusted adult cannot be exaggerated (see the final section of this chapter).

When we turn to examine the *kinds of situation* that are reported to arouse fear we find remarkably little change between the second and the fifth years. From the mother's day-to-day records reported by Jersild six situations stand out as being likely to arouse fear at least occasionally in a fairly large proportion of the children at each age-level:
– noise, and events associated with noise
– heights
– strange people or familiar people in strange guise
– strange objects and surroundings
– animals
– pain or persons associated with pain.
In each of these six situations some 40 per cent of all the children were recorded as having shown fear behaviour on some occasion during the three-week spell. In so far as there was any reduction

with age in the proportion of children showing fear the reduction occurred after the third birthday.[4]

Among the many other situations recorded as having aroused fear, but in a smaller percentage of these children, were sudden unexpected movements, especially when an object was both approaching and noisy, and also bright lights, flashes, etc. Together, these kinds of situation elicited fear in nearly 30 per cent of the one- and two-year-olds; but of the older children no more than about 10 per cent had shown fear in those situations. The dark, especially being alone in the dark, was recorded as having aroused fear in about 10 per cent of the children during the three-week period of observation: here there was no change with age. Fear of being left alone or abandoned was recorded for about 10 per cent of the children at each of the age-levels. Only after the second birthday were any of the children recorded as having shown fear of imaginary creatures, the proportion being about 6 per cent. The origin and nature of such fears are discussed in Chapters 10 and 11.

The *forms of behaviour* recorded as shown by these children when afraid differed very little between the younger and the older ones. The behaviour most frequently recorded was crying in its various forms, from whimpering to screaming and including explicit cries for help. In each age-group no less than one-third of the episodes of fear recorded by mothers were signalled by crying of one sort or another. Another form of behaviour also frequently recorded was either turning towards an adult or running to him or her, with or without clinging: in each age-group about one-sixth of the fear-producing situations were said to elicit behaviour of that sort. Avoiding action or running away was

4. When analysed by age the picture from these six situations is as follows. Of the one-year-olds, 60 per cent were recorded as having shown fear of noise, 52 per cent fear of pain or potential pain, and from 35 to 40 per cent as having shown fear in each of the other four situations, of which one was the presence of animals. Of the four-year-olds, only 23 per cent were recorded as having shown fear of noise and events associated with noise, but no fewer than 40 per cent had shown fear of animals, the same percentage as for the one-year-olds. In each of the other situations, however, including the possibility of pain, only about 15 per cent of the four-year-olds had shown fear.

recorded in about one-fifth of the episodes. In the remainder, fear was inferred because a child trembled or jumped, showed a frightened expression, hid his head, or stayed unwontedly still. Occasionally a child was aggressive, or protective of another.

In this catalogue of forms of behaviour held by mothers to be indicative of fear it should be noted that two of the commonest are crying for or turning towards a protective figure. This finding resembles that of Anderson (1972a) when he interviewed the mothers of eighteen two-year-olds in London. The forms of fear behaviour most commonly described to him were screaming, crying, turning to mother, clinging to or following mother, and staying close to her. Withdrawing from the frightening object was referred to less frequently.

When, however, Anderson was himself observing the fear behaviour of another but very similar sample of toddlers while they were with mother in a London park (see p. 134 above), rather different forms of fear behaviour were seen. In the dozen episodes observed, the fear-arousing object was an approaching animal (eight cases), an approaching child (three cases), and noise (one case). In such conditions a toddler would suddenly cease his activity, back away from whatever it was that was frightening him while continuing to fixate it, and simultaneously edge towards his mother. Crying was not observed. Once the object had moved away, the child would advance again but continue to fixate it.

The differences in forms of behaviour exhibited turn presumably on the intensity of fear. At high intensity crying and clinging are common; at low intensity withdrawing from the object and backing towards mother.

A limitation of records kept by parents and also of naturalistic observations such as those of Anderson is that, when a child is not described as having shown fear of a particular class of situation during the period his behaviour was recorded, it remains uncertain whether he is never afraid in such situations or whether it just happened that during that span of time he was never confronted by one when his mother or the observer was about. The experiments devised by Jersild & Holmes help to clarify this matter, though they too have obvious limitations.

Experimental Findings

It is evident that ethical considerations limit severely the kinds of experiment it is legitimate to do in order to explore the situations that arouse fear in humans, especially in young children.

In their experimental work with children between their second and sixth birthdays, therefore, Jersild and Holmes took many precautions. In the first place, each child was throughout with an adult who was experienced with children, and who had made a friendly contact with him before the experiments began. In the second, each situation with which a child was confronted was one that many children hardly find frightening. In the third, a child was introduced to the situation by easy stages. And finally, if a child refused to take part, the experiment was ended.

There were eight potentially fear-provoking situations. Four were presented on the first day, extending over about fifteen minutes; two on the day following; and two about four weeks later. For a few minutes between each fear-inducing situation a child was allowed to play with toys. Since it appears that the situations were presented to every child in the same order, there is a serious possibility that responses to later situations may have been influenced by the experience of earlier ones; though in which direction such influence may have been exerted it is difficult to know. On the one hand is the possibility that, through habituation, responses to later situations may have been less than they would otherwise have been. On the other is the possibility that, as the series progressed, a child may have become increasingly sensitized and therefore have shown more fear in some of the later situations than he would otherwise have done. The finding that a larger proportion of children showed fear in the later experimental situations than in the earlier ones is in keeping with the latter possibility.

The eight situations were chosen because earlier studies had shown that they were likely to elicit at least a little fear in a substantial proportion of young children. Details are as follows:

1. *Being left alone:* When the child is seated at a table playing with a toy, the experimenter names a pretext for leaving the room (which until the time of the experiment was unfamiliar to the child). The experimenter remains outside the room for

two minutes. The child's behaviour is recorded by concealed observers.

2. *Sudden displacement or loss of support:* A bridge-like piece of apparatus, consisting of two boards laid end to end at a height of about two inches above the floor, was used. The first board is securely supported, but when the child steps onto the second board, which is supported only at the middle, it gives way and descends to the floor.

3. *Dark passage:* While playing ball with the child, the experimenter seemingly inadvertently throws the ball into a dark passage, 18 ft long, leading from one corner of the room. The child is asked to retrieve the ball.

4. *Strange person:* While the child is temporarily withdrawn from the room an assistant, dressed in a long grey coat, a large black hat, and a veil that obscures her features, seats herself in one of the two chairs near the entrance. The child returns and his reactions are observed when he notices the stranger and when he is asked to obtain toys placed near the stranger's chair.

5. *High board:* A board 12 in. wide, about 8 ft long, and 2 in. thick, held firmly in place at the ends by two stationary holders, is arranged at various heights from the ground and the child is asked to walk from one end of the board to the other to obtain a box of brightly coloured toys. The board is first placed at a distance of four feet from the floor; it is subsequently lowered if the child refuses to walk across at this height and is raised if he performs at the four-foot level.

6. *Loud sound:* An iron pipe 2 ft long and $2\frac{1}{4}$ in. diameter, suspended from the ceiling in a corner of the room behind a screen, is struck a sharp blow with a hammer while the child and the experimenter are seated at a table containing toys. The child's response to the unexpected noise from an unseen source is first observed and then, pointing to the screen, the experimenter asks the child to 'Go and see what made that noise'.

7. *Snake:* A snake, harmless and about 2 ft long, was placed in a box sufficiently deep to ensure that it could not immediately climb out when the top was removed. In the box was placed a small coloured toy. The child's attention is directed to the box, the lid is uncovered, and the child is allowed to look

in; if he raises any questions the experimenter simply says 'It is a snake', and then points to the toy and asks the child to reach in and get the toy.

8. *Large dog:* While the child is seated at a table with toys a large collie dog is brought into the room on a leash by a familiar person. The dog is led to a certain point in the room and, after preliminary comment by the experimenter, the child is asked to go and pat the dog.

The subjects were 105 children, half from a private nursery school for better-off families and half from a public nursery school for poorer families. Fifty-seven were boys and forty-eight girls. Children were tested only when they were fit, willing, and in a good humour; and the experiments were never combined with any other sort of examination. On each occasion when tests were carried out, two-year-olds and three-year-olds were well represented (never fewer than twenty-one children tested and usually between thirty and forty-five); but four-year-olds and five-year-olds were rather few (numbers tested varied between seven and fourteen children).

Each experiment, except the first, was presented to a child in four stages: first he was given directions what to do; then, if he was hesitant, he was given reassurance and encouragement; then, if he still refrained, the experimenter offered to accompany him in the task; finally, if a child was still reluctant to take part, the experiment was abandoned.

A child's performance was scored on a five-point scale:

0 performs without hesitation
1 performs after hesitation and with caution
2 performs alone, but only after protesting and seeking reassurance
3 refuses to perform alone but does so when accompanied
4 complete refusal.

Good reliability was obtained between independent observers.

In presenting their findings Jersild & Holmes use stringent criteria for their assessment of fear: only refusal to perform alone and refusal to perform at all (categories 3 and 4) were held to be responses indicative of fear. Had the children who performed alone but only after seeking reassurance (category 2) been included also, the percentages showing fear responses would, the authors report, have been raised by about one-third. Results are given in the table below.

Proportions of children showing fear responses (categories 3 and 4) in experimental situations:[a]

Situation	Age: N:[b]	2·0–2·11 21–33	3·0–3·11 28–45	4·0–4·11 7–14	5·0–5·11 12–13
		%	%	%	%
1. Left alone		12	16	7	0
2. Loss of support		24	9	0	0
3. Dark passage		47	51	36	0
4. Strange person		31	22	12	0
5. High board		36	36	7	0
6. Loud sound		23	20	14	0
7. Snake		35	56	43	43
8. Large dog		62	43	43	not tested

[a] Source: Jersild and Holmes (1935a).
[b] Number of children varies by experiments.

The proportion of children showing fear according to these criteria in these experiments differs little when two-year-olds are compared with three-year-olds. After the fourth birthday, however, there is a marked reduction, which becomes particularly noticeable after the fifth birthday.

Because, as remarked earlier, the experimental situations were presented to each child in the same order, it is difficult to be confident how they compare with each other in their fear-inducing potential. The three situations that stand out in the series as being frightening to a high proportion of children up to the fifth birthday are nos. 3, 7, and 8: the dark passage, the snake, and the large dog. In each of these situations never less than one-third of the children refused to perform alone, and in certain groups more than half refused. When the children who were scored in category 2, having performed only after receiving reassurance and encouragement, are included the percentages range from about 50 to 80 per cent. And had the children who hesitated and performed with caution (category 1) been included also, an overwhelming majority would have been found to have exhibited some trace of fear in these three situations. Thus, even when the proviso about the effects of test order is borne in mind, the experiments go some way towards confirming a commonly held view that a very large proportion of young children are apt to be afraid of the dark and of animals.

The Findings in Relation to Age

A study of the data reviewed so far suggests that, if we leave aside fear of separation as a special problem, the whole medley of situations that can be observed to arouse fear in children during their first five years can be listed in four main categories, whose fear-arousing properties vary to some extent with the age of the children:

(a) Noise and situations associated with noise; sudden change of illumination and sudden unexpected movement; an object approaching; and height. These situations are especially liable to arouse fear during the first, second, and third years of life.

(b) Strange people and familiar people in strange guise; strange objects and strange places. Strangeness is especially liable to arouse fear during the last quarter of the first year and through the second and third years, and then tends to diminish.

(c) Animals: not only did animals commonly elicit fear in children of each of the age-groups for which parents kept records (35 per cent in the second year and 40 per cent or above in the older children), but the presence of an animal was the experimental situation that aroused fear most frequently. All other relevant studies, some to be described shortly, also report a high incidence of fear of animals.

(d) Darkness, especially being alone in the dark. Occurrences of fear in such situations were recorded by mothers for about 20 per cent of the children at each age-level, and, if anything, the incidence seems to rise with age. Furthermore, fear of the dark and of being alone in the dark was seen in about half the children tested in the experimental situations. Again, as with fear of animals, a high incidence of fear in these situations is reported in several other studies.

The situations listed in categories (a) and (b) above are simple and require little or no learning. They tend to elicit fear in the youngest children especially and to do so less as children get older. Those in categories (c) and (d) are more complex and may include some reference to potential events. The fear-inducing properties of these situations do not diminish during the early years of childhood; indeed, those of some situations tend to increase.

These conclusions regarding changes with age are based on the cross-sectional studies discussed so far, in which each age-group comprises a distinct group of children. It is therefore reassuring to find that they are confirmed when a single group of children is followed longitudinally over a period of a year or more.

In another of their many studies Jersild and Holmes (1935b), relying on information from parents, compared changes in situations feared in a sample of forty-seven children (thirty-three aged initially three or four years and fourteen aged initially five or six years). The follow-up period varied between thirteen and thirty-five months for different children. As they got older, many children earlier reported to be afraid of noise, sudden change of stimulation, strangeness and strangers were reported as no longer afraid. Conversely, children who had earlier not been reported as afraid of the dark or of anticipated events, such as accidents or robbers, were later reported to have become so. These shifts are in keeping with a child's increasing, though still very limited, capacities for appraising current events in terms of their significance for the future, a topic considered further in Chapter 10.

A Note on Fear of Strangers

The tendency for something or someone strange to elicit fear has been much discussed. Whether fear is or is not aroused in a particular instance evidently turns on a great number of conditions that are still not fully understood. In his observations of toddlers in a park with mother (see p. 134 above), what impressed Anderson was that the presence of a passing stranger seemed to go almost unnoticed. On the other hand, in his discussions with mothers of another group toddlers (see p. 136 above), he found that eight out of eighteen children were reported as having at some time shown fear of a stranger. This information was volunteered spontaneously by the mothers who had plainly been much struck by it. The most usual situation was when a relative or friend, well known to mother but perhaps little known to the child, visited. Unlike total strangers, who would naturally stay at a distance, relatives and friends are apt to approach mother and child enthusiastically, and mother herself reciprocates. It was in situations likely to have been of this kind that a number of the children had become very frightened. (Not infrequently, some unusual aspect of the visitor was picked upon – spectacles, wrinkles, beard, or a loud voice.) The conclusion to which Anderson's findings point is that what young children find especially frightening is the combination of strangeness and approach (cf. the findings of Morgan and Ricciuti (1969) described on pp. 148–9 below).

If that conclusion is correct, it would go some way to explain why the children studied by Heinicke and Westheimer (1966) in a residential nursery so often showed fear of the observer (see Chapter 1 above, p. 28. First, the children were without mother; second, the observer remained a relative stranger to them; third, the observer 'actively though cautiously approached the child to see how he would react'.

Fear of Animals and of the Dark

It is remarkable with what regularity being afraid of animals and of the dark is reported for children from the age of three years upwards. In the Macfarlane longitudinal study, for example, more than 90 per cent of the hundred children in the sample were reported by mother to have shown fear of some specific situation at one or another age during the period in which they were studied, which was from the age of twenty-one months to fourteen years. At each yearly examination up to the age of eleven years between one-third and one-half of the children were reported as having shown fear of a particular situation; and of the situations most frequently reported as feared, dogs and the dark were the commonest, especially in the younger age-groups (Macfarlane, Allen and Honzik 1954). Comparable findings, also based on mothers' reports, are presented by Lapouse and Monk (1959) who made a cross-sectional study of a representative sample of 482 children between the ages of six and twelve years in New York State.

Similar findings emerge again from two further studies conducted by Jersild. In one of them he and his colleagues interviewed some four hundred children between the ages of five and twelve years (twenty-five boys and twenty-five girls at each of eight age-levels). Starting each interview on neutral topics the interviewer went on to inquire of the child about the things that scared or frightened him. In a second, questionnaires were issued to some three hundred students and members of staff aged between seventeen and thirty-five years (mostly between eighteen and twenty-six). Subjects were asked to describé situations that had frightened them as children and to indicate which was the earliest they could remember, which they were most intensely afraid of, and which they were most persistently afraid of; a single situation might of course qualify under all three heads.

The situations that these adults recalled as having aroused fear were closely in line with those described by the five- to twelve-year-old children. In both groups fear of animals bulked large. Among the children it was clearly highest at the younger age-levels: fear of animals was described by 27 per cent of the five- and six-year-olds, by 22 per cent of the seven- and eight-year-olds, and by 11 per cent of the older children. Among the adults, about one in six reported fear of animals as the earliest fear they recalled, and/or the most intense and/or the most persistent.

Fear of the dark is frequently a mixture of being afraid when alone in the dark, especially of strange noises or other happenings, and being afraid of being attacked in the dark, perhaps by imaginary creatures, such as ghosts or characters out of story-books, or perhaps by burglars and kidnappers. Being afraid in such situations and ways was reported by about 20 per cent of the five- to twelve-year-olds, the incidence not changing greatly with age, and it was recalled also by about the same proportion of young adults; among the latter fear of the dark resembled fear of animals in being recollected as having been very intense and very persistent.

Fear of Damage, Illness, Death

In both series some 10 per cent of subjects reported or recalled being afraid of getting damaged in an accident or a fight, though fear of pain as such was rarely mentioned.

Fear of becoming ill or dying was conspicuous by its infrequency. It was mentioned by none of the 200 children under nine years of age and by only six of the 200 from nine to twelve. About 3 per cent of the young adults recalled fear of illness or death as their most intense or their most persistent fear. Absence of fear of death among children under ten is in keeping with Anthony's study reported in *The Child's Discovery of Death* (1940). After examining the steps by which a child gradually acquires the concept of death as an irreversible departure, Anthony concludes that death acquires its emotional significance through its equation with separation (see Appendix I, p. 433n).

Fear of the illness or death of a parent was rarely mentioned by either the children or adults questioned by Jersild; the proportion was about 3 per cent in each group.

It is interesting to note how infrequently the situations observed most regularly to arouse fear during the first two or three years of life are referred to by the older children or recalled by the young adults. In neither series do more than 5 per cent of the subjects report or recall being afraid of noise, sudden movement, falling, strange objects or strange people – so long as it is light. During darkness, however, as already described, the position is very different.

Clinicians will inevitably be sceptical whether interviews, even if skilfully conducted, or questionnaires can possibly elicit from either children or young adults an accurate and comprehensive account of all the situations that frighten or have frightened them. The fact that the younger children (five- and six-year-olds) described fewer such situations than did the older ones suggests, indeed, that their accounts were especially inadequate. Nevertheless, though some fear-arousing situations were no doubt underreported, it seems probable that such positive information as was given can be regarded as valid.

In this chapter all that is attempted is a description of the situations that commonly arouse fear in humans and a rough indication of how these situations tend to change as a child grows towards adulthood. Possible explanations of the findings are postponed until later chapters. Meanwhile there is more to be said about the situations themselves.

Compound Situations

Again and again it is found that a child or adult is especially apt to be frightened in a situation characterized by two or more potentially alarming features: for example, a stranger who suddenly approaches, a strange dog that barks, an unexpected noise heard in the dark. Commenting on the records made by parents over a period of twenty-one days of situations that aroused fear in their children, Jersild and Holmes (1935a) note that two or more of the following features were frequently reported to have been present together: noise, strange people or surroundings, the dark, sudden and unexpected movement, and being alone. Whereas a situation characterized by a single one of these features might only alert, when there are several present together fear, more or less severe, may well be aroused.

Because the response to a combination of features is often dramatically greater than, or different from, what it is to any one singly, it is proposed to refer to such situations as 'compound', a term chosen to echo the chemical analogue.

We have seen that situations that are especially likely to elicit fear not only during childhood but during later years also are those involving animals and those involving darkness. Their fear-arousing property, it seems likely, is to be explained by the fact that both types of situation commonly constitute a source of two or more of the potentially alarming features already considered. A discussion of how fear responses to these two types of situation develop during the early years will be found at the end of Chapter 10.

Being Alone

The situational feature of special interest to us in this work is, of course, being alone. Probably nothing increases the likelihood that fear will be aroused more than that. Finding oneself alone in a strange place, perhaps in darkness, and met by a sudden movement or mysterious sound, few of us would be unafraid. Were we to have with us even one stout companion, however, we should probably feel much braver; and given many our courage would quickly return. Being alone, like conscience, 'doth make cowards of us all'.

The immense difference made to a child who is in a potentially frightening situation by the presence of an adult was, it will be noted, taken for granted by Jersild and Holmes when they devised their experiments. Not only was the experimenter present with the child in all of them (except the first), but the scoring system was based on the extent to which a child required encouragement or support from the experimenter in carrying out the task. Had the experimenter not been present, it is evident, a far higher proportion of children would have been scored as having been afraid than were so scored. This is shown by the fact that, of the children scored as *not* having shown fear, many had carried out the task, for example to find the ball down the dark passage or to pat the dog, only after they had been given much reassurance and encouragement from the experimenter. Furthermore, almost all of those who were scored as having shown fear, because despite encouragement they refused to carry out the task on their own, were ready to do it when the experimenter accompanied them.

These findings are so much in keeping with common experience that it may seem absurd to labour them. Yet there is abundant evidence that, when psychologists and psychiatrists come to theorize about fear and anxiety, the significance of these phenomena is gravely underestimated. The same is true of most psychoanalysts, with Freud a conspicuous exception.

Fear behaviour and the development of attachment

As long ago as 1920 Watson and Rayner reported that it was not possible to elicit fear responses, which had been conditioned to a white rat, in a small boy of eleven months, Albert, so long as he had his thumb in his mouth; and in 1929 English described how a little girl of fourteen months showed no fear of strange objects as long as she was in her familiar high chair, though she became afraid of them when she was placed on the floor.

Others of these early workers also note the phenomenon. Valentine (1930) remarks that 'the presence of a companion is a well-known banisher of fear'. Freud's view, as presented for example in the *Three Essays* (1905b, *SE* 7: 224) and quoted at the head of Chapter 3, is not very different. In more recent times Laughlin (1956) has proposed a new term, 'soteria', as an obverse of phobia, to denote the intense sense of reassuring comfort that a person may get from a 'love object', be it toy, charm, or talisman.

There is still much to be learnt about the extent to which, at different ages, the situation in which a child finds himself in relation to his attachment figure affects the way he responds to stimuli that are potentially fear-arousing. A step towards greater understanding comes from the findings of Morgan and Ricciuti (1969). In their developmental study of fear of strangers they show that, during the first eight months of life, little difference is made to the form or intensity of response by whether an infant is seated on his mother's lap or on a chair a few feet from her. Thereafter, however, and especially from twelve months of age, proximity to mother becomes a most important variable.

Morgan and Ricciuti studied eighty infants, falling into five age-groups (four and a half, six and a half, eight and a half, ten and a half, and twelve and a half months). Each infant was tested for his response to a stranger (a) when seated on mother's lap and (b) when seated in a little chair four feet from her. After entering, the stranger[5] behaved according to a regular routine. First he sat silent but smiling about six feet from the infant; next he spoke to the infant; then he moved quietly to a distance of about two feet, where he knelt and talked further; finally, he touched the infant's hand. After a half-minute pause, the stranger began his withdrawal, proceeding as before but in reverse order. The infant's

5. Each infant was tested with two strangers, one male and one female. At each age-level there was a tendency for the response to the male stranger to be less friendly and more fearful than that to the female. Whether this was due to the sex difference or to some other difference between them it is not possible to know.

behaviour was observed from behind a one-way screen. Positive marks were given for smiling, babbling, cooing, and reaching out towards the stranger; negative marks for frowning, pouting, fussing, whimpering, crying, turning towards mother, and avoiding or withdrawing from the experimenter. Sobering or merely looking at the stranger or mother scored zero.

Three-quarters of the infants in the two youngest age-groups (four and a half and six and a half months) responded warmly to the stranger by smiling, cooing, and reaching out; and whether they were seated on mother's lap or not made little difference. Only one showed signs of fear. Infants in each of the three older age-groups, however, were not only increasingly more likely to show fear but also increasingly more sensitive to mother's whereabouts. Thus, of those in the two intermediate age-groups (eight and a half and ten and a half months), a quarter withdrew or showed some other sign of fear; and of those aged twelve and a half months no fewer than half withdrew or were otherwise afraid. The effect of mother's whereabouts on the response was only just apparent in the two intermediate age-groups. In infants of twelve and a half months, however, it was abundantly clear. Only when seated on mother's lap did any of these one-year-olds welcome the stranger; when, by contrast, they were seated four feet from her, every one of them showed fear.

Rather similar findings are reported by Bronson (1972) from his short longitudinal study, referred to above (p. 127), of infants between three and nine months of age. He observed how the response to a stranger is influenced (a) by the infant's being held by mother and (b) by the infant's being able to see her.

At the age of four months there was little indication that being held by mother reduced wariness when the stranger approached to within two feet and called the baby. But by six and a half months being held by mother reduced wariness considerably and it did so at nine months also.

Presence of an infant's mother within sight, about four feet from him, made little difference to the degree of wariness of the stranger shown by the infant at four and a half or six and a half months. By the age of nine months, however, visual contact with mother was found to reduce wariness. Moreover, at that age it was not uncommon for a baby to crawl over to his mother when the stranger approached.

In the light of these findings it is instructive to consider afresh the much-quoted case of Albert on whom Watson and Rayner reported fifty years ago. In a series of experiments this eleven-month-old infant was conditioned to fear a white rat and, through generalization, a rabbit, a piece of seal fur, and human hair. The unconditioned stimulus was a loud noise made by hitting a long steel bar with a hammer just behind his head. Learning theorists have argued that many cases of phobia are to be traced to conditioning of this kind.

Deductions drawn from the case have often been challenged (e.g. see Marks 1969). In the context of this work the following points deserve mention. First, Albert had been 'reared almost from birth in a hospital environment' and was selected for the experiment because he seemed so 'stolid and unemotional'. Second, the conditioning took place with Albert placed on a mattress on top of a small table, and with no familiar figure towards whom he could turn. Some of his responses, nevertheless, were those used by a child in turning to a mother figure: for example, raising his arms as if to be picked up and, later, burying his head in the mattress. In addition, Albert was very apt when upset to suck his thumb. To the experimenters this proved most inconvenient, since 'the moment the hand reached the mouth he became impervious to the stimuli producing fear. Again and again ... we had to remove the thumb from his mouth before the conditioned response could be obtained.' From these observations the experimenters themselves reached a very significant conclusion: 'the organism ... apparently from birth, when under the influence of love stimuli, is blocked to all others.'

Thus the results of this early experiment by Watson & Rayner as well as those of the recent ones by Morgan and Ricciuti and by Bronson are consistent with the picture of the growth of attachment behaviour given in the first volume. They are consistent also with two findings by Schaffer described earlier in this one. The first (reported in Chapter 3) is that, before the age of twenty-eight weeks, infants do not protest when removed from mother to the strange surroundings of a hospital but that, from seven months onwards, they do so. The other finding (noted earlier in the present chapter) is that, whereas an infant of twelve months when confronted with strange objects refers constantly to his mother if she is seated behind him, an infant of six months appears oblivious of her being there.

Thus in general it can be said that, just as attachment to a mother figure is becoming steadily better organized during the latter half of the first year, so also is withdrawal from a fear-arousing situation. Furthermore, because by twelve months a child's cognitive equipment has developed sufficiently for him to be well able to take account of objects and situations briefly absent, he has become able so to organize his behaviour that he moves simultaneously both away from one type of situation and towards another type. Hence he enters his second year equipped to respond in the dual way that is typical of well-organized fear behaviour. In the next chapter a description is given of how young monkeys pass through the same developmental phases but at a faster rate.

Fear of Future Contingencies

In this chapter attention has been focused mainly on the nature of the immediate situations that can be observed to give rise to fear behaviour in children. Nevertheless, during the course of human life the situations that are apt to arouse fear include not only those that are actually present but others, more or less likely, that are forecast. Thus children and adults are frequently apprehensive about events that they believe may be going to occur and of objects and creatures that they suspect may be going to appear. Such fear is concerned with future contingencies.

Because so many of the situations feared by humans are of that nature and because they bulk so very large in clinical work, it is necessary to examine them in some detail. This is done in Chapters 10 and 11, after the immediate situations that arouse fear behaviour have been considered in the light of the behaviour's biological function.

We turn now to consider what is known about situations that arouse fear in animals.

Chapter 8
Situations that Arouse Fear in Animals

Natural clues to potential danger

Although the stimulus situations that arouse fear in other species are not identical with those that arouse fear in humans, there is much overlap. Overlaps are especially evident, moreover, in the case of the non-human primates, to which much of this chapter is given.

Ethologists take for granted that many of the stimulus situations that arouse fear in animals can be regarded as naturally occurring clues to events that constitute a potential danger to the species in question. This applies especially to situations that arouse fear on the first occasion that an individual encounters them.

Distance receptors are commonly employed for sensing these naturally occurring clues. Depending on the species, an animal may rely mainly on visual clues and receptors, mainly on auditory ones, or mainly on olfactory ones; or on any combination of them.[1] Only when the distance receptors have failed to detect potential dangers in time are the proximal receptors, those for touch and pain, called into action – and by then it may be too late. Thus, in eliciting fear behaviour, distal clues and distance receptors play a crucial role.

Of all the possible stimulus situations that could act as clues to potential danger and can be sensed at a distance, there are certain ones that are exploited by a very wide array of species. Among the best known are strangeness and sudden approach, both of which regularly evoke fear responses in birds and mammals. Another is the 'visual cliff' to which young mammals of all species so far tested respond by taking avoiding action.

Situations of other kinds, by contrast, arouse fear responses in animals of only a few species; and sometimes, perhaps, of only

1. For discussions of fear responses in animals see Tinbergen (1957), Marler and Hamilton (1966), and Hinde (1970).

one. For example, in some species of bird the sight of mammalian fur elicits fear responses; in others, the sight of a pair of staring eyes or of something falling from the sky. In some species of night-flying moth the high-pitched echolocating calls of predator bats lead to instant flight or, alternatively, to 'catalepsy'. Thus, like drugs, the naturally occurring distal clues to potential danger can be classified into 'broad-spectrum' clues, to which animals of a wide array of species are sensitive, and 'narrow-spectrum' clues, to which animals of only one or a few species are sensitive.

Many of the alarm calls of birds and mammals act as broad-spectrum clues since they are responded to with fear not only by members of the species that emits them but by members of other species as well. This is in part because the alarm calls of different species have come to resemble each other, presumably through a process of natural selection.

In a number of animal species olfactory stimuli, some of broad but many of narrow spectrum, are especially effective in eliciting fear behaviour. Such 'warning scents' arise from one of two sources: from enemies or from friends. On the one hand, as is well known, the scent of an approaching predator, man or wolf, can elicit fear responses in a broad array of grazing mammals, zebras, deer, and antelope. On the other, an 'alarm scent' emitted by an animal when frightened or wounded can elicit fear responses in other animals (exactly as an alarm call can), but in this case the effect is likely to be confined to members of its own species.

Thus animals of every species are born genetically biased so to develop that they respond with one or another form of fear behaviour whenever they sense a stimulus situation that serves as a naturally occurring clue to one of the particular dangers that beset members of their species. Since some categories of potential danger are common for a wide array of species, clues to them act as broad-spectrum clues. Since other potential dangers affect only a few species, clues to them are likely to be narrow-spectrum.

Just as in man the forms of behaviour that can conveniently be labelled as fear behaviour are diverse, so are they in non-human species. Responses include, on the one hand, crouching, curling up, freezing and taking cover, and, on the other, calling, escaping, and seeking proximity to companions. The precise response shown turns on many factors – the animal's species, its sex and age, its physiological condition, and also the particular type of situation that has aroused the fear.

For example, Hinde (1970) reports a finding by Hogan that, in chicks, withdrawal occurs from stimuli at high intensity (and some others) whereas freezing is elicited by stimuli that are strange, novel, or surprising. Again, both Lorenz (1937) and Tinbergen (1957) have pointed out how, in many species of bird, distinctive situations can elicit distinctive sorts of response. The Burmese jungle fowl (and also the domestic chicken) possess two distinct warning calls uttered in response to the sight, respectively, of a flying raptor and a terrestrial predator. When heard by another fowl, the raptor-type warning call elicits a downwards escape, ending, where possible, beneath cover of some kind. When, by contrast, the predator-type warning call is heard a fowl takes off and flies into a tree. These distinctive types of behaviour in response to distinctive warning calls are further evidence that, as is indicated in Chapter 6, we are dealing, not with some single and comprehensive 'instinct of fear', but with a heterogeneous collection of interrelated forms of behaviour, each elicited by a slightly different set of causal conditions.

Fear behaviour, it has been emphasized, may not only remove an animal from situations of certain kinds but take it towards, or into, situations of other kinds. Depending on the warning call heard, a fowl flies *down* to ground cover or *up* to a tree. A form of behaviour shown by animals of a great many species, and one of especial interest to our thesis, is movement that takes an animal towards his companions. For example, when a peregrine is overhead, lapwings not only take flight but keep close together as a flock; starlings do the same. (By contrast, in the same situation partridges crouch close to the ground.) Most of the group-living mammals also edge closer together when alarmed. Movement of this kind is particularly evident in young mammals which, with only few exceptions, habitually run to mother and stay close to her.

Let us return now to the situations that arouse fear. It is probable that all the examples of distant situations mentioned so far in this chapter are responded to by fear behaviour of one kind or another on the very first occasion that an individual of a particular species encounters them. In such cases no special opportunities for learning that the situation is potentially dangerous are required. In the case of other stimulus situations, however, the position is quite different. Only after the situation has become associated with some other clue to potential danger is a fear response aroused. A clue universally known to lead to such learnt associations, though not the only one, is pain.

Pain receptors are proximal and therefore their role is in many ways different from that of the distal receptors. In the first place, pain receptors are usually called into action as a last resort and only when the distal receptors, or the fear responses they may have elicited, have failed to ensure the animal's withdrawal. In the second place, the sensation of pain leads commonly to immediate and urgent action. In the third place, the sensation of pain may well mean that the danger has already materialized. For these reasons it is easy to suppose that pain and danger are in some way identical, which of course is not the case (see next chapter), and thus to give pain far too great a prominence in theories of fear behaviour.

Because by being a proximal clue to potential danger pain is very late in acting, it is of great biological advantage to an animal to learn to recognize potentially painful situations from associated distal clues. The investigation of such learning has for long been a principal interest of experimental psychologists, and in consequence much is known about it. In particular, it has long been known from conditioning experiments in which a neutral stimulus is coupled with a painful one that, in a great variety of mammalian species, a fear response to a stimulus hitherto neutral is both quickly established and very hard to extinguish.

A high concentration of interest on the fear-arousing properties of pain, and on the learning to which it gives rise, has at times led to a neglect of the immensely important and prior role of distal clues and distal receptors, both in animals and in man. As a result it is not always realized that in many species a new distal clue to potential danger can be learnt as readily by watching how companions respond to it, and then copying them, as by its becoming associated with pain. In mammals, indeed, a principal means whereby new situations come to be categorized as potentially dangerous, and so to be responded to by fear behaviour, is that of copying older animals, especially parents. In no kinds of mammal does imitative behaviour of this sort play so large a part as it does in primates.

Fear behaviour of non-human primates

Some years ago, as a result of long experience with chimpanzees in captivity, Yerkes and Yerkes (1936) wrote: 'The stimulus characters which early and late are dominant in the determination of avoidance responses are: visual movement, intensity, abruptness, suddenness and rapidity of change in stimulus or stimulus complex.' Although this description needs a little elaboration the nub of the matter is there.

Field Observations

Field observers of the primates are well aware that sudden noise or sudden movement is immediately effective in alarming their subjects and leading to their rapid disappearance. Describing her experiences in watching langur monkeys in the forests of India, Jay (1965) writes: 'Forest groups gradually became used to me and I could follow them at a distance of about 50 feet. However, if any sudden movement in the brush startled them, they immediately fled from sight.' Sudden sounds have the same effect.

For a forest-dwelling species, such as the langur tends to be, safety lies anywhere in the tree-tops. For ground-living species, by contrast, safety may lie in only one special place. For example, in East Africa the home range of each band of olive baboons must contain at least one clump of tall trees to the tops of which the band retreats whenever alarmed and in which it sleeps (DeVore and Hall 1965). Further north, in Ethiopia, family parties of the related species of Hamadryas baboon must live within reach of precipitous cliffs to which they similarly can retreat (Kummer 1967). The location of their haven of safety is a supreme determinant of the behaviour of these animals: 'Where large predators such as lions are numerous . . . the absence of trees in some areas may deny baboons access to rich food sources when food items in general are scarce' (DeVore and Hall 1965).

In the field studies of non-human primates so far published, systematic attention is not always given either to the situations that evoke fear behaviour or to the forms that the behaviour commonly takes. The long-term study of wild chimpanzees undertaken in Tanzania by van Lawick-Goodall (1968) presents far more detail than most.

Van Lawick-Goodall starts by emphasizing that the form that fear behaviour takes 'depends on the situation and the individual or individuals concerned'. When a chimpanzee is startled by a sudden noise or movement nearby, its immediate response is to duck its head and to fling one or both arms across its face; alternatively, it may throw both hands in the air. Occasionally these startle reactions are followed by a hitting-away movement with the back of the hand towards the object, at other times by flight. When the alarming object is another and more dominant chimpanzee, flight is accompanied by loud screaming; when it is anything else, flight is quite silent. An alternative to flight is cautious withdrawal out of sight, combined with an occasional peering-out to see what is going on.

The situations van Lawick-Goodall reports as having evoked startle responses involved sudden noise or movement, for example a low-flying bird, a large insect, or a snake. Fear responses were very often aroused in a chimpanzee when another, more dominant, animal was making threatening gestures. Before the chimpanzees got used to her presence the observer herself was a common source of both fear and flight. After a year or so many of them carried on their normal activities when she was as close as thirty to fifty feet from them. Nevertheless, they quickly became uneasy if she began to follow them; often, too, she had to conceal her interest in them by diversionary activity, such as pretending to eat leaves or to dig.

Since so many species of animal give an alarm call when frightened, van Lawick-Goodall was surprised that the chimpanzees she studied never did so (except when fleeing from one of their own kind). Instead, each one moved away silently on its own. Nevertheless, they were quick to be alerted by the alarm calls of other species: they 'were invariably alerted by the alarm barks of baboons and also by the alarm calls of other monkeys, of bush buck and of some species of birds; after hearing such calls, they peered round to ascertain the nature of the disturbance'.

As in so many other species, to move away from an alarming situation or event is, in chimpanzees, only half the picture of fear behaviour. The other half is to move towards some place treated as though safe or to make physical contact with companions. The latter was seen in adults as well as in young. Van Lawick-Goodall describes how adult animals when frightened move towards and hug one another. This behaviour she believes to be a direct extension of what is seen so regularly in the infant:

Thus a mature chimpanzee may embrace, reach out to touch, or mount another animal under similar circumstances and in more or less the same manner as a frightened or apprehensive infant runs to embrace or be embraced by its mother, reaches out to grasp or touch her hair, or stands upright behind her grasping her rump . . . ready to climb on if the situation warrants it.

The calming and reassuring effects of contact with another animal are discussed by van Lawick-Goodall in some detail. A touch, a pat, or an embrace from a dominant animal was quickly effective in calming a subordinate, and occasionally the reverse occurred. One mature male was seen to find comfort by embracing a female only three years old, once when he had a sudden fright from seeing his own reflection in a glass and twice after he had been attacked by another male.

Field observers of other primate species have also noted the strong propensity of a frightened or agitated animal to touch or cling to a companion. For example, in his description of the behaviour of wild Hamadryas baboons, which live in stable family units of one male with up to three females and their young, Kummer (1967) remarks that not only infants but adults also when under stress are strongly disposed to cling to a companion. Thus an adult female, when alarmed, clings to the back of her husband or is embraced by him. Conversely, when he is under stress during a fight, a male is likely to embrace one of his wives. When an animal that has left its mother but is still not fully mature becomes frightened it seeks out the highest-ranking individual within range. Since not infrequently it is the threats of this animal that aroused the fear in the younger animal the result is paradoxical: the young animal runs to and clings to the very individual that aroused its fear. Among many interesting features of Kummer's study is the evidence he presents that in this species the relationship of a mated male and female is patterned closely on the relationship of a mother and her infant.

The persistence into adult life of patterns of behaviour seen first and at greatest intensity during infancy is found, then, to be a regular feature of the behavioural repertoire of other primate species. It warns us against supposing that, whenever something similar is observed in humans, as it so often is, it must be treated as an example of regression.

In wild animals it is never possible to be sure whether an individual would respond to a particular situation with fear were it to encounter it for the first time or whether it does so only after having learnt to do so. Fear of snakes is a case in point. Van Lawick-Goodall reports that the wild chimpanzees she observed showed fear both of a fast-moving snake and of a dying python. Yet it seems that chimpanzees brought up in zoos do not always show such fear.[2]

Apparently incompatible findings of this kind are not difficult to reconcile. In a social species, to respond with fear to a situation, once learnt, is handed on by tradition. This point is well illustrated by an observation made in Nairobi Park (Washburn and Hamburg 1965). A large band of some eighty olive baboons were sufficiently tame to be approached easily in a car. Two of these baboons were then shot (by a local parasitologist). Thenceforward the baboons fled on sight of man or car, and eight months later

2. A great many zoologists, including Charles Darwin, have been interested in the marked tendency for monkeys and apes to respond to snakes by strong fear, often amounting to panic, and many observations are on record. The evidence is reviewed by Morris and Morris (1965), who also record striking observations of their own. While some measure of learning cannot be ruled out, it is evident that in old-world monkeys and apes the tendency to fear snakes is very pronounced, is relatively specific and, if learnt, is remarkably long-lived in the absence of any further experience.

they still could not be approached although they had seen 'harmless' cars almost daily during the interval. This example is in keeping with the common finding that a response learnt as a result of a single violent experience does not extinguish quickly. It illustrates, further, that it is not necessary for more than a few animals in a band actually to have been exposed to the alarming experience, since it is customary for all the animals in a band to flee as soon as they either hear an alarm bark or see a dominant animal running off. Thus, by following a tradition once set by their elders, members of a band may for years treat whatever happens to have frightened one of their number, present or past, as potentially dangerous. By these means, a tradition that snakes, or men, or cars are to be avoided may develop and persist in one social group though not in another.

Until recent years there was a tendency to suppose that maintenance within a social group from generation to generation of special ways of behaving was a skill confined to man. Now it is recognized that cultural traditions occur also in many other species and affect many forms of behaviour: how to sing (Thorpe 1956), what to eat (Kawamura 1963), where to nest (Wynne-Edwards 1962). It is no surprise, then, to find that in a bird or mammal species cultural traditions exist regarding what to avoid.

The part played in human development by culturally determined clues to potential danger is discussed further in Chapter 10. Here it may be noted that recent experimental studies of monkeys demonstrate clearly that an animal may learn to fear a situation solely by observing how a companion responds. For example, Bandura (1968) refers to a study by Crooks which shows that monkeys that initially played freely with certain play objects ceased to do so after they had witnessed another monkey (apparently) emit cries of fear whenever it touched one of the objects.[3]

Experimental Studies

Many other studies of captive animals, including experimental studies, fill out our knowledge of the fear behaviour of non-

3. In fact the distress vocalizations were played on a tape-recorder each time the monkey touched an object.

human primates and of the situations that are likely to evoke it.

Two visual situations that arouse fear in young rhesus monkeys are a looming stimulus and the visual cliff. Both experimental situations are described in the previous chapter where the fear responses of human infants are discussed.

Schiff, Caviness and Gibson (1962) studied the behaviour of twenty-three rhesus monkeys of varying age when confronted by a looming stimulus; eight were infants of between five and eight months, and the remainder adolescent or adult. Each animal was tested alone in its own cage at a distance of five feet from the screen on to which the expanding (looming) shadow was projected. All but four of the animals responded immediately by either withdrawing or ducking. A number of animals sprang to the rear of the cage, often bumping hard against the back. Other and less active animals were quick to duck head and upper part of body. Younger animals often gave alarm calls as well. (The four animals that failed to respond were thought to be looking elsewhere when the stimulus was presented.) No age differences were shown. The speed and form of the stimulus appeared irrelevant. No habituation occurred when two animals were each exposed to a series of fifteen looming trials at intervals of ten seconds.

When the same animals were confronted by a contracting (receding) shadow the response was quite different. All but four remained at the front of the cage and appeared interested as the shadow contracted. A general brightening of the screen also aroused interest. A darkening screen produced no particular response, except when it was presented after a looming stimulus: then it produced a few slight flinches, much milder than those that occurred to looming.

The number of young rhesus monkeys tested on the visual cliff is few, but responses are unambiguous. Walk and Gibson (1961) report on a male infant tested at ten days, and again at eighteen and forty-five days, and on a female infant tested at twelve and thirty-five days. During their second week both infants proved only fairly reliable in avoiding the 'chasm'. By the ages of eighteen and thirty-five days, respectively, the two showed pronounced discrimination and effectively avoided the 'deep' side at every test. Thus, in this species, avoidance of the deep side is only

partly efficient when locomotion begins, but it improves rapidly.
The results of similar experiments on another small sample of
rhesus infants, reported by Fantz (1965), are of a similar kind.

Strangeness has been used as a fear-arousing stimulus in many
experiments with primates.

Harlow and his colleagues have conducted a number of experiments on the fear behaviour of young rhesus monkeys.[4] Before
about twenty days of age an infant rhesus shows no sign of fear
of strange visual stimuli; for example, it will confidently approach
a moving toy animal it has never seen before. After that age,
however, and especially after six weeks, the presence of such a
toy leads an infant immediately to rush away from it. Infants
that have been reared on a cloth dummy 'mother' not only flee
from the alarming toy but return promptly *to* the familiar dummy
mother, to which they then cling tightly. Often a rather older
infant, of twelve weeks or more, having fled from the alarming
toy and clung tightly to its familiar dummy mother, relaxes. Then
it may leave the dummy mother and cautiously approach the
fear-inducing toy; it may even explore it manually. The behaviour
of the same infant when its familiar dummy mother is absent is,
however, very different. It is likely then to curl up on the floor and
scream (see below, p. 165).

Mason (1965) has carried out rather similar experiments with
chimpanzees, also using strangeness as a main form of fear-
arousing stimulus situation. In this species also behaviour is very
different according to whether an animal is with others or alone.
This leads to a consideration of the effects on non-human primates of compound situations, and especially of the striking
effects of being alone.

Compound situations

Monkeys and apes are like humans in that, when confronted by
a situation compounded of more than one alarming feature, they
are apt to exhibit fear at an intensity far greater than they would

4. An account of some of Harlow's experiments is given in Volume I,
Chapter 12. See also Harlow and Zimmermann (1959); Harlow (1961);
Harlow and Harlow (1965).

were any one of the features to be present singly. Being alone in the presence of a fear-inducing stimulus, moreover, greatly intensifies the fear behaviour seen.

Being Alone

An experimental study reported by Rowell and Hinde (1963) gives quantitative data for a sample of seventeen rhesus monkeys, thirteen adult (three male and ten female) and four sub-adult (two of each sex). These animals live together in stable groups of a male with three or four females and young. The tests, each of which lasted for three minutes, consisted of very simple situations. In each test the tester, who was well known to the animals, stood close to the cage. In one he offered them pieces of banana; in another he stood quietly watching but not staring; and in a third he dressed up in mask and cloak and made slight movements. Before being tested each animal was observed for half an hour and its behaviour was recorded. Thereafter the three tests followed, separated by intervals of five minutes.

In the first series of tests the animals were tested while living together in their regular groups. Each time the tester appeared they showed a characteristic change in behaviour compared with what they had shown before the testing started. There was a great increase of threat noises and of activities, such as lip-smacking, scratching, and yawning, that are associated with stress. In addition, they urinated more frequently, their hair stood on end, and they showed a frightened facial expression. (Attacks were sometimes made by the adult males towards the tester but were not made by the other monkeys.)

Most of these forms of behaviour were considerably more in evidence when the observer wore the mask and cloak and moved than when he stood quietly by. Of responses seen in the mask test, significant increases in frequency were recorded for low aggression threat noises, hair standing on end, urinating, frightened expression, and yawning. In general terms it seems that, whereas the monkeys were merely 'made uneasy' when the observer quietly watched, when he wore the mask they became 'alarmed and angry'.

In a second series of tests each animal was tested alone. For a period of six hours before testing began the remainder of its group was locked into an indoor cage while the animal under test remained alone in its familiar outdoor cage; it could, however, hear its companions and see them through a window, so that it was far from being isolated. Nevertheless, for every animal, fear responses to the simple tests were far more frequent when it was alone than when it was with its group. Increased scores ranged from threefold to fiftyfold. The response showing the greatest increase in frequency was that of looking into the window where it could see its absent companions.

Summing up their findings, Rowell and Hinde write:

Thus isolation is best regarded not merely as an additional stress-producing factor acting equally under all circumstances, but rather as one which, while producing relatively little effect on undisturbed animals, can strongly accentuate the effect of other stress-producing agents. It is as though isolation multiplied their effects, rather than summating with them.

The results of Harlow's experiments on young rhesus monkeys brought up on dummy mothers strongly support this conclusion (Harlow and Harlow 1965). In one series of experiments four infants raised on cloth dummy mothers were introduced, singly, to a strange 'room', six feet square, containing various objects known to be of interest to young monkeys. Each week two tests were given to each infant. In one the infant's dummy mother was present in the 'room', in the other it was absent. According to whether its dummy mother was present or absent the behaviour of an infant was utterly different.

When the dummy mother was present an infant, on entry to the strange room, rushed to it and clutched it tenaciously. The infant then relaxed and, showing little sign of apprehension, began climbing over the dummy mother and manipulating it. After several such sessions, the infants began to use the dummy mother as a base from which to explore. Leaving the dummy, an infant moved to a toy, picked it up and handled it, and then moved back to the dummy. Sometimes a monkey would bring its plaything with it. Exploration of an object away from the dummy mother alternated with rapid return to base. Throughout, the monkey seemed relaxed and confident.

In the absence of the familiar dummy mother, behaviour was radically changed. An infant either curled up on the floor rocking and crying, or else ran around clutching hold of itself. Exploration of the objects, when it occurred at all, was 'brief, erratic and frantic'. The impression given to an observer was of an infant in a state of distress and misery.[5]

The results of Mason's experiments with young chimpanzees point in the same direction (Mason 1965). In one experiment twelve African-born animals were, singly, given electric shocks to the foot, both when held by an observer and when alone. Whereas when an animal was alone it whimpered and screamed some 60 per cent of the time, when held by an observer it was practically silent. Comparable results were obtained when the animals, instead of being shocked, were confronted by a novel situation.

In yet another series of experiments, conducted by Gantt in a Pavlovian tradition, it is shown that anxiety, induced experimentally in dogs, is much reduced by the presence of a human companion, especially someone well known to the animal. Patting and petting the dog is particularly efficacious; and the effect is more pronounced on animals made 'neurotic' by frequent experimental procedures than on more normal animals. Findings are reviewed by Lynch (1970).

Fear, attack, and exploration

Stimulus situations that are likely to arouse fear in humans and other animals can also, when circumstances are a little changed, evoke behaviour of quite different sorts. Attack is one of these alternative forms of behaviour; exploration another.

Whether an animal flees from a potentially fear-inducing stimulus object or goes in to attack it turns on very many factors,

---

5. Infants that had been reared on a wire dummy mother were little influenced by whether it was present or absent. In both conditions they showed very distressed behaviour, which was at a level of intensity significantly greater even than that of the infants reared on a cloth dummy mother when the dummy was temporarily absent. Thus the wire dummy mother proved entirely ineffective as a base from which to explore.

some organismic, others situational. Of the organismic factors, the individual's species, age, and sex play major parts. In many species, including the ground-living primates, older animals, especially males, are more likely to attack, whereas immature animals and females are more likely to withdraw. Ill health and fatigue may also play a part in tipping the balance towards withdrawal. Hunger often tips it towards attack. Of the situational factors, being on familiar territory makes for boldness, being elsewhere for withdrawal. When escape routes are blocked, attack is the rule. Not infrequently, behaviour of both sorts is clearly aroused: even in the act of attacking, an individual may show signs of also being afraid. Because of the close association between them, attack, threat, flight, and submission are sometimes lumped together by ethologists and termed 'agonistic behaviour'. The reason for the close association between these forms of behaviour is that, of the many causal conditions necessary to elicit each one of them, some are shared in common (Hinde 1970).

This circumstance is the explanation also of the close link there is between withdrawal and exploration, discussed in Chapter 13 of Volume I. It is well known that a single kind of stimulus situation, namely strangeness or novelty, can elicit either withdrawal or exploration or both together. In animals of many species a small change in the environment elicits investigation whereas a larger one arouses fear behaviour. Not infrequently an interested approach and an alarmed withdrawal are shown either simultaneously or in rapid succession. Which of the two classes of behaviour becomes dominant turns on many factors – the details of the novel stimulus, the environment in which it is met (familiar or unfamiliar terrain, companions present or absent), the age and sex of the individual, its hormonal condition, and no doubt other factors besides.

The fact that small changes in a situation can have great influence on the form of behaviour shown cannot be over-emphasized. If a population of animals is to survive in the wild each one needs to show, according to its age, sex, and social status, a nice balance between discretion and valour.

Chapter 9
Natural Clues to Danger and Safety

I left my darling lying here,
a-lying here, a-lying here,
I left my darling lying here,
To go and gather blaeberries

I found the wee brown otter's track,
The otter's track, the otter's track,
I found the wee brown otter's track,
But ne'er a trace of baby-O

I found the track of the swan on the lake,
The swan on the lake, the swan on the lake,
I found the track of the swan on the lake,
But not the track of baby-O

I found the trail of the mountain mist,
The mountain mist, the mountain mist,
I found the trail of the mountain mist,
But ne'er a trace of baby-O

– From the Gaelic

Better safe than sorry

None of the stimulus situations so far considered – strangeness, sudden change of stimulation, rapid approach, height, being alone – is intrinsically dangerous. Each one is no more than an indicator of potential danger or, more precisely, of an increased risk of danger, and, as such, of only moderate accuracy. As a result, much fear is aroused in situations that later turn out not to have been dangerous at all; while, by contrast, certain truly dangerous objects and events are heralded by no fear-arousing natural clues. This imperfect correlation of natural clues with actual dangers has proved confusing for clinicians and a trap for unwary theorists.

The heart of the theory here advanced, which derives directly from ethology, is that each of the stimulus situations that man is genetically biased to respond to with fear has the same status as a red traffic light or an air-raid siren. Each is a signal of potential danger; none is intrinsically dangerous. In a similar way, each of the stimulus situations that man, when alarmed, is genetically biased to approach and cling to has the same status as sanctuary on sacred ground. Each signifies potential safety; none is intrinsically safe. Whereas the signal value of the red light and the sacred ground is conferred by human convention and transmitted by word of mouth, that of the natural clues is conferred by statistical association and transmitted by genes. Strong genetically derived biases to respond differentially to these two classes of natural clue either by withdrawal or by approach have, during the course of evolution, become a characteristic of the human species because of their survival value. Most clearly apparent during childhood and old age, sometimes disguised or discounted during adult life, these biases nevertheless remain with us. From the cradle to the grave they are an intrinsic part of human nature.

This theory, it will be seen, explains well why, in modern Western environments, fear can be readily aroused in situations that are not, in fact, the least dangerous; and also why fear can be readily allayed by actions, such as clutching a teddy bear or sucking a pipe, that do nothing effective to increase safety. Though to the eye of an intellectual city-dweller such behaviour may seem irrational and childish, and may even be attributed to pathological fancy, to the eye of a biologist a deeper wisdom is apparent. Examination shows, indeed, that, so far from being irrational or foolhardy, to rely initially on the naturally occurring clues to danger and safety is to rely on a system that has been both sensible and efficient over millions of years.

For, it must be remembered, we have but one life. Though on occasion risks are run, either for potential gain or merely for fun, in the ordinary run of days it is better by far when natural clues are perceived to take what on ninety-nine occasions proves to be unnecessary action than, by habitually ignoring them, to fall victim on the hundredth. Were we regularly to ignore red traffic lights we might not meet our doom for a time; but our days would be numbered.

A natural clue to potential danger signals merely *an increased risk of danger* and gives no information regarding the absolute degree of risk. For animals of different species, of different ages and sex and in different environments, the absolute risk indicated by one or another clue can vary from high to quite low. For example, certain natural clues that are closely linked to predators, such as staring eyes, may perhaps in certain natural environments be associated with a very high degree of risk, whereas in some other environments the risk might be low. Similarly, certain other natural clues, such as being alone, might be associated with either a high or a low degree of risk depending on the particular circumstances and the particular individual. Nevertheless, whatever the absolute levels of risk may be, a natural clue is associated as a rule with a *raised* degree of risk. The increase may be from moderate to very high or perhaps from near zero to a mere 1 per cent. Without a great deal of knowledge of the total situation the absolute degree of risk in any one case cannot be known. What seems clear, however, is that in every case the degree of risk is likely to be raised.

The great advantage of our being biased to respond, by prompt withdrawal, to the natural clues to an increased risk of danger is that between them they act as indicators to a high proportion of all the dangerous situations into which we might stray; while in combination their potential value for the purpose is vastly increased, in a way that Broadbent (1973) describes.[1] No matter that they embrace also a great many situations that are not dangerous at all. Far better to be safe than sorry.

In an analogous way it is also an advantage when running away from a potential danger to run towards a potential haven of

1. Broadbent discusses the various ways in which unreliable or in other respects insufficient items of evidence can be utilized by the brain for purposes of decision-making and action. When a number of such items are received together there are two main ways in which they can be processed. One way is to process them independently and serially, in which case maximum advantage for decision-making is unlikely to be obtained. Another is for the items to be processed simultaneously. In that case not only is maximum advantage obtained but the effects on decision-taking, and therefore action, are likely to be dramatically different from those of the first method. In view of the data regarding the striking effects on behaviour of a combination of natural clues to danger, it seems probable that combinations are usually processed simultaneously.

safety: for small animals ground cover, for monkeys the tree-tops, for group-living species the social band, for weaker animals their stronger companions. No matter if such action is taken unnecessarily: once again, better safe than sorry.

By this point some readers may have become impatient. However true the principles outlined may be for monkeys and apes, and perhaps even for young human children, adult humans are a great deal more sophisticated than to attend merely to natural clues. Thought and imagination, rational or irrational, conscious or unconscious, are the stuff of human fear. Why waste time on these primitive mechanisms? The reason is, of course, that much of the sophisticated superstructure of cognitive and feeling processes characteristic of Western man in the realm of fear is intelligible only in terms of the primitive genetically biased groundwork that evolved in a different environment and that we share with other primate species. A failure to understand this primitive groundwork, it is argued, has led to many and serious misunderstandings. Not only is the behaviour of every human adult influenced by these primitive processes but so also are his most sophisticated cognitive structures and his most sensitive ways of feeling. Whether suddenly alarmed or chronically anxious, whether temporarily comforted or steadily confident, the way a man or woman thinks and feels is determined in significant degree by these strong genetic biases to respond unthinkingly to the natural clues.

In the chapters that follow attention is given, first, to showing that the strong tendency to respond to the natural clues accounts for most of the more elaborate situations that humans come to fear, and, subsequently, to the way in which increasingly refined processes of appraisal lead to a broad spectrum of human feeling states. Before proceeding, however, let us consider further the genetically biased groundwork. We begin with the special place of physical pain as a natural clue.

The Limitations of Pain as a Natural Clue

In the past there have been theorists who have postulated that almost the only type of stimulus to which there is any genetic bias to respond with fear is physical pain, and that all other stimuli derive their fear-arousing properties from becoming associated with pain. Not only is the theory false, but a moment's thought shows it to be hardly plausible.

As a natural clue to potential danger, the experience of physical pain is in a special category. The clues to which attention has so far been directed are distal clues perceived by the distance receptors, eye, ear, and nose. By giving warnings while potential danger is still more or less remote, these clues enable an animal or man to take precautions in good time. By contrast, as noted in the previous chapter, to await events until pain is experienced may well be to wait too long. Whereas the distance receptors can be likened to advance look-outs, physical pain has the status of last ditch.

The special property of pain is that, being so late in acting, it leads to immediate and urgent action. The phase of alert wariness, so characteristic of many animals after a distal clue is first sensed, is absent. Instead, there is immediate and unthinking retreat, or, alternatively, attack.

Another special property of pain is, of course, its power to promote learning. Countless experiments demonstrate how rapidly and firmly an animal learns to recognize a situation in which it has experienced pain and to respond thenceforth by avoiding it. After such learning, an animal no longer relies on the hazardous proximal clue of pain but comes instead to use some distal clue that gives time and space in which it can take precautions. The advance look-outs are alerted to identify and beware of a new clue.

Even though physical pain may be more highly correlated with potential danger than are some of the other natural clues, it is not infallible. For example, medical attention may be painful but is usually not dangerous; whereas a truly dangerous condition, such as internal haemorrhage, may be accompanied by no pain. That is but one example of a serious danger that is either without natural clues or heralded by faint ones only.

Dangers that have no Natural Clues

Earlier it was noted that the natural clues to which we react with fear are, singly and especially together, indicators of a high proportion of all the dangerous situations into which we might stray. Nevertheless, there are some dangerous situations that present no clue to which we have a natural bias to respond by escape. Some, indeed, even emit no signal that our sense organs can detect.

Among naturally occurring hazards, infectious illnesses are cases in point. Where infection is airborne there is usually no naturally occurring clue that we are able to sense and from which we are genetically biased to withdraw. (In contrast, by producing bad smells or tastes, food- and water-borne infections are often much less silent.) In modern times, moreover, man has added a number of other dangers that also emit no clues to which human nature is sensitive. Examples are carbon monoxide gas and X-rays. Since in such cases evolution has as yet had neither time nor opportunity to provide us with natural means for their detection, we have to rely instead on man-made indicators.

Thus, although by exploiting the natural clues to danger and safety our genetic endowment provides us with a remarkably sensitive and efficient means of protection, it is far from fool-proof. On countless occasions we are led unnecessarily to avoid wholly harmless situations; on a few others we are permitted to blunder into truly dangerous ones.

Potential danger of being alone

The natural clue to increased risk of danger with which this volume is especially concerned is being alone. Statistically, being alone is less safe than being with a companion. That that should be so during childhood, during sickness, and in old age may not be too difficult to grasp. That it is also the case for the ordinary healthy grown-up man and woman may at first sight seem unexpected. Yet there is good reason to believe that it is so, especially in certain situations; even though in Western countries the situations may be few and the absolute risk not high. The thesis of this section is, therefore, that, as it was throughout man's earlier history, in many circumstances still today it is as appropriate to avoid being alone as it is to avoid any of the other natural clues to potential danger. That we should be so constructed that we find comfort in companionship and seek it, and that we experience greater or less degrees of anxiety when alone, is, therefore, in no way surprising.

In the previous volume (Chapter 4) it is argued that, if we are to understand human behavioural equipment, it is necessary to view it in the light of what we know of man's environment of evolutionary adaptedness. Later, following this line of thought (Chapter 12), the theory is advanced that in man's environment of evolutionary adaptedness the function of attachment behaviour, which of course promotes proximity to special companions, is protection from predators, and that this is as true for humans as it is for other species of mammal and bird. For all ground-living primates, safety lies in being with the band. To become separated from it is to provide a more or less easy meal for a lurking leopard[2] or a pack of hunting dogs. For weaker members, especially females and young, the old and the sick, isolation often spells speedy death.

By practical people this theory is sometimes treated as an academic curiosity. Yes, it may be said, there may well have been a time in man's history when separation entailed danger from predators. But that was long ago. For such responses to persist into modern times is an irrelevant nuisance. It is time to rid ourselves of such archaic superstition.

This line of reasoning has several defects. In the first place, even if we wished it, genetic biases built in over millions of years cannot be eradicated overnight. In the second, reflection suggests that to try to eradicate them might be most unwise. For in many parts of the world today the absolute risk attendant on being alone is still fairly high; and even in Western societies the risk may be higher than we like to imagine.

In Western countries today, it is true, injury and death are no longer due to predators. But there are other dangers. In place of predators, power-driven motor cars and household equipment

2. Since publication of the first volume further evidence has come to light of the dangers of leopards to early man. According to Brain (1970) the fossilized bones of *Paranthropus robustus* found in a cave in the Transvaal are fragmented in ways typical of leopard prey. One of the better-preserved skulls (of a juvenile) bears two holes the right size and distance apart to fit the canine teeth of a leopard.

provide novel hazards and take their toll. Young children newly mobile and the elderly are among the principal victims. Yet, though ordinary experience strongly suggests that those most at risk are children and old people left on their own, researchers concerned with accident prevention seem to have given the matter little attention. Statistics of traffic accidents for one of the London boroughs and also for Sweden are, however, revealing.

Traffic Accidents to Children

During 1968 in the London borough of Southwark,[3] injuries to pedestrians numbered 901, of which twenty-seven were fatal. Of the total injuries, 411, or nearly half (46 per cent), were to children under the age of fifteen. This represents an incidence of injury to children about three times that to adults.

The most vulnerable age-group were children between their fourth and eighth birthdays. At these ages the risk of injury was about five times that for adults. The incidence for those a little younger and a little older (the three- and the eight-year-olds) was only slightly lower. The age distribution was as shown in the table below.

Age in years	No. of injuries
0– 2·11	14
3– 5·11	125
6– 8·11	124
9–11·11	81
12–14·11	67
Total	411

Of all the children injured, almost two-thirds (62 per cent) were entirely alone. Even in the case of the younger children more than half were alone. Many of the others were with other children, often no older than themselves. Only one in eight of the injured children was with an adult.

A similar picture emerges from Sweden (Sandels 1971). The

3. I am indebted to Mr V. E. Golds, Road Safety Officer for the borough, for these figures.

incidence of injury to pedestrians is especially high in children between their third and tenth birthdays. A special study of 177 accidents occurring to children under the age of eleven years at pedestrian crossings shows that 44 per cent of the children were alone and another 34 per cent with peers; only one in five was with an adult.

Although we still lack the crucial data regarding differences in the incidence of accidents to children who are with and to children who are without an adult, it nevertheless seems safe to conclude that the great excess of traffic accidents to children when compared with adults is due to their being out in the street either alone or with peers.[4] To anyone who has had the care of small children in an urban district this conclusion will hardly cause surprise.

Risk to Adults

It is perhaps easy to understand that for a young child or an old person to be alone is a risk. But, it may be protested, that can hardly be true also for a healthy adult. Reflection, however, strongly suggests that it is.

It seems very probable that, were comparative figures available, it would be found that even for healthy men and women in Western countries there are many situations in which risk of injury or death is greater when a person is alone than when in company. Walking in city streets at night is a case in point. It is not for nothing that in certain areas policemen patrol in pairs. Those who take part in active sports, moreover, are aware that to be alone carries added risk. Whether climbing mountains, swimming, exploring caves, or sailing the seas, to be alone is hazardous, sometimes because in detecting danger two heads are better than one, sometimes because an injury that would present no problem to a pair can prove fatal to a singleton.

4. Studies of the family background of children who are injured in traffic accidents (Backett and Johnston 1959; Burton 1968) cast light on why these children are not being looked after by a parent. When compared with children in a control group, more of the injured children are found to be unwanted and unloved and/or to have a mother who, currently, is anxiously preoccupied with other matters, e.g. illness in herself or in others in the household, younger siblings, elderly relatives, or her own pregnancy. Similar findings for children who sustain burns are reported by Martin (1970).

Yet another hazard to a man alone comes when he is overtaken by fatigue. Once asleep he cannot protect himself should danger threaten. When, by contrast, he has companions, each can take his turn on watch. The practice of alternating watches on board a ship at sea is, indeed, the organized and human version of a sleeping pattern common in birds that roost together in flocks and in primates that sleep together in bands. Because every animal is awake for some part of the night, at any one moment, while the majority of animals are asleep, a few are likely to be awake ready to give the alarm (Washburn 1966).

It is true that in recent years great feats of single-handed navigation have been performed. That interest in their success should be so high is an earnest of the public's recognition, not only of the difficulties to be solved, but of the risks to be surmounted. Safety lies in numbers, especially in the companionship of familiars.

Potential safety of familiar companions and environment

Throughout these chapters it is emphasized that what is feared includes not only the presence, actual or imminent, of certain sorts of situation but the *absence*, actual or imminent, of certain other sorts of situation. Throughout life we tend to be drawn towards certain parts of the animate and inanimate environment, mainly people and places we are familiar with, and to be repelled by certain other parts of the environment, especially those that exhibit one or more of the natural clues to potential danger. Since two of the natural clues that tend to be avoided are strangeness and being alone, there is a marked tendency for humans, like animals of other species, to remain in a particular and familiar locale and in the company of particular and familiar people.

It has long been obvious that animals of any one species tend to restrict their movements so that they remain within those parts of the earth's surface to which they are physiologically adapted. Such parts can be defined in terms of various physical measures, such as earth, air or water, temperature gradients, rainfall, and also in terms of biological measures, such as presence or absence of certain foodstuffs. Only by regulating their movements in these ways are members of a species able to maintain the physiological measures on which life depends within certain critical limits. The types of behavioural system, activation and termination of which result in an animal's remaining within its ecological niche, are of the kind traditionally termed instinctive.

Yet, great though ecologically determined limitations may be, they are nothing in comparison with the limits constantly found in nature. It is still too little realized, perhaps, that the individuals of a species, so far from roaming at random throughout the whole area of the earth's surface ecologically suitable to them, usually spend the whole of their lives within an extremely restricted segment of.it, known as the home range.[5] For example, a vole lives within its few hundred square yards of thicket, a troup of baboons within its dozen square miles of savanna, a band of human hunters and gatherers within its few hundred square miles of forest or plain. Even flocks of migrating birds, which may travel thousands of miles between nesting and wintering grounds, use only special parts of each: many birds nest each year at or very near the place they were born.

In a similar way birds and mammals do not mix indiscriminately with others of their kind. Individual recognition is the rule. With certain individuals close bonds may be maintained for long stretches of the life-cycle. With a number of others there may be a less close but none the less sustained relationship. Yet other individuals may either be of little interest or else be carefully avoided. Thus each individual has its own relatively small and very distinctive personal environment to which it is attached.

While the survival value of an animal's predisposition to remain within an ecologically suitable environment is clearly not in doubt, the survival value of its strong tendency to remain within its own special and familiar environment may at first sight seem debatable. Yet examination of the issue shows that to do so

5. The concept of the home range embraces that of territoriality but is much broader. Whereas very many species of bird and mammal show marked preferences for a particular home range (see Jewell and Loizos 1966), far fewer maintain and defend an exclusive territory. For a discussion of the probable functions of territory holding, which may differ between species, see Crook (1968).

in all likelihood confers distinct advantage, especially when conditions turn unfavourable. By remaining within a familiar environment an animal, or a human, knows at once where food and water are to be found, not only at different seasons of the ordinary year but also during those exceptionally bad years that occur from time to time; he knows, too, where shelter from the weather can be got, where there are trees or cliffs or caves that provide safety, what are the common dangers and from what quarter they are likely to come. By remaining in company with familiar companions, he can benefit from established and therefore relatively successful customs, for example food preferences, and also, when threatened by a predator, from co-ordinated social action. Thus, by remaining within his personal and familiar environment an individual stays within an arena that is comparatively safe and is kept well clear of many hazards that might otherwise endanger him.

Maintenance of an individual within his familiar environment is, it is postulated, the result of the activation and termination of behavioural systems that are sensitive to such stimulus situations as strangeness and familiarity, being alone and being with companions. On the one hand, behavioural systems mediating fear behaviour tend to remove the individual from situations that are potentially dangerous. On the other, those mediating attachment behaviour tend to lead him towards, or retain him within, situations that are potentially safe.

This brings the discussion back to attachment behaviour. The behavioural systems that maintain a younger or weaker individual in more or less close proximity to another discriminated and stronger individual can now be seen as a part of a larger set of systems that have the effect of so regulating the whole of a creature's movements that he remains as a rule within his familiar environment. Attachment to a parent figure is, in most species, ontogenetically the first form in which this type of behaviour develops.

In the next chapter and in Chapters 18 and 19 is is argued that many of the difficulties that have dogged psychiatric and psychoanalytic theories of anxiety have arisen because insufficient recognition has been given to the enormous roles that an individual's personal and familiar environment, including his familiar companions, plays in determining his emotional state. Only when it is realized that each man's environment is unique to himself can how he feels be understood.

Maintaining a stable relationship with the familiar environment: a form of homeostasis

Those trained in physiology may find it illuminating to view the behaviour under consideration as homeostatic. Whereas the systems studied by physiologists maintain certain physico-chemical measures, internal to the organism, within certain limits, the systems mediating attachment behaviour and fear behaviour maintain the whole individual within a defined part of the environment. In the one case the states held steady are interior to the organism, in the other the states held steady concern the relationship of the organism to the environment.

A principal advantage of casting the theory of fear and anxiety presented here in terms of homeostasis is that by so doing it becomes possible to relate it to two other bodies of theory, both of which commonly invoke homeostatic principles. On the one hand, the theory can be linked to theories of stress and stress diseases, most of which invoke concepts of physiological homeostasis. On the other, it can be linked to a theory of defensive processes, which also, traditionally, have been conceived as contributing to the maintenance of some form of homeostasis. In place, however, of Freud's postulate that defensive processes help to reduce the level of stimulation in the mental apparatus to a steady low level, the theory advanced here conceives them as contributing to the maintenance of what can conveniently be termed a steady 'representational' state.[6]

In the view presented here, maintenance of a steady relationship between an individual and his familiar environment occurs

6. A theory of defensive processes incorporating these ideas is to be sketched in the later part of the third volume, in which also a comparison will be made with certain other concepts of homeostasis that from time to time have been proposed by psychoanalysts.

hardly less automatically and unthinkingly than does maintenance of his physiological steady states. In the case of each form of homeostasis, an individual is conceived as being born with a strong genetic bias to develop biological systems that, by being sensitive to certain types of stimuli, come into action whenever some particular measure deviates from certain set limits and cease action as soon as it is restored within those limits. Thus the theory proposed places the maintenance of a steady relationship between organism and familiar environment on a level of biological importance only one step lower than the maintenance of the much better understood physiological steady states.

Furthermore, the systems maintaining each of the two forms of homeostasis are seen as complementary. For it is clear that, so long as the systems that maintain an individual within his familiar environment are being successful, the loads placed on the systems that maintain physiological states steady are being eased. This is because, so long as an individual remains within his familiar physical environment and with familiar companions, he is more likely than he would be otherwise to find food and drink, and to achieve reliable and continuing protection from natural hazards—from predators, from eating poisonous foodstuffs, from falling and drowning, from exposure and cold. Conversely, so long as the systems maintaining physiological homeostasis are successful, the healthier will the individual be and the easier will it be for him to maintain himself effectively within his familiar environment. Looked at in this light the regulatory systems that maintain a steady relationship between an individual and his familiar environment can be regarded as an 'outer ring' of life-maintaining systems complementary to the 'inner ring' of systems that maintain physiological homeostasis.

It must, of course, be stressed that, whatever category of homeostasis is being considered, states are never maintained more than relatively stable nor, except rarely, do set-points and limits persist unchanged throughout the life-cycle. So long as the unit of study is the individual, indeed, processes of growth are the antithesis of processes of homeostasis. The principle of homeostasis is, therefore, only one among several. The reason for emphasizing it here is that homeostasis is held to be a key concept for understanding not only fear and anxiety but also grief and mourning.

While special attention is directed to the tendency for an individual to maintain a steady relationship between himself and his familiar environment, the important roles of exploratory and investigative behaviour, which tend to be antithetical to it, are not overlooked (see Volume I, Chapter 13). Nor are the developmental changes that occur in regular procession during the life-cycle.

Chapter 10
Natural Clues, Cultural Clues, and the Assessment of Danger

Innately, children seem to have little true realistic anxiety. . . . They will run along the brink of the water, climb on to the window-sill, play with sharp objects and with fire – in short, do everything that is bound to damage them and to worry those in charge of them. When in the end realistic anxiety is awakened in them, that is wholly the result of education; for they cannot be allowed to make the instructive experiences themselves.
– SIGMUND FREUD (1917b)

Clues of three kinds

Initially during infancy the only stimulus situations to which a child responds with fear are the natural clues. During the second and third years other situations are added, notably presence of animals, and darkness (with its associated happenings), both of which situations, it is argued, are readily learnt derivatives of the natural clues. From his second year, in addition, a child is much influenced by observing the behaviour of significant adults and imitating it. Among the great array of behaviour a child learns in this way, all of it culturally determined, is to respond with fear to a range of stimulus situations he has hitherto treated as neutral, or even interesting. These new stimulus situations are conveniently referred to as 'cultural clues'. In many instances, it is evident, imitative fear behaviour of this sort is entirely without insight into the nature of the danger being avoided. Because of this, fear aroused by a cultural clue has much in common with fear aroused by a natural clue. In neither case can the fear be regarded as 'realistic' in Freud's sense of the term.

Only very slowly and as his cognitive capacities develop does a child begin to distinguish natural or cultural clues from real danger and to learn methods of his own for calculating risk. During the same phase of growth all his behaviour is becoming organized increasingly in terms of goal-corrected plans, and with it his fear behaviour. As a result of these linked developments his fear behaviour is becoming, as it is said, more 'rational' and 'realistic'. Thenceforward, during later childhood and adolescence, and into adult life, his capacity to assess real danger and to respond appropriately is likely steadily to improve.

Nevertheless, important though these new developments in the organization of fear behaviour may be, the bias to respond with fear to both the cultural and the natural clues persists. Indeed, not only throughout childhood but throughout adolescence and adult life as well the natural clues and their derivatives remain among the most effective of all the stimulus situations that arouse fear. Even the most courageous is not immune to fear on seeing some extraordinary apparition or a sudden rapid approach, or on hearing some piercing scream or finding himself alone in darkness in a strange place.

In intellectual circles both the persisting bias to respond to the natural clues and the value of that bias are all too often overlooked. As a result much human fear comes to be seen in a false perspective. For example, Arnold (1960), rightly impressed by the role of appraisal in the regulation of behaviour, goes so far as to assert that 'genuine fear develops only when the child is old enough to estimate the possibility of harm'. Elsewhere in scussions of fear in human beings, there is commonly to be found the assumption more or less explicit that, whereas fear of real danger is a healthy and often desirable response, fear of anything else is childish or neurotic. Throughout psychiatry that assumption has for long been powerful and persuasive. It is found not only in the psychoanalytic tradition from Freud himself onwards (see above, Chapter 5) but in other traditions of psychiatry also (e.g. Lewis 1967). It is a main reason why the fear of separation from a loved figure is still so often, and so erroneously, held to be both neurotic and childish.

A principal thesis of this work is that the assumption that mature adults are afraid only of real danger, plausible though it may seem, is profoundly mistaken. Naturally enough an adult man, or woman, does what he, or she, can to calculate the prospects of real danger and to take the necessary precautions. Yet to make those calculations is often far from easy, and on some occasions would take dangerously long to do. By contrast, to respond to the natural and cultural clues is quick and simple. To respond to the natural clues, moreover, especially when two or more people are present together, provides, as described in the previous chapter, an efficient, if crude, system for minimizing danger and maximizing safety. No wonder, therefore, that alongside the more sophisticated measures for calculating danger, adult man continues to respond, at least tentatively, to each one of the natural clues and, when faced with compound situations, to respond especially strongly.

Thus, in adult man fear behaviour comes to be elicited by clues that derive from at least three sources:
- natural clues and their derivatives
- cultural clues learnt by observation
- clues that are learnt and used in more or less sophisticated ways in order to assess danger and avoid it.

Behaviour based on clues of the first type develops very early and is apt to be referred to as 'childish' and 'irrational'. Behaviour based on clues of the third type develops much later and is commonly referred to as 'mature' and 'realistic'. Behaviour based on clues of the second type is intermediate: whether it is referred to as childish or mature, rational or irrational, turns on whether the onlooker shares or does not share the cultural norm reflected in the behaviour. For example, fear of ghosts is judged realistic by an observer from one culture and childish by an observer from another.

A true evaluation of behaviour based on these three distinct types of clue is held to yield a picture very different from the popular one. Behaviour based on clues of the first and second types no less than behaviour based on those of the third is plainly consistent with normal development and mental health. In a healthily functioning individual, indeed, responses to clues of all three types are present; they can occur simultaneously or sequentially, and be either compatible with one another or in conflict.

In this chapter we consider the role of behaviour elicited by each of these three types of clue. Because so much attention has already been given to the natural clues we begin by considering the more sophisticated methods of assessing and avoiding danger.

Real danger: difficulties of assessment

Psychiatrists often speak as though it were easy to assess real danger. This is not so.

Both in ordinary life and in clinical practice there are two distinct types of problem. One is the difficulty that each of us has in assessing what is and what is not a real danger to his own interests. Another is the difficulty that each of us has in assessing what is and what is not a real danger to another person.

Difficulties are met as soon as we try to define what we mean by 'real danger', whether to self or to another. There are a number of problems. One concerns how widely each of us draws the boundary of where his interests lie. A second concerns our understanding of what can, or cannot, cause injury. A third concerns the very varying ability of individuals to protect themselves and their interests: whereas a strong man might well be able to protect himself in a certain dangerous situation, a weaker one, or a woman or a child, might not.

We start with the problem of where each draws the boundary of his interests. Plainly, any situation that might lead to our own injury or death is classifiable as dangerous. The same would be agreed for anything that threatens injury or death to members of our family and to close friends. Beyond that, definition becomes more difficult. How widely do we extend the circle of friends and acquaintances whose safety we are concerned about? To what extent do we identify ourselves with the safety and well-being of the institution in which we work or the recreational club to which we belong? How do we rate threat to personal possessions, to house, and to favourite haunts?

Experience shows that a human being is constantly made afraid and anxious by threats of damage to a circle of persons, possessions, and places some way beyond himself and his body. For that reason it is necessary to include, within the concept of real danger, threat of injury or damage not only to the person himself but to the whole of his personal environment, as it is defined in the previous chapter.

All too often the need to include within the boundary the whole of an individual's personal environment is not recognized or, even if the principle is recognized, the nature and extent of the personal environment of a particular individual are not properly known. As a result, what is truly a danger for that person may go unnoticed by an onlooker.

Furthermore, not only is the nature of threat strictly relative to the person concerned but, as already remarked, means of protection are so too. Strong and competent people are able to protect themselves in situations in which weaker and less competent ones cannot.

Even when a definition of real danger is agreed, however, there remain great difficulties for each of us in assessing it. For example, for an individual to calculate accurately when and in what degree he and his interests are endangered requires him to have a comprehensive knowledge of the world about him and to be able reliably to predict results. How many of us are qualified in these respects? It is easy to talk of real danger, but very difficult to estimate it.

It is indeed easy to forget that what is held to be publicly and permanently real is never more than some schematic representation of the world that happens to be favoured by a particular social group at a particular time in history. To some people during some periods to be afraid of ghosts is realistic. To other people during other periods to be afraid of germs is realistic. In matters of reality we all stand in danger of being arrogantly parochial.

That, however, is not to assert that everything is subjective, that there is no reality. The difficulty in using reality as a criterion lies, not in there being no reality, but in our imperfect capacity to comprehend it. That a child has an imperfect capacity to comprehend what is or may be truly dangerous is usually taken for granted. That the capacity of an adult is greater often by only a small margin tends to be forgotten.

To assess a risk of danger accurately requires us to take into account simultaneously a number of factors. Consider, for example, how we calculate the risk of being attacked by a particular dog. The ordinary dog, it will be agreed, is a harmless and amiable creature. Yet some dogs are dangerous to some people sometimes. What then are the criteria to be applied? On reflection we realize that they are numerous and complex. An accurate forecast rests partly on the sort of dog it is, partly on the situation in which we encounter it, partly on its behaviour and partly on how we estimate our own strength. Thus, we need to take into account the dog's age and sex, its breed, and perhaps also its probable training. Simultaneously, we should take into account whether the dog its on its home ground or elsewhere, whether with or without is master, and whether, in the case of a bitch, it has puppies. At the same time we should consider whether the dog is familiar with us, how it greets us, and how effective we judge ourselves to be in countering threat with threat and protecting ourselves should it attack. It is in fact a complex appraisal requiring considerable knowledge of dogs and accurate perception of the current situation. No wonder many adults as well as children despair of making it and behave as though all dogs are dangerous until proved safe. Others, simplifying the situation in an opposite direction, may make the opposite assumption.

Consider again the difficulty of estimating accurately the danger of food-poisoning. To do so requires intimate knowledge of the food's origin, who has handled it, whether or not it has been cooked and the capabilities of various organisms to survive heating to various temperatures and for varying lengths of time. No wonder the ordinary housewife bases her behaviour on a limited number of culturally derived clues and practices.

In his capacity to assess and forecast real danger a child is of course even worse placed than an adult. Not only is he likely to be ill informed but, as Piaget has repeatedly shown (see Flavell 1963), his capacity to take into account more than a single factor at a time grows only slowly. It is fortunate that a child responds so readily to the natural and the cultural clues. Were he not to do so he would soon be dead.

'Imaginary' dangers

Assessment of danger always takes the form of a forecast. Sometimes the dangerous situation foreseen is judged to be imminent, at other times to be remote. In either case the likelihood of the situation's eventuating is of every degree. Dangerous situations that almost every adult in a society forecasts as probable present no problem. It is those situations that almost every adult forecasts as highly improbable or even impossible that are the challenge. Scoffingly, fear arising from such forecasts is dubbed 'exaggerated' or 'imaginary'; in more sober vein it is termed 'inappropriate'. For long, fear exhibited about such possibilities has constituted one of the principal riddles of psychopathology.

Yet, once the difficulty of making accurate forecasts of danger is grasped and once it is realized that if living beings are to survive there can be no great margin for error, the so-called imaginary fears come to be seen in a different and more sympathetic light. That children, still with a very imperfect model of the world, should at times gravely underestimate a danger may at times alarm us but is no surprise. That they should as frequently make an error of the opposite kind, foreseeing danger when we foresee none is, when viewed in this perspective, no surprise either. Thus, when the bathwater goes down the plughole, how is a toddler to know he will not go down too? When, later, he hears tales of robbers and red indians intercepting coaches or robbing mailtrains, how is he to know that he and his family may not be the next victims? The very great difficulty a child has in appraising at all accurately the degree of danger in which at any moment he may stand accounts, it is argued, for a much larger proportion of the so-called imaginary fears of childhood than is often supposed.

Sometimes 'imaginary' fear arises because of a simple misunderstanding, as when a small boy of six and a half, acting as a photographer's model, ran hurriedly off stage each time the photographer was about to press the button. Not until the next day was it revealed that, as soon as he heard the word 'shoot', he had run for his life. A similar type of misunderstanding led a boy of twelve, referred for stealing, to insist on having a sixpence in his pocket when he came to the clinic. The mystery was solved after some weeks when it transpired that he believed the clinic to be a penal establishment, and that he had plans that if incarcerated he would escape, and he would then need the money for his bus fare home.

At other times 'imaginary' fear is a consequence of generalizing from too small a sample. If granny can die today, perhaps mother or father may die tomorrow. If a mother's first infant has died, is it surprising that she fears her second may die also?

The examples so far given are of erroneous or disproportionate forecasts of danger that arise from inaccurate or inadequate data. Until the source of an individual's erroneous forecast is known, his tendency to fear a particular situation will appear to another person to be absurd; it will also persist. Once the source is known about, however, the tendency is quickly seen by the other person to be far from unreasonable, even if misguided; and there is then a chance of its being corrected or modified.

In other cases fear of a situation that it may seem ridiculous to an outsider to fear can be explained in other ways. One source of such fear that has been greatly underestimated in the clinical literature is a forecast of danger that is in fact well based but remains inexplicable to an outsider because it is derived from information of the greatest secrecy. An example is seen in a child or adolescent one of whose parents is given to uttering dire threats – of suicide, leaving home, even murder – during emotional outbursts that, though real enough at the time, may be infrequent and in general out of character. While child or adolescent, not unnaturally, takes the threat seriously, the notion that such threats could ever be made may be discounted or even denied by the parents. The key role that such family situations can play in accounting for the greatly intensified degree of separation anxiety suffered by some patients is considered in later chapters.

Another source of apparently unreasonable fear is a forecast of danger that derives from an individual's knowledge, conscious or unconscious, of certain desires of his own; for example, hostile wishes directed against someone he loves. Here again, to be afraid ceases to be unreasonable once the facts are known.

Yet other sources of fear that is or appears to be ill based lie in processes of projection and rationalization, to which brief attention is given in the next chapter.

In Chapters 18 and 19 further attention is given to some of the so-called irrational fears of anxious children and adults. These few paragraphs are intended to show only that the theoretical approach adopted can encompass without difficulty clinical problems of the greatest concern to every practising clinician and that a biological perspective in no way negates Freud's profoundly important discovery that fear can arise, not only from forecasts of how the external world and the people in it may behave, but also from forecasts of how we ourselves may possibly act.

Perhaps the most fundamental lesson to be learnt by anyone who wishes to understand the situations that other people fear is that forecasts of future dangers are as often as not strictly individual. Though forecasts of some sorts of event are public and shared with others, forecasts of other sorts of event are intrinsically private and personal. In particular, forecasts of how our personal relationships are likely to fare are not only of vastly more concern to ourselves than to anyone else but are based on past experience and present information that are ours and ours alone. Thus, as regards the future, each one of us has his own personal forecasts of what good and what harm may befall. This is the private world of future expectations that each of us carries within. This theme is resumed in Chapter 14 in which attention is given especially to a person's forecasts of how his attachment figures are likely to behave and the immense influence these forecasts have on his propensity to be anxious or confident.

Cultural clues learnt from others

For long it has been suspected that children tend to 'catch' fears from their parents. Nevertheless, the extent to which there is a correlation between what is feared by children and what by their parents is still little understood, and it is only during the past decade or so that the basic tendency to learn through observation has been the subject of systematic attention.

As a result of research it is now well established that learning through observation plays a significant part in the behavioural development of many species of bird and mammal (Hinde 1970). In the case of humans, Bandura (1968), a leading exponent of social learning theory, claims that virtually anything that can be learnt through direct experience can be learnt vicariously through observing how others behave in particular situations and, especially, what the consequences of their behaviour are for them. In this way innumerable skills can be acquired. Observational learning provides a powerful means for the cultural transmission of which situations are to be avoided and which can be regarded as safe.

People concerned with children sometimes speak as though they thought it would be better were a child not to be influenced in what he fears by imitating[1] his parents. A moment's reflection, however, shows that on the contrary this is a wise provision of nature. Just as members of a band of non-human primates extend the range of the stimulus situations they avoid through imitating the behaviour of other animals (see Chapter 8), so do humans. Admittedly the consequence could on occasion be that some harmless situation was treated through several generations as though it were dangerous; yet more often, we may suppose, the tendency to imitate results in a young individual's being inducted quickly into the traditional wisdom of his social group and thereby avoiding hazards that might otherwise prove fatal.

Furthermore, to learn through imitating encompasses in the case of fear behaviour far more than learning to fear situations formerly not feared. It can equally well have an opposite effect. Thus the fear-arousing properties that a situation has for a child or an adult can be much reduced, or even extinguished, by his witnessing another person deal with the situation without fear and without harmful consequences. The restriction of the situations that arouse fear in an individual is discussed in Chapter 13.

Reports of studies in which the degree to which situations feared by children are correlated with situations feared by their parents are unexpectedly scarce. Four can be quoted. In a study of seventy pre-school children, aged from two to six years, and their mothers, Hagman (1932) found significant correlations between the children who feared dogs and the mothers who feared dogs, and also between children and mothers who feared insects. A correlation was also present, though of lower degree,

---

1. There is a growing tendency in scientific literature to restrict the term 'imitation' to cases in which a new motor pattern is developed. In what follows, however, the term is used in an everyday sense to denote that an individual observes the ways in which others respond to particular stimuli and then responds similarly, even though no new motor pattern is involved.

between children and mothers who feared thunderstorms. Not unexpectedly, when a child's fear of a situation was shared by his mother, the child was more likely to continue to be afraid of that situation than was a child whose mother was unafraid. In a comparable but better-controlled study, Bandura and Menlove (1968) also found a significant correlation between pre-school children who were afraid of dogs and parents (one or both) who were afraid of dogs. The third study concerns fear of dentistry. Shoben and Borland (1954) found that a most important factor in determining whether an individual will react with fear to the prospect of dental treatment is the attitude and experiences of members of his family. The fourth study concerns a hundred pre-school children evacuated with their mothers from a bombed area during the second world war. John (1941) reports a correlation of 0·59 between the intensity of fear a child was reported to have shown during the raids and the intensity of fear his mother was reported to have shown. (Although the primary source of information was in most cases the mother herself, the existence of independent evidence for a few cases led the investigator to give the finding credence.)

Though the extent to which the situations that arouse fear tend to run in families and communities needs much further investigation, the ease with which fear of a previously neutral stimulus can be acquired vicariously is now well documented. For example, experiments in which the sound of a buzzer comes to arouse fear in a subject after he has observed that it is followed by an apparently painful shock to another person[2] are reported by Berger (1962) and also by Bandura and Rosenthal (1966). To observe another person apparently undergoing a shock whenever the buzzer sounds is found by many to be a most disagreeable experience. In Bandura's experiment some of the observers tried to decrease their discomfort by concentrating on other things. One remarked: 'When I noticed how painful the shock was to him I concentrated my vision on a spot which did not allow me to focus directly on either his face or hands.' That the observers

2. In these experiments the model who is observed is not in fact exposed to shock. Instead he acts as though he has received a shock, e.g. by suddenly flexing his arm, dropping his pencil and wincing.

came also to respond to the stimulus with fear (as measured by their galvanic skin response) is therefore hardly surprising.

In the experimental situations described it is demanded that a subject observe what is going on. In real life we are free to observe or not as we wish. Though few systematic records are available, it seems probable that whenever we are in a strange or otherwise potentially dangerous situation we commonly make a point of observing how others are responding and take our cue from them, especially when we believe them to be more experienced than we are ourselves. Children certainly do so. In the study referred to above (p. 191), Hagman (1932) conducted a series of simple experiments with his sample of pre-school children. He reports that, at the moment a fear-arousing stimulus was presented, nearly half the children looked up at the adult who was with them. Schaffer (1971), it will be remembered, reports the same behaviour as early as twelve months (see p. 128 above).

Plainly this is a large area and very inadequately explored. It is also complex, since it is well known that the correlation between situations feared by children and those feared by adults is far from perfect. For example, a mother who is afraid of dogs and horses can have a daughter who is as bold as they come. Conversely, a father who is conspicuously unafraid can have a timid son. Many factors are evidently at work.

One point to which too little attention has so far been given in this exposition is that individuals learn to fear situations of certain types much more easily than they do others. This takes us back to the natural clues.

Continuing role of the natural clues

Already in this and the preceding chapter it has been emphasized that throughout our lives we tend to respond with fear to the natural clues – to strangeness, sudden change of stimulation, rapid approach, height, being alone – and to respond especially strongly to compound situations in which two or more natural clues are present together. Fear of animals and fear of darkness, both so common, are, it seems likely, to be explained by the fact that animals and darkness frequently constitute sources of two or more of the natural clues.

Fear of Animals

During the first eighteen months of life few children show fear of animals. Thenceforward, however, fear becomes increasingly easily aroused by animals so that during the third, fourth, and fifth years a majority of children are likely to show fear, at least on some occasions. Although thereafter the tendency for animals to arouse fear diminishes, it continues to be extremely common both in older children and in adults. (These findings were presented above, see Chapter 7.)

On occasion, of course, a child may be threatened or even attacked by an animal, but it is unlikely that such events account for more than a very small proportion of the children who develop fear of animals. All the evidence suggests that in great part the readiness of children to develop such fear can be explained by the fact that animals are so frequently a source, simultaneously, of at least three of the natural clues that arouse fear, namely rapid approach, sudden movement, and sudden noise. This is well illustrated by an observation by Valentine (1930) who was among the first to study the ontogeny of human fear responses.

Valentine reports that one of his sons first showed fear of a dog at the age of twenty months. On this occasion a dog tripped over the string of the little boy's toy horse and yelped. In so doing it presented, of course, a combination of approach, sudden movement, by tripping, and sudden noise, by yelping. At this the little boy cried and thenceforward was afraid of the dog.

In that episode the dog belonged to a neighbour and so was presumably familiar to the child. On many other occasions, however, an animal behaving in this kind of way is a stranger. Whenever it is so, yet another natural clue is added to the constellation. Small wonder, then, that fear of animals is so widespread.

Not only do animals frequently present simultaneously several of the natural clues but there is reason to believe that they may present also some additional stimulus properties that increase the likelihood of a child's learning to fear them. Being furry is possibly one; a wriggling movement probably another; certain visual patterns may be still others.

Valentine had been struck by the ease with which young children seem to develop a fear of animals in comparison with fear of other things. He therefore conducted a little experiment with one of his daughters, Y, 'an exceptionally healthy, strong and jovial youngster', aged at the time twelve and a half months (Valentine 1930). In a first test the little girl, seated on her mother's knee, was given a pair of opera glasses which were then placed on a table in front of her. Each time she reached for them a wooden whistle was blown as loudly as possible behind her. Each time, she turned round quietly as if to see whence the noise had come. In these conditions the whistle aroused no fear. When the same afternoon, however, the same experiment was conducted, this time with a woolly caterpillar in place of the opera glasses, 'at once Y gave a loud scream and turned away from the caterpillar. This was repeated four times with precisely the same effect.' Later the same day, while seated on her mother's knee and with no whistle being sounded, Y vacillated between showing interest in the caterpillar and turning away from it. When her brother picked up the leaf on which the caterpillar was crawling the little girl seemed to gain confidence and went to seize it (an example very probably of observational learning).

From these experiments Valentine draws three conclusions. In the situation described:

- sight of opera glasses and sound of whistle together were not alarming, nor was there reason to think that either singly would be
- sight of the caterpillar aroused interest which alternated with slight fear
- sight of caterpillar and sound of whistle together were alarming.

From observations such as these Valentine suggests that there is a much readier bias to develop fear of objects like caterpillars than fear of objects like opera glasses.[3]

3. A defect of this experiment was that during the second test when the caterpillar was presented and the whistle blown Y was seated on her father's knee, not her mother's. It is therefore possible that a change in the person caring for her was responsible for the results.

An Ethological Approach to Human Fear

The extreme ease with which monkeys and apes develop a fear of snakes is remarked on above (Chapter 8, p. 159). The same is true of humans. As already reported in Chapter 7 (pp. 137–41), in the experiments conducted by Jersild and Holmes (1935a) between one-third and a half of the children aged between two and six years showed marked fear of the snake. A comparable finding is reported by Morris and Morris (1965). In a children's television programme in England children were invited to compete for a prize by proposing future programmes. To qualify, however, they had to name the animal they liked most and the animal they disliked most. Altogether nearly twelve thousand children aged from four years upwards replied. Of the animals most disliked the snake was an easy first: it was named by 27 per cent of the children. Spiders came next, given by under 10 per cent; then lions and tigers, together, were named by about 7 per cent. Up to the age of nine years, at least one child in three expressed dislike of snakes. At all ages a slightly higher proportion of girls than boys expressed the fear.

It seems likely that to the development of a fear of animals in general and of snakes in particular several factors make an interlocking contribution. First are several of the common natural clues, including often strangeness. Second, there may also be certain specific natural clues, for example crawling or wriggling. Third, there is the behaviour of others. Because of their appearance and behaviour, including their vocalizations, animals arouse simultaneously both lively interest and incipient fear. In such conditions the behaviour of a companion is likely to have a maximum effect, tipping the balance either towards decreased fear and approach or towards increased fear and withdrawal.

Fear of Darkness

Every study shows that fear of darkness is as common at every age as fear of animals and that during ontogeny it runs a roughly parallel course. In all likelihood the development of fear of darkness is to be explained in a comparable way to that of fear of animals; though the natural clues concerned are usually not the same ones.

In conditions of darkness the two natural clues that are apt to be present together are strangeness and being alone. During darkness visual stimuli that, if viewed in daylight, would be recognized as familiar are often ambiguous and difficult to interpret. Endless examples come to mind: the pattern of movement of light shining through bedroom curtains; the shapes of the trees in a wood at night; the shadowy recesses of a dimly lit cellar. In each case the visual stimuli available are barely adequate for accurate perception and it is therefore as easy to perceive something unusual as something familiar. In addition, without visual cues, sounds are far more difficult to interpret accurately or with confidence. Thus in conditions of darkness much seems uncertain or strange and in consequence alarming.

Yet, mere strangeness would probably of itself arouse comparatively little fear were it not so regularly accompanied by being alone. Sometimes a person is in reality alone; sometimes, because his companion is unseen, he may merely feel himself to be. In either case the situation is compound: it combines sights and sounds that are not easily interpreted and the situation of being alone.

Freud, it is interesting to note, was greatly struck by the way in which darkness leads a child to feel alone, and it is an observation of a small boy's behaviour in the dark, together with inferences from it, that lies at the heart of his theory of anxiety. This is therefore a good point at which to compare Freud's theory with the one presented here.

In *Three Essays* (1905b, *SE* **7**: 224n) and again in the *Introductory Lectures* (1917b, *SE* **16**: 407) Freud tells the story of a three-year-old boy. He recounts how he once heard this child

calling out of a dark room: 'Auntie, speak to me! I'm frightened because it's so dark.' His aunt answered him: 'What good would that do? You can't see me.' 'That doesn't matter,' replied the child, 'if anyone speaks, it gets light.' Thus [comments Freud] what he was afraid of was not the dark, but the absence of someone he loved . . .

Reflection on that episode, Freud tells us, led him to the view that the prototypic situation that gives rise to anxiety in children is simply separation from mother. Neurotic anxiety, he then argues, can best be understood as a persistence beyond childhood of the tendency to be anxious when alone, though fear of being alone often masquerades as fear of something else, for example of the dark. In all these regards the theory advanced here is very close to Freud's. Where the two differ is that Freud did not recognize that strangeness is intrinsically frightening or that both strangeness and being alone can usefully be regarded as two members of a class of natural clues to increased risk of danger. As a consequence he held that to be afraid when alone (and also when confronted by any of the other natural clues) is irrational and neurotic; whereas in the theory put forward here to be afraid in such conditions is held to be in general adaptive.

Fear of Being Alone

Repeatedly in these chapters it is stressed that being alone is one of several natural clues to increased risk of danger and that it occurs very commonly as a component in a compound situation. Not only does it occur in combination with other natural clues, moreover; it can occur equally well with cultural clues and also in situations realistically assessed as being dangerous. Thus, throughout life, being alone is a condition that either stimulates fear or greatly intensifies fear aroused in other ways. Concomitantly, being with a companion greatly reduces fear. In no conditions is the reassuring effect of the presence of companions more evident than during and after a disaster.

Behaviour in disaster

The role of a companion in reducing fear in children is very obvious and it is also readily acknowledged by children. Adults, by contrast, are less likely to acknowledge it. During and after a disaster, however, people are less reticent (Baker and Chapman 1962).

When the impact of disaster comes members of a family commonly cling together:

When sirens scream of approaching disaster, minds turn to loved ones. If they are near enough mothers run to protect their children, and men seek their families. They huddle together and support one another through the stress, and when it is passed they resume and nurse those they love (Hill and Hansen 1962).

Wolfenstein (1957) describes how a woman who had been with her fifteen-year-old daughter when a tornado struck recounted her experience:

And she said, 'Mother, its coming – a cyclone.' And I said, 'Mary, I'm afraid it is. But,' I said, 'we're together.' And she said, 'Mother, I love you and we're together.' I shall never forget those words. And we – our arms were around each other, and I said, 'Whatever happens, Mary, let's cling together.'

Whenever members of a family happen to be apart at the time of impact they are unlikely to rest until they have found each other; then, again, physical embraces are the rule. 'Just being together is deeply important following impact even in loosely-knit families' (Hill and Hansen 1962).

Survivors agree that to be alone during a disaster is extremely frightening, whereas the advent of a companion, however inadequate, is likely to transform the scene. Wolfenstein refers to another episode, one in which, following an explosion, two injured men were trying to crawl out of a burning factory. Describing their experiences, one of the men, who had suffered a broken leg, explained:

Then Johnny and Clyde came along. I said, 'Johnny, help us – we can't walk.' His arms were broken and he said, 'I can't help you, but I'll stay with you. If you can crawl, I'll guide you.' Talk about cheer! That helped me more than anything – just when he said, 'I'll stay with you.'

Not only is there a strong tendency for members of a family or other social group to remain together during the height of a disaster but the tendency is likely to persist for days or weeks after it is over. This heightened tendency to attachment behaviour is commented on in a number of reports.

For example, Bloch, Silber and Perry (1956) studied the effects on children of a tornado that struck a town in Mississippi, affecting in particular a cinema in which children were attending a Saturday afternoon programme. Altogether, information was obtained during the succeeding weeks from interviewing the parents of 185 children between the ages of two and twelve years.

About one-third of the children were reported to be showing signs of increased anxiety, which typically took the form of clinging to or remaining close to parents and wishing to sleep with them. They were made anxious by noise and also tended to avoid situations associated with the tornado. Children aged six to twelve were more disturbed than younger ones. A possible reason for that was that more of them had probably been in the impact zone. Another possible reason, though it is not commented on by the researchers, was that the older the child the more likely was he to have been away from his parents. Boys were as much affected as girls.

Experiences that were significantly associated with increased anxiety were the child's presence in the impact zone, personal injury, and the death or injury of a family member. Not unexpectedly the reaction of children reflected the reaction of parents. In nine cases parents described themselves as having 'gone to pieces' and, instead of having supported their child, as having sought help from him. Eight of these children were disturbed and, about the ninth, the mother could not be induced to talk. Further discussion of the contribution to a child's anxieties of parents who invert the relationship by requiring their child to care for them will be found in Chapters 18 and 19. Many cases diagnosed as school phobia and agoraphobia can be understood as being caused by such inversions.

Reports on the effects of the Mississippi tornado of 1953 (Bloch *et al.* 1956) and of the Los Angeles earthquake of 1971 (*Time*, 8 March 1971) both make it clear that, after a disaster, parents are almost as eager to retain their children close to them as the children are eager to remain close to their parents. Since these responses are adaptive, it is unfortunate that the concept of regression is so frequently invoked to explain them. Investigation shows that, in run-of-the-mill cases as well as in those that follow a disaster, behind behaviour dubbed regressive by clinicians there exist situations that, once known about, explain at once why a child or an adult should cling relentlessly to another member of his family.

Chapter 11
Rationalization, Misattribution, and Projection

All round the house is the jet-black night;
It stares through the window-pane;
It crawls in the corners, hiding from the light,
And it moves with the moving flame.

Now my little heart goes a-beating like a drum,
With the breath of the Bogie in my hair;
And all round the candle the crooked shadows come,
And go marching along up the stair.

The shadow of the balusters, the shadow of the lamp,
The shadow of the child that goes to bed –
All the wicked shadows coming, tramp, tramp, tramp,
With the black night overhead.
– ROBERT LOUIS STEVENSON, *A Child's Garden of Verses*

Difficulties in identifying situations that arouse fear

When a person is afraid and claims that something in particular, for example thunder or a dog, has made him so, doubt is often expressed whether he has identified the right stimulus situation. This is especially likely to happen when fear is shown or reported by children and by emotionally disturbed adults. Among psychoanalysts there is a long tradition of claiming that what a person is really afraid of is something very different from what he claims to be afraid of. Indeed, psychoanalytic theorizing about anxiety and fear reflects a prolonged hunt for some primal danger situation that is thought to arouse a primal anxiety or fear.[1] Arising out of that tradition, also, is the practice of invoking the process of projection whenever a fear appears not to be appropriate to the situation presenting.

In the approach adopted here, no less than in the traditional ones, misattribution is held to be very common. The difference in the present approach lies in the explanations it offers of why

1. See Chapter 5 and Appendix I.

misattribution should occur. The concept of a primal danger situation is dispensed with, and projection is given a much smaller role as an explanatory principle. A solution is found in the relationship that the natural clues bear to danger and safety.

The very fact that fear is first aroused in human beings not by any rational appraisal of danger but by stimulus situations that are no more than clues to an increased risk of danger invites misunderstanding and misattribution; for, as has been made clear, a natural clue is in no sense inherently dangerous. Because that is so, however, and because in Western culture (and perhaps also in others) a human being is expected to be afraid only of real dangers, there is a strong bias both in the frightened subject and in an onlooker to attribute the fear response to something other than the natural clue. For example, since it is thought absurd for anyone to be afraid merely of thunder, the fear is 'explained' as a fear really of being struck by lightning. Similarly, since it is thought absurd to be afraid merely of a dog, the fear is 'explained' as a fear really of being bitten by a dog.

Rationalizations of these sorts are no doubt very common. They are commented upon by all who have made a study of fear, irrespective of theoretical orientation. For example, Marks (1969) suggests that a child's fear of monsters in the dark may be no more than a rationalization of his fear of the dark, 'a genuine rationalization of an irrational fear on the same lines that any post-hypnotic suggestion is rationalized'. The Newsons (1968) point out that such rationalizations are often and easily encouraged by other children, or even by adults, who tease a child about what he might meet when in the dark on his own. Jersild (1943) calls attention to the fact that when a child is already frightened, from whatever cause, he 'may formulate his fear in terms of an imaginary or anticipated danger', such as criminal characters or bogeys or some other sinister circumstances he has encountered or, more probably, heard or read about.

Though simple rationalizations of this kind are probably common, even commoner perhaps are mistaken or biased attributions stemming from the special properties of compound situations. In compound situations, two or more stimulus conditions, by being present together, have the effect of arousing far more intense fear than would any one were it to occur separately. In such a case there is a marked tendency to single out one component of the compound situation as the one that arouses the fear and to ignore the other(s). For example, a person is alone in the dark and hears strange noises. Whereas in fact all three conditions – being alone, being in the dark, and hearing the strange noises – may well be necessary to account for the fear aroused, in all likelihood attention is focused solely on the strange noises and the other components of the situation are almost ignored. Furthermore, from there it is only a short step to rationalize the fear, aroused in fact by what is little more than a combination of two or three natural clues, and to claim that what is feared is burglars or ghosts.

Which one of several components present in a compound situation is fastened on as the fear-arousing one and which are neglected needs examination. Presumably, the component selected is usually the one that most readily lends itself to being interpreted as indicative of real danger. If that is so, being alone would habitually be neglected, or at least given a subordinate position. That is, in fact, very close to what Freud believed to happen, though he expressed his views in terms of libido theory and not of attachment theory.

In 1917, at the end of a discussion of the psychopathology of phobias, Freud summed up his position:

Infantile anxiety has very little to do with realistic anxiety, but, on the other hand, is closely related to the neurotic anxiety of adults. Like the latter, it is derived from unemployed libido, and it replaces the missing love-object by an external object or by a situation (1917b, SE 16:408).

Since Freud regards the unemployed libido as constituting an internal danger, his formulation is that fear of an internal danger is replaced by fear of an external one. An alternative rendering of his position would run: when a child or an adult is afraid of some external object or situation, what he is really afraid of is the absence of someone he loves.

In Chapters 18 and 19, in which misattributions are discussed further, reasons are given for believing that many intense fears attributed to all sorts of common situations and termed phobias are best understood as being aroused in compound situations, a main component of which is the expectation of being separated from a principal attachment figure. The famous and theoretically influential case of 'Little Hans', who was afraid of being bitten by a horse, appears to be a good example (Freud 1909, *SE* **10**). Evidence is presented (Chapter 18) for believing that fear of separation played a much larger part in this case than Freud at the time realized.

Misattribution and the role of projection

In some psychoanalytic traditions the concept of projection has been used very extensively in an attempt to explain any fear that is not readily intelligible as a response to a real danger. Since the term is itself used in several ways the resulting theory is often confused.

One usage of projection is to denote our propensity to perceive an object in terms of some preconceived notion, in other words to 'project onto' the object characteristics we suppose it to have, even though they are not apparent to the sense organs and may in fact be absent. In so far as this process is integral to all perception, it is normal. Although as a rule the resulting percept is reasonably valid, on some occasions seriously false percepts result.

A second usage is to denote the process whereby a person (male or female) attributes to another (male or female) some features of his own self, especially some aspect of himself that he dislikes or is afraid of. This process must, almost inevitably, lead to false and unfavourable attributions being made about the other person and his motives.

There are two reasons for confining the term projection to the second usage. One reason is that another term, 'assimilation', introduced many years ago by Piaget, is already in wide currency to denote our propensity to perceive any object in terms of some model we already have, even though that model may fit the object imperfectly: the new object of perception is said to be assimilated to the existing model. The second reason is that in the various psychoanalytic traditions the most frequent usage of the term projection is to denote our propensity to attribute our failings to others and to be blind to them in ourselves, to see motes in the eyes of others and to be blind to beams in our own.

Using the term in its second sense, we find that the process of projection is invoked extremely frequently by psychoanalysts to explain how it comes about that children and adults should be so afraid, as we know they are, of the wide array of situations that are not intrinsically dangerous. This trend in theorizing has been carried furthest by Melanie Klein who has postulated that the process of attributing to others undesired and frightening features of the self occurs on a major scale during the earliest phases of normal development, with far-reaching effects on later personality. During his first year of life, in the Kleinian view, an infant regularly attributes to parent figures impulses that are in fact his own and then introjects (namely creates working models of) parent figures already distorted by these misattributions. In this view, then, the reason a child develops working models of hostile, rejecting, or unresponsive parents ('bad introjected objects') is not so much because of any actual experience he may have had of being unsympathetically or adversely treated by them as principally because, almost from the first, his perception of his parents is gravely distorted by his own prior projections. Since the death instinct is a special aspect of the self that Klein believes is always projected during the earliest months, she is led to a theory of anxiety she sums up in the following sentence: 'I hold that anxiety arises from the operation of the death instinct within the organism, is felt as fear of annihilation (death) and takes the form of fear of persecution' (Klein 1946).

It will be clear that this blanket application of the concept of projection is alien to the present approach. Not only is the Kleinian system of thought rooted in a non-evolutionary paradigm that bears no relation to modern biology, but in clinical work it has the effect, inimical to good practice, of directing attention away from a person's real experiences, past or present, and treating him almost as though he were a closed system little influenced by his environment. Another unfortunate effect of applying the concept of projection in this uncritical way is the danger of bringing a useful concept into disrepute. Let us therefore consider the problem afresh.

Not infrequently a person is afraid that someone else intends him harm, but to another's eye this expectation seems misplaced. In such circumstances, as we have seen, psychoanalysts are very apt to postulate that the person who is afraid is projecting onto the other hostile intentions that are in himself but that he denies exist. Though there can be no doubt that this can happen it probably happens much less often than is supposed.

In fact a situation of the kind described is explicable in at least four ways; and it is necessary to examine the evidence in each case before deciding which explanation, or which two or more together, is most likely to apply:

1. The subject has rightly detected harmful intent in the other person and in so doing has been more sensitive to the situation than the onlooker.

2. The subject during childhood has learnt that significant people are often hostile when they claim to be friendly, and is therefore apt, through a process of assimilation, to suppose that figures met with in later life are hostile also when they are not.

3. The subject, aware that he is no friend of the other person and even that he is disposed to do him harm, not unnaturally expects his ill intent to be reciprocated.

4. The subject, unaware of his own ill intent, maintains that, whereas he is friendly to the other, the other is hostile to him.

Of these four possible explanations only the process postulated in the fourth can properly be called projection when the term is used in the restricted sense of attributing to others unwelcome features of the self. That the process can be a source of misattributions is not in doubt. How large a proportion of misattributions have this sort of origin is a matter for inquiry.

The case of Schreber: a re-examination

The urgent need for fresh thinking in this area of psychopathology is shown by the findings of a re-examination by Niederland (1959a and b) of the case from which all psychoanalytic theorizing about paranoia and paranoid symptoms derives. Freud's original study of the Schreber case, based solely on the patient's published memoirs, appeared in 1911 (*SE* 12: 9–82). Although he later published other papers on paranoia, according to Strachey (1958) Freud never modified his earlier views in any material way.

Daniel Paul Schreber was born in 1842, the second son of an eminent physician and pedagogue. By 1884 he was serving as a judge. He then developed a psychiatric illness from which he recovered after some months. He resumed his legal post but after eight years fell ill again. This time he remained in an asylum for nine years (1893–1902) towards the end of which he wrote his memoirs. In 1903, shortly after his discharge, they were published, and soon became a subject of psychiatric interest. A principal theme concerns a number of bodily experiences that were extremely painful and humiliating to him. These experiences he construed as 'miracles' performed by God by means of 'rays':

> From the first beginnings of my contact with God up to the present day my body has continuously been the object of divine miracles. . . . Hardly a single limb or organ in my body escaped being temporarily damaged by miracles, nor a single muscle being pulled by miracles, . . . Even now the miracles which I experience hourly are still of a nature to frighten every other human being to death.[2]

Freud's analysis of Schreber's delusions of persecution takes account of no material except that of the memoirs. Freud notes that Schreber's feelings towards God are intensely ambivalent, being on the one hand critical and rebellious and on the other reverential towards someone of whom he stands in awe. Freud calls attention also to the frankly homosexual attitude Schreber sometimes adopts towards God, including Schreber's belief that he had a duty to play the part of a woman for God's enjoyment. From material of this kind Freud postulates that delusions of

2. In addition to Freud's paper and Strachey's editor's note in the Standard Edition, an English translation of the memoirs is now available and also a paper by Baumeyer (1956) in which he summarizes and quotes from the original case records of Schreber's illnesses. Niederland's bibliography gives references to the above and to the published works of Schreber's father.

persecution are attempts to contradict the proposition 'I (a man) love him (a man)', and to replace it by 'I do not *love* him – I *hate* him', and, finally, by 'I *hate* him, because he persecutes me'.

An internal perception is suppressed, and, instead, its content, after undergoing a certain kind of distortion, enters consciousness in the form of an external perception. In delusions of persecution the distortion consists in a transformation of affect; what should have been felt internally as love is perceived externally as hate.

To this process Freud gives the name *projection* (*SE* 12: 63–6).

In his re-examination of the case Niederland (1959a and b) draws attention to the fact that Schreber's father held extraordinary views about the physical and moral education of children and published a number of books describing his methods. In them he asserts the vital importance of starting the prescribed régimes during infancy and states repeatedly that he has applied his methods to his own children. It is safe therefore to conclude that Schreber the son had been subjected to his father's educational methods from his earliest years.

The physical methods, recommended for application daily throughout childhood and adolescence, include a number of exercises and harnesses whereby posture is to be controlled. An example of a harness, designed to prevent a child's head from falling forwards or sideways, consisted of a strap clamped at one end to the child's hair and at the other to his underwear so that it pulled his hair if he did not hold his head straight. Because the device was apt to produce a stiffening effect it was recommended that its use be restricted to one or two hours a day. An example of an exercise is to place two chairs facing each other with a gap between of a few feet. A child is instructed to put his head on the seat of one chair and his feet on that of the other and to stiffen his back to make a bridge, in which position he must remain. The dire results that Schreber senior ascribed to bad posture included impeded circulation and, later, paralysis of arm and foot. Of one of his devices, an iron crossbar designed to ensure that a child sits straight, he comments that, besides its physical benefits, it provides an effective moral corrective.

Schreber senior held the sternest of views regarding moral

discipline. Bad elements of the mind he regarded as 'weeds' to be 'exterminated', and he describes the threats and punishments by which, starting at five or six months, a parent should make certain that he becomes 'master of the child for ever'. The strong impression given that Schreber senior was a psychotic character is supported by a note made by a hospital psychiatrist and based, it is thought, on information from a member or close acquaintance of the family. It states that the patient's father 'suffered from obsessional ideas with murderous impulses'.

Niederland compares the son's descriptions of the fearful 'miracles' he had to suffer at God's hands with the father's prescriptions of how children should be treated for their physical and moral welfare. Point by point the resemblances are traced. The son complains of miracles of heat and cold. The father prescribes that, in order to toughen an infant, he should be washed in cold water from the age of three months and also subjected to various local cold applications. The son complains that his eyes and eyelids are the target of uninterrupted miracles. The father prescribes repeated visual exercises and advises spraying the eyes with cold water should there be irritation and fatigue following over-stimulation. The son describes a miracle in which his whole chest wall is compressed. Father prescribes a harness consisting of an iron bar that presses against the collar bones should a child not sit straight and upright.

In view of these remarkable resemblances, Niederland's hypothesis, in keeping with the second of the four possible explanations listed above (p. 206), is that Schreber's delusory beliefs regarding the way God was treating him were derived from memories of how his father actually treated him when he was a child. The delusory character of the beliefs is then regarded as due to (a) the patient's attributing the origin of his sufferings to the activities of God in the present instead of to his father in the past, and (b) his attributing the mechanism of his sufferings to 'rays' and miracles instead of to actual manipulations of himself by parent figures. As Niederland (1959a) himself remarks, the hypothesis is in keeping with ideas that Freud was entertaining towards the end of his life (but which still have been little exploited). In hallucinations, Freud (1937) suggests, 'something

209

that has been experienced in infancy and then forgotten returns . . .'

If this approach to understanding paranoid delusions is adopted, many problems remain still to be solved. How comes it that the patient has no recollection of how his parents treated him as a child? Why is it that, instead, childhood experiences are misplaced in time and the agent responsible for them is misidentified? Possible answers to these questions invoke hypotheses regarding the kinds of injunction, explicit or implicit, a parent may issue to a child; for example, an injunction on a child to construe whatever happens to him as beneficial, an injunction to see his parent as above criticism, an injunction neither to perceive nor to remember certain acts that he none the less witnesses or experiences. These hypotheses, with much evidence to show that they apply to the case of Schreber, are advanced in a recent paper by Schatzman (1971). Yet a further hypothesis, not discussed by Schatzman, is that children wish to see their parents in a favourable light and often distort their perceptions accordingly.

In Chapter 20 these matters are pursued further. Meanwhile, enough has been said to show that, when the actual experiences they have had during childhood are known and can be taken into account, the pathological fears of adult patients can often be seen in a radically new light. Paranoid symptoms that had been regarded as autogenous and imaginary are seen to be intelligible, albeit distorted, responses to historical events.

Chapter 12
Fear of Separation

Hypotheses regarding its development

It is now time to draw together ideas regarding fear of separation and how it develops.

At the end of Chapter 1 it is pointed out that 'presence' and 'absence' are relative terms that can give rise to misunderstanding. By presence is meant 'ready accessibility', by absence 'inaccessibility'. The words 'separation' and 'loss' as used in this work imply always that the subject's attachment figure is inaccessible, either temporarily (separation) or permanently (loss). Thus in what follows we are concerned with the developmental processes that lead a young child to respond with fear when he finds, or believes, his attachment figure to be inaccessible.

Among the many questions raised and not yet answered are the following:

1. Is inaccessibility of mother in itself a situation that arouses fear in human children without its being necessary for any learning to have taken place?
2. Or is such fear elicited in an individual only after he has come to associate her inaccessibility with a distressing or frightening experience?
3. If the latter, what is the nature of such distressing or frightening experience, and by what type of learning does it become linked with separation?

Whatever the answers to these questions may be, because being alone carries an increased risk of danger, especially for young individuals and others who are weak, the fear response to inaccessibility of mother can usefully be regarded as a basic adaptive response, namely a response that during the course of evolution has become an intrinsic part of man's behavioural repertoire because of its contribution to species survival.

If that is so, there is no *a priori* reason to assume that fear elicited by mother's inaccessibility can be explained only in terms of an individual's having experienced something distressing or frightening while separated from her, an assumption that has commonly been made. On the contrary, it is entirely possible that the response to mother's inaccessibility develops during ontogeny without learning of any sort having to take place. Let us call this hypothesis A.

Whether or not hypothesis A applies in the human case remains an open question. For, as was emphasized repeatedly in the first volume, there are many forms of behaviour that, like this one, can usefully be classed as instinctive but that develop functionally only when the environment provides opportunity for learning of some specific kind to occur. In other words, to hold the hypothesis that fear behaviour in a situation of maternal inaccessibility is instinctive in no way rules out the possibility that learning of some kind is necessary for its development. All that such a view requires is that, when an individual is reared in the species' environment of evolutionary adaptedness, opportunity for the necessary learning is always present.

Reflection suggests that there are at least three hypotheses that are consistent with that proviso and merit attention. Let us call them hypotheses B1, B2, and B3.

The first, B1, is Freud's hypothesis of 1926 which postulates that fear of mother's absence results from an infant's learning that, when she is absent, his physiological needs go unmet, and learning, further, that this results in the accumulation within him of dangerous 'amounts of stimulation' which, unless 'disposed of', bring about a 'traumatic situation'. Since, moreover, the infant finds that, left to himself, he is unable to dispose of such accumulations, the danger situation that he comes intrinsically to fear is 'a recognized, remembered, expected situation of helplessness'.[1]

Reasons for not adopting Freud's hypothesis will already be apparent. One is that it is embedded in a paradigm very different from the one adopted here (see Chapter 5). Another is that it seems to postulate a degree of insight into cause and effect that not only is improbable in an infant of a year or so of age but that we now know to be unnecessary to account for the findings.

1. Quotations are from *Inhibitions, Symptoms and Anxiety* (*SE* 20: 137–8 and 166). Freud's theory is described more fully in Appendix I.

For the fact that so many of the responses shown by a human infant when separated from his mother are to be seen also in infants of non-human primate species demonstrates that it is quite possible for such responses to be mediated at a primitive and presumably infra-symbolic level.

Objections of a similar sort apply to the theories advanced by Klein, which presuppose even more sophisticated cognitive functioning (see Appendix I).

A second hypothesis, B2, not very different from Freud's but simpler and implying no insight learning, is compatible with the theory of attachment behaviour proposed in the first volume. In Chapter 14 of that volume an account is given of the conditions that terminate crying during the early months of life:

... when a baby is not hungry, cold, or in pain, the most effective terminators of crying are, in ascending order, sound of voice, non-nutritive sucking, and rocking. These findings readily explain why babies are said to cry from loneliness and to have a desire to be picked up. Although to attribute such sentiments to babies in the early months of life is almost certainly not warranted, the statements none the less contain more than a grain of truth. When they are not rocked and not spoken to infants are apt to cry; when they are rocked and spoken to they cease crying and are content. And by far the most probable agent to rock and talk to a baby is his mother figure.

In view of this, it could be argued, an infant comes to learn that presence of mother is associated with comfort while absence of mother is associated with distress. Thus, through a fairly simple process of associative learning, an infant comes to associate mother's absence with distress, and so to fear her being inaccessible. This hypothesis is close to one advanced by Kessen and Mandler (1961).

A third hypothesis, B3, derives from the fact that an infant is much more intensely afraid of fear-arousing situations, such as strangeness, or sudden approach, or loud noise, when his mother is absent than when she is present. After a few such experiences, it could be postulated, mother's absence might of itself come to elicit fear, again through a process of associative learning. This hypothesis is similar to one suggested by Rycroft (1968a) and referred to in Chapter 6 above.

On present evidence it is not possible to decide between hypotheses A, B2, and B3; each is plausible.

Hypothesis A, that an anxiety response to mother's inaccessibility develops during ontogeny without learning of any sort having to take place, is difficult to test. Furthermore, even if it were true, it would not make hypotheses B2 and B3 irrelevant, since learning of the kinds proposed by these two hypotheses could still occur and might be of much significance in accounting for degrees of separation anxiety above a minimum.

Whether hypothesis A is valid or not appears, at present, to be of no great clinical importance. This is because, were the forms of learning postulated by hypotheses B2 and B3 to occur at all, which they probably do, they would be taking place during the latter half of the first and during the second year of life and, except where a child had no mother figure, would be virtually unavoidable. As a situation that arouses fear, therefore, separation from an attachment figure would still be nearly universal, almost as much as it would were hypothesis A to apply.

Support for the view that associative learning of the kinds postulated by hypotheses B2 and B3 does take place comes from studies of individual differences in susceptibility to respond with fear, especially to separation. These show, as is discussed in detail in later chapters, that children who have been well mothered, and therefore, in all likelihood, protected from the experience both of intense distress and of intense fear, are those least susceptible to respond with fear to situations of all kinds, including separation; whereas children who have had intensely distressing and frightening experiences when away from mother are apt to show an increased susceptibility to fear, especially to fear of being separated again.

Should, as therefore seems likely, both these forms of associative learning occur during infancy and early childhood, their effects on personality development might possibly be rather different. For example, were a child, because of his particular experiences, to come to associate mother's absence with high degrees of discomfort and distress, he might perhaps grow up to respond to separation and loss, either actual or forecast, with psychosomatic troubles and general tension; whereas a child who, because of his particular experiences, came to associate mother's absence with being more or less intensely afraid might grow up prone to respond to any fear-arousing situation with more marked fear than would other individuals. Whether or not differences of these kinds occur in fact can be determined only by further research.

Need for two terminologies

Throughout recent chapters a sharp distinction has been drawn between situations that arouse fear and situations that are intrinsically dangerous. Whereas situations that arouse fear can be regarded as constituting either natural or cultural clues to an increased risk of danger, they are certainly not infallible indicators of actual danger. How we feel in a situation bears therefore only an indirect relationship to the degree of risk present in that situation.

Because the world as reflected in feeling is distinct from, though correlated with, the world as it is, two terminologies are necessary.

At the end of Chapter 6 three terms, 'anxious', 'alarmed', and 'afraid' are introduced and the way in which they are used here is described. All three belong to the world as reflected in feeling. By contrast, 'dangerous' belongs to the world as it is.

At this point it is necessary to settle on some analogously distinct terms suitable to refer, on the one hand, to a state of feeling antithetical to feeling afraid and, on the other, to a situation antithetical to one of danger. Etymology suggests 'feeling secure' for the one and a 'situation of safety' for the other.

The original meaning of the English adjective 'secure' is 'free from care, apprehension, anxiety or alarm' (*Oxford English Dictionary*). Historically, therefore, 'secure' applies to the world as reflected in feeling and not to the world as it is. By contrast, the original meaning of 'safe' is 'free from hurt or damage'. As such it applies to the world as it is and not to the world as reflected in feeling. The distinction is neatly illustrated by a seventeenth-century saying, quoted in the *OED*, 'The way to be safe is never to bee (*sic*) secure', namely feel secure.

An Ethological Approach to Human Fear

By using the terms in their original senses, it is possible accurately and without ambiguity to make statements such as:
- although the situation was safe enough he became very frightened, or
- I could see the situation was dangerous but somehow the captain's behaviour made us all feel secure.

The distinction drawn here between feeling secure and being safe is not always made so that a number of terms current in the literature do not conform to the usage proposed. This applies both to Harlow's 'haven of safety', termed here 'secure base', and to Sandler's 'feeling of safety' (Sandler 1960), termed here 'feeling of security'.

Use of the word 'secure' in the sense proposed has, of course, for long been customary in clinical practice. For example, with reference to states of feeling, children and grown-ups are habitually described as being either secure or insecure. Moreover, because any person who is acting as an attachment figure for another is commonly referred to as providing that other with a sense of security, it is often convenient to describe an attachment figure also as a security figure or as providing a secure base. At the same time, it must be emphasized that a secure base, however much it may lead someone to feel secure, is no guarantee of safety, any more than a natural clue, however frightening we find it, is a certain indicator of danger. As a guide to what is safe and what is dangerous the kind of feeling a situation arouses in us is never more than rough and ready.

Part III: Individual Differences in Susceptibility to Fear: Anxious Attachment

Chapter 13
Some Variables responsible for Individual Differences

Constitutional variables

That individuals differ enormously in their susceptibility to respond to situations with fear is a commonplace. Why they should differ in such extreme ways remains a puzzle. In this chapter and those following an attempt is made to identify some of the many variables that are operating. The main focus, of course, is on the part played by a person's relationship to his attachment figure(s). This is held to be pervasive and still too little understood. Let us consider first some of the other variables.

It must be assumed that genetic differences play some part in accounting for variance between individuals with regard to susceptibility to fear. Very little is yet known about their role in humans, but it is well documented in the case of other mammals, e.g. dogs (Scott and Fuller 1965; Murphree, Dykman and Peters 1967).

A difference in susceptibility in humans that is likely to be in part genetically determined is one between men and women.

Sex Differences

Feminist opinion notwithstanding, it is very commonly believed that there are some differences in susceptibility to fear as between men and women. This view is plausible and there is some evidence to support it. At the same time it is clear that in this regard there is much overlap between any population of women and a comparable population of men. Culture, moreover, can either magnify such potential differences as there may be, for example by sanctioning the expression of fear by members of one sex but not by those of the other, or else try to reduce them.

Evidence from four sources supports the idea of a difference in susceptibility between the sexes:

1. In the experiments with nursery-school children, carried out by Jersild and Holmes (1935a) and described in Chapter 7, a

higher percentage of the girls were afraid than of the boys. The situations in which the difference was most marked were going into the dark passage and approaching the two animals, snake and dog. In these three situations the percentages of boys who showed fear were respectively 36, 40, and 46. The comparable percentages for girls were 48, 50, and 59.

2. In interviews of mothers of children aged six to twelve years Lapouse and Monk (1959) found that the proportion of girls reported as being afraid of strangers and animals, notably snakes, was higher than that of boys. In two other studies in which children of about the same age were interviewed, girls reported more situations as feared than did boys (Jersild, Markey and Jersild 1933; Croake 1969).

3. In questionnaires given to students there is a consistent tendency for women to report more situations as feared than men (for references and comment see Marks 1969).

4. In epidemiological studies of psychiatric casualties women are reported to suffer from anxiety states about twice as frequently as men (Leighton *et al.* 1963; Hare and Shaw 1965). Two-thirds of agoraphobic patients seen by psychiatrists are women (Marks 1969).

A difference in the opposite direction – that females tend to show less fear than do males – seems not to have been reported.

Viewed in an evolutionary perspective these findings are not surprising. In most races of man, as in other species of ground-living primates, males are larger and stronger than females (Cole 1963). While males bear the brunt of defence against predators, as well as attacking them when necessary, females protect young and, unless prevented from doing so, are more likely to retire from dangerous situations than to grapple with them. It would be strange were such long-standing differences between the sexes in respect of body structure and social role not to be reflected in complementary differences in behavioural bias.

Minimal Brain Damage

In Chapter 16 of the first volume an account is given of a longitudinal study of twenty-nine pairs of boys (Ucko 1965), which shows that children who at birth are noted to be suffering from asphyxia are much more sensitive to environmental change than are matched controls. When the family went on holiday or changed house, boys who had suffered from asphyxia were more likely to be upset than were the controls. The same was true when a member of the family – father, mother, or sibling – was absent for a time. These differences were apparent during each of the first three years of life (though not significantly so during the third). A comparable difference was seen when some of the children started nursery school.

Soon after his fifth birthday every child started infant school, making this the only event that was common to them all (though of course they went to many different schools). Here again the difference between the two groups was striking and significant. On a three-point scale (reduced from five points), the children distribute as shown below:

	Asphyxiated at birth	Controls
Enjoyed school from the start or at least accepted it	8	17
Mild apprehension and protest disappearing within one week	8	10
Mild apprehension or marked disturbance lasting more than a week	13	2
Totals	29	29

Childhood Autism

The behaviour of an autistic child shows a complete absence of attachment together with many indications of chronic fear. Tinbergen and Tinbergen (1972), adopting an ethological approach, suggest that the underlying condition may be one of chronic and pervasive fear, which cannot be allayed by contact with an attachment figure because the child also fears humans. If this is so, the syndrome could be conceived as resulting from a persistently lowered threshold to fear-arousing stimuli combined with delayed development of and/or inhibition of attachment. Causal factors might then include any of the following: (a) genetic factors, (b) brain damage, (c) inappropriate mothering. A combination of two or more factors seems likely. Clancy and McBride (1969) describe a treatment programme based on this type of theory.

Blindness

Nagera and Colonna (1965) report that blind children are apt to be more than usually afraid of such common fear-arousing situations as animals, mechanical noises, thunder and wind, and to live in a state of permanent alertness. A principal reason for this is probably that, being blind, they are likely to be out of contact with their attachment figure far more often than are sighted children, and thus often to be effectively alone when something frightening occurs. Their tendencies on some occasions to remain rigidly immobile and, on others, to seek very close bodily contact with an adult are in keeping with this explanation.

Great difficulties arise for such children after a brief separation because a blind child cannot track his mother visually and keep close to her as a sighted child commonly does on such occasions. Fraiberg (1971) describes the very acute reaction of a blind boy of fourteen months after his mother had been absent for three days, during which he had been cared for by various friends and relations. During the first fortnight after mother's return he screamed for hours at the highest pitch, 'something between terror and rage', or else shouted and chanted perpetually. Only when his mother held him was there any respite; and then he would crawl relentlessly all over her. Because the screaming was so distressing to mother it was suggested she give him pots and pans to bang together instead. This the child did with great gusto and the screaming ceased.

Fraiberg describes also another blind child, a little older, who was cared for by familiar grandparents while mother had a new baby. When reunited with his mother he was markedly ambivalent at first but responded quickly when she, an affectionate mother, gave him plenty of cuddling. The main reason for the far more acute reaction in the younger child is likely to have been that his mother was a disturbed woman whose mothering was erratic both before and after her absence; another factor may have been that he was cared for by several different people while she was away.

Changes during Development in a Child's Susceptibility to Fear

While every infant comes into the world with biases to respond in some ways more than in others, how he develops turns on a process of interaction between himself and his environment. In regard to a susceptibility to respond fearfully, there are certain developmental trends sufficiently buffered to environmental variation to be seen in a huge majority of individuals. For example, as related in Chapter 7, all descriptive studies agree that, whereas during the first two years of life a child is broadening the range of situations he fears – to include especially strangeness, animals, darkness, and separation – from his fifth birthday onwards, and often before, he is likely to become steadily more discriminating in what he fears and more confident and competent in dealing with situations that would formerly have frightened him. Because change towards greater discrimination and confidence represents the norm, we start by considering the nature of the experiences and processes likely to be responsible for it. Subsequently we consider experiences and processes that have an opposite effect, for example, those that interfere with the usual tendency for susceptibility to diminish, or even enhance the susceptibility, and others that have the effect of increasing the range of situations feared.

Experiences and processes that reduce susceptibility to fear

The experiences that occur and the processes at work during the ordinary course of a person's life that tend to reduce his susceptibility to fear are of many kinds. A principal process, increasing confidence in the availability of his attachment figure(s), is the subject of the next chapter. Of the others the main ones can be

described, in everyday language, as getting used to situations that are initially alarming, discovering that in many such situations other people are not afraid, and learning to tackle a situation actively and thereby discovering that nothing ill befalls. In the language of learning theory they are termed:
- habituation
- observational learning leading to vicarious extinction
- observational learning combined with guided participation.

Other processes are likely to be at work as well, though it is not clear how large a part they play during the ordinary course of development. For example, it may well be that there is some naturally occurring version of the procedure developed by behaviour therapists, and known variously as 'reciprocal inhibition', 'counter-conditioning', and 'desensitization', in which an association is gradually built up between a stimulus situation that is feared and something that the subject finds pleasant.[1]

Yet another process, and one that it is easy to forget, is that as an individual grows up he becomes stronger and more skilful so that situations that might once have been, or at least seemed, dangerous to him cease to be so.

Knowledge of some of these processes has been greatly extended in recent years by the work of learning theorists and behaviour therapists. As Marks (1969) is at pains to stress, a large majority of these studies have been conducted with healthy individuals who happen to be intensely afraid of some delimited object or situation, such as a snake or a dog, and not with psychiatric patients who commonly suffer not only more generalized anxiety but usually difficulties in personal relationships and a tendency to depression as well. It is for this reason that many clinicians suspect that the findings of the learning theorists may prove to be of only limited value in psychiatric practice. Yet it is for this same reason that their findings are in all likelihood of much relevance in understanding how it happens that the tendency to respond fearfully recedes during the ordinary course of healthy development.

Let us consider further the three processes already listed.

1. A full description of desensitization and related techniques is given in Marks (1969).

Habituation

This is a process of learning *not* to respond to a situation when it is followed by nothing of consequence. It presumably plays a major part in restricting an infant's initial tendency to respond with fear to all and any strong or sudden stimulation. Later, habituation, perhaps in more sophisticated forms, also restricts the range of situations that are responded to with fear because they are strange; for much of what is strange today will not only have become familiar tomorrow but also have been found to lead to no untoward consequence. Thus habituation greatly limits the range of situations responded to with fear. It should none the less be noted that habituation in no way affects the basic and persistent tendency to respond with fear, as well as with curiosity, to anything perceived as strange.

Observational Learning leading to Vicarious Extinction

It has already been remarked that observational learning can work in either of two directions: either the observer learns to fear situations that formerly he did not fear or else he learns not to fear situations that formerly he did fear. The most important component in learning not to fear situations formerly feared, Bandura (1968) finds, is that the observer should see that the feared situation can be approached and dealt with without there being any bad consequences. The identity of the person observed (model) and the degree to which the observer can identify with him are found to be of much less significance. Even watching a sequence on film can have a reassuring effect, provided that the consequences of the model's actions are clearly depicted.

The process of learning that something is harmless from direct observation of the experience of others is very different, it should be noted, from merely being informed by another person that a situation is harmless. All those who have made a systematic study of the problem report that simple explanation and reassurance have only very limited effect, a finding that will come as no surprise to clinicians.

Fortunately, in the ordinary course of events, a child growing up in a family has endless opportunities to learn from observation that many of the situations that make him afraid are in fact harmless. Parents, older brothers and sisters, neighbours and schoolfellows are continually and without knowing it providing a child with this indispensable information.

Observational Learning combined with Guided Participation

This method requires much more from the model than giving the subject opportunity for simple observational learning. It is evident none the less that every sensible parent is constantly providing it. The method consists in the model's first demonstrating in action that the feared situation holds no danger and then encouraging the other person – child or adult – to tackle the situation himself. Once again it appears that the crucial part of the process is that the learner should discover, this time for himself, that approaching and tackling the situation can be done without untoward consequences. The efficacy of the method was commented on by several of the early students of children's fear behaviour (e.g. Jones 1924a; Jersild and Holmes 1935a), and their findings have been amply confirmed by Bandura and his colleagues in a number of recent experiments.

In one experiment, reported by Bandura (1968), a study was made of a group of adolescents and adults who suffered acute fear of snakes. The subjects were divided into four subgroups and given four different sorts of treatment:

(a) the now standard desensitization procedure of imagining increasingly alarming situations with snakes and at the same time engaging in deep relaxation exercises;

(b) observing a graduated film depicting young children, adolescents, and adults engaging in progressively more fear-provoking interactions with a large harmless snake;

(c) observing the therapist engage in a carefully graduated series of such procedures and at each step being aided by the therapist to engage in the same procedures, so that gradually the subject is himself led first to touch and stroke the snake, then to grasp the snake round the middle while the therapist holds its head and tail, and so on step by step until the subject is able to allow the snake in the room with him, to retrieve it, and finally to let it crawl freely over him; only when a subject has accomplished one step without fear is he encouraged to go on to the next;

(d) receiving no treatment but, like subjects in the other subgroups, being tested for fear of snakes both at the start of the experiment and at the end of it, thus providing a control group.

When subjects in the four subgroups were tested at the end of their treatment by being required to engage in increasingly daring activities with snakes, those who had both observed the therapist interact with the snake and themselves taken part in the graduated exercises with it showed much the least fear. Subjects in subgroups (a) and (b) were less fearful than before but had not benefited as much as had those in subgroup (c). Finally, those in the control group showed as much fear of snakes at the end of the proceedings as they had done at the beginning.

In commenting on his results Bandura suggests that the striking efficacy (for these subjects) of observational learning combined with guided participation rests on two features of the method: first, the subject's fear is reduced sufficiently to enable him to start a process of interaction with the feared object; and second, after he begins to interact, he discovers for himself that it has no disagreeable consequences. Bandura lays emphasis on the point that to be successful the method has to be carefully graduated so that at no stage is fear of more than modest intensity aroused.

In the context of this work, perhaps the most important aspect of Bandura's findings is the key role played in his technique by a trusted and encouraging companion. Not only does the therapist perform the fear-arousing acts, but he stands by while the subject tries the same measures himself, encouraging him at every success and reassuring him after any failure. Only in the presence of such a companion is a subject likely to feel confident enough to tackle the problem in active fashion and so to discover for himself what the consequences really are.

A second valuable lesson from the work of behaviour therapists is that it is essential to work forward in small steps so that the fear aroused is never beyond low intensity. Once fear at high intensity is aroused, it is found, the subject may well be back where he began. It is of interest that the careers of men who later become astronauts appear to be built in a similar way, moving steadily from one modest success to another in unbroken series (Korchin and Ruff 1964). These findings are referred to again in Chapter 21.

It is fortunate that most parents seem to know intuitively that no good comes from allowing a child to become acutely frightened. They also know that what allays fear more certainly than anything else is their own presence. As the Newsons write of their sample of four-year-olds and their mothers:

> Two out of three of all our children have definite and recurrent fears of which the mother is aware. Once she realizes that the child is frightened, she will go through a series of remedies until she finds one that works: and that a remedy is effective is the main consideration to most mothers, even if it does upset the household, for few are unsympathetic to fear. There are no certain methods, and some fears are immune to endless ingenious expedients: the parents can only hope that the child will eventually 'grow out of it'. In general, mothers tend to favour a mixture of explanation and simple cuddling; and these usually at least have a soothing effect, even if they do not always drive the fear away (Newson and Newson 1968).

Experiences and processes that increase susceptibility to fear

It is argued in Chapter 6 that 'it is no less natural to feel afraid when lines of communication with base are in jeopardy than when something occurs in front of us that alarms us and leads us to retreat'. As a consequence, an individual's increased tendency to respond to situations with fear can be a result of either (or both) of two distinct types of experience. One is an experience in a particular situation that has led the person henceforward to become especially prone to avoid or withdraw from that situation. The other is uncertainty about the availability of his attachment figure(s). As a rule a specially alarming experience is likely to lead to an increased susceptibility to respond with fear in that specific situation only; whereas uncertainty about the availability of attachment figures results in increased susceptibility to respond with fear to such a wide range of situations that the person concerned is often referred to as suffering from 'free-floating anxiety'.

Since the remaining chapters of this volume are concerned with susceptibility to anxiety about the availability of attachment figures, here we deal mainly with experiences that increase a person's susceptibility to be afraid of specific situations.

Frightening Experiences

Jersild and his colleagues and also the Newsons present evidence that in very many cases when an individual exhibits unusually intense fear of a particular situation the origin can be traced to a specific experience connected with that situation.

In describing their four-year-olds the Newsons remark that, when a child's previous experiences are known, his fear is often seen to be 'reasonable', even though it may now seem exaggerated. As examples, they describe: a child who had intense horror of mud which dated from a summer holiday during which her feet were trapped in wet sand so that, when the other children ran off, she was unable to follow; a child who would not go near water after she had fallen into a river; and a child terrified of anyone in a white coat after he had been shouted at and held down while being X-rayed (Newson and Newson 1968).

Evidence of a similar sort and from two separate sources is reported by Jersild and Holmes: (a) from parents about factors that may have contributed to a child's having developed unusually intense fear of some particular situation (Jersild and Holmes 1935b), and (b) from young adults about what factors they believe have been responsible for their having themselves developed intense and/or persistent fear of some situation (Jersild and Holmes 1935a). For obvious reasons neither source is adequate and a great deal of further research is required.

Like the Newsons, Jersild and Holmes describe a number of cases in which a child's fear of a specific situation is reported by a parent to have developed in a thoroughly intelligible way. Examples are a child frightened of all objects resembling a balloon, whether on earth or in the air, following an operation during which a gas balloon had been used for an anaesthetic; and another child afraid of a familiar pet canary after having been frightened by the sudden hooting of an owl in the zoo. All such cases can be understood as due to a child's generalizing from too small a sample.

Similarly, the group of young adults report that in many instances fear of a particular situation had followed an alarming experience they had had as children. Examples include witnessing an accident, returning home to find the house had been burgled, witnessing an explosion, and mother being ill.

Since not all children become persistently afraid after a particularly alarming experience, specific conditions are presumably responsible. Of possible candidates, compound situations of which one component is being alone seem especially likely. It is perhaps noteworthy that in none of the examples quoted above is it stated whether the child was alone or with a trusted companion. In future studies of what appear retrospectively to have been traumatic situations, therefore, exact details of all the conditions obtaining are necessary.

There is, of course, a large literature regarding experiences that have led individual animals to become persistently afraid of specific situations (Hebb 1949). Animals, however, cannot be made afraid by stories heard or by threats uttered, as humans can.

Stories Heard

A major cause of persistent and/or intense fear was said by the young adults questioned by Jersild and Holmes (1935a) to have been hearing lurid tales, some true and some fictional. Other evidence suggests that this may be a more frequent cause of certain individuals coming to fear certain situations than is often supposed. An example given by Jersild and Holmes (1935b) is of an unprecedented number of young children reported to be afraid of wolves during the period when the song 'Who's afraid of the big bad wolf?' was popular. In view of the difficulties a child has in distinguishing fact from fiction and in making realistic assessment of potential danger, already touched upon in Chapter 10, this finding should not surprise us. It seems likely that fear arising from such misunderstandings, though intense enough at the time, usually becomes modified once the individual's grasp of the world improves.

Situations of several sorts that are feared by some children and adults and not by others can be understood as culturally determined. For example, several studies report a difference of incidence in regard to fear of certain situations dependent on socio-economic class. In interviews of 400 children aged between five and twelve years in the vicinity of New York City a higher proportion of children from public schools than from private schools reported fear of robbers and kidnappers and also of supernatural happenings (Jersild and Holmes 1935a). In their study of 482 children aged from six to twelve years in Buffalo, New York, based on interview data from mothers, Lapouse and Monk (1959) report a higher incidence of fear of wars, floods, hurricanes and murders, of fire and of being kidnapped among whites of lower socio-economic class than among upper-class whites. A difference in the same direction is reported by Croake (1969) who interviewed 213 children between the ages of eight and twelve years in South Dakota and Nebraska.

Many other differences in incidence between groups reported in the literature seem likely to be due to cultural influences.

Threats

In answering the questionnaire administered by Jersild and Holmes (1935a) many of the young adults were unable to give any clear account of how or why they had developed intense and/or persistent fear of some situation. Nevertheless, in examining the reasons that were given, the researchers were struck by how large a part deliberate threats of horrifying consequences seemed to have played in a number of cases. Some of those threats had been made by older children, sometimes perhaps to tease but at other times with serious intent. Other threats had been made by parents, or occasionally a schoolteacher, as a means of discipline. Some of these threats were of physical punishment. More often they were an exploitation of a child's tendency to fear one of the natural clues, notably darkness, isolation, or abandonment.

231

Unfortunately Jersild and Holmes found that it was not possible to make an exact count of 'apparently deliberate attempts to frighten' but they record some of the more extreme instances. It is a disturbing list. For example, if the answers to the questionnaire are to be believed, a child's fear of the dark had been exploited either by his having been punished by being locked in a dark room or cellar, or by his having been threatened that that would be done. In a few cases a child's fear of the dark had been amplified by its being alleged that the dark room was filled by such things as vicious rats or dreadful monsters.

Another type of threat used for disciplinary purposes, reported both by Jersild and Holmes (1935a) and by the Newsons (1968), is one entailing separation from parents. The threat can take one of several forms. A child can be threatened that he will be sent away, or that some alarming figure will come to take him away, or that his mother will go away and leave him. There is reason to believe that many children are exposed to threats of this kind and also that such threats play a far larger part in increasing a person's susceptibility to separation anxiety than has yet been realized by psychiatrists. Evidence for these statements is given in later chapters (15, 18, 19), and some of the reasons why the role of these threats has been so seriously underestimated are discussed in Chapter 20.

The Key Role of Experience

In clinical circles great emphasis is often placed on the existence of cases in which a much raised susceptibility to respond with fear in a situation cannot be accounted for, apparently, by any experience of the kind so far discussed. Resort is then had to more complex explanations, often turning on fear of 'internal dangers'. The position taken here is that such explanations are invoked far too readily. In some cases highly relevant experiences are unknown to the patient or his relatives; in others they are known about but for one of many reasons are deliberately not reported. In yet other cases, experiences are known about but go unreported because they are thought not to be relevant or because the clinician appears uninterested or unsympathetic. In other cases again experiences are mentioned but the clinician hardly registers them because he is guided by theories that give them no place. Finally, it is not uncommon for fear that is aroused by one situation to be attributed erroneously either by patient or by clinician to another.

A major theme of this volume is that no fear-arousing situation is missed or camouflaged as often as is fear that an attachment figure will be inaccessible or unresponsive.

Chapter 14
Susceptibility to Fear and the Availability of Attachment Figures

Throughout all this ordeal his root horror had been isolation, and there are no words to express the abyss between isolation and having one ally.
– G. K. CHESTERTON, *The Man Who Was Thursday*

Forecasting the availability of an attachment figure

Enough has been said about the conditions that arouse fear to make plain how crucial a variable it is to be with or without a trusted companion. In the presence of a trusted companion fear of situations of every kind diminishes; when, by contrast, one is alone, fear of situations of every kind is magnified. Since in the lives of all of us our most trusted companions are our attachment figures, it follows that the degree to which each of us is susceptible to fear turns in great part on whether our attachment figures are present or absent.

But man does not live entirely in the present. As a child's cognitive capacities increase he becomes capable of foreseeing the possible occurrence of many sorts of situation, including those that he knows would arouse fear. And, of the many fear-arousing situations that a child, or older person, can foresee, none is likely to be more frightening than the possibility that an attachment figure will be absent or, in more general terms, unavailable when wanted.

It has already been noted (Chapter 1) that, in reference to an attachment figure, presence is to be understood as implying ready accessibility rather than actual and immediate presence, and absence implies inaccessibility. Still further amplification is required, however, since accessibility in itself is not enough. Not only must an attachment figure be accessible but he, or she, must be willing to respond in an appropriate way; in regard to someone who is afraid this means willingness to act as comforter and protector. Only when an attachment figure is both accessible and potentially responsive can he, or she, be said to be truly available. In what follows, therefore, the word 'available' is to be understood as implying that an attachment figure is both accessible and responsive.

In this chapter three distinct propositions are introduced, each of which is basic to the thesis of this work. The first is that, when an individual is confident that an attachment figure will be available to him whenever he desires it, that person will be much less prone to either intense or chronic fear than will an individual who for any reason has no such confidence. The second proposition concerns the sensitive period during which such confidence develops. It postulates that confidence in the availability of attachment figures, or a lack of it, is built up slowly during the years of immaturity – infancy, childhood, and adolescence – and that whatever expectations are developed during those years tend to persist relatively unchanged throughout the rest of life. The third proposition concerns the role of actual experience. It postulates that the varied expectations of the accessibility and responsiveness of attachment figures that different individuals develop during the years of immaturity are tolerably accurate reflections of the experiences those individuals have actually had.

Each of these three propositions is controversial, though each is much more controversial in some quarters than in others.

To psychoanalysts who adopt an object-relations theory of personality the first proposition is familiar enough: in terms of that theory, a person's confidence, or lack of it, in the availability of an attachment figure is regarded as resulting from his having either introjected, or failed to introject, a good object. By contrast, to those unfamiliar with object-relations theory, or perhaps alternatively with ethology, the proposition may be novel and even surprising.

The second proposition lies somewhere between, on the one hand, a view that attributes a high degree of plasticity to personality structure even during mature years and, on the other, a view, stemming especially from the work of Melanie Klein, that regards plasticity of personality as diminishing rapidly after the earliest months of infancy and as falling to a low ebb as soon as the first year or two are past. The view adopted here contrasts with both. It holds that the period during which attachment behaviour is most readily activated, namely from about six months to about five years, is also the most sensitive in regard to the development of expectations of the availability of attachment figures; but that nevertheless sensitivity in this regard persists during the decade after the fifth birthday, albeit in steadily diminishing degree as the years of childhood pass.

The third proposition, which concerns the role of experience, may seem fairly self-evident to many but has nevertheless been extremely controversial in psychoanalytic circles. It is a crucial question, since on how it is answered turn not only preventive measures but also therapeutic techniques. The controversy is referred to repeatedly in this and later chapters.

These three propositions, each of which can in principle be tested, provide the scaffolding for the rest of the volume. It is claimed that each is inherently plausible, that none is contradicted by evidence of weight, and that together they enable the evidence available to be fitted together in a way that makes sense.

Working models of attachment figures and of self

The states of mind with which we are concerned can conveniently be described in terms of representational or working models. In the first volume it is suggested that it is plausible to suppose that each individual builds working models of the world and of himself in it, with the aid of which he perceives events, forecasts the future, and constructs his plans. In the working model of the world that anyone builds, a key feature is his notion of who his attachment figures are, where they may be found, and how they may be expected to respond. Similarly, in the working model of the self that anyone builds a key feature is his notion of how acceptable or unacceptable he himself is in the eyes of his attachment figures. On the structure of these complementary models are based that person's forecasts of how accessible and responsive his attachment figures are likely to be should he turn to them for support. And, in terms of the theory now advanced, it is on the structure of those models that depends, also, whether he feels confident that his attachment figures are in general readily available or whether he is more or less afraid that they will not be available – occasionally, frequently, or most of the time.

Intimately linked to the type of forecast a person makes of the probable availability of his attachment figures, moreover, is his susceptibility to respond with fear whenever he meets any potentially alarming situation during the ordinary course of his life.

The theory proposed can be formulated in two steps: from the early months onwards and throughout life the actual presence or absence of an attachment figure is a major variable that determines whether a person is or is not alarmed by any potentially alarming situation; from about the same age, and again onwards throughout life, a second major variable is a person's confidence, or lack of confidence, that an attachment figure not actually present will none the less be available, namely accessible and responsive, should he for any reason desire this. The younger the individual the more influential is the first variable, actual presence or absence; up to about the third birthday it is the dominant variable. After the third birthday forecasts of availability or unavailability become of increasing importance, and after puberty are likely in their turn to become the dominant variable.

Although the concepts of working models and forecasts derived from working models may be unfamiliar, the formulation adopted is no more than a way of describing, in terms compatible with systems theory, ideas traditionally described in such terms as 'introjection of an object' (good or bad) and 'self-image'. The advantages claimed for the present concepts are that they allow for greater precision of description and provide a framework that lends itself more readily to the planning and execution of empirical research.

Reflection shows that working models of attachment figures and of self can vary along many dimensions. One is that of simplicity versus sophistication (see Volume I, Chapter 17). Another is that of validity, which is discussed briefly later in this volume (Chapter 20). Yet another is the extent to which the roles of attachment figures, on the one hand, and of self, on the other, are differentiated. Let us consider the last.

Confidence that an attachment figure is, apart from being accessible, likely to be responsive can be seen to turn on at least two variables: (a) whether or not the attachment figure is judged to be the sort of person who in general responds to calls for support and protection; (b) whether or not the self is judged to be the sort of person towards whom anyone, and the attachment figure in particular, is likely to respond in a helpful way. Logically these variables are independent. In practice they are apt to be confounded. As a result, the model of the attachment figure and the model of the self are likely to develop so as to be complementary and mutually confirming. Thus an unwanted child is likely not only to feel unwanted by his parents but to believe that he is essentially unwantable, namely unwanted by anyone. Conversely, a much-loved child may grow up to be not only confident of his parents' affection but confident that everyone else will find him lovable too. Though logically indefensible, these crude over-generalizations are none the less the rule. Once adopted, moreover, and woven into the fabric of the working models, they are apt henceforward never to be seriously questioned.

Whereas common sense might suggest that a person would operate with only single models of each of his attachment figures and of himself, psychoanalysts from Freud onwards have presented a great deal of evidence that can best be explained by supposing that it is not uncommon for an individual to operate, simultaneously, with two (or more) working models of his attachment figure(s) and two (or more) working models of himself. When multiple models of a single figure are operative they are likely to differ in regard to their origin, their dominance, and the extent to which the subject is aware of them. In a person suffering from emotional disturbance it is common to find that the model that has greatest influence on his perceptions and forecasts, and therefore on his feeling and behaviour, is one that developed during his early years and is constructed on fairly primitive lines, but that the person himself may be relatively, or completely, unaware of; while, simultaneously, there is operating in him a second, and perhaps radically incompatible, model, that developed later, that is much more sophisticated, that the person is more nearly aware of and that he may mistakenly suppose to be dominant.

How and why multiple models originate and persist raises difficult questions of defensive processes, to which attention is given in the third volume. The hypothesis of multiple models, one of which is highly influential but relatively or completely unconscious, is no more than a version, in different terms, of Freud's hypothesis of a dynamic unconscious.

In terms of the present theory much of the work of treating an emotionally disturbed person can be regarded as consisting, first, of detecting the existence of influential models of which the patient may be partially or completely unaware, and, second, of inviting the patient to examine the models disclosed and to consider whether they continue to be valid. In pursuing this strategy an analyst finds that how the patient perceives him (the analyst), and what forecasts the patient makes about his likely behaviour, are particularly valuable in revealing the nature of the working models that exert a dominant influence in the patient's life. Because certain of these perceptions and forecasts appear to the analyst so clearly to be based on a patient's preconceptions about him and to be derived from working models that stem from experiences with other people during earlier years, rather than from current experience, how the patient perceives and conceives the analyst is often known as 'transference'. When an analyst interprets the transference situation he is, among other things, calling the patient's attention to the nature and influence of those models and, by implication, inviting him to scrutinize their current validity and, perhaps also, to revise them.

Seen in the perspective of Piaget's theorizing, the concept of transference implies, first, that the analyst in his caretaking relationship to the patient is being assimilated to some pre-existing (and perhaps unconscious) model that the patient has of how any caretaker might be expected to relate to him, and, second, that the patient's pre-existing model of caretakers has not yet been accommodated – namely, is not yet modified – to take account of how the analyst has actually behaved and still is behaving in relation to him.

Some analysts argue that only those features of the model that are inappropriate to the current situation should be referred to as transference. In practice, however, it is often very difficult to disentangle what parts of a complex model are mistakenly applied to the analyst and what parts are in some degree truly applicable. As a result a tradition has grown up of referring to all aspects of a patient's conception of and attitude towards the analyst as transference. There is perhaps no harm in this, provided that the issue of which parts of the model are inapplicable to the analyst and which parts are in some degree applicable is kept constantly in mind.

Not infrequently, a striking feature of a patient's forecasts is his strong expectation of being abandoned by his analyst, an expectation by no means always fully conscious. During weekends and holidays, and especially during unexpected separations due to illness or other contingency, the way in which a patient behaves and the thoughts and feelings he expresses may be intelligible only on the hypothesis that he forecasts that the analyst will not return, and often also on the assumption that the analyst no longer wishes to see him. Not infrequently these forecasts, either conscious and expressed as fear or not conscious and expressed in some distorted form, persist in spite of assurances that they are mistaken. What is far more important, moreover, they persist often in spite of repeated falsification in real life.[1]

At the same time as he is drawing the patient's attention to the nature of the forecasts he (the patient) appears to be making, the analyst is striving, jointly with the patient, to understand how the models on which the forecasts are based may have come into being. During those inquiries it is often found that a model, currently active but at best of doubtful current validity, becomes reasonably or even completely intelligible when the actual experiences that the patient has had in his day-to-day dealings with attachment figures during all his years of immaturity are known. This leads again to the controversial question of the

1. Although responses of these kinds are referred to in numerous case reports, I am unaware of any systematic empirical record of how one (or more) patient(s) responded to the separations, planned or unplanned, that occurred during the course of his (or their) analysis.

extent to which actual experience is of influence in the development of working models of self and others.

The role of experience in determining working models

There was a time when psychoanalysts were as loath as a Kraepelinian psychiatrist might be to attribute a patient's unfavourable models of attachment figures to his actual experiences. To make such attributions was deemed to be naïve, to be underrating the role of projection, and to be failing to give due weight to the contribution that the patient himself had made, and was making, to the misfortunes he experienced. Nowadays, thanks to the influence of Fairbairn, Winnicott, and others, fewer psychoanalysts take that view, which, it is held, is tenable only so long as a clinician limits himself to treating isolated patients, usually adults, and is uninterested in considering systematically what their day-to-day experiences have actually been: to what extent and in what ways has a patient had his attachment behaviour met, not only during early infancy, about which information is usually uncertain and often entirely speculative, but throughout all the later years of childhood also?

Probably no one who has worked for long in a family clinic, in which disturbed children and their parents are treated, still holds the traditional view that actual experience is of little consequence. On the contrary, in the course of that work it is found repeatedly that, when information about a child's experiences of interaction with parents and parent figures is obtained – usually partly from first-hand observation of members of the family who are interviewed together and partly from the family's history as it is pieced together, often only slowly and from a diversity of sources – the forecasts the child makes of how attachment figures are likely to behave towards him are not unreasonable extrapolations from his experiences of the way in which they have behaved towards him in the past, and may perhaps still be behaving towards him in the present. Thus, whatever contributions to variations of personality are made by genetic biases and physical traumata, the contribution of family environment is certainly substantial.

Individual Differences in Susceptibility to Fear

From the viewpoint of the position adopted, adult personality is seen as a product of an individual's interactions with key figures during all his years of immaturity, especially of his interactions with attachment figures. Thus an individual who has been fortunate in having grown up in an ordinary good home with ordinarily affectionate parents has always known people from whom he can seek support, comfort, and protection, and where they are to be found. So deeply established are his expectations and so repeatedly have they been confirmed that, as an adult, he finds it difficult to imagine any other kind of world. This gives him an almost unconscious assurance that, whenever and wherever he might be in difficulty, there are always trustworthy figures available who will come to his aid. He will therefore approach the world with confidence and, when faced with potentially alarming situations, is likely to tackle them effectively or to seek help in doing so.

Others, who have grown up in other circumstances, may have been much less fortunate. For some the very existence of caretaking and supportive figures is unknown; for others the whereabouts of such figures have been constantly uncertain. For many more the likelihood that a caretaking figure would respond in a supportive and protective way has been at best hazardous and at worst nil. When such people become adults it is hardly surprising that they have no confidence that a caretaking figure will ever be truly available and dependable. Through their eyes the world is seen as comfortless and unpredictable; and they respond either by shrinking from it or by doing battle with it.

Between the groups of people with extremes of either good or bad experience lie groups of people with an almost infinite range of intermediate sorts of experience, who grow up to have expectations of the world to match. For example, some may have learnt that an attachment figure responds in a comforting way only when coaxed to do so. They grow up supposing that all such figures have to be coaxed. Others may have learnt during childhood that the wished-for response can be expected only if certain rules are kept. Provided the rules have been moderate and sanctions mild and predictable, a person can still come confidently to believe that support will always be available when needed. But when rules have been very strict and difficult to keep, and when sanctions on breaking them have been severe and especially when they have included threats to withdraw support, confidence is likely to wilt.

Sanctions of a damaging kind, which are used by many parents, include both refusing to respond to a child's approaches, for example by sulking, and threatening to leave the home or to send the child away. When used repeatedly, or even only occasionally but with intensity, such sanctions or threats of sanctions can have calamitous effects on a developing personality. In particular, because they deliberately cast grave doubt on whether an attachment figure will be available when needed, such threats can greatly increase a person's fear that he will be abandoned, and thereby greatly increase also his susceptibility to respond to other situations fearfully.

Admittedly the influence that these sorts of experience have on the development of personality and especially on susceptibility to fear and anxiety is still controversial. Evidence in support of the position adopted, introduced already in Chapter 16 of the first volume, is presented more fully in the coming chapters. It is hoped that those who adopt a different position, for example that experiences of the kinds described play at most a subordinate role in accounting for variations in personality development, will be stimulated to present the evidence on which they base their views. Only in this way can progress be made.

A note on use of the terms 'mature' and 'immature'

In many clinical circles the practice has developed of referring to personalities as 'mature' or 'immature'. A person who approaches the world with confidence yet who, when in difficulty, is disposed to turn to trusted figures for support is often said to be mature. In contrast, both someone who is chronically anxious and permanently in need of support and someone who never trusts anyone are said to be immature.

The theory underlying this use of immature is that adult personality structures so described are held to be a consequence of arrested development and to have remained in a state that, though normal for early childhood, is passed through during the course of healthy growing up and left well behind.

The theory advanced here and discussed further in the final chapter is different. It disputes that mental states either of chronic anxiety or of persistent distrust are characteristic of normal or healthy stages of development. Instead, it holds that the main cause of such deviations is that, during childhood, an individual's attachment behaviour was responded to in an inadequate or inappropriate way, with the result that throughout later life he bases his forecasts about attachment figures on the premise that they are unlikely to be available.

The resemblance of certain of these types of personality to the personalities typical of young children, especially in so far as individuals of both sorts require and often demand the constant presence and support of attachment figures, is held to be superficial only. In the case of a young child he has no means by which to make forecasts except over short spans of time. In the case of an 'immature' personality he not only has the means to make forecasts but the forecasts he makes, and makes with conviction, are that attachment figures will be unavailable unless he maintains constant watchfulness or is constantly humouring them.

Thus the common usage of the terms mature and immature is held to be inaccurate and misleading. A particularly adverse effect of using immature in this way is that it can, on occasion, lead a clinician to take a humouring patronizing attitude to the persons concerned, instead of recognizing that their behaviour is a legitimate product of bitter experience.

Chapter 15
Anxious Attachment and Some Conditions that Promote it

> If there are quarrels between the parents or if their marriage is unhappy, the ground will be prepared in their children for the severest predisposition to a disturbance of sexual development or to a neurotic illness.
> – SIGMUND FREUD (1905b)

'Overdependency' or anxious attachment

In the opening pages of this volume vignettes are given (quoted from Burlingham and Freud 1944) of children, aged between two and four years and resident in the Hampstead Nurseries, who showed intensely possessive behaviour towards one or another nurse. Jim, for example, who had been in the nursery since the age of seventeen months, is described as having formed 'strong attachments' first to one young nurse and then to another who had successively looked after him. Towards each he was intensely clinging and possessive, and he refused to be left by them for a minute. Numerous other observers, including my colleagues Robertson and Heinicke, have also noted this type of behaviour whenever small children in a nursery setting are given opportunity to make an attachment to a member of staff, and the same behaviour is shown towards mother after they return home.

Clinging behaviour, either literal or figurative, can be seen at every age, during childhood, during adolescence, and during adult years. It goes by many names. Among adjectives used to describe it are 'jealous', 'possessive', 'greedy', 'immature', 'overdependent', and 'strong' or 'intense' attachment. For scientific and clinical purposes, it is argued, each word has drawbacks: because it derives from and implies obsolescent theory, or because it is ambiguous, or, and perhaps most important of all, because it carries with it an adverse value judgement that is held to be inappropriate and unhelpful.

Both 'jealous' and 'possessive', though accurate, are apt to be pejorative. The same is true of 'greedy', which is used mainly by

245

those whose thinking is still influenced by the assumption that attachment derives from food and being fed.

'Strong' attachment and also 'intense' attachment are ambiguous: both of them, and the former especially, might be thought to imply a satisfactory state of affairs.

'Immature' derives from a theory of regression which, as indicated at the end of the previous chapter, is held to be out of keeping with the evidence.

Some of the ambiguities and false values concealed in the terms 'dependency' and 'overdependency' are emphasized in the first volume (Chapter 12).[1] Let us look further at their deficiencies and also propose an alternative term.

Perhaps no terms are used more frequently in the clinical literature than 'dependent' and 'overdependent'. A child who tends to be clinging, an adolescent reluctant to leave home, a wife or husband who maintains close contact with mother, an invalid who demands company, all these and others are likely sooner or later to be described with one of these words. Always in their use there is an aura of disapproval, of disparagement. Let us consider more closely the behaviour to which these terms are applied and how we are to evaluate the persons who come to be described by them.

Viewed in the perspective of this work, most persons described by clinicians as dependent or overdependent are ones who exhibit attachment behaviour more frequently and more urgently than the clinician thinks proper. Inherent in the terms, therefore, are the norms and values of the observer using them. This leads to many difficulties. One is that norms and values differ greatly not only between individuals but from culture to culture and from subculture to subculture. To take a crude example, behaviour that in some parts of the East might pass unnoticed, or even be encouraged, might in the West be condemned as childishly dependent. Another difficulty is that, even within a single culture, no useful evaluation of the behaviour can be made without knowledge of the conditions, organismic and environmental, in

1. For a discussion of how the concepts of dependency and attachment are related to one another see Ainsworth (1972); overlap in their meanings is not complete.

which it is shown. Ignorance of a child's age, of whether he is well or ill, of whether or not a person has recently experienced a shock, can play havoc with an observer's judgements. Individuals who are notoriously apt to be wrongly judged as overdependent are children who look older than they are, who are tired or unwell, or who have recently acquired a new sibling, and adults recently bereaved. Another example is a young woman during pregnancy or while caring for small children. In all such instances attachment behaviour is likely to be shown more frequently and/or more urgently than would otherwise be the case. In other words, in the conditions obtaining the behaviour may be well within normal limits and no adverse conclusions on the personality development of the individuals concerned would be appropriate.

There are, however, persons of all ages who are prone to show unusually frequent and urgent attachment behaviour and who do so both persistently and without there being, apparently, any current conditions to account for it. When this propensity is present beyond a certain degree it is usually regarded as neurotic.

When we come to know a person of this sort it soon becomes evident that he has no confidence that his attachment figures will be accessible and responsive to him when he wants them to be and that he has adopted a strategy of remaining in close proximity to them in order so far as possible to ensure that they will be available. To describe this as overdependency obscures the issue. Even the term 'separation anxiety' is not ideal. A better way to describe the condition is to term it 'anxious attachment' or 'insecure attachment'. This makes it clear that the heart of the condition is apprehension lest attachment figures be inaccessible and/or unresponsive. For these reasons, therefore, and especially because it can be expected to enlist our sympathy, anxious attachment is the term to be used. It respects the person's natural desire for a close relationship with an attachment figure, and recognizes that he is apprehensive lest the relationship be ended.

The thesis of the present work is that, even though other causal factors may play some part in the development of this condition, those about which by far the most evidence is at present available are experiences that shake a person's confidence that his attachment figures will be available to him when desired.

Alternative theories, some long entrenched, are considered in the next chapter.

The following descriptions by two working-class mothers of occasions when their young children went through a phase of 'overdependency' reveal the condition in what is believed to be its true light. The descriptions are taken from the survey of 700 four-year-old children in Nottingham undertaken by Newson and Newson (1968).

Asked whether her daughter sometimes wanted to be cuddled, a miner's wife replied:

Ever since I left her that time I had to go into hospital (two periods, 17 days each, child aged 2 years), she doesn't trust me any more. I can't go anywhere – over to the neighbours or in the shops – I've always got to take her. She wouldn't leave me. She went down to the school gates at dinner time today. She ran like mad home. She said, 'Oh, Mum, I thought you was gone!' She can't forget it. She's still round me all the time.

When asked the same question a lorry-driver's wife, whose husband had deserted three months earlier, replied:

Yes, all the time just lately – only since he left. (What do you do?) Well, if I'm not busy I sit down and nurse her, because – you know – she's continually clinging round me, she keeps saying, 'Do you love me? You won't leave me, Mummy, will you?' – and so I sit down and try to talk to her about it, you know; but I mean, at her age [about four], really you can't explain. And she used to dress herself; but since my husband's been gone, she's relied on me for – well, every mortal thing I've had to do for her. At the moment I'm more or less letting her do what she wants. I mean, she's been upset in one way, and I don't want to upset her again. Because I did put her in a nursery just after he went, because I thought it might take her mind off things, you see, but anyhow the matron asked if I'd mind taking her away, because she said she just sat and cried all day long. I think she'd got it into her head that because her Daddy's gone, and me taking her there and leaving her all day, she p'raps thought I'd left her too, you see. So she was only there a fortnight, and then I took her away. But she's afraid of being left on her own, I mean, if I go to the toilet, I have to take her with me, she won't even stay in the room then on her own. She's frightened of being left.

In summing up their findings on children who exhibited overdependency and fear of separation the Newsons write: 'Most of these children's separation fears are reality-based, in that they or their mothers have been hospitalized or some other separation has already taken place.' Nevertheless, there were some children who had had such an experience without apparently having been left prone to separation anxiety, and other children who were prone to such fears without having had such an experience. Important though experience of actual separation is, therefore, it is clear that variables of other kinds contribute as well.

Among the most influential of these other variables, it seems likely, are, first, threats to abandon a child, made for disciplinary purposes, and, second, a child's recognition that parental quarrels carry with them the risk that a parent may depart. In the light of present evidence, it seems extremely probable that, as Suttie (1935) and Fairbairn (1941) long ago suggested, threats to abandon a child are the most influential of all. None the less, it must not be forgotten that those threats have the tremendous power they do have only because for a young child separation is itself such a distressing and frightening experience, or prospect.

For that reason, therefore, we return once more to our point of departure, the effects on a young child of being separated from his mother figure.

In the two sections that follow we consider, first, children who are being reared in a residential setting without any permanent mother figure and, second, children who are being reared mainly at home with mother but who, for various reasons and for shorter or longer periods, have been separated from her.

Anxious attachment of children reared without a permanent mother figure

The most systematic data yet available on the attachment and fear behaviour of children reared without a permanent mother figure are provided by Tizard and Tizard (1971). They compare the social and cognitive development of two-year-old children cared for in residential nurseries in England with that of children brought up in ordinary families.

In recent years there have been great changes in the organization of residential nurseries in Britain. Not only are links with a child's family encouraged but, within the nursery itself, attempts are made to provide living conditions that are nearer than in the past to ordinary family living. Apart from babies under twelve months, who are cared for in a separate unit, children live in groups of six, of varying ages up to about five or six years, and are cared for in 'private' accommodation by their own nurse and her assistant. In addition, in some nurseries a system obtains whereby each nurse is encouraged to give special attention to one or two children, as a rule from a group other than the one in which she usually works; she takes the child out in her free time, buys him little presents, sometimes puts him to bed, or takes him to her home for weekends.

Although this type of régime is a big advance on some of the impersonal régimes of the past, examination shows that, so far as mothering care goes, it still falls very far short of what obtains in an ordinary working-class home in present-day London.

For their study Tizard and Tizard selected fifteen boys and fifteen girls (ten white and five coloured in each case), aged two years, who had been healthy full-term babies, whose health had throughout been good, and who had entered a nursery before the age of four months and had remained there since. All but one were illegitimate. Half were visited by mother, who still hoped to be able to care for them; the others had been offered for adoption, but for various reasons adoption had been delayed.

A contrast group, similarly composed by age, sex, and health record, but confined to white English children, was selected from among working-class children living in their own homes and in intact families. For reasons of research convenience, any child whose mother was working full time and who had an older sibling of less than school age was excluded.

The aim of the study was to compare children in the two groups in respect of both their cognitive and their social development. Various cognitive tests were therefore administered,[2] and oppor-

2. Results of the cognitive tests showed the mean of the nursery children to be two months below the norm and three months below the mean of the family children. The inferiority of the nursery children was due mainly to their failures on the verbal subtests (Tizard *et al.* 1972).

tunity was taken to observe the children's responses first to the advent of a stranger and then to the brief departure of the caretaker from the room. In addition, to obtain further information regarding attachment behaviour, a child's caretaker was asked a series of detailed questions about it and also certain particulars regarding the child's experiences with potential attachment figures and with other persons. Both research workers engaged in the project were women.

In reporting results it is useful to begin with particulars of the opportunities that children in each of the groups had to make attachments. Comparison shows there were great differences.

For the thirty two-year-olds living in their families, mother was principal attachment figure for twenty, father for four, and both parents equally for five. In one case, where father was away from home, it was a maternal uncle. The total number of figures towards whom attachment was shown was strictly limited, with an average of four per child in the group. Following an attachment figure around the house was reported as a regular activity for all but four of the children.

In contrast to this picture of focused attachment, the attachment behaviour of the nursery children was directed diffusely. By most of them the behaviour was shown in some degree towards a large, indeed an indeterminate, number of people, including usually 'anyone he knows well'. Despite this, however, each of the children had a preference. Provided a child's natural mother visited once a week or more, she was said always to be the preferred figure: 'the child would be very excited to see her and distressed when she left'. Similarly, when a child had a 'special nurse' who took him out (and no mother who visited regularly) the special nurse was always the child's preferred figure, despite the fact that she would probably see him for only a few minutes on most days. Thus, whereas the family children had almost constant contact with their preferred attachment figures, the nursery children saw very little of theirs. Furthermore, the nursery children were not permitted to follow anyone out of the room in which they were.

Despite every endeavour by the nursery authorities to stabilize the children's social relationships the results were found to be disappointing. Since entering the nursery twenty months earlier, a majority of the nursery children had had at least twenty different people caring for them for periods of a week or longer, in comparison with an average of two in all for the family children. Even during the course of a single week the average number of nurses looking after the nursery children was found to be six. Furthermore, in the lives of nursery children members of staff were found to come and go at irregular intervals, often disappearing for days or weeks at a time, and sometimes never returning.

When data on attachment and fear behaviour for children in the two groups were compared the nursery children proved to be significantly more anxious[3] in their attachments and significantly more afraid of a stranger.

Information given by the nurses showed that the attachment behaviour of the nursery children both to the preferred figure and to the rest of the staff was much more anxious than that of the family children (as reported by mothers). For example, twenty-four of the thirty nursery children were apt to cry when their favourite caretaker left the room compared with thirteen of the thirty family children; those who cried regularly numbered ten and two respectively. When the caretaker returned, all but two of the nursery children would run to be picked up (and most of them did so usually), in comparison with only four of the family children (none of them usually). Thus, whereas about two-thirds of the family children took mother's coming and going from the room as a matter of course, all but a handful of the nursery children were upset when an attachment figure left and wanted to be picked up by her when she returned.

For children in each group a standard procedure was used to measure fear of strangers. Every child was assessed in his own living-room with his own caretaker (nurse or mother) present. During the first five minutes the child sat on his caretaker's lap, while the research worker chatted to the caretaker. Then the research worker made a series of standardized overtures to the

3. In their report Tizard and Tizard refer to the 'intensity' of the nursery children's attachment behaviour as being 'much greater' than that shown by the family children.

child: she started with a greeting; as a second step she invited him to come over to look at a picture book; and lastly she invited him to sit on her lap. The child's response to each move was rated on a seven-point scale.

When, during the second phase, the research worker invited the child to come over, only fifteen of the thirty nursery children did so in comparison with twenty-six of the family children. When the nursery children were invited to sit on her lap only eight accepted, while six of them cried and ran away. Of the family children sixteen accepted the invitation and none ran away.

After the researcher had made her initial overtures to a child she engaged the caretaker in a few minutes' further conversation and then asked her to leave the room briefly and to leave the door ajar. The child's response to this was rated on a four-point scale. Towards the end of the session the caretaker was again asked to leave the room and the child's response was again rated. When left alone with the research worker on the first occasion, six of the nursery children ran out of the room; and even on the second occasion later in the session five of them were still unwilling to stay with her. On both occasions every one of the family children was ready to stay with the researcher.

Finally, at the end of the session, the research worker again invited the child to sit on her lap. The nursery children, although most of them were bolder by now, remained much more cautious than the family children. Two of the nursery children still ran away and cried; and none of them smiled and chatted as did eleven of the family children as they climbed up onto the research worker's lap.

Whereas all the findings cited so far from this study support our hypothesis, there are one or two others that do not. In particular, fearfulness, for example of dogs, was reported by nurses and mothers respectively 'with equal frequency' for children of the two groups. Considering the very different responses of the children to the strange research worker, we are perhaps entitled to question the validity of this information, which comes from informants whose standards may well not be comparable.

In this context a case report by Schnurmann (1949) is of interest. This describes how a little girl of two and a half years, who was being cared for in the Hampstead Nurseries, developed fear both of going to bed and of dogs. Although the symptoms are described as phobic and the writer seeks to explain them in terms of castration anxiety resulting from the child's observation of sex differences, it is apparent from the record that the onset of symptoms was closely related in time to the cessation of her mother's daily evening visits, and the remission of symptoms to the resumption of visits. The relation of phobic symptoms to anxious attachment is considered at length in Chapters 18 and 19.

In view of the very different experience with attachment figures that children in a residential nursery have compared with children in a family setting, it is hardly surprising that the attachment behaviour of the nursery children should be so much more anxious or that they should be more prone to fear strangers. Nor would it be surprising were there to be a substantial difference between the working models of attachment figures built by children in the two groups and used by them as the basis of their future predictions about the accessibility and responsiveness of such figures. For, whereas a family child lives in a stable and predictable world with accessible and usually responsive attachment figures, a nursery child, even in a modern nursery, lives in a highly unpredictable world in which his preferred attachment figure is usually inaccessible, while subsidiary ones come and go almost at random.

Anxious attachment after a period of separation or of daily substitute care

After a period of separation, especially when it has been spent with strange people, it is usual for small children who are being brought up in families to be more anxious and clinging than they were before. This finding, which constitutes part of the basic data on which the present thesis rests and which is well illustrated by the two examples (quoted from Newson and Newson 1968) given in the first section of this chapter, has perhaps ceased to be a matter of controversy. What is debatable concerns the factors that lead one child to recover confidence and another not to.[4]

Effects of a Brief Stay in Hospital

A study by Fagin (1966) of the behaviour of two groups of children after return home from a short stay in hospital (varying from one to seven days) casts some light on this problem. The thirty children of one group had had mother staying with them in hospital, the thirty of the other group were there without her, though they were visited daily. The children were matched for age, between eighteen and forty-eight months, but not for sex. Interviews held with the mothers prior to the hospitalization suggested that attitudes towards child-rearing did not differ between mothers in the two groups, nor did the mothers differ in regard to their desire to remain with their child in hospital.

For each child, behaviour at one week and again at one month after his return home, as reported by mother at interview,

4. Scepticism is sometimes expressed about whether a period in hospital or residential nursery has effects in the long term as well as the short. In this connection the findings of a recent analysis by Douglas (in press) of data collected some years ago in the course of a longitudinal study of over four thousand children are of interest. When the children were assessed during adolescence, those who had been in hospital before the age of five years, either for longer than a week or on two or more occasions, were found to differ from other children in the following four ways. They were:
- more likely to have been rated by teachers as troublesome at ages thirteen and fifteen years
- more likely, in the case of boys, to have been cautioned by police or sentenced between the ages of eight and seventeen years
- more likely to have scored low on a reading test
- more likely, in the case of school-leavers, to have changed jobs four or more times between the ages of fifteen and eighteen years.

The tendencies to delinquency and unstable employment record are significantly increased for children who experienced a further period in hospital between the ages of five and fifteen. All these differences remain significant when the rather atypical backgrounds of children who are admitted to hospital before the age of five years – e.g. as regards health, large families – are taken into account.

These findings tend to support the belief expressed earlier, in Chapter 4, that the effects of separations from mother during the early years are cumulative and that the safest dose is therefore a zero dose.

was compared with what it had been before he entered hospital, as reported by her at that time.

Both at one week and at one month following return home the behaviour of the unaccompanied children was reported as markedly disturbed in comparison with what it had been prior to hospital. Significant differences occur in all the usual fields. In particular, these children were reported as being much more upset by a temporary brief separation than they were before hospital and as more 'dependent'. By contrast, children who had been accompanied in hospital by mother showed none of these adverse changes. Indeed, mothers' reports showed them to have developed favourably in all these respects, which suggests that, as MacCarthy and his colleagues (1962) have found, mother's presence on a potentially upsetting occasion had given a child additional confidence that she would always be available in emergency.[5]

These findings are in keeping with those of similar studies. What is of particular interest in Fagin's study is the differential effect on children in the two groups of having a mother who was rated by the interviewer as being very 'irritable'. Of the accompanied children who had an irritable mother none showed any adverse effects of their stay in hospital; whereas, of the unaccompanied children, those who had an irritable mother were even more affected by their experience than were those whose mother was rated as more equable.

A number of other studies point firmly to the view that a separation has a specially adverse effect on children whose parents are inclined to be hostile or to threaten them with separation as a disciplinary measure, or whose family life is

5. Limitations of Fagin's study are that data were derived entirely from mothers' reports and that, in regard to ailment and length of stay, the two groups were not matched. Twenty-one of the accompanied children were in hospital for hernia operation or tonsillectomy and were out again within two days. Only nine of the unaccompanied children had a similar experience; thirteen had had respiratory or alimentary infections and had been away for between three and five days. It is therefore possible that these differences of experience might account for some of the reported differences in subsequent behaviour, though the findings of MacCarthy, Lindsay and Morris (1962) do not support that interpretation.

unstable. Indeed, evidence is accruing fast that parent-child relations, both before and after the event, play a very large part in accounting for the differential outcome of a separation.

Effects of Periods of Residential Substitute Care

Moore (1964; 1969a and b) has reported a number of findings of much interest to our thesis. In a longitudinal study of London children, starting at birth with 223 cases and reducing to 167 at the age of six years, Moore was able to investigate the short-term effects on children of separations and other discontinuities of care, and also differences in the behaviour, at the age of six or seven years, of children who, during their early years, had had different types of experience. Information regarding behaviour was obtained: (a) from interviews with mothers (two before the child was born, five during the child's first year, four during the next two years, and annually thereafter); (b) from psychological tests and observations of the children carried out regularly at the Study Centre; and (c) from interviews with the heads and staffs of any day nurseries or nursery schools that the children attended. Most of the results are expressed in terms of differences between the average frequencies of behaviour in children in a series of samples differing in regard to previous experience.

A number of the children had spent periods of a week or two with relatives, by way of a holiday for the child or for the parents or both. The commonest behaviour of children under three on reunion with mother was clinging around her, sometimes after initial reserve. Although such clinging often passed off after two or three days, in 30 per cent of cases it persisted for a matter of weeks. Moore (1969b) concludes: 'It is clear that for most young children separation from the mother is in itself a stressful experience', and that they are especially vulnerable during their second and third years.

Moore reports much evidence that shows that whether disturbances persist or fade turns in great measure on the stability of the home and the attitudes of the parents. Details are given of three of his comparisons.

(a) There were six children who had experienced one or more stays in a residential nursery between the ages of nine and thirty months. All but one, who was backward, were upset on return home, 'showing it in aggressive behaviour, head banging, fear of strangers and/or increased dependence on their mothers'. Four other children had had a similar experience before the age of nine months; of these, two were similarly upset. When all these ten children had reached the age of eight years, two were found to be 'reasonably well-adjusted' and eight were not. It was noted that, whereas the two who were reasonably well adjusted came from homes in which family relationships were good, the eight who presented difficulties, mainly of an aggressive uncontrolled sort, came from homes which were breaking up (two cases) or where relationships were otherwise disturbed.

(b) Fifteen children who came from stable homes had experienced episodic separations during their first four years. Separations had been in various settings and of varying lengths. In many cases a child had stayed with relatives; in others he had been in a hospital or nursery. When the lengths of time away were summed for each child, summed lengths ranged from five to twenty-three weeks. Not only did these children come from stable families but, apart from the separations, they had been cared for throughout by mother. At the age of six years their behaviour could be compared with that of two similar groups of children:

(i) those who had been cared for by mother throughout without having experienced any separations;

(ii) those who had not only experienced a variety of separations but whose home life had been generally unsettled, including frequent changes of daily caretaker during the pre-school years.

(i) Judged by mothers' reports, the children from stable homes who had experienced these episodic separations were rather less given to attention-seeking than were those who had not been separated. This suggests that, for children cared for as a rule by mother in a stable family, episodic separations of the length and kinds described, although in many cases reported to have been very distressing at the time, do not leave obviously adverse effects on the children's later attachment behaviour. Nevertheless in drawing conclusions it is necessary to be cautious since we do not know how such children would react to a new fear-arousing situation. The findings of Hinde and Spencer-Booth, for example, on the effects two years later of a week's separation on young rhesus monkeys when exposed to a fear-arousing situation (see Chapter 4) are a warning against premature confidence.

(ii) Whereas the children from stable homes who had experienced episodic separations appeared to have developed favourably, those from unstable homes had not. At the age of six they are reported to have shown many typical signs of insecurity: overdependence, anxiety, sleeping problems, and nail-biting.

Effects of Daily Substitute Care

Moore (1969a) deals in some detail with the effects on a child's behaviour at the age of six years of different types of daily substitute care experienced before the age of five. About half the mothers of his sample had worked outside their homes for at least three months before the child was five, but patterns both of mother's work and of child care while mother worked varied enormously. At one extreme were mothers who, during their child's fourth and fifth years, did part-time work while the child attended nursery school; at the other were women who were doing full-time or near full-time work from early in their child's life while the child attended day nursery or a child-minder. Inevitably variables were much confounded. In most cases in which daily substitute care had started early in a child's life, care had been unstable, so that the child had been looked after first by one set of people and then by another. Conversely, when care began after the third birthday, often at nursery school, it had tended to be stable. Another complication, not surprisingly, is that instability in arrangements for care tended to be correlated with instability of parental personality.

Despite these problems, Moore is able to identify two samples, each of about fifteen children, matched for sex and reasonably well matched in other respects, all of whom had received some daily substitute care before the age of five years. In one sample substitute care had been stable and in the other unstable. For each sample the age at which the children first received daily substitute care varied from a few weeks to about three years.

Sample with unstable daily substitute care: The fifteen children who had experienced unstable and changing daily substitute care, in most cases starting before the second birthday, were conspicuously insecure and anxious in later years. Judged by mothers' reports when the children were six, they showed

far more dependent clinging behaviour – wanting to sit on mother's knee, hating her to leave, being very upset if she was cross and demanding attention at bedtime. . . . This behaviour was obvious at the Centre, where the group received higher ratings for dependence and nervousness and lower for initial adjustment to the situation. They showed more fears, especially of doctors and hospitals and the dark . . . (Moore 1969a).

In addition to unstable daily substitute care, these fifteen children had experienced more periods in hospital and elsewhere than had children in the other sample. Moreover, some of their anxious attachment, though not all of it, was probably attributable to the treatment they received from their parents, many of whom were rated as 'unstable personalities'.

Sample with stable daily substitute care: There were only a few cases in which daily substitute care had begun before the second birthday and had also been stable. At the age of six or seven years, these children tended to seek extra attention from mother; and some of the mothers had failed to establish a close relationship with their child.

The children whose daily and stable substitute care had not begun before their third birthday, by contrast, showed no evident emotional difficulties at the age of six. This finding is in keeping, of course, with common everyday experience. During their time away from mother these three- and four-year-olds had either been attending nursery school (for not more than six hours a day) or else been cared for in another family, both of them arrangements that are not only widespread at that age but are usually enjoyed by the children and have never seemed to give rise to any difficulty.

The findings of Moore's study thus strongly support the theory that anxious attachment develops not because a child has been excessively gratified, as is sometimes held (see next chapter), but because his experiences have led him to build a model of an attachment figure who is likely to be inaccessible and/or unresponsive to him when he desires her. The more stable and predictable the régime the more secure a child's attachment tends to be; the more discontinuous and unpredictable the régime the more anxious his attachment.

To this conclusion one major proviso must be added. Some children subjected to an unpredictable régime seem to despair. Instead of developing anxious attachment, they become more or less detached, apparently neither trusting nor caring for others. Often their behaviour becomes aggressive and disobedient and they are quick to retaliate. This type of development occurs much more frequently in boys than in girls; whereas anxious clinging is commoner in girls than in boys.

That separations and instabilities of maternal care should lead to responses of two opposed types, anxious attachment and aggressive detachment, and sometimes a mixture of the two, is a little confusing. So also, perhaps, is the finding that in respect of these responses the sexes differ. Nevertheless, that finding is in keeping with the differential incidence between the sexes of certain types of personality disorder in adult life. Anxiety is commoner as a neurotic symptom in women than in men; conversely, delinquency is commoner in men than in women.

Follow-up inquiries when the children were eleven and fifteen years old showed that whatever pattern of attachment behaviour had become established during the first five years tended to persist, whether it was secure attachment, anxious attachment, or some degree of detachment (Moore 1971).

Moore's data do not permit of any conclusions regarding the effects on a child of starting full-time day care during his third year of life, a matter about which there is still controversy. Clinical experience suggests that, whereas there are children who enjoy attending a very small playgroup a few mornings a week towards the end of their third year, there are strong reasons for caution about full-time attendance, the more so when it begins soon after the second birthday. The case of Lottie, who started nursery school when she was two years and three months old and attended only two half-days a week (see Chapter 3), illustrates the danger. So also do the findings of van Leeuwen and Tuma (1972) referred to in the same chapter.

In a recent study of children who spend many hours daily in day care Blehar (1974) has thrown further light on the question. Blehar studied four sub-samples of middle-class children and their mothers by means of Ainsworth's strange situation procedure (see Chapter 3). Children in two of the sub-samples had been attending privately organized day nurseries[6] for between eight and ten hours a day for five days a week during the preceding four months: children in one of these sub-samples had begun attendance at age twenty-six months and were tested at thirty months; children in the other sub-sample had started at age thirty-five months and were tested at thirty-nine months. The other two sub-samples, which acted as controls, comprised children of equivalent age and sex who were being cared for in their own homes.

A month prior to testing, the research worker paid a visit to the home of each child during which Caldwell's inventory of home stimulation was completed; this draws mainly on data from first-hand observation of mother–child interaction. Analysis of these data showed no differences in the mean amounts or forms of stimulation received in their homes by the day-care and the home-care children respectively.

Nevertheless, there were clear differences between the children in the two groups in respect of their behaviour in Ainsworth's strange situation procedure, the differences being especially noticeable during the episodes when mother was out of the room and those when she returned. During mother's absence children in all four groups explored less than when she was present. The decrease was most marked in the older day-care children and least marked in the comparable group of home-care children. Furthermore, during mother's absence the older day-care children cried far more than did their home-care counterparts (who hardly cried at all) and more even than either group of younger children. When mother returned both younger and older day-care children

6. Blehar describes these as 'four private day nurseries in Baltimore. They followed a traditional nursery school regime and had been recommended as being of high quality, having staffs receptive to research, and serving primarily middle-class families. The child to adult ratio ranged between six and eight to one.' The nurseries were open from 7.30 a.m. to 5.30 p.m.

avoided her to a greater degree than did the home-care children, a form of behaviour, Blehar points out, that has been found in Ainsworth's studies to be characteristic of one-year-olds whose mothers were rated as relatively insensitive, unresponsive, and/or inaccessible during the infant's first year of life (see Chapter 21 of the present volume for details and references).

Behaviour towards the stranger also differed significantly between the day-care and the home-care children. At both ages day-care children avoided the stranger more than did their home-care counterparts. Furthermore, during the course of the test procedure, day-care children tended increasingly to avoid the stranger in contrast to the home-care children who became progressively more accepting of her. Such a finding is utterly at variance with the commonly expressed hope that day care will make a child more adaptable and independent.

There is, however, a finding from Moore's follow-up study (1971) that raises opposing considerations. This is that some of the children in his sample who had remained with mother until the age of five and had never attended nursery school or playgroup were apt in later years to be over-sensitive to criticism and timid with peers. This finding, if confirmed, supports the widely held view that, from about their third birthday, children benefit from play with peers within an ordered environment, and this especially when the alternative is confinement within limited living space in an urban environment, and in many cases with a rather controlling and possessive mother, as in Moore's sample.

Anxious attachment following threats of abandonment or suicide

Already in previous chapters reference is made to the effects on a child of being threatened by his parents that they will not love him or even will abandon him if he is not good. Clinical experience suggests that threats of these kinds, especially threats to abandon, including threats of suicide, play a far larger part in promoting anxious attachment than has usually been assigned to them.

Threats by parents that, if a child is not good, they will not love him any more have, of course, frequently been referred to as playing a part in the genesis of anxiety. In *Inhibitions, Symptoms and Anxiety* (1926a) Freud discusses them. Yet, although a threat of loss of love is far from being of negligible importance, the threat actually to abandon a child plainly carries immensely greater weight. Reference to such threats rarely appears in case reports, and suggestions in the literature that they play a significant, let alone a key, role are few and scattered. Nowhere do they seem to have been the subject of systematic study and discussion. The reason for their comparative neglect is almost certainly that parents are loath to talk about them.

A threat to abandon a child can be expressed in a variety of ways. One is that if a child is not good he will be sent away, for example, to a reformatory or to a school for bad boys, or that he will be taken off by a policeman. A second, made also in a disciplinary context, is that mother or father will go away and leave him. A third, which plays on the same anxiety, is that if a child is not good his mother or father will be made ill, or even die. A fourth, probably of great importance, is an impulsive angry threat to desert the family, made usually by a parent in a state of despair and coupled often with a threat to commit suicide. Finally, there is the anxiety engendered in a child when he overhears his parents quarrelling and fears, not unnaturally, that one or other of them is going to leave.

Evidence suggests that threats of these kinds, whether punitive or incidental, are not infrequent and that they almost always have an extremely frightening effect upon a child.

Let us start with threats that are used as part of disciplinary policy. The proportion of parents who use such threats no doubt varies greatly from culture to culture and subculture to subculture. In their study of 700 children and parents in Nottingham, Newson and Newson (1968) report that *no less than 27 per cent of all the parents interviewed admitted using threats of abandonment as a means of discipline*. The incidence was lowest in social classes I and II, the professional and managerial, in which it is reported as 10 per cent. In parents from the remaining social classes it is in the region of 30 per cent. The Newsons are particularly struck that white-collar workers of the shop and clerical groups should show an incidence (34 per cent) at least as high as skilled, semi-skilled, and unskilled manual workers, and perhaps higher.

Naturally enough, threats of these kinds can vary in the seriousness with which they are made and believed. Some are plainly no more than teasing. But probably to interviewers like the Newsons, who are inquiring about techniques of discipline, parents would hardly refer to such threats unless they used them seriously and believed in their efficacy. In any case the children concerned in the study were only four years old and to a young child a threat needs very little elaboration to be taken in deadly earnest. Nevertheless, some parents, intent on teaching their children a lesson, clothe their threats in impressive play-acting, as the following examples from the Newsons' records show.

In reply to inquiries regarding the techniques of discipline she employed with her four-year-old son, a packer's wife replied:

I used to threaten him with the Hartley Road Boys' Home, which isn't a Home any more; and since then, I haven't been able to do it; but I can always say I shall go down town and see about it, you know. And Ian says, 'Well, if I'm going with Stuart (7) it won't matter'; so I say, 'Well, you'll go to different ones – you'll go to one Home, and *you'll* go to another'. But it really got him worried, you know, and I really got him ready one day and I thought I'll take him a walk round, *as if* I was going, you know, and he really *was* worried. In fact, I had to bring him home, he started to cry. He saw I was in earnest about it – he *thought* I was, anyway. And now I've only got to threaten him. I say 'It won't take me long to get you ready'.

To the same question a miner's wife first denied using such threats to her small girl and then corrected herself:

No – oh, I tell a lie, I once did – and upset her that much that I've never said it any more. (What did you say?) Well, she was having an argument with me, and she says to me 'You don't live here! Hop it!' So I says, 'Oh, well, I can do that! Where's my coat? I'm moving!' So I got my coat from the back, and I was gone. I just stood outside the door, and she cried so bitter, she did. As soon as I came in, she got hold of my leg and wouldn't let go, sort of thing, I'll *never* say it no more.

Another miner's wife also had qualms about using such methods with a four-year-old:

I have said that if he makes me poorly when he's naughty I shall have to go away, and then he'll have no Mummy to look after him, and he'll have to live with someone else, I know that's all wrong, but I do. His Daddy'll say to him 'Pack his bags – get that bag out, and get his toys, he's going!' And he has one time put some of his clothes and toys *in* the bag; and it made him nearly demented – it upset me, but I didn't like to interfere, you see. And I asked him after, I said '*Don't* do that again, I don't like it, it'll make him feel unsafe, and he belongs here as much as we do. Find another way to punish him, I don't like him to think that.' I thought it was going *too* far.

In the last case, although mother drew the line at father's packing the child's bag, she was prepared to threaten that she might become ill and have to go away.

Since the most complete information about the use of threats to abandon a child comes from the Newsons' study conducted in England there may be danger that citizens of other countries will shrug off its findings. Any tendency to complacency is not encouraged by some, more limited, findings reported for parents in New England.

When interviewing some hundreds of mothers regarding their child-care practices, Sears, Maccoby and Levin (1957) found that such was the reluctance of mothers to acknowledge that they used threats to withdraw love or to abandon a child that information was inadequate in half their cases. In the other half, for which information was believed to be adequate, two out of every ten mothers were assessed as making considerable use of threats to withdraw love and/or to abandon the child, and a further three out of every ten as making moderate use of them. Taken together that makes half of all cases that could be assessed. Examples given in which five-year-old children are described by mothers as becoming 'hysterical' or as weeping 'a rain of tears' when threatened with being sent away from home – e.g. back to the hospital where he was born – differ in no way from those reported by the Newsons.

The fact that in a representative sample of lower-middle- and working-class homes in midland Britain today 30 per cent of mothers admit to using threats of abandonment, and another 12 per cent to threatening that they won't love a child any more if he is naughty (and that New England figures appear comparable), may come as a surprise to those brought up in professional-class homes in which such threats are much less common.[7] Yet, once the frequency and effects of such threats are firmly grasped, a great many cases of separation anxiety and anxious attachment that otherwise appear inexplicable become intelligible. Furthermore, it becomes easy to understand why so many children who have to go to hospital or residential nursery should suppose that they are being sent there as a punishment.

It is of course true that a majority of parents do not threaten to abandon their children and, as the Newsons found, refrain from doing so as a matter of principle. As a publican's wife remarked: 'It takes the child's security away. You're the whole of their security, and you must not take that away.' Yet the Newsons also came across mothers who, though sure that such threats were wrong, admitted that none the less they occasionally used them when they were upset.

Such shamefaced admissions by parents may well include the most frightening threats of all. There is certainly a minority of parents who, in fits of exasperation and temper, say the most horrifying things which they later greatly regret. Threats to abandon the home and/or to commit suicide, made perhaps only at rare intervals but with an angry vehemence, are likely to have an effect entirely out of proportion to their frequency. Their effect, moreover, is magnified should the parent, father or mother, subsequently be so ashamed of having made such a threat that he or she cannot acknowledge either what was said or how frightening it must have been to the child. In such families the child has no opportunity to check his inevitable fears against the real risks, whatever they may be.

Furthermore, when families of this sort reach a psychiatric clinic, there is small likelihood that the true facts will be divulged. It is then very easy to attribute the child's fears either to his own guilty phantasies or to his having projected onto others his own

7. Nevertheless, sanctions of professional ostracism to coerce younger and weaker members of a profession to accept the theories held by their seniors are not unknown.

guilty wishes. Long familiarity with how easy it is even for experienced clinicians to be misled in such cases suggests that, whenever a child or adult is inexplicably afraid, it is always wise to assume that there is no smoke without fire.

Since the way a parent treats a child is usually modelled on the way his (or her) parents treated him (or her) as a child, it is almost inevitable that the use of such threats should run in families. This was made dramatically clear during the treatment of an acutely anxious and depressed mother and her young son.

An Illustrative Case

Mrs Q and her son, Stephen, were referred originally when Stephen was eighteen months old, because he refused to eat and was seriously underweight. It was soon apparent that Mrs Q was in a chronic state of anxiety and depression which had begun at the time of Stephen's birth. Mrs Q was taken into once-a-week analytically oriented treatment and made good progress. Once Stephen's mother was able to refrain from constantly pressing him to eat, Stephen began to do so, and after a month or two was putting on weight satisfactorily.

In view of the severity of Mrs Q's condition, she remained in once-a-week treatment for some years. Her father was a skilled artisan, now retired, and her husband a ticket collector on the railway. She herself was an intelligent woman who had had to leave school early in order to earn but who had later become a successful technician. The account she gave of her childhood was lucid and consistent, though for many months, indeed years, she had the utmost difficulty in divulging its more distressing and frightening aspects.

Pieced together the following picture emerged. Mrs Q's father had fought in the 1914–18 war and had been invalided on account of 'shell shock'. His neurosis appeared to have developed after his section had been blown up on a bridge, leaving him the sole survivor. Thereafter, he had been subject to long phases of depression and ill temper during which he could treat his family very badly. Mrs Q's mother was an active capable woman of strong opinions, whose own mother had been a chronic alcoholic for many years. Throughout Mrs Q's childhood her parents had

had violent quarrels, during which dreadful things were not only said but often done. Crockery was smashed, knives drawn, and furniture set alight. Mrs Q recalled long sleepless nights listening to the battles and dreading the outcome. Yet by breakfast next morning all was quiet. Putting all the horrors of the night behind her, Mrs Q's mother went out to her daily domestic work the picture of peaceful respectability. On no account was any of the trouble at home to be divulged to outsiders; and it was deeply impressed on Mrs Q that she must whisper it to no one – neighbours, teachers, or schoolfriends. This explained why she hid its full horror from her therapist for so long.

There were a number of occasions when Mrs Q's mother had attempted suicide, and many more when she had threatened it. Twice Mrs Q had returned home to find her mother with her head in the gas oven and once she had found her collapsed after having drunk household disinfectant. Not infrequently her mother, after having threatened to desert the family or to commit suicide, would disappear. On some occasions she would leave the house and not return until after midnight. On others she would hide, perhaps in a cupboard. In view of all this it is hardly surprising that Mrs Q grew up an acutely anxious girl, constantly afraid to go far from home, and that she experienced spasms of violent anger.[8]

Although it seemed evident that the anger was aroused by her parents', mainly her mother's, violent behaviour, Mrs Q during treatment found it very difficult to accept this possibility. Instead, she claimed for a long while not only that her feelings for her mother were of love, which was true since her mother had many good qualities, but that that must exclude hatred. But, as she gained confidence, Mrs Q recalled how, as a child, after a bad row with her mother, she would sometimes go to her room and wreak violence on her dolls, throwing them at the walls and trampling them underfoot.

8. In her relationships both with her mother and with her son Mrs Q showed all the features found by Melges (1968) to be typical in cases of postpartum disturbance. They include intense conflict with own mother, and repudiation of own mother as someone to be imitated, together with a strong tendency nevertheless to behave like her.

It was in this context that Mrs Q's problems with Stephen became intelligible. After Stephen's birth, Mrs Q had experienced strong impulses to throw the baby out of the window and, not unexpectedly, had become acutely anxious lest Stephen should die. Her frantic and ineffective efforts to make him eat were a direct result. It seemed evident that Mrs Q's hostility, still often aroused by her mother, had become redirected (displaced) towards Stephen. Even during the period of treatment, Mrs Q admitted shamefacedly, she still had occasional outbursts of violence, when crockery was smashed, saucepans dented, and Stephen's pram damaged. It was not always clear what precipitated these outbursts because Mrs Q was eager to forget about them as soon as possible and for long she hardly referred to them during treatment.

When Stephen was seven and a half Mrs Q reported that he sometimes expressed fear that she might die, and was afraid to go to school. For some months the origin of this fear remained obscure. Then the solution became clear. Having herself grown up in such deeply distressing circumstances, Mrs Q had been determined that her own son should fare better. She had therefore done everything she could to make Stephen's life secure and happy, and had in many respects succeeded. Yet, during her outbursts of violence, her good resolutions vanished. On those occasions, she now admitted, she said the most dreadful things, the very same things, in fact, that her mother had said to her when she was a girl. Stephen's fear that his mother might die was a direct reflection of his mother's threats of suicide, made during comparatively rare outbursts but with an intensity that might alarm anyone.

Once the facts were known it was possible to arrange some joint sessions with mother and son during which mother, with real regret, acknowledged making the threats and Stephen explained how terrified they made him. Mother assured Stephen that she would never do it really. All was not well thereafter, but recognition that Stephen's fears were well based and an opening of communication between mother and son eased the situation.

There can be little doubt that great numbers of parents are extremely reluctant to admit to a professional person that they sometimes threaten their child in the ways described. Many are aware that it is a bad thing to do and are ashamed of it. Others may themselves have mixed feelings about it, but are aware that professional people would disapprove. For these reasons it is probable that parents hardly ever volunteer the information and, until they have gained much confidence, are likely to deny it if questioned. Children, moreover, habitually take their cue from their parents and are similarly reluctant to divulge the truth. Even when she was in her mid-thirties, Mrs Q was still intent on protecting her mother's reputation. Not only is a child afraid of what a parent might say and do should he discover that the child had 'split' on him, but children are deeply reluctant to admit even to themselves that their own mother or their own father can behave in these frightening ways. Thus children are often willing conspirators in silence, even though simultaneously they may be yearning for someone to come to their aid.

Incidence of 'Attempted' Suicide by Parents

The incidence of completed suicide among parents of children under the age of eighteen years is low because most suicides occur in the older age-groups. By contrast, the incidence of so-called 'attempted' suicide among parents in this category is relatively high because such acts occur most frequently in both sexes between the ages of twenty and thirty years. Since most attempts are not intended to end in death but to frighten or coerce others, the term is placed in quotation marks in the heading of this section.[9]

Figures for attempted suicide in the city of Edinburgh are available for the past decade, and from them a number of rough estimates can be made.[10] For all women between the ages of

9. To deal with the difficulty Kreitman and his colleagues (1969) have proposed 'parasuicide'; but Walk (1972) has raised serious etymological objections.

10. I am indebted to Norman Kreitman, Director of the MRC Unit for Epidemiological Studies in Psychiatry, for making some recent figures available. Owing to rising rates and for other reasons, the estimates given for mothers and fathers over a twenty-year period are extremely rough. They have been calculated by me, and are given on my sole responsibility, in order to show the order of magnitude of the problem.

fifteen and thirty-four years there was an average annual incidence of attempted suicide of about 0·3 per cent and there is reason to think that this figure holds for women with children as well as for those without. Over a twenty-year period, during which children are being born and are reaching mature years, it can be estimated that about 4 per cent of mothers will have attempted suicide and, of these, one-third will have done so more than once. The incidence for men is lower and seems likely, over a similar twenty-year period, to amount to between 2 and 2·5 per cent. Even allowing for the possibility that in some families both mother and father will have attempted suicide, it seems that not less than one in twenty of all children growing up in Edinburgh during recent years will have had experience of a suicidal attempt by a parent. For most children the attempt will have occurred before they have reached their tenth birthday.

The incidence of attempted suicide is not spread evenly throughout a population, so that in some sectors the rate, with age and sex held constant, may be several times what it is in others. Whereas the incidence in socio-economic classes I, II, and III is below average for the population of Edinburgh, that for class V is much above. Children growing up in certain subcultural groups are therefore at high risk of being exposed to the suicidal attempts of their parents. There is evidence also that in certain family networks a very high rate of attempted suicide may be due to its having become a recognizable mode of social communication. Women below the age of thirty-five years seem especially likely to be influenced by such family patterns (Kreitman, Smith and Tan 1970).

Since no figures appear to be available to indicate the incidence of *threats* to commit suicide, we can only speculate. Presumably very many children who are exposed to suicidal attempts by a parent are exposed also to threats. Mrs Q is a case in point. In addition, there must be many others who, like Stephen Q, are exposed to threats but not to attempts. All in all the proportion of children who are exposed to threats or attempts, or to both, must be considerable. Both clinical experience and common sense suggest not only that such people will be more than usually prone to anxiety about the availability of attachment figures while they are still children but that they will often continue so long after they are grown up.

What is so surprising is that, as a source of heightened susceptibility to anxiety, threats of and attempts at suicide by parents should have attracted so little attention, whether from psychoanalysts, psychiatrists, or those engaged in child psychiatry.

Fear of Parental Desertion after a Quarrel

When parents quarrel seriously a risk that one or other will desert is always there. Not infrequently, moreover, it is made explicit. In such conditions children usually hear a great deal more than parents like to believe. Although, therefore, the kind of situation that leads a child to fear abandonment is different from one in which threats to abandon him are directed punitively at him, the effects may still be very unsettling.

Here again it is not unusual for professional workers whom parents may consult about their child's behaviour to be kept in the dark about what is happening at home, and for such workers, ignorant of the true situation, to resort to 'deep' interpretations invoking projection and the inner world to explain a child's symptoms. During the practice of child and family psychiatry and also in work with adolescents and adults it is prudent always to assume that only after some months of work, including joint family interviews, are we likely to have obtained even a reasonably accurate picture of how members of a family behave towards one another and what they say. When after much patience the facts become known, it is usually far less difficult to understand how a child has come to be disturbed and why he fears whatever he does.

Earlier in this chapter it was pointed out that, in studies of the effects on a child of separation, the factors that lead the effects to persist in one child and not to do so in another have in the past been difficult to identify. Review of evidence available today suggests that we may be nearer a solution. We can indeed be confident that when a child is threatened with being abandoned by his parents, either as a disciplinary measure or because of marital discord, the effects on him of any actual separation will not only be magnified but be likely to persist.

Individual Differences in Susceptibility to Fear

When the high incidence of such threats in the lives of children is borne in mind, along with the cumulative effects of actual separations, of threats of separation, of unstable substitute care, and of unstable family life, the fact that many children grow up to be anxiously attached becomes explicable. In the light of these findings, moreover, a number of clinical syndromes can be better understood (see Chapters 18 and 19).

Chapter 16
'Overdependency' and the Theory of Spoiling

The child is all the more clinging the more it has an inner conviction that separation will repeat itself.
— BURLINGHAM AND FREUD (1944)

Some contrasting theories

Following presentation of some of the evidence on which the theoretical position adopted here is based, it is useful to consider briefly the whole array of hypotheses that have been proposed to account for why a particular individual is prone to a high degree of overdependency or separation anxiety, the terms by which anxious attachment is usually known. Hypotheses advanced by psychoanalysts and others working in a psychoanalytic tradition not only give varying weight to constitutional and environmental factors but also inculpate different and in some respects contradictory factors in each class. The five main hypotheses, each of which has adherents, are outlined briefly below.

Two lay emphasis on *constitutional* factors, as follows:

1. Some children have inherently a greater amount of libidinal need in their constitution than others, and so are more sensitive than others to an absence of gratification (Freud 1917b).

2. Some children have inherently a stronger death instinct than others, which manifests itself in unusually strong persecutory and depressive anxiety (Klein 1932).

Three lay emphasis on *environmental* factors:

3. Variations in the birth process and severe traumata occurring during the first weeks of postnatal life may increase the (organic) anxiety response and heighten the anxiety potential, thereby causing a more severe reaction to later (psychological) dangers met with in life (Greenacre 1941; 1945).

4. Some children are 'spoiled' by excess of early libidinal gratification; they therefore demand more of it and, when not gratified, miss it more (Freud 1905b; 1917b; 1926a).

5. Some children are made excessively sensitive to the possibility of separation or loss of love through experiencing either actual separation (Edelston 1943; Bowlby 1951) or threats of abandonment or loss of love (Suttie 1935; Fairbairn 1941).

It should be noted that whereas hypotheses 1, 4, and 5 are framed to account for a person's liability to a high degree of anxiety about separation in particular, hypotheses 2 and 3 are intended to account for liability to a high degree of anxiety of any kind.

In regard to the first two of these hypotheses there is no evidence either to support or to refute them since, with present research techniques, there is no way of determining differences of these kinds in constitutional endowment. That heritable differences play some part in determining why some people grow up to be more anxious than others is not unlikely; but whether either Freud's or Klein's formulation of the nature of the difference will prove useful seems doubtful.

Clear evidence in support of a hypothesis of the third type comes from the work of Ucko (1965) who found that children suffering from neonatal asphyxia are unusually prone to respond to separations and other changes of environment with anxiety. Her findings are described in Chapter 13. While supporting the third hypothesis, they do not conflict with either of the remaining hypotheses.

The fourth and fifth hypotheses, because they raise immediate and practical issues of how to treat children, are perhaps the most controversial of the set, and particularly so since the lessons they hold for how to rear children are of exactly opposite kinds.

The fourth hypothesis, that an excess of parental affection spoils a child by making him exceptionally demanding and intolerant of frustration, is one that was very widely held during the first half of this century and that still dies hard. Freud not only committed himself to it at an early stage of his work but held to it firmly and consistently until the end. Since this view of Freud's has had a deep and lasting influence on psychoanalytic theory and practice, quotations may be useful.

Freud's first reference to spoiling is in his *Three Essays on the*

Theory of Sexuality, first published in 1905. There, after commending the mother who strokes, rocks, and kisses her child and thereby teaches him to love, he nevertheless warns against excess: '... an excess of parental affection does harm by causing precocious sexual maturity and also because, by spoiling the child, it makes him incapable in later life of temporarily doing without love or of being content with a smaller amount of it' (*SE* 7: 223). The same theme runs through much of Freud's theorizing about 'Little Hans' (1909); though, paradoxically, it is in his discussion of this small boy's separation anxiety that he comes nearest the view adopted here. He attributes part of the anxiety to the fact that Little Hans had been separated from his mother at the time of his baby sister's birth (*SE* 10: 114 and 132). Nevertheless, both in the *Introductory Lectures* (1917b, *SE* 16: 408) and in his late work, *Inhibitions, Symptoms and Anxiety* (1926a), Freud makes no reference to such origins and instead explicitly adopts the theory of spoiling:

The undesirable result of 'spoiling' a small child is to magnify the importance of the danger of losing the object (the object being a protection against every situation of helplessness) in comparison with every other danger. It therefore encourages the individual to remain in the state of childhood ... (*SE* 20: 167).

The theoretical context within which Freud advanced these views is referred to in an earlier chapter (Chapter 5) and described rather more fully in Appendix I.

Despite its wide popularity, no evidence of substance has ever been presented to support the theory that anxious attachment is a result of an excess of parental affection. As already indicated, all the evidence points the other way, a conclusion reached also by Maccoby and Masters (1970) in their definitive review. The same holds for other primates (Jolly 1972). The question arises, therefore, why Freud (and many others[1] also) should have favoured

1. In a recent work Anna Freud (1972), in considering the origins of intensified separation anxiety in later years, gives weight to an infant's experience of a mother who proves unreliable as a stable figure, including actual separations from her. Yet she also states her continuing belief that 'excessive gratification in the anaclitic phase' can have similar consequences.

the theory. Possible answers are offered at the end of the chapter. Meanwhile, let us consider further the fifth type of theory, the one favoured here.

However cogent the evidence may be that some cases of anxious attachment are a consequence of separation, or of threats of being abandoned, or of risks of losing a parent inherent when parents quarrel, it is still possible that not all cases are to be explained in this way. Are there perhaps other cases that arise from causes other than those so far considered? To answer this question it is necessary to turn to the results of studies conceived on different lines from the studies discussed so far.

Studies of 'overdependency' and its antecedents

Despite very frequent references to overdependency in the clinical literature there seem to be few studies in which a clinician has selected a sample of adult patients on the criterion of over-dependency and then examined the family experiences these individuals have had during their childhood and compared them with the experiences of an appropriately selected contrast group. Some of the literature on agoraphobia is in fact relevant (see Chapter 19) although the criterion for patient selection, namely fear of leaving home without a companion, is ostensibly quite different.

Studies of the family backgrounds of children selected as being overdependent are also few in number. With regard to these, moreover, a difficulty that has to be borne in mind is the ambiguity of the term overdependent, for it is found to cover two distinct conditions. One comprises children who are exhibiting typically anxious attachment. The other comprises children who are less able than are others of their age to do ordinary little tasks, such as feeding or dressing, for themselves and, instead, ask mother to do them for them.

This distinction emerges clearly in a study undertaken by Stendler (1954). A group of twenty six-year-old children, selected by teachers as being markedly overdependent, was found to fall into two subgroups. On the one hand were six children who turned to mother to do everything for them. On the other was a group of fourteen who had no difficulty in doing things for themselves but who were upset by mother's absence and created a scene whenever she went out and left them behind. Not unexpectedly, the family experiences of these two subgroups were radically different.

The six children who constantly turned to mother for help came from stable homes. All six, however, had a mother who was excessively protective and tended to discourage her child from learning to do things for himself.

Of the fourteen children who were anxiously attached eleven had had a very unsettled home life. Changes of caretaker, from mother to grandmother and back again, father constantly coming or going, frequent shifts of residence, and similar instability had been the rule. For the fourteen anxiously attached children taken as a group, the total number of such discontinuities that had occurred during the period between nine months of age and the third birthday was fifty-two, an average of nearly four apiece. For a control group of twenty children, picked from the same school classes, the equivalent total was twenty-six, giving an average of 1·3 apiece.

So far as they go, therefore, the results of this small study are consistent with the view that most, if not all, cases of anxious attachment can be understood as being the consequence of a series of separations and similar experiences. A much larger study, by McCord and others (1962), gives strong support to this type of hypothesis.

In their study McCord and his colleagues draw on the detailed case records of some 255 boys aged between nine and seventeen years who constituted the 'treatment group' of the Cambridge–Somerville project. All lived in a high-density industrial area and were mainly from the working classes. Half of these boys had been selected, when between the ages of nine and thirteen, by teachers and others in the community as potential delinquents. The other half were selected similarly as developing in a relatively normal way. All these boys and their families were then given such support and help as could be arranged in order to see whether delinquent development could be averted. Since supportive work continued for five years, a great deal of information was amassed both about the boys themselves and about their families.[2] Some years later the information was rated by independent raters who had taken no part in the study. For purposes of this analysis a sub-sample, of forty-three boys, was identified as showing 'overdependent behaviour' and another, of 105 boys, as showing, in this respect, the normal culturally expected pattern of development.

Three-quarters of the overdependent boys showed markedly dependent behaviour towards adults and can almost certainly be regarded as anxiously attached. A minority (eleven) showed dependent behaviour only towards peers and were rather remote from adults; it is an open question whether that behaviour can be regarded as anxious attachment. In the presentation of the results, however, findings for the majority are not distinguished from those for the minority.

When compared with the control group, the overdependent boys were found to be more likely to express feelings of inferiority (51 per cent against 12 per cent) and to be more prone to 'abnormal fears' (56 per cent against 36 per cent), though unfortunately details of the fears are not specified.

When the family backgrounds and attitudes of parents of boys in the two groups were compared a set of highly consistent findings was obtained. Nearly twice as many of the dependent boys as of the controls were rated as being rejected by father (51 per cent compared with 28 per cent) and/or by mother (39·5 per cent and 20 per cent). No less than 56 per cent of the dependent boys were found constantly to be compared unfavourably with their siblings; that proportion compares with only 17 per cent of the controls. No data on separations and losses are given. Quarrels between parents and mutual disparagement were reported for almost every home in the overdependent sub-sample; though it must be admitted that in this working-class neighbourhood a fairly high incidence of such happenings is reported also in the families of the controls. Not unexpectedly, the feelings expressed by some of these overdependent boys towards their mothers were the reverse

2. Included in the study also were a comparable pair of samples who were not given support. Because little information on them and their families became available these cases cannot be used for the present analysis.

of warm: one-third of them expressed active dislike, or fear, or contempt of her.

Such other evidence as is available on conditions associated with overdependency, or anxious attachment, is consistent with the findings so far considered. For example, in the previous chapter reference is made to two studies that focus attention on parental behaviour when the children are four or five years old and describe the variety and incidence of different methods of child care used in a particular community; these are the studies by Newson and Newson (1968) of families in the English midlands and by Sears, Maccoby and Levin (1957) of families in New England. Although in neither study are the effects on the children of different family experiences at the centre of interest, each presents some data relevant to our problem.

The Newsons' findings on overdependency are given in the previous chapter (pp. 248-9). Most of the children who at four years of age were afraid of separation were found to have experienced a separation: either they or their mothers had been hospitalized, or some other separation had taken place.

Sears, Maccoby and Levin (1957) report the results of interviewing 379 mothers of five-year-old children attending kindergarten in the suburbs of a large metropolitan area in New England. Among the questions they asked about the children were four designed to give information about 'dependency'. No evidence was found that separations had played any part in the development of those children who, on the basis of mothers' reports, were assessed as most dependent; but the authors point out that the incidence of separation in the sample was very low.

The principal finding of Sears's study in regard to dependency is that the more irritable, scolding, and impatient a mother was when her child was clinging or desirous of attention the more 'dependent' he was likely to be. This significant correlation is appreciably increased in the case of mothers who were initially rejecting but later gave in. The researchers also found a significant correlation between a high degree of dependency and parents who used withdrawal of love as a disciplinary measure, including threats to abandon a child. These findings are consistent with the present hypothesis.

Another of their findings, however, could be taken to support the theory of spoiling. A small group of mothers were assessed as being 'exceptionally demonstrative' of affection, and these were more likely than others to have children rated as 'quite dependent'; the correlation is low but significant.

An explanation of this finding that seems not unlikely is that the children assessed by the researchers as overdependent fell, like Stendler's, into two groups, those who showed anxious attachment and those who looked to mother to do everything for them. If this was so and if Stendler's findings were confirmed, then a number of the mothers assessed by Sears and his colleagues as exceptionally demonstrative would have been found to be not only affectionate but inclined also to discourage their child from doing things for himself.

Further and substantial evidence that strongly supports the hypothesis favoured here, and equally strongly challenges the theory of spoiling, comes from studies of the family backgrounds of children, adolescents, and young adults who, relative to their age, are growing up confident and self-reliant. This is presented in the penultimate chapter.

How came it, then, that Freud should have adopted the theory of spoiling? Apart from the likelihood that he was more influenced than he realized by the accepted opinion of his day, there is some evidence that he was misled by the show of affection and over-protection that is so frequently present either as an over-compensation for a parent's unconscious hostility to a child or as part of the parent's own desire to cling to the child. This explanation is suggested by a passage in *Three Essays*, immediately following that quoted earlier, in which he refers to 'neuropathic parents, who are inclined as a rule to display excessive affection, [as] precisely those who are most likely by their caresses to arouse the child's disposition to neurotic illness' (*SE* 7: 223). In fact, when such cases are investigated in a psychoanalytically oriented family clinic, it is found, probably invariably, that the child's heightened anxiety over separation and loss of love is a reaction not to any real 'excess of parental affection' but to experiences of an almost opposite kind. On the one hand are threats by a parent either to withdraw love or to abandon the child, threats that, as already discussed, are apt to be kept very secret. On the other are cases in which a parent demands, either overtly or covertly, that the child act as a caretaker to him (or her), thereby inverting the normal parent–child roles. In such cases it is the parent, not the child, who is overdependent or, to use the better term, anxiously attached. These cases are discussed in Chapters 18 and 19.

To some it may seem a trifle absurd to go to such lengths to demonstrate that uncertainty regarding the availability of an attachment figure commonly results in anxious attachment. Yet, so long as terms such as 'overdependent' and 'spoiled' are in use to describe the individuals in question and a theory is current that attributes their condition to an excess of gratification during their early years, children and especially adults who manifest this type of behaviour will meet with scant sympathy or understanding. Once it is recognized that the condition is one of anxiety over the accessibility and responsiveness of attachment figures, and that it develops as a result of bitter experience, there is good prospect not only of helping those who have grown up insecure but of preventing others from doing so.

Chapter 17
Anger, Anxiety, and Attachment

Anger: a response to separation

Time and again in preceding chapters reference is made to the anger that is engendered towards a parent figure by a separation or a threat of separation. It is time now to consider this response more systematically and in particular how it is related to attachment and fear.

In the first chapter an account is given of the systematic study by Heinicke and Westheimer (1966) of ten children aged from thirteen to thirty-two months during and after a stay of two or more weeks in a residential nursery. When comparisons were made between the separated children and a contrast group of children who remained in their own homes the increased tendency of the separated children to respond aggressively was clear. For example, during their stay in the nursery a doll-play test was administered to the separated children on at least two occasions, at an interval of eight days; and the same tests were administered to the children in the contrast group at the same interval at home. On each occasion episodes of hostile behaviour occurred four times as frequently in the doll play of the separated children as they did in the play of the children living at home. Objects attacked tended to be the parent dolls. Of the separated children eight attacked a doll that had already been identified by the child as a mother or father doll; none of the children living at home did so.

Six weeks after the separated children had returned home, and after an equivalent period for the non-separated children, doll-play tests were again administered; and they were repeated ten weeks later. On neither of these occasions, however, were significant differences in hostility found between the children in the two groups. The reason for this was that, six weeks and more after reunion, the children who had been separated were no longer particularly aggressive in their play, a change for the better that was itself significant.

Nevertheless, it was apparent from mothers' reports that during the months after return home a number of the separated children were still behaving hostilely in the home, especially towards mother. During the period from the second to the twentieth week after reunion six of the ten separated children behaved towards mother with an intensity of ambivalence reported for none of the children who had remained in their own homes.

Other observers to have reported notably aggressive and/or destructive behaviour *during* a period of separation are Burlingham and Freud (1944), Robertson (1958b), Bowlby (1953), Ainsworth and Boston (1952), and also Heinicke in an earlier study (1956) in which he compared the behaviour of a small sample of children during a short stay in a residential nursery with that of a similar group starting to attend a day nursery.

Others to have noted intensely ambivalent behaviour *after* a child has returned home include Robertson (1958b), Robertson and Robertson (1971), and Moore (1969b; 1971).

Anger: functional and dysfunctional

Although sometimes the aggressive behaviour of a child who has experienced a separation appears to be directed towards all and sundry, often, as in the doll-play sessions mentioned above, it is plainly directed towards a parent or parent-substitute and is an expression of anger at the way he has been treated. Sometimes it is the anger of hope; sometimes the anger of despair.

On occasion a child's hostility to a parent takes the form of a reproach for his having been absent when wanted. For example, Robertson (1952) describes the angry reproaches of Laura, a child of two years and four months whom he had filmed during an eight-day stay in hospital for a minor operation. Some months after her return home Robertson was showing an early version of his film to her parents for their comments, while Laura was in bed believed asleep. As it happened, she awoke, crept into the room and witnessed the last few minutes of the film, in which she is seen on the day of her return from hospital, at first distressed and calling for her mother, later when her shoes are produced delighted at the prospect of going home and finally departing from hospital with her mother. The film over and the lights switched up, Laura turned away from her mother to be picked up by her father. Then, looking reproachfully at her mother, she demanded 'Where *was* you, Mummy? Where *was* you?' Similarly, Wolfenstein (1957), in her study of responses to disaster, relates how a small girl who had been apart from her father during a tornado, when reunited with him afterwards, hit him angrily and reproached him for having been away from her.

Both these little girls seemed to be acting on the assumption that parents should not be absent when their child is frightened and wants them there, and were hopeful that a forceful reminder would ensure that they would not err again.

In other cases a child's anger is the anger of despair. For example, in Chapter 1 there is a description (quoted from Burlingham and Freud 1944) of Reggie who was being cared for in the Hampstead Nurseries and who, by the age of two and a half years, had already had a number of mother figures. Then, two months later, the nurse to whom he was attached left to get married. Not only was Reggie 'lost and desperate' after her departure, but he refused to look at her when she visited him a fortnight later. During the evening after she had left he was heard to remark: 'My very own Mary-Ann! But I don't like her.'

In the case of Reggie we are dealing with a response, not to a single temporary separation, but to repeated prolonged separations each of which amounts to a loss. Although loss is the topic of our third volume, it is useful at this point to trespass briefly across the boundary.

In several papers (e.g. Bowlby 1960b; 1961b; 1963), the present writer has drawn attention to the frequency with which anger is aroused after a loss, not only in children but in adults also, and has raised the question of what its biological function might be. The answer proposed is that whenever separation is only temporary, which in the large majority of cases it is, anger has the following two functions: first, it may assist in overcoming such obstacles as there may be to reunion; second, it may discourage the loved person from going away again.

Whenever loss is permanent, as it is after a bereavement, anger and aggressive behaviour are necessarily without function. The reason that they occur so often none the less, even after a death, is that during the early phases of grieving a bereaved person usually does not believe that the loss can really be permanent; he therefore continues to act as though it were still possible not only to find and recover the lost person but to reproach him for his actions. For the lost person is not infrequently held to be at least in part responsible for what has happened, in fact to have deserted. As a result, anger comes to be directed against the lost person, as well as, of course, against any others thought to have played a part in the loss or in some way to be obstructing reunion.

Further research on responses to bereavement supports this line of reasoning. In her study of the responses of children and adolescents to the death of a parent, Wolfenstein (1969) confirms that anger is extremely common, certainly in disturbed children, and endorses the view that it is linked to strong hopes of recovering the lost parent. Parkes (1970) likewise in his study of the responses of widows to loss of husband finds anger to be common, though not universal. He also sees it as part of the bereaved's attempts to recover the lost person.

Thus, whenever a separation has proved to be temporary, and also whenever it is believed that a separation now in train will prove only temporary, anger with the absent figure is common. In its functional form anger is expressed as reproachful and punishing behaviour that has as its set-goals assisting a reunion and discouraging further separation. Therefore, although expressed towards the partner, such anger acts to promote, and not to disrupt, the bond.

Angry coercive behaviour, acting in the service of an affectional bond, is not uncommon. It is seen when a mother, whose child has run foolishly across the road, berates and punishes him with an anger born of fear. It is seen whenever a sexual partner berates the other for being or seeming to be disloyal. It is seen, again, in some families when a member becomes angry whenever his approaches to another member are met by an unresponsive silence (Heard 1973). It occurs also in non-human primates. For example, when he sights a predator a dominant male baboon may behave aggressively towards any wandering members of his own group who may be at risk. Frightened thereby, their attachment behaviour is aroused and they quickly come closer to him, so obtaining the protection inherent in proximity (Hall and DeVore 1965).

Dysfunctional Anger

Angry behaviour that has coercion as its function and is compatible with a close tie has tended to be neglected by clinicians. Very probably this is because it can so readily become dysfunctional and it is the dysfunctional forms that are usually met with clinically.

Dysfunctional anger occurs whenever a person, child or adult, becomes so intensely and/or persistently angry with his partner that the bond between them is weakened, instead of strengthened, and the partner is alienated. Anger with a partner becomes dysfunctional also whenever aggressive thoughts or acts cross the narrow boundary between being deterrent and being revengeful. It is at this point, too, that feeling ceases to be the 'hot displeasure' of anger and may become, instead, the 'malice' of hatred.[1]

Clinical experience suggests that the situations of separation and loss with which this work is concerned are especially liable to result in anger with an attachment figure that crosses the threshold of intensity and becomes dysfunctional. Separations, especially when prolonged or repeated, have a double effect. On the one hand, anger is aroused; on the other, love is attenuated. Thus not only may angry discontented behaviour alienate the attachment figure but, within the attached, a shift can occur in the balance of feeling. Instead of a strongly rooted affection laced occasionally with 'hot displeasure', such as develops in a child brought up by affectionate parents, there grows a deep-running resentment, held in check only partially by an anxious uncertain affection.

The most violently angry and dysfunctional responses of all, it seems probable, are elicited in children and adolescents who not only experience repeated separations but are constantly subjected to the threat of being abandoned. In Chapter 15 descriptions are given of the intense distress produced in young children

1. Definitions given in the *Oxford English Dictionary.*

by such threats, especially when the threats are given a cloak of verisimilitude. During the treatment of Mrs Q it seemed that nothing had caused her greater pain and distress than her mother's realistic threats either to abandon the family or to commit suicide. From experiencing such intense pain it is only a short step to feeling furiously angry with the person who inflicts it. It was in this light that the intensity of anger that Mrs Q felt at times towards her mother seemed most readily understood.

A similar conclusion was reached some years ago by Stott (1950), a British psychologist who lived for four years in an approved school studying the personalities and home backgrounds of 102 youths aged fifteen to eighteen years who had been sent there because of repeated offences. The information he gathered was derived from long interviews with the boys themselves and with their parents, and also from many informal contacts he had with the boys during their stay in the school. The boys, he found, were deeply insecure and their delinquencies in many cases seemed to have been acts of bravado. Adverse parental attitudes and disrupted relationships were found to have been common, as is usual in such studies, and were thought to account for much of the boys' sense of insecurity. Nevertheless, what impressed Stott more than anything else was evidence that in many cases mother, and in a few cases father, had used threats to desert as a means of discipline and how intensely anxious and angry these threats had made the boys. Although Stott gives particulars of some typical cases, he expresses himself reluctant to give numbers, partly because it was only late in the inquiry that he realized how immensely important such threats probably are and partly because there were a number of cases in which he felt fairly confident that threats had played an important role despite the fact that their use in these cases had been strenuously denied by both boy and parents.

Stott draws attention to the combination of intense anxiety and intense conflict inevitably aroused by threats of this kind. For, while on the one hand a child is made furiously angry by a parent's threat to desert, on the other he dare not express that anger in case it makes the parent actually do so. This is a main reason, Stott suggests, why in these cases anger at a parent usually becomes repressed and is then directed at other targets. It is a reason also why a child or adolescent who is terrified of being deserted tends instead to complain of being afraid of something else, perhaps of the dark or of thunder or of an accident. In the next two chapters a shift of exactly this kind as regards the situation allegedly feared is held to explain the symptomatology of a large proportion of patients at present diagnosed as phobic.

It seems not unlikely that a number of individuals who become literally murderous towards a parent are to be understood as having become so in reaction to threats of desertion that have been repeated relentlessly over many years. For example, in an early paper that calls attention to the traumatic effects of separation, Kestenberg (1943) describes a girl of thirteen who had been deserted by her parents and who had been cared for by a succession of other people. She trusted no one and responded to any disappointment by some vengeful action. During the course of treatment this girl pictured herself as grown up and so able to revenge herself on her mother by killing her. Many analysts who have treated patients with this type of background could give similar examples.

In another paper that also relates anger to separation, Burnham (1965) makes brief reference to two patients who actually engaged in matricide. One, an adolescent who murdered his mother, exclaimed afterwards 'I couldn't stand to have her leave me'. Another, a youth who placed a bomb in his mother's luggage as she boarded an airliner, explained 'I decided that she would never leave me again'. The hypothesis proposed makes these statements less paradoxical than they appear.

These admittedly are no more than clinical anecdotes, and no adequate history of previous family relationships is given for any case. Furthermore, so far as is known, no researcher since Stott has made a systematic study to test a possible causal link between violent anger directed towards an attachment figure and a history of being subjected by that figure to repeated threats of being abandoned. At present, therefore, the suggested link is hardly more than a conjecture; but as a lead for research it seems promising.

A Test for Appraising Responses to Separation

Psychoanalysts and others who adopt an object-relations approach have for many years regarded the balance of a person's disposition to love, to become angry with, and to hate his attachment figure as a principal criterion in making a clinical assessment. In recent years Hansburg (1972), by taking as his starting-point certain measures of how a person responds to separation, has begun to put this onto a more systematic footing.

The clinical test Hansburg is developing comprises a dozen pictures, all but three of which depict a situation in which either a child is leaving his parents or a parent is leaving his child. Some of the situations, such as a child leaving to go to school or mother leaving her child at bedtime, are of a kind that any child of over six would be expected to take in his stride. Others are of a more disturbing character. They include a picture in which the child's mother is being taken by ambulance to hospital, and another in which the child is going off to live permanently with his grandmother. Under each picture is written a title making explicit what the picture represents.

In its present form the test is suitable for children and young adolescents in the age-range ten to fifteen years. Hansburg reports that, despite the upsetting nature of some of the scenes, administering the test has not created difficulties. Should the test prove as useful as it promises to be, versions suitable for younger children and also for older adolescents and adults could readily be designed.

In presenting each picture the clinician asks the child being tested, first, 'Did this ever happen to you?' and then, if the answer is no, 'Can you imagine how it would feel if it did happen?' The child is then presented with a series of seventeen statements of how a child might be expected to feel in such a situation, and is invited to tick as many of them as he thinks would fit. Although for each picture the seventeen statements are phrased a little differently, the range of feelings described is similar. The following selection of eight statements illustrates part of the range of feeling covered:

291

'feeling alone and miserable'
'feeling sorry for his parents'
'feeling that he doesn't care what happens'
'feeling he will do his best to get along'
'feeling angry at somebody'
'feeling that, if he had been a good child, it would not have happened'
'feeling that his house will now be a scary place to live in'
'feeling that it is not really happening, it's only a dream'.

Preliminary findings show, among other things, that children growing up in stable families give two or three times as many responses that express distress and concern at what is happening as responses that express anger and blame. By contrast, disturbed children who have experienced long and/or repeated separations, many of whom come from rejecting families, give at least as many angry and fault-finding responses as they do responses expressing distress and concern. This very marked difference in the balance of responses is especially evident in respect of pictures that represent a major disruption of a child's bond with his parents; in respect of pictures that represent only a routine and transient separation the difference in balance is less evident.

Another interesting difference of balance, also seen especially in response to pictures representing a major disruption, is in the proportion of responses that indicate that the child will do his best to get along on his own or that he will be happier as a result of the event. While these form only a small minority of the responses given by children from stable homes, they are much in evidence in the responses of children who have experienced long and repeated separations or who come from unhappy homes. There is reason to believe that most such responses are expressions of a forced and premature attempt at autonomy that will prove brittle, a condition described by Winnicott (1955a) as a 'false self'. Some characteristics of persons who, by contrast, show a stable autonomy, and the conditions in which such autonomy develops, are the subject of Chapter 21.

Anger, ambivalence, and anxiety

In the schema proposed, a period of separation, and also threats of separation and other forms of rejection, are seen as arousing, in a child or adult, both anxious and angry behaviour. Each is directed towards the attachment figure: anxious attachment is to retain maximum accessibility to the attachment figure; anger is both a reproach at what has happened and a deterrent against its happening again. Thus, love, anxiety, and anger, and sometimes hatred, come to be aroused by one and the same person. As a result painful conflicts are inevitable.

That a single type of experience should arouse both anxiety and anger need cause no surprise. At the end of Chapter 8 it is pointed out that students of animal behaviour have observed that in certain situations either form of behaviour may be aroused and that whether an animal responds with attack or withdrawal, or with a combination of both, depends on a variety of factors that have the effect of tipping the balance either one way or the other. Between anxious attachment and angry attachment an analogous type of balance appears to obtain. A child who at one moment is furiously angry with a parent may at the next be seeking reassurance and comfort from that same parent. A similar sequence may be seen in lovers' quarrels. It is not by chance that the words 'anxiety' and 'anger' stem from the same root (Lewis 1967).[2]

Psychoanalysts have for long been especially interested in the interrelationships of love, fear, and hate, since in clinical work it is common to find patients whose emotional problems seem to spring from a tendency to respond towards their attachment

---

2. It is of interest that in one of the reports of an infant chimpanzee brought up by humans this same mixture of anger and anxiety is described as occurring when separation threatens (Kellogg and Kellogg 1933). The authors, who adopted a female chimpanzee, Gua, at the age of seven months, discuss the nature of what are commonly described as 'temper tantrums', and the situations that elicit them. 'By far the most frequent occasion for the appearance of a tantrum', they report, 'was when she was left alone or when . . . it was momentarily impossible for her to get into the protecting arms of one of the experimenters. . . . In the more violent type of tantrum, such as that which resulted when we ran away faster than Gua could follow, she seemed to become "blind with fear" and would utter a series of shrill vibrant screams. . . .' She would then run almost at random and occasionally bump headlong into bushes or other obstacles. Ultimately she would fall to the ground, and grovel in the sand. In their discussion, the Kelloggs are in doubt whether to regard the tantrum as expressing rage or fear. Their account suggests that it contains elements of both.

figure with a turbulent combination of all three: intense possessiveness, intense anxiety, and intense anger. Not infrequently vicious circles develop. An incident of separation or rejection arouses a person's hostility and leads to hostile thoughts and acts; while hostile thoughts and acts directed towards his attachment figure greatly increase his fear of being further rejected or even of losing his loved figure altogether.

To account for the intimate connections found between attachment, anxiety, and anger, a number of hypotheses have been advanced. Some are based on an assumption that the aggressive component is reactive to frustration of some kind; others hold that aggressive impulses well up within and find expression almost irrespective of what an individual's experience may be. Among leading analysts who have regarded ambivalence to a loved figure as a key issue in psychopathology and have proposed solutions, Fairbairn (1952) advocates a frustration–aggression type of hypothesis; while Melanie Klein (1932; 1948b) holds that all aggressive feeling and behaviour is an expression of a death instinct that wells up within and must be directed outwards.

Because of the great influence that Melanie Klein has had on many psychoanalysts and child psychotherapists we consider her views first.

The clinical phenomenon to which Klein drew especial attention during the 1920s and 1930s is that some children who are attached to mother with unusual intensity are, paradoxically, possessed of strong unconscious hostility also directed towards her. In their play they may express much violence towards a mother figure and then become concerned and anxious lest they have destroyed or alienated mother herself. Often after an outburst a child runs from the analytic room, not only for fear of consequences from the analyst, but also, it is suggested, to assure himself that mother is still alive and loving. Observations of this kind are now amply confirmed; and much other evidence demonstrates without doubt that the presence of hostile impulses, whether conscious or unconscious, directed towards a loved figure can greatly increase anxiety. (Witness Mrs Q's acute anxiety for her son's safety arising from her own impulses to throw the child out of the window, recounted in Chapter 15.) Thus the value of many of Klein's observations remains intact whether or not we accept her ideas in regard to the origin of anger and aggression.

It must, however, be remembered that just as hostility directed towards a loved figure can increase anxiety, so can being anxious, especially that an attachment figure may be inaccessible or unresponsive when wanted, increase hostility. It is of both great theoretical and great practical importance to determine how these vicious circles begin. Does increased anxiety precede increased hostility, is it the other way round, or do they spring from a common source? When looking backwards from data provided by a patient in analysis it is notoriously difficult to unravel the sequence, as Ernest Jones noted many years ago (Jones 1929); and this difficulty holds no less during the treatment of young children than it does for older patients. Neglect of this methodological difficulty and insufficient attention to family relationships have, it is held, led Klein to one-sided conclusions.

Logically it is clearly possible for intense anxiety to precede intense hostility in some cases, for the sequence to be reversed in others, and for them to spring from a single source and so be coincidental in yet a third group. Such possibilities, however, are not allowed for by Klein's formulation. Instead, her basic tenet is that increased anxiety is always both preceded by and caused by increased hostility; that anxiety may sometimes be independent of, sometimes itself provoke, and often be aroused by the same situation as, increased hostility is not conceded.

Fairbairn addresses himself to the same clinical problem as Klein but proposes a very different solution. In the absence of frustration, he holds, an infant would not direct aggression against his loved object. What leads him to do so is 'deprivation and frustration in his libidinal relationships – and more particularly . . . the trauma of separation from his mother' (Fairbairn 1952).

The position consistently adopted by the present writer (e.g. Bowlby 1944; 1951; 1958a), and, as will already be apparent, adopted also in this work, is close to Fairbairn's.[3] Anger and

3. A principal point of difference is that in much of his work Fairbairn tends to identify attachment with feeding and orality and so to attribute proportionally greater significance to a child's first year or two than is attributed by the present writer.

hostility directed towards an attachment figure, whether by a child or an adult, can be understood best, it is held, as being in response to frustration. Frustration, it is true, can affect motivational systems of any kind. But there is reason to believe that the motivational systems with which this work is concerned, namely those mediating attachment behaviour, are those affected in a very large proportion of the most severe and persisting cases of frustration, especially when the agent of frustration is, wittingly or unwittingly, the attachment figure himself/herself.

The reason that anxiety about and hostility towards an attachment figure are so habitually found together, it is therefore concluded, is because both types of response are aroused by the same class of situation; and, to a lesser degree, because, once intensely aroused, each response tends to aggravate the other. As a result, following experiences of repeated separation or threats of separation, it is common for a person to develop intensely anxious and possessive attachment behaviour simultaneously with bitter anger directed against the attachment figure, and often to combine both with much anxious concern about the safety of that figure.[4]

Because of the tendency for anger and hostility directed towards a loved person to be repressed and/or redirected elsewhere (displaced), and also for anger to be attributed to others instead of to the self (projected), and for other reasons too, the pattern and balance of responses directed towards an attachment figure can become greatly distorted and tangled. Furthermore, because models of attachment figures and expectations about their behaviour are built up during the years of childhood and tend thenceforward to remain unchanged, the behaviour of a person today may be explicable in terms, not of his present situation, but of his experiences many years earlier. It is, indeed, because of these complexities that the nature and origin of our feeling and behaviour are often so obscure, not only to others but to ourselves as well. These are all matters to be considered further in the third volume.

4. Frustrations of another kind that can engender much anger towards a parent occur when a parent demands that his (or her) child act as a caretaker to him (or her), thus as noted above (p. 283), inverting the usual parent and child roles.

Chapter 18
Anxious Attachment and the 'Phobias' of Childhood

Often and often afterwards, the beloved Aunt would ask me why I had never told any one how I was being treated. Children tell little more than animals, for what comes to them they accept as eternally established.
– RUDYARD KIPLING, *Something of Myself*

Phobia, pseudophobia, and anxiety state

It is argued earlier (Chapter 14) that an individual's susceptibility to respond with fear whenever he meets a potentially alarming situation is determined in very large part by the type of forecast he makes of the probable availability of attachment figures, and that these forecasts derive from the structure of the working models of attachment figures and of self with which he is operating. In the same chapter it is argued, further, that these models are probably built up throughout the years of childhood and adolescence and that they tend thereafter to remain comparatively stable; and, finally, that the particular forms that a person's working models take are a fair reflection of the types of experience he has had in his relationships with attachment figures during those years, and may perhaps be having still. Evidence regarding the nature of the experiences that lead to increased susceptibility to fear is considered in Chapters 15 and 16.

In this chapter and the next the potential usefulness of the theory is illustrated by applying it to certain clinical syndromes in which overt anxiety and fear are prominent. The conditions selected are those commonly grouped under the label 'phobia', a label which, as currently used by psychiatrists and psychologists (e.g. Marks 1969; Andrews 1966), includes a broad range of conditions in which anxiety and fear are the main symptoms. Principal instances to be examined are 'school phobia' and 'agoraphobia'.

Although when the condition is of recent onset some patients so labelled respond to fairly simple therapy (e.g. Friedman 1950; Kennedy 1965), others pose a much greater problem. A majority of those whose condition has been present for a long time, it is now agreed, suffer also from a wide variety of other emotional troubles. Most are timid individuals prone not only to fear situations of many kinds but to become depressed, and apt to develop various psychosomatic symptoms as well. In all such cases the feature to which the term phobia is applied, for example fear of school (school phobia) and of crowded places (agoraphobia), is found to be only a small, and sometimes even negligible, part of a deep-seated disturbance of personality that has been present for many years.

There is, however, a small minority of long-standing cases of phobia that appear to be very different. The individuals concerned, to whom Marks (1969) has drawn attention, are intensely afraid of some particular animal but, in all other respects, are stable personalities not given to psychological disturbance. Marks presents evidence that, in regard to personality functioning and psychophysiological responses, these individuals not only resemble people who are psychiatrically healthy but differ markedly from those diagnosed agoraphobic. They differ from agoraphobics also in the age when difficulty begins. Whereas agoraphobic symptoms usually appear after the age of ten years, a specific and limited animal phobia has usually been present since before the age of seven years. The specific phobia appears to be due to the persistence into later life of the tendency to fear animals that is found commonly during the early years of childhood but usually diminishes to moderate or negligible proportions before or during adolescence.

Discussion here concentrates on the majority group, namely people who suffer from deep-seated disturbances of personality. The minority group, comprising people who suffer from specific animal phobias, probably present a different type of problem and are touched on only briefly.

In what follows the term phobia is used only because so much of the descriptive material with which we are concerned is to be found in the literature under that head. It is placed in quotation marks in the chapter title in order to indicate a belief that, when applied to patients in the majority group, it is being misapplied.

Others also have held that many of the cases commonly

labelled phobic are mislabelled. Brun (1946) distinguishes a group that he terms 'pseudophobic', and includes in it all cases of agoraphobia. Snaith (1968) similarly argues that agoraphobia is best regarded as a pseudophobia (although he uses the term in a way different from Brun). In the present work it is argued that not only is agoraphobia best regarded as a pseudophobia but so also is school phobia. By contrast, intense fear of a specific animal or of some other discrete situation in a person of otherwise healthy personality can sometimes be regarded as a case of true phobia.

The distinction between the two conditions is readily defined in terms of the present theory. In the case of a phobic person, what is most feared is the *presence* of some situation that other people find much less frightening but that he either takes great pains to *avoid* or else urgently *withdraws from*. In the case of a pseudophobic person, what is most feared is the *absence or loss* of an attachment figure, or some other secure base, that he would normally *move towards*. Whereas in the case of phobia the clinician identifies the feared situation correctly, in the case of pseudophobia the true nature of the feared situation often goes unrecognized and the case is misdiagnosed as one of phobia.

Although the label pseudophobia helps to draw attention both to the problem itself and to the tangled misconceptions about underlying psychopathology that abound in the literature, it is hardly suitable for regular use. A far better way to deal with the pseudophobias is to classify them simply as anxiety states and thereby to combine them with the many cases in which anxiety is said to be 'free-floating'. For cases of pseudophobia and anxiety state not only have in common the same age-range of onset but 'overlap considerably in their clinical features' (Marks 1969). Indeed, once the role that anxious attachment plays in these conditions is firmly grasped, it becomes clear that patients said to be suffering from free-floating anxiety, no less than those labelled here as pseudophobic, are in an acute or chronic state of anxiety about the availability of their attachment figure(s).

This leads to the conclusion that a patient's emotional responses remain puzzling, and are labelled symptoms, only so long as they are seen divorced from the situation that elicited them.

In support of our thesis we devote most of this chapter to an examination of school phobia, about which there is a large and revealing literature; subsequently we consider afresh two cases of childhood phobia that have long been classics in the literature of psychoanalysis and of learning theory respectively. Special attention is given to the patterns of interaction that appear to have characterized the children's families. In the chapter following we examine agoraphobia in the light of our discussion of school phobia.

'School phobia' or school refusal

During the past fifteen years there has grown up an extensive literature on a condition known usually as school phobia (Johnson *et al.* 1941) or, and better, school refusal (Warren 1948). These terms apply when children not only refuse to attend school but express much anxiety when pressed to go. Their non-attendance is well known to their parents, and a majority of the children remain at home during school hours. Not infrequently the condition is accompanied by, or masked by, psychosomatic symptoms of one kind or another – for example, anorexia, nausea, abdominal pain, feeling faint. Fear is expressed of a variety of situations – of animals, of the dark, of being bullied, of mother coming to harm, of being deserted. Occasionally a child seems to panic. Tearfulness and general misery are common. As a rule, the children are well behaved, anxious, and inhibited. Most come from intact families, have not experienced long or frequent separations from home, and have parents who express great concern about their child and his refusal to attend school. Relations between child and parents are close, sometimes to the point of suffocation.

In all these respects the condition differs from truancy. Truants from school do not express anxiety about attending, do not go home during school hours, and usually pretend to their parents that they are attending. Often they steal or are otherwise delinquent. Commonly they come from unstable or broken homes, and have experienced long and/or frequent separations or changes of mother figure. Relations between a truant and his parents are likely to be quarrelsome or distant.

The validity of the distinction between school phobia and

truancy is well attested, notably by the study of Hersov (1960a), who compares a series of fifty cases of school refusal with a matched series of fifty truants and with another contrast group, also drawn from a clinic population. Although several other studies are based on a series of cases seen in clinical practice, in none of them are results treated statistically. Instead, observations are presented descriptively and interwoven with a greater or less measure of theoretical interpretation. Among such studies, each based on a series of between twenty and thirty cases, are those by Talbot (1957), Coolidge and his colleagues (1957; 1962), Eisenberg (1958), and Davidson (1961). For her two papers Sperling (1961; 1967) draws on experiences with fifty-eight children, some of whom had long analytic treatment. Kennedy (1965) reports on fifty cases of recent and acute onset dealt with by simple brisk methods. Weiss reports on fourteen children and adolescents treated as inpatients, and on their follow-up some years later (Weiss and Cain 1964; Weiss and Burke 1970). A number of empirically based articles on the family background of school refusers are published in the *Smith College Studies in Social Work* and reviewed by Malmquist (1965). A book by Clyne(1966), based on fifty-five cases seen in general practice, gives a vivid description of the many and varied clinical pictures encountered. Among other publications are early papers by Broadwin (1932) and E. Klein (1945), a book by Kahn and Nursten (1968), reviews by Frick (1964), Andrews (1966), and Berecz (1968), and several papers reporting on small numbers of cases that have been treated by one or another method, including some by behaviour therapy (e.g. Lazarus 1960; Montenegro 1968).

At an empirical level there is substantial agreement among these many authors, both in regard to the personalities, behaviour, and symptoms presented by the children and in regard to the personalities, behaviour, and symptoms presented by the parents. Furthermore, there is widespread agreement that what a child fears is *not* what will happen at school, but leaving home. With the exception of Frick (1964), who expresses doubt, almost all students of the problem conclude that disagreeable features of school, for example a strict teacher or teasing or bullying from other children, are little more than rationalizations. In keeping

301

with this view, Hersov (1960b) found that only a minority of his fifty school-refusing children made any complaint about teacher or schoolmates. Many of the children he studied stated that once in school they felt quite secure. Thus, unlike what occurs in genuine phobias, exposure to the alleged phobic situation does not exacerbate the sufferer's fear. Several other authors confirm this finding, and also that fear is often at its height either just before leaving home or on the journey to school. The subjects of a follow-up study by Weiss and Burke (1970), looking back on their problem, confirm that it arose from difficulties in family relations.

Because the situation feared is that of leaving home, the term school phobia is an obvious misnomer.[1] In order to emphasize the family dynamic which she, like others, holds to be all-important, Johnson abandoned the term school phobia, which she herself had advocated in 1941, and replaced it with that of 'separation anxiety' (Estes, Haylett and Johnson 1956). As a name for a clinical syndrome, however, separation anxiety is ill fitted. Of the terms at present in use 'school refusal' is probably the best, by virtue of its being at once the most descriptive and the least laden with theory.

In the course of these empirical studies a considerable body of theory has been elaborated. Three main influences are apparent.

One, that stems from Freud's classical paper on the analysis of a phobia in a five-year-old boy known as Little Hans (Freud 1909), is couched in terms of the child's individual psycho-pathology and gives a central role to the process of projection. In that tradition concepts frequently drawn upon include those of dependency and overdependency, over-gratification and spoiling, linked as a rule to a theory of fixation at, or regression to, one or another level of psychological development. Sperling (1967), for example, points to the anal erotic (especially anal sadistic) stage of libidinal development, and Clyne (1966) to Winnicott's con-

---

1. In the early 1920s the term school phobia was applied by Burt, and applied appropriately, to a very different condition, namely to children who were afraid of going to school because of having gone there for shelter during air-raids (referred to by Tyerman 1968).

cept of an infantile transitional stage in the development of object relations.

The second main influence on theory stems from a seminal paper by Johnson and her colleagues (1941). Basing their views on experience gained in the practice of child and family psychiatry, they lay especial emphasis on family interactions and the role that one or other parent is playing in instigating and maintaining the condition. They describe parents who, for emotional reasons, cling to their child and, in effect, stop him from going to school.

The third main influence is learning theory which, like traditional psychoanalysis, is conceived in terms of individual psychopathology. Nevertheless, as Andrews (1966) points out, the practitioners of behaviour therapy are often far more alive to the importance of interpersonal relations and family dynamics than their theory would lead us to expect.

Four Patterns of Family Interaction

A reading of the clinical literature shows that, although workers may approach the problem of school refusal from very different theoretical standpoints, when they come to assess actual cases the features to which they draw attention tend to be much the same. It is therefore possible to treat the array of clinical findings as reasonably well authenticated and to proceed to consider how they can be understood in terms of the theory of anxious attachment outlined in earlier chapters.

When viewed in that light a large majority of cases of school refusal can be understood as the products of one or more of four main patterns of family interaction:

Pattern A – mother, or more rarely father, is a sufferer from chronic anxiety regarding attachment figures and retains the child at home to be a companion

Pattern B – the child fears that something dreadful may happen to mother, or possibly father, while he is at school and so remains at home to prevent it happening

Pattern C – the child fears that something dreadful may happen to himself if he is away from home and so remains at home to prevent that happening

Pattern D – mother, or more rarely father, fears that something dreadful will happen to the child while he is at school and so keeps him at home.

Though in most cases one or another of these four interaction patterns is dominant, the patterns are not incompatible and mixed cases occur. Pattern A is the commonest and may be combined with any of the other three.

Family Interaction of Pattern A

A family pattern in which a mother or father suffers from anxiety over attachment figures and retains the child at home to be a companion is now widely recognized. In a majority of cases mother is the principal agent and for that reason, and to simplify exposition, it is mothers who are referred to in what follows. Yet it must not be forgotten that a father can also be a principal agent in the condition: Eisenberg (1958), Choi (1961), Clyne (1966), and Sperling (1967) are among those who describe illustrative cases.

A mother who retains her child at home to act as a companion for herself may do so deliberately and consciously or may be unaware of what she is doing and why.

An example of the former is the mother of a ten-year-old boy who had been kept at home for more than a year when the family was referred to a clinic. Although initially mother claimed that she pressed her son to return to school, after the family had been in treatment for some months she admitted frankly that she did not want him to go. In a burst of candour she explained how for many years during her childhood she had been away in an institution and had had no one to love, how her son was the first person she had ever had to love in her life, and how she could not be expected to relinquish him now. The boy's father was aware of what was happening but preferred to stay inactive to avoid upsetting his wife. The boy also, it emerged, was well aware of the situation.[2]

More often a mother is unaware, or only partly aware, of the pressures she is putting on her child and believes more or less sincerely that she is doing everything possible for his benefit. In

2. I am grateful to my colleague, Dr Marion Mackenzie, for information about this family.

some cases the train of events begins when the child contracts some minor ailment, and mother treats the condition as of much more consequence than it really is. The child is kept at home, ostensibly to convalesce, but is gradually presented with a picture of himself as being unfitted for the rough world of school and as being, therefore, in constant need of his mother's care. Unkind teachers, bullying boys, and chronic ill health are inculpated as the villains of the piece. This pattern and its many variants, in which a mother exploits some temporary upset or anxiety of her child, are described in almost every paper on the topic. Eisenberg (1958) gives vignettes of mothers who, on arrival at school with their child, exhibit intense reluctance to relinquish him and behave in such a way that he is made anxious about school and perhaps guilty at enjoying the company of anyone but mother. Weiss and Cain (1964) describe mothers who, while claiming to protect their children from the horrors of the world, not only burden them with their personal and marital worries but seek their undivided support. Clyne (1966) describes cases in which a mother develops psychosomatic symptoms herself after her child has returned to school. Others (Estes, Haylett and Johnson 1956) have noted how, after one child has been released from his parent's grip, another child is sometimes fastened on and held.

Whenever a family pattern of this kind is present, the parent concerned is found to be intensely anxious about the availability of her own attachment figures and unconsciously to be inverting the normal parent–child relationship by requiring the child to be the parent figure and adopting the role of child herself. Thus the child is expected to care for the parent and the parent seeks to be cared for and comforted by the child. As a rule the inversion is camouflaged. Mother claims that the person who is in special need of care and protection, and who is receiving it, is the child; and a clinician inexperienced in family work may even come to believe that the trouble arises because the child is being 'spoiled' by having his 'every whim gratified'. In effect what is happening is very different and much sadder. Unknown to herself, mother (or father) is seeking belated satisfaction of her desire for the loving care she either never had as a child or perhaps lost, and, simultaneously, is preventing the child from taking part in play or school activities with his peers. So far from being 'over-indulged', such children are chronically frustrated and, because allegedly given everything, are not even free to expostulate. During treatment one nine-year-old boy illustrated how he felt by repeatedly winding the window cord around himself and explaining, 'See, I'm in a spider's web and can't get out' (Talbot 1957). Another boy, aged eleven, drew a dog on a tight leash led by a lady and made clear he felt the dog was himself, furious at being tied to his mother (Colm 1959).[3]

To present the picture thus may seem one-sided and to be unfairly biased against parents. Yet, once the parents' own difficulties are examined and the origins of these difficulties traced to the very troubled childhoods that they too have experienced, not only does their behaviour as parents become intelligible but our sympathy is enlisted. Time and again it is found that the pathological behaviour of a parent is a reaction against, or a reflection or residue of, a deeply disturbed relationship that she has had, and is perhaps still having, with her own parents. Recognition of this quickly dispels any disposition to see the parent as a villain, even though the way she is treating her child may be patently pathogenic. Instead, she is seen as the unhappy product of an unhappy home and, as such, a person fully as much sinned against as sinning.

For an adequate understanding of the dynamics and historical origins of families in which a parent inverts the relationship with the child by requiring him to care for her we should need to have far more systematic data than are yet available regarding the personalities and childhood histories of the parents and grandparents concerned. On grandparents no data appear to be on record, except anecdotally. As regards parents, not only are systematic data on representative samples of the parents of school-refusing children scarce, but in so far as there are any they

---

3. Sometimes the term 'symbiosis' is used to describe these suffocatingly close relationships between mother and child. The term is not happily chosen, however. since in biology it is used to denote an adaptive partnership between two organisms in which each contributes to the other's survival; whereas the relationship with which we are concerned here is certainly not to the child's advantage and often is not to the parent's either.

do not distinguish between parents in terms of the four patterns of family interaction considered here. Such systematic data as are available are presented therefore only after all four patterns have been considered (see pp. 323–4).

Nevertheless it is not too difficult, in the light of the theory outlined, to discern the main features of the *psychopathology of parents in families showing pattern A*. Once again it must be remembered that, although reference continues to be made to mothers and maternal grandmothers, almost exactly the same dynamics can occur with a father and a paternal grandmother in the principal roles, and also with one or other grandfather.

Very commonly a mother who inverts the relationship with her child has had, and may still be having, a close but intensely anxious and ambivalent relationship with her own mother. In such cases a mother believes, often with good reason, that she was unwanted or at least less wanted than one of her siblings. As a result she has felt that she has always had to fight for such affection and recognition as she has got. Yet in only a few cases in which pattern A obtains has she been wholly rejected. Far more often the maternal grandmother's feeling for her daughter is ambivalent; and not infrequently the older woman seems to be making strong, insistent, and unjustified demands upon her daughter. Thus, while on the one hand mother has never had the spontaneous care and affection a child desires, and usually receives, on the other she has often been put under duress to provide care for her own dominating and demanding mother. Responding to these pressures, mother may meet her mother's demands but only at the price of feeling bitter with suppressed resentment against her.

It will perhaps be noticed that the intensely ambivalent relationship between mother and grandmother, of the kind sketched above, is likely itself to be an example of an inverted parent–child relationship. For in many cases maternal grandmother is demanding from her daughter just that same parental-type care and affection that mother, in her turn, is demanding from her school-refusing child. That this is truly so in some instances is shown by the fact that, in every series studied, there are cases reported of mothers (or fathers) who, when children, had themselves been school refusers. For example, in a study by Goldberg (1953) of seventeen cases, about half the parents are reported to have had symptoms during their childhood identical with those shown by their children. In Davidson's study (1961) of thirty cases, mother had herself been a school refuser in three, and three other mothers had had to remain at home to look after their own sick mother or younger siblings. Sperling (1967) reports the case of a father who was in analysis for phobic anxieties when his son began refusing to go to school. Although at first it appeared that John was clinging to his father, it soon became clear that father was demanding that the boy keep him company. During analysis father began to recognize that his own father had treated him in exactly the same way that he was now treating his son, using him thus, presumably, in an attempt to deal with his own anxieties. Whenever possible, then, it is desirable that in future studies the childhood histories and psychopathology of grandparents should be explored.

Not unexpectedly, the marital relations of the parents of school-refusing children are usually very disturbed. Forms of disturbance vary greatly and it would take us too far from our theme adequately to discuss their variety. One form frequently described is of a wife locked in mutually ambivalent relationships both with her own mother and with her school-refusing child, and having a rather passive husband who tends to opt out of his roles as husband and father. The way this relationship comes into being is not accidental. Few men other than passive ones are willing to marry and stay married to a woman who not only consistently gives preference to the never-ending demands of her own mother but may also try to dominate her husband in the same way that her mother dominates her. As it was put by Mrs Q, who had evidently had many admirers as a girl, only her husband among them had been willing to tolerate the extent to which she was daily entangled with her own very disturbed mother and to put up with the hysterical outbursts that, engendered in her relationship with her mother, she had been wont to vent on each of her boyfriends successively.

No doubt the mirror-image of this relationship, in which the husband is entangled with his mother and the wife is the passive one, also occurs. In either case sexual relations are likely to be sparse or absent.

Let us return to our main theme, the relationship of one or other parent, usually mother, to the school-refusing child. When that is examined it is found, time and again, that mother treats the child as though he were a replica of her own mother, the child's maternal grandmother. Not only does mother seek from her child the care and comfort she had sought, perhaps in vain, from maternal grandmother, but she may behave towards him as though he were the dominant figure. While at one moment she may be smouldering with resentment at what she feels to be her child's rebuff, as she does at those from her mother, at the next she may be treating him with the same anxious deference that she shows an elderly mother who rules the family by means of invalidism.

Examples of parents who are part of a family showing one or another variant of pattern A are to be found throughout the literature. Talbot (1957) calls attention to the mother who allows her child to dominate her in exactly the same way that she has always allowed her own mother to. In their account of the case of a boy of nine, Johnson et al. (1941) describe a mother whose own mother had been in bed for years with a hysterical disorder and had demanded her daughter's constant attention. The boy's mother was hypochondriacal about him, on the one hand, insisting on endless medical examinations, and, on the other, under the guise of believing that he was in greater need of love from her than were her other children, she made extreme demands upon him. During a late phase of her treatment, however, this mother was able to describe how she had always longed for love herself, how she felt she was unable to give it, and how she even competed with her son for attention. In describing another variant of the pattern Davidson (1961) reports how a mother referred to her school-refusing daughter protectively as 'small and white like Grandma'. Weiss and Cain (1964) observe that a mother is inclined to treat her child as her confidant in regard to her difficult family relationships and that the child is apt to respond by adopting an inappropriately grown-up manner, both to his parents and to strangers.

Although in such cases it may appear at first sight that a

mother's attitude to her school-refusing child is one of undiluted loving care, greater knowledge of the family may show another side. Clyne (1966), who writes from experience in general practice, notes that, whereas the mother's 'need for dependence' remains fairly constant, her child's response alternates: at times he is clinging, at others he is obviously striving towards independence. To the latter, mother can respond in various ways, by clinging to him more intensely, by inducing him to feel guilty, or by becoming angry with him or even rejecting him. When the facts become known it is sometimes found not only that a mother's relationship to her child is intensely ambivalent, but that she is treating him far more violently than anyone had imagined. Talbot (1957) describes how a mother may be observed to swing from one extreme to the other in her way of treating her child, kissing him one moment and beating him the next. In fact, as we shall see when we consider family patterns B and C, which often coexist with pattern A, many school-refusing children are being subjected to great duress.

Before considering these other patterns it may be useful to list some of the processes that, singly or together, account for the hostile treatment that many a school-refusing child receives from an emotionally disturbed parent.

A mother's hostile treatment of her school-refusing child can be understood as a product of one or more of at least three closely related processes:

(a) redirecting (displacing) anger, engendered initially by own mother, against the child;

(b) misattributing to child the rejecting characteristics and/or the demanding characteristics of own mother, and being angry with the child accordingly;

(c) modelling angry behaviour towards child on the angry behaviour exhibited by own mother.

Let us consider each of these processes in turn.

(a) Inevitably, a mother brought up and caught in a disturbed family network keenly resents her own mother's meagre affection for her and also the intense demands that are made upon her. At the same time, however, she feels unable to express her anger openly, either because she is terrified of how her parent will respond or else because she fears making her ill. Either way, mother boils with unexpressed resentment and sooner or later finds a figure on whom to vent it. Not infrequently it is her school-refusing child who becomes the target.

(b) In some cases it is apparent that the charges a mother levels against her child are replicas of those she levels, overtly or covertly, at grandmother. For example, a mother may first attribute dreadfully unreasonable demands to her child and then lash out at him for the demands he is alleged to make; when to an external observer the child is behaving little differently from any other child of the same age who is placed in similar circumstances. Similarly, a mother may misattribute rejection or ingratitude to her child. Such misattributions can be understood as the result of the parent's treating her child as an attachment figure, and, in so doing, assimilating the child to the model she has of how attachment figures can be expected to behave. This process is identical to what happens in the transference relationship during psychoanalytic treatment (see Chapter 14).

(c) In Chapter 15 the process is described by which a mother may come unwittingly to model her behaviour towards her child on the way her own mother has treated her. As an illustration the case was described of Mrs Q who, during hysterical outbursts, was apt to threaten her son, Stephen, with the same dire threats she had herself suffered from her mother. In the literature on school refusal several writers, and notably Estes, Haylett and Johnson (1956), invoke that process as an explanation of why a mother's angry behaviour takes the particular form it does.

In the families of school-refusing children, threats by a parent against a child, or perhaps against members of the family in general, are common. Indeed, once their frequency and effects are appreciated, threats are found to be the key to an under-standing of most of the clinical problems presented by families showing patterns B and C.

Family Interaction of Pattern B

In families showing pattern B a child fears that something dread-ful may happen to mother, or possibly father, while he is at school and remains at home in order to prevent it. The pattern is probably the second most frequent of the four; and it occurs fairly often in conjunction with pattern A.

Empirical studies show that it is common for school-refusing children to state that the reason they do not go to school is a fear of what may happen to mother while they are away from home. Talbot (1957) in her study of twenty-four children writes: 'Over and over again we are told by every child studied, whether five years old or fifteen, that he is afraid something dreadful will happen to mother or other close relative, such as grandmother or father.' Hersov (1960b), in his careful study of children aged from seven to sixteen years, reports that fear of some harm befalling mother was the commonest single explanation given by children of why they did not attend school; it was given by seventeen out of fifty children. Among others to describe such cases are E. Klein (1945), Lazarus (1960), Kennedy (1965), Clyne (1966), and Sperling (1961; 1967).

Though the finding is no longer in question, there remains much disagreement as to why a child should come to fear such happenings. Explanations are of two main types. Though the processes each type invokes are very different, they are not incompatible, so that it is possible that in some cases both types of explanation are applicable.

The first type of explanation, and one habitually advanced by psychoanalysts, of why a child should become afraid of harm befalling his mother is that he harbours unconscious hostile wishes against her and is afraid lest his wishes come true. This is the explanation explicitly favoured by Broadwin (1932), E. Klein (1945), Waldfogel, Coolidge and Hahn (1957), Davidson (1961), Clyne (1966), and Sperling (1967), and also by those holding the views of Melanie Klein.

A second type of explanation is more mundane: it attributes what a child fears to his real experiences. For example, a child may come to fear that his mother may become seriously ill or die after seeing or hearing about the illness or death of a relative or neighbour, especially when mother is herself in ill health. Alternatively, a child may come to fear some disaster after hearing his mother make alarming threats about what may happen to her in certain circumstances. For example, if her child does not do what is asked of him, she will become ill; or, because 'things at home are so awful', she will desert the family or commit suicide.

Much of the scanty evidence available is open to an interpretation of either of these principal types; but it seems most unwise to adopt an explanation solely in terms of unconscious wishes before an explanation in terms of experience has been thoroughly investigated and shown to be inadequate. In point of fact, evidence suggests that in an overwhelming proportion of cases the eventualities a child fears can be understood wholly, or at least in part, in terms of his actual experiences. The extent to which unconscious hostile wishes may or may not also be making a contribution becomes then a matter for investigation in each individual case.

Experiences that can lead a child to fear that something dreadful may happen to mother are of two main kinds: first, actual events, such as illnesses or deaths, and, second, threats. Not infrequently the effects of the two are interlaced.

As regards actual events, many workers have reported that an episode of school-refusing often begins at a time when, or soon after, mother herself has been ill or a close relative or friend has died. Talbot (1957) cites the case of an adolescent girl who, on going to kiss her grandmother goodbye before leaving for school, suddenly realized her grandmother was dead. Sperling (1961) reports a rather similar case. Lazarus (1960), writing from the viewpoint of a behaviour therapist, describes as typical the case of a girl of nine whose 'central fear was the possibility of losing her mother through death' and whose refusal had been preceded by no fewer than three deaths, that of a schoolfriend by drowning, of a neighbouring friend by meningitis, and of a man killed in a car accident before her eyes. Hersov (1960b) reports 'the death, departure or illness of a parent, most often the mother', as the precipitating factor in nine out of his fifty cases. Davidson (1961), who gave especial attention to this factor, reports that, in her series of thirty cases, mother herself had been dangerously ill in six, and, in another nine, a close relative or friend had died within a few months of the child's refusal to attend school. Thus half her cases were preceded by an event of this kind.[4]

Davidson is one of those who adopt the wish-fulfilment theory of the child's fears and she draws on her own findings to support it. Mother's actual illness or a friend's death, she argues, heightens the child's fear that his unconscious hostile wishes are coming true or might come true. Yet it will be seen that the facts are no less compatible with a theory of the second type. For example, when mother herself is ill, it is not unnatural for a child to be afraid that she may become worse. When a grandmother or neighbour dies suddenly, it is not unnatural for a child to fear that mother may die equally suddenly. Therefore factors external to the child as well as factors internal to him must always be considered.

Although it is natural enough for a child to feel some measure of fear when mother is ill or a relative dies suddenly, especially when the two events occur together, it must be recognized that not all children exposed to such conditions develop intense or prolonged fear that mother will come to harm; nor do they often remain at home to make sure that she does not. Clearly, then, further factors are operative. Though in some cases they may be internal to the child, there is good evidence that in a great many cases these further factors that make for intense and prolonged fear that mother will come to harm derive also from the child's actual experience.

One such factor may be misplaced attempts to conceal from a child the seriousness of a parent's illness or the truth about the death of a relative or friend. The more concealment the more a child is likely to worry. Both Talbot (1957) and Weiss and Cain (1964) remark on the extent to which the parents of school-refusing children are apt to dissemble and evade. As one of the patients in the latter study put it, 'I never know who to believe

4. Davidson strongly emphasizes how easy it is for a clinician inexperienced in the field to overlook vital information. Not only do parents often fail to volunteer information about illness or death that may later seem highly relevant, but they may even deny such occurrences when first asked about them.

in my family. There are too many white lies told. I have to watch and listen when they don't know I'm around.'

Another factor, and one likely to enhance to a much higher degree a child's anxiety about harm befalling his mother, is his having been threatened that, if he is not good, she will fall ill or die. In such a case, mother's illness seems to show the child all too clearly that what mother has always said would happen is in fact coming to pass; and a friend's death is taken as a lesson that mother's predictions are not idle ones: illness and death are real and may strike mother at any time.

It is already argued in Chapter 15 that the high incidence and intensely frightening effects of parental threats have hitherto been gravely neglected as likely explanations of children's fears; and the case of Stephen Q, himself a school refuser for a time, is reported to show how easy it is for parents and children to hide from clinicians information of the greatest relevance. On this issue the perspective adopted by Talbot (1957) and by Weiss and Cain (1964), who are among the very few to refer to the role of threats in cases of school refusal, is nearest that adopted here. Talbot in particular describes the many and varied threats to which some of these children are subjected – that mother will beat the child, kill him, desert him; or, alternatively, that the child by his inconsiderate and wicked ways will be the death of his mother. 'My mother wants me to stay home but she tells me I'm killing her,' was the way one little girl described her predicament.

A case of protracted school refusal in which threats of several kinds were being used, including mother's threats to desert her children, has been reported recently by two of my colleagues at the Tavistock, Paul Argles and Marion Mackenzie (1970). By identifying the problem as one of disturbed family relationships and treating it as such, not only were the clinicians able to help the family to reorganize its way of living but they were able also to gain access to crucial information about the pathological interactions that were current in the family.

The family, a multi-problem one, had been known to medical and social agencies for several years. At the time when systematic therapeutic work was begun Susan, aged thirteen, had been refusing to go to school for eighteen months. She lived with her mother, aged forty-seven, who had worked as a charwoman but was now incapacitated with ulcerated legs, and a younger brother, Arthur, aged eleven. Father, who had always had a chronic physical disability, had been dying of cancer at home during the preceding year. By her first marriage mother had had two sons, now in their twenties. Shortly before Susan began refusing school and following friction, mother had evicted the elder son with his wife and two small children from the house.

Prior to father's death, which occurred just before casework began, all attempts to help the family over Susan's non-attendance at school had been rebuffed. At the time of father's death, however, a new initiative was taken, conceived in terms of crisis intervention (Caplan 1964); and this met with a more hopeful reception. At this time the child care officer responsible for Susan arranged that all three members of the family would be present when a clinical team visited the home in order to make an assessment and, if possible, to plan a therapeutic programme.

During the assessment interview mother began with bitter recriminations against Susan for not attending school, interspersed with threatening remarks to the effect that Susan was responsible for her (mother's) physical ailments. Many other mutually disparaging remarks were passed and only towards the end of the interview, and with much skilled assistance from the team, was it possible for members of the family to describe their loneliness and anxiety, and their concern for each other. They agreed to regular weekly visits from the caseworker for a set period of three months, and also that all three members would always be present. Both in making these arrangements and in subsequent work the caseworker played a very active part.

During the first half-dozen sessions, during which the caseworker had himself to broach the problems stemming from father's illness and death, the pattern of family interaction became clear. Prominent in this pattern were the threats that accounted for Susan's non-attendance at school. Frequently, when mother tried to exert discipline, she would blame the children for their father's death and imply that the same would happen to her if they did not behave. She also admitted threatening to desert them and giving her threats substance by putting on her coat and leaving the house. In response to these threats both children became more defiant and disobedient. During these sessions not only did each of the three members of the family express strong hostility towards the other two, but at times all three banded together and turned angrily on the caseworker.

At the seventh session Susan for the first time was absent. It then transpired that she was at school but that Arthur was unwell and had stayed at home. Gradually it became clear that, for a year or more, the two children had been taking it in turns to stand guard over mother to make sure that she did not desert them. Susan stayed at home by day and visited friends during the evenings; whereas Arthur went to school by day and stayed at home after he had returned. Many of the children's quarrels, about which mother complained bitterly, turned on which of them should be on duty.

Once it became clear that Susan's school refusal was a response to mother's threats to desert, and it became possible to discuss in the family how these threats were affecting the children, much changed. Already by the eighth session it emerged that, for the first time for eighteen months, both children were attending school simultaneously. When, during that session, Arthur returned from school, he was most solicitous as to how his mother had been faring while left on her own; and she was able to reassure him.

A month later, at the end of the agreed three-month spell of work together, Susan was attending school three or four days a week. At a visit six months later, during the summer holidays, the family was found in much better shape. Mother's ulcers had healed and she had renewed contact with her married son. Arthur was helping mother to redecorate the flat; Susan was on holiday with relatives. When school began again both children attended more or less regularly.

This and other cases illustrate how, as soon as family interviewing is adopted as a regular practice, the family origins of many intractable childhood problems are brought to light; whereas as long as each member of the family is seen only separately, interaction patterns of the greatest pathogenic significance can remain hidden. Inappropriate clinical techniques, together with strongly held theory that gives no place to the effects of family pathology, go far to explain why, with only few exceptions, those practising child psychiatry and psychoanalysis have been so very slow to recognize that a majority of children who are referred for psychiatric problems have been, and often are still being, subjected to strong pathogenic influences within their families.

Recognition of the crucial role that parents' threats play in many cases of school refusal makes it possible to read many a published case report in a new light. In some of these, for example those of E. Klein (1945), children are described who have a parent who is threatening that he or she will leave home or else that the child's bad behaviour will lead the parent to become ill or die; despite the evidence presented, however, when the psychopathology of the children's condition is discussed, the threats are given little or no weight. In other reports cases are discussed in which it might be thought that by far the most likely explanation of why a child is afraid that harm will befall his mother is that he has heard her threaten to desert the family or to commit suicide. Yet it is clear that that possibility was never considered by the clinician, even when a child was giving the most explicit hints. As an example, one of our authors gives an interesting account of a boy of ten who told him, 'very confidentially', that one reason for his occasional reluctance to go to school was his dislike of leaving his mother alone as it was 'just possible that she might run away' and he might not find her when he returned. Yet the possibility that the boy had heard his mother make such a threat seems never to have crossed the author's mind. Another author tells of a boy who, on hearing music that reminded him of the funeral of a neighbour who had committed suicide while the child was at school, suddenly felt 'funny' and very sad, and had an irresistible urge to see his mother. The writer, after confidently explaining the fear in terms of the wish-fulfilment theory, adds, almost as an afterthought: 'There was a rather strong probability that Peter might have sensed the depressive mood of his mother and that his sudden phobia was also a sort of realistic protection of her.' Let a spade be called a spade: it seems more than likely that Peter had heard his mother threaten suicide.

So far in our consideration of cases falling into pattern B both the evidence presented and the argument have strongly favoured the view that refusal to go to school in such cases is a response mainly to events at home. Does this mean, then, that the wish-fulfilment theory is totally discarded? Or is it possible that the theory may have some application, even if only a limited one?

Those who support the wish-fulfilment theory very naturally point to evidence that many school-refusing children do in fact entertain hostile wishes towards a parent. And it can be agreed that, in so far as this is so, there are valid reasons for expecting the child's anxiety about his parent's safety to be increased. In some cases, therefore, the wish-fulfilment theory may apply as a partial explanation. Nevertheless, even in those cases it is necessary to probe further, since children do not become hostile to parents for no reason.

In cases where a child is anxious about his parent's safety, not only are those who adopt the wish-fulfilment theory apt to neglect the part played by mother's threats, but they are apt also to over-look the immense frustration and provocation to which school-refusing children are often subjected. For any child to be required day after day to stay at home to keep his mother company or to make sure that she does not desert or commit suicide is the greatest of strains; and almost inevitably angry feelings are engendered. That point is made repeatedly by Johnson. In one of her papers (Johnson *et al.* 1941) she describes the treatment of a nine-year-old boy and his mother. During treatment Jack expressed much rage against his mother because of her demands upon him and because of her resentment when he strove to be independent. Almost simultaneously, during her own treatment, mother came to recognize that Jack's rages against her were an exact replica of how she herself had always reacted to the insistent demands made upon her by her own mother, who had also begrudged her doing anything on her own.

In conclusion, therefore, it can be said that, whenever a school-refusing child expresses anxiety about the continuing presence or safety of a parent, it is likely to be a fairly straightforward response to events occurring in his family; and that, in so far as an increased degree of anxiety stems from fear that unconscious hostile wishes may be realized, these unconscious wishes are themselves likely to arise in response to events within the family. For these reasons, events within the family have first claim to a clinician's attention.

The remaining two patterns of family interaction probably occur less frequently than patterns A and B and can be dealt with more briefly.

Family Interaction of Pattern C

In families of pattern C a child is afraid of leaving home for fear of what might happen to *himself* were he to do so. Here again threats by parents, either overt or covert, usually provide the explanation.

Wolfenstein (1955) gives a vivid account of a case in which threats to get rid of the child were overt and, in her view, accounted for his symptoms.

Tommy, aged six years, refused to stay in nursery school or to be separated from his mother in any other way. About the time of his birth mother had lost both her parents by death, and a few months later her husband deserted. Thenceforward mother and child had lived an isolated life together. Throughout, mother was in two minds whether to keep Tommy with her or to place him in a foster home: 'While she thought constantly of getting rid of Tommy, she also clung to him desperately. He was, as she said, all she had, her whole life.' Mother's relationship to her own mother had evidently been an extremely disturbed one; internal evidence suggests that she herself may also have been subjected to threats of being abandoned.

Mother's threats to abandon Tommy were no secret: 'Tommy not only overheard his mother discuss with neighbours the possibility of placing him, he also was repeatedly threatened with this when he misbehaved.' Tommy's response was one of intense anxiety combined with overactive provocative behaviour and hectic laughter. During therapy he was deeply concerned that he might be sent away and often played a game in which he abandoned the therapist. To his teachers he was sometimes violent, and he shouted at them to 'Get out of here!' In both these regards his behaviour seems clearly to have been modelled on that of his mother towards himself. Wolfenstein is in no doubt that 'the central and overpowering anxiety' in Tommy's life 'was the well-justified fear of being abandoned by his mother'. His refusal to go to school was thus a simple and intelligible response.

Robert S. Weiss (personal communication), who is studying mothers who are struggling to bring up children without a partner to help them, reports that a large proportion of them admit that, at times when they are more than usually anxious or depressed, they entertain ideas of getting rid of their children. This being so, it seems not unlikely that, in fits of desperation, many of them express these ideas within earshot of their children and thereby engender deep anxieties. Unless she has very great confidence in an interviewer, however, a mother is most unlikely to admit to this.

There is in fact reason to suspect that, as in cases of pattern B, there are many children who are being subjected to threats the existence of which is kept a closely guarded secret from all those who may be called upon to help. An example, in which the secret was divulged by the child when drugged, is given by Tyerman (1968):

Eric was thirteen, a conscientious pupil at the technical school, and popular with both teachers and classmates. He went to church regularly with his parents and was a welcome member of the youth club. Then suddenly he refused to go to school, saying he was frightened that on the way his heart would stop beating and he would die. . . . He had read in the newspapers, he said, of people dropping dead in the street, and he was frightened that this was going to happen to him. He was eating and sleeping normally, his mother reported; but nothing seemed to interest him, and he was very preoccupied with thoughts of death. . . . His parents seemed to love each other and to love him. It appeared a happy home, and no source of tension could be discovered. There was no sign of hostility towards Eric in the school or at home, and his behaviour remained a mystery. He was not improved by taking phenobarbitone, or by talking to the psychiatrist or myself; and so an abreaction with sodium pentothal was carried out by the consultant psychiatrist.

During the abreaction Eric described a distressing event which had occurred about a week before he complained of this fear of dying. Apparently his father had accused him of stealing money out of his pockets. When Eric denied it, his father said he was going to punish him – not for stealing, but for lying. Eric told the psychiatrist that he had not taken the money, but that he had later confessed to having done so in order to escape being beaten. When he had made his confession – which was, in fact, his only lie – his father said he must be punished. He drew up a document which said that he and his wife irrevocably gave up all rights to Eric, and that they wished the children's officer to take him into one of the local authority's homes. They then put Eric into the car and drove to see the children's officer. It was lunch-time and his office was closed. The boy was thereupon taken backwards and forwards from office to car until he was in tears and almost hysterical. His father then told him that as he seemed to be suitably sorry he could stay at home.

The parents did not accept invitations to come for further interviews and the boy's story remained uncorroborated. Nevertheless, those with experience in the field are likely to think the boy's story to be true, at least in substance.

Tyerman remarks that neither the parents nor the boy had mentioned the incident in earlier interviews, presumably because the parents were ashamed of their actions and the boy was afraid to tell. If we are right in thinking the boy's story true, the case illustrates yet again how very easy it is even for experienced clinicians to be misled into supposing that a child's fears have no basis in reality. It calls attention also to a main reason why clinicians have resorted so readily to theories that invoke unconscious wishes, phantasy, and projection and have been correspondingly so slow to recognize the role of situational factors, either of the present or of the past.

Family Interaction of Pattern D

In families showing this pattern mother, or more rarely father, fears that something dreadful will happen to the child and so keeps him at home. In many such cases the parent's fear has been much exacerbated by the child's having been ill, occasionally seriously but more often only slightly.

Explanations of why a parent should have fears for his child again fall into two types. One, traditionally adopted by psychoanalysts, is the wish-fulfilment theory, namely that what a parent fears is that his own unconscious hostile wishes towards the child may come true. The other is that a parent is unusually apprehensive of danger befalling his child because he is reminded of some tragedy that happened in the past.

As we saw when considering the converse case of why a child should fear that harm will befall his parents, the two theories are not incompatible. In any one case either or both may apply.

Many cases of pattern D are on record in which the parent's anxiety stems from some past event. For example, Eisenberg (1958) describes a father whose anxiety about his son's safety was closely linked to the sudden death of his brother at the age of seventeen, for which he had felt responsible. Other examples are given by Davidson (1961). In one, the case of a girl of eleven, it emerged after ten months of treatment that mother's sister had died at the age of eleven. The girl herself offered this as the explanation of why she thought her maternal grandmother had suddenly become so fussy and over-protective of her. Talbot (1957) refers to parents still deeply preoccupied with deaths in the family that had occurred years earlier. Almost everyone practising family psychiatry who is alive to the issue will have met with similar cases.

Yet there are also cases in which the wish-fulfilment theory is certainly applicable. An example from my own experience is the intense apprehension felt by Mrs Q that Stephen might die, which was found to be a direct reaction to her own impulse to throw her baby out of the window, an impulse she had been both wholly conscious of and horrified at. What Mrs Q had not been aware of was that her hostility to Stephen arose, in all probability, from her having redirected (displaced) towards her infant angry feelings engendered in her initially by the way her own mother behaved.

Parents of School-refusing Children: Results of Psychiatric Examination

In view of all that has been said it will come as no surprise to find, when a sample of parents of school-refusing children is examined psychiatrically, that the incidence of psychiatric disturbance is high and that, with the exception of the least severe cases, marital disharmony is universal.

Of fifty mothers studied by Hersov (1960b) eight had had previous psychiatric treatment (five for depressive and three for hysterical conditions) and a further seventeen were found to suffer from anxiety and depression of marked degree. Of the series of thirty mothers studied by Davidson (1961) twelve showed symptoms of depression, including two who had been hospitalized. In a series of eighteen cases of children showing marked anxiety over separation, Britton (1969) reports that ten mothers had been under psychiatric treatment and another six exhibited psychiatric symptoms.

The incidence of disturbance among fathers is less pronounced though by no means negligible. Of the fifty fathers studied by Hersov (1960b) eight showed psychiatric symptoms: two had had severe depressions with suicidal attempts, two others had suffered less severe depression, and another four suffered from anxiety symptoms. Davidson (1961) reports that eleven out of thirty fathers suffered from neurotic symptoms.

In his valuable review of the literature Malmquist (1965) gives much evidence of a similar kind. He is insistent that the problem is one that involves the whole family and he protests at the tendency to give too little attention to the role of father.

This completes our review of what is known of the families of children who refuse to leave home to go to school. When cases are considered in the light of the four patterns of family interaction described, it is seen, first, that, once the facts are known and the family pattern is identified, a child's behaviour is usually readily intelligible in terms of the situation he finds himself in; and, second, that many of the judgements hitherto made about such children by clinicians – that they have been spoiled by overindulgence, that they are afraid to grow up, that they are importunately greedy, that they wish to remain a baby tied to mother for ever, that they are fixated and regressed – are as mistaken as they are unjust.

Two classical cases of childhood phobia: a reappraisal

In the light of our review of the family patterns that lie behind almost every case of school phobia, it is of interest to look afresh at two cases of childhood phobia that, reported during the first quarter of this century, have shaped all later theorizing. In the tradition of psychoanalysis, the classical case is that of the five-year-old Little Hans, described by Freud (1909). In the tradition of learning theory, a classical case is that of Peter, aged two years and ten months, described by Mary Cover Jones (1924b), a student of Watson.

In view of the key role that anxious attachment is held in this work to have played in all the cases of childhood phobia so far considered, is there evidence, we may ask, of its having played a part also in either of these famous cases? In what follows it is argued that in both cases there is clear presumptive evidence that it did and that, because theoretical expectations led each researcher to attend to other aspects of the case, those aspects on which weight is placed here were either overlooked or relegated to a subordinate position.

In both children the presenting symptom was an animal phobia. The pattern of family interaction present in the first case is likely to have been pattern B, and that in the second case pattern C.

The Case of Little Hans

A key paper in the development of psychoanalytic theorizing is Freud's study of a horse phobia in a five-year-old boy. The theory that Freud advances in that paper (1909) is that Little Hans's fear of being bitten by a horse had resulted from the repression and subsequent projection of his aggressive impulses, comprising hostility directed towards his father and sadism directed towards his mother. Later, he concluded: 'The motive force of the repression was fear of castration' (1926a, *SE* **20**: 108). Although the origin of the hostility, oedipal or pre-oedipal, may have been debated by other analysts, the outline of the theory has persisted and remains the basis for all later psychoanalytic theorizing about phobias.

What evidence, we may now ask, is there that anxiety about

the availability of attachment figures was playing a larger part in Hans's condition than Freud realized?

When the case report is read afresh in the light of our discussion of school refusal, it seems probable that anxious attachment was indeed contributing a great deal to Little Hans's problem. Most of his anxiety, it is suggested, arose from threats by his mother to desert the family. This view is advanced on two grounds:
- the sequence in which symptoms developed and statements made by Little Hans himself (*SE* **10**: 22–4)
- evidence in father's account that mother was in the habit of using threats of an alarming kind to discipline the boy and that those included threats to abandon him (*SE* **10**: 44–5).

Although the title of the paper is the 'Analysis of a Phobia in a Five-year-old Boy', Freud himself saw the child only once and the 'analysis' was conducted by Hans's father. The published paper comprises father's stenographic protocol, with a running commentary and a long concluding discussion by Freud.

The parents themselves had for some years been supporters of Freud, were in fact among his first (Jones 1955), and Freud had treated mother for a neurosis before her marriage. There was a younger sister, Hanna, born three and a half years after Hans and of whom he was jealous.

Hans was four and three-quarters when father became worried about him and consulted Freud. The problem as presented was Hans's fear that a horse would bite him in the street. Father recounted how a few days earlier Hans had been out to Schönbrunn with his mother, which he usually enjoyed. On this occasion, however, he had not wished to go, had cried, and had been frightened in the street going there. On the return journey 'he said to his mother, after much internal struggling: "*I was afraid a horse would bite me*."' That evening before bedtime he had remarked apprehensively: 'The horse'll come into the room.'

The symptoms, as might be expected, had not come out of the blue. According to father's record, Hans had been upset throughout the preceding week. It had begun when Hans had woken up one morning in tears. Asked why he was crying he had said to his mother: 'When I was asleep I thought you were gone and I had no Mummy to coax with.' (Coax was Hans's expression for cuddle.) Some days later his nursemaid had taken him to the local park, as usual. But in the street he had begun to cry and asked to be taken home, saying that he wanted to 'coax' with his mother. When later that day he had been asked why he had refused to go any further, he would not say. During that evening he had again become very frightened and cried, and he had demanded to stay with his mother. The next day, his mother, eager to find out what was wrong, had taken him on the visit to Schönbrunn, when the horse phobia was first noticed.

Looking back further into the history, we find that the week preceding the onset of the phobia had not been the first time that Hans had expressed fear that his mother might disappear. Six months earlier, during the summer holiday, he had made remarks such as 'Suppose I was to have no Mummy' or 'Suppose you were to go away'. Looking further back still, Hans's father recalled that, when Hanna was born, Hans, aged three and a half, had been kept away from his mother. In father's opinion, Hans's 'present anxiety, which prevents him leaving the neighbourhood of the house, is in reality the longing for [his mother] which he felt then'. Freud endorses that opinion and describes Hans's 'enormously intensified affection' for his mother as 'the fundamental phenomenon in his condition' (*SE* 10: 24–5; also 96 and 114).

Thus, both the sequence of events leading up to the phobia and Hans's own statements make it clear that, *distinct from and preceding any fear of horses*, Hans was afraid that his mother might go away and leave him. Since, in the light of present knowledge, the expression of such fear should alert to the possibility that mother might have uttered threats, explicit or implicit, to leave the family, it is of interest to ask whether there is any evidence of her having done so.

Early in the record it becomes apparent that mother is inclined to use rather alarming threats. For example, when Hans is only three she is described as having threatened him that, if he touched his penis, she would send for the doctor to cut it off (*SE* 10: 7–8). And we know too that, over a year later, at the time the phobia was first reported, mother was still trying to break him of the habit (p. 24). She is said to have 'warned him' not to touch his penis, though we are not told the nature of the warnings she was then uttering.

Three months later, however, and buried deep in the 'analytic' record, Hans lifts the curtain. He had come into father's bed one morning and in the course of talk had told his father: 'When you're away I'm afraid you're not coming home.' Father expostulates: 'And have I ever threatened you that I shan't come home?' 'Not you,' retorts Hans, 'but Mummy. Mummy's told me she won't come back.' Father concedes the point. 'She said that', he replies, 'because you were naughty.' 'Yes,' assents Hans (*SE* **10**: 44–5).

In the passage following father reflects, reasonably enough: 'His motive for at the most just venturing outside the house but not going away from it, and for turning round at the first attack of anxiety when he is half-way, is his fear of not finding his parents at home because they have gone away.' Soon after, however, father reverts to an explanation along oedipal lines.

Even Hans's expressed fear that a horse might bite him is consonant with the view that fear of mother's departure was the principal source of his anxiety. This is shown by an incident that had occurred during the summer holiday of the previous year and to which Hans referred, by way of refutation, when father was trying to reassure him that horses do not bite. When Lizzi, a little girl who was staying in a neighbouring house, had gone away, the luggage had been taken to the station in a cart pulled by a white horse. Lizzi's father was there and had warned her: 'Don't put your finger to the white horse or it'll bite you' (*SE* **10**: 29). Thus, we find Hans's fear of being bitten by a horse is closely linked in his mind to someone's departure. There is other evidence also that horses are identified with departures (e.g. p. 45).

On all these issues, it is evident that Freud was thinking along lines very different from those proposed here. Hans's insistent desire to remain with his mother is seen, not in terms of anxious attachment, but as the expression of his love for his mother, held to have been genitally sexual in character, having reached an extreme 'pitch of intensity' (*SE* **10**: 110–11). The dream that his mother had gone away and left him is held to have been, not an expression of Hans's fear that his mother would carry out a threat to desert the family, but an expression of his fear of the punishment due to him for his incestuous wishes (*SE* **10**: 118). The episode when Hans heard a neighbour warn that the white horse might bite is linked to a postulated wish that his father should go away, not to a fear lest his mother desert. Mother's displays of affection to Hans and her allowing him to come into bed with her are seen, not simply as a natural and comforting expression of motherly feeling, but as actions that might have encouraged, in a rather unfortunate way, Hans's oedipal wishes (*SE* **10**: 28).

A tailpiece that tends to support the present hypothesis is that, subsequent to these events, Hans's parents separated and later divorced (*SE* **10**: 148). (The fact that Hans was separated from his younger sister suggests that mother may have kept the little girl with her and left Hans with his father.)

There the matter must be left since there is no way of knowing which of the alternative constructions is nearer the truth. In the light of the evidence, both from the case itself and from other cases of childhood phobia reviewed earlier, the hypothesis advanced here seems no less plausible than the one adopted by Freud: it is not implausible to believe that the presenting symptom in the case of Little Hans can best be understood in terms of family interaction of pattern B.

The Case of Peter

In the literature on behaviour therapy the case of another young child, Peter, aged two years and ten months, who also suffered from intense fear of animals, has achieved some fame because it is the first recorded example of fear being deconditioned. Although the therapist, a student of Watson, assumes that the child had come to be afraid of animals through having been conditioned to fear them at some time unknown, explicit evidence regarding the way his mother treated him suggests that threats from his mother had probably played a principal part.

'When we began to study him', writes Mary Cover Jones (1924b), 'he was afraid of a white rat, and this fear extended to a rabbit, a fur coat, a feather, cotton wool etc., but not to wooden blocks and similar toys.' At the sight of a white rat in his crib

'Peter screamed and fell flat on his back in a paroxysm of fear', and he proved to be even more afraid of a rabbit. Since other children of the same age were not particularly afraid of these creatures the researchers decided to see whether they could help Peter to become less afraid of them.

A principal procedure used to 'decondition' Peter was for him to play each day with three other children chosen because of 'their entirely fearless attitude toward the rabbit'; during a part of the play period the rabbit was brought in. After about nine sessions, a second procedure was added: each time before the rabbit appeared Peter and the other children were given candy. Altogether some forty-five sessions were given, strung out over a period of nearly six months, during which there was a two-month interruption while Peter was in hospital for scarlet fever. From time to time Peter's progress was tested by presenting him with the rabbit when he was alone. At the end of the process Peter was no longer afraid of the rabbit or of the feather and he was much less afraid of the rat and the fur coat.

From the viewpoint of this work two aspects of the case command attention.

First, Peter is described as having come from a disturbed family that was living in impoverished conditions. Throughout the experiment, it seems, he was in a residential nursery[5] or else a hospital. His mother is described as 'a highly emotional individual who cannot get through an interview without a display of tears'. Peter's older sister had died and the parents were said thenceforward to have lavished 'unwise affection' on him. Discipline was 'erratic' and in her attempts to control him mother is said to have resorted to threats: the example given is 'Come in Peter, someone wants to steal you'. The pattern of family interaction suggested by this limited information is pattern C.

The second point of interest is the effect on the deconditioning process of the presence or absence of a particular student assistant of whom Peter was fond and who he insisted was his father. On each of two occasions when this assistant was present Peter became

5. Although it is not stated explicitly that Peter was resident in the nursery in which deconditioning took place, a phrase (near the end of the paper) that 'he has gone home to a difficult environment' suggests that this was so.

decidedly less afraid, although the assistant made no overt suggestions. On this phenomenon Jones comments, 'it may be that having him there contributed to Peter's general feeling of well-being and thus indirectly affected his reactions'.

Animal phobias in childhood

There is no disposition to argue here that every case of animal phobia in childhood and later life is but the tip of an iceberg the great bulk of which comprises intense fear of losing an attachment figure. In some individuals, no doubt, an animal phobia has developed because as children they had some frightening experience in which they were attacked by an animal of that species. In other cases, seeing or hearing about such events, perhaps in dramatic circumstances and at an age when misunderstanding and fallacious over-generalization are common, may be responsible. In yet others, prolonged exposure to a parent or other adult who habitually responds with fear to a particular species of animal may play a part. Whatever the causes, Marks (1969) presents evidence suggesting that there are individuals who are acutely afraid of a particular species of animal but who do not suffer from any other form of emotional disturbance.

Yet, although cases of true and limited animal phobia may well exist, there can be little doubt that, in very many children and probably adults also who are more than usually afraid of animals, the principal source of anxiety lies in the home and not outside it. It is already suggested that the cases of Little Hans and Peter can usefully be considered in that light. Further and substantial evidence stems from the finding that, as already described, many school-refusing children number among their heterogeneous symptoms a fear of animals. Furthermore, just as any expressed fear of school sinks into oblivion once the disturbed family situation is recognized and dealt with, so does any expressed fear of animals. Because that is so and because difficulties at home are so frequently kept a secret, it is wise when confronted by a patient complaining of animal phobia always to examine carefully the pattern of interaction within the family from which the patient comes.

The wisdom of this course is well illustrated by a case of animal phobia in an adult reported by Moss (1960). The patient was a woman of forty-five who had suffered since childhood from an intense fear of dogs. After seeing a film (*The Three Faces of Eve*) in which a woman is treated for phobia by means of hypnosis, she sought hypnotic treatment for herself.

During the course of treatment the patient recalled a tragic event that had occurred when she was aged four. It appeared that she had been playing in the backyard of her home with her younger sister when the family dog, Rover, knocked the little sister down. A splinter entered the child's cheek, the wound went septic and a few days later the child died. The patient recalled how her mother had accused her of having knocked her sister down and had openly blamed her for the death, and also how thenceforward she had deeply disliked Rover and had become afraid of dogs of every kind. A few years later, after another sister had been born, she recalled that she had been much afraid lest a puppy attack that sister also.

After the patient had recalled how her mother had blamed her for her sister's death, much in her life seemed to her to fit into place. For example, the episode seemed to explain, at least in part, why she had always felt misunderstood by her mother, why she had suffered from a chronic sense of guilt and a compulsive desire to please, and why her relationship to her mother had been so deeply ambivalent.

When an event that a patient recalls has occurred many years previously it is extremely difficult to be sure how valid the recalled details may be. In this case it was possible to obtain limited corroboration of the patient's story. An elder brother confirmed the presence of Rover and also that at the time of the fatal accident his two little sisters had been alone, because he and his brother, who seem to have been left in charge, had gone off to watch a fire. The patient's youngest sister recalled how in later years the patient had anxiously protected her from the approach of any and every dog. There was, however, no corroboration that mother had blamed the patient for the accident, and mother herself, who was still alive, denied having done so.

Experience in family psychiatry shows, nevertheless, that,

when a young child dies, it is by no means uncommon for a parent, distraught by what has happened and perhaps feeling guilty over failure to have taken some precaution, impetuously to attribute blame to an older child. In some families the older child then becomes a scapegoat; in others the parent, after recovering from the shock of acute grief, may forget, and then deny, having ever made the accusation. But in either case the accusation cuts deep, even when memory of it is repressed.

That is what seems likely to have occurred in the case described. If that were so, there would be little wonder that the accused child had come to hate and fear the animal that she believed responsible for her disgrace. Nor would there be wonder that she should have felt thenceforward that her mother, and therefore all others to whom she might look for comfort and support, would disown her and treat her with nothing but contempt.

Enough has been said perhaps to show that the theory of anxious attachment outlined in earlier chapters can illuminate many a case in which a child is intensely and persistently afraid of some situation in circumstances that are perplexing to all around him and perhaps also to the child himself. In the next chapter the problem of agoraphobia in adults is considered in the light of the same theory.

Chapter 19
Anxious Attachment and 'Agoraphobia'

It follows from the nature of the facts ... that we are obliged to pay as much attention in our case histories to the purely human and social circumstances of our patients as to the somatic data and the symptoms of the disorder. Above all, our interests will be directed towards their family circumstances ...
– SIGMUND FREUD (1905a)

Symptomatology and theories of 'agoraphobia'

When a psychiatrist used to dealing with children and families examines the problem of 'agoraphobia'[1] he is at once struck by its resemblance to school phobia. In both types of case the patient is alleged to be afraid of going into a place filled with other people; in both the patient is apt to be afraid of various other situations as well; in both the patient is prone to anxiety attacks, depression, and psychosomatic symptoms; in both the condition is precipitated often by an illness or death; in both the patient is found to be 'overdependent', to be the child of parents one or both of whom suffer from long-standing neurosis, and frequently also to be under the domination of an 'over-protective' mother. Finally, a significant number of agoraphobic patients were school refusers as children.

Although minor degrees of agoraphobia are probably common and, when of recent origin, probably have a high remission rate (Marks 1971), patients who come to the attention of psychiatrists are usually those who are suffering either from a chronic condition of some severity or else from an acute attack. Often a patient is intensely anxious, apt to panic when unable to get home

1. The condition under discussion appears in the literature under many names, including anxiety hysteria, anxiety neurosis, anxiety state, and phobic anxiety–depersonalization syndrome (Roth 1959). The name most widely adopted at present is agoraphobia (Marks 1969). Since criteria used to select cases differ from study to study, the extent to which findings are comparable remains in doubt.

quickly, and to be afraid of an extraordinarily broad range of situations (typically, crowded places, the street, travelling) or of collapsing or even dying when out on his own. From among this heterogeneous and variable collection of situations feared it is possible, none the less, to identify two that are feared in virtually every case and are also the most feared. These situations are, first, leaving familiar surroundings and, second, being alone, especially when out of the house. Since the argument advanced here turns on the fact that fear of these situations is at the heart of the syndrome, let us consider the evidence.

During the past decade there has been very active interest in the syndrome by psychiatrists in the United Kingdom. Roth and his colleagues in Newcastle upon Tyne describe two series of cases, each numbering over one hundred (Roth 1959; 1960; Harper and Roth, 1962; Roth, Garside and Gurney 1965; Schapira, Kerr and Roth 1970). Special aspects of the condition to which they give attention are: the high incidence of traumatic precipitating events, notably actual or threatened physical illness, bereavement and illness in the family; the high incidence of depersonalization; and the close relation of the condition to states of anxiety and depression. Another programme of research into the condition, with special reference to the efficacy of different methods of treatment, is one conducted at the Maudsley Hospital, London, by Marks and Gelder (for references to their numerous papers see Marks 1969 and 1971). A third study of value is by Snaith (1968) who reports on forty-eight cases of phobia in adult patients, twenty-seven of whom were typically agoraphobic. Roberts (1964) describes results of a follow-up of thirty-eight patients, all married women.

Although none of these workers approaches the problem from a standpoint in any way similar to that adopted here, each endorses the view that a principal feature of the condition is fear of leaving home. Roth (1959) speaks of 'a fearful aversion to leaving familiar surroundings'; Marks (1969) holds that 'fear of going out is probably the most frequent symptom from which others develop'; Snaith (1968) finds that, in twenty-seven of his forty-eight cases, the principal source of fear is leaving home and its attendant circumstances. Furthermore he reports, first, that the more anxious an agoraphobic patient becomes the more intense grows his fear of leaving home and, second, that when a patient becomes more anxious his fear of leaving home is magnified in intensity by a factor many times greater than is his fear of anything else. These findings lead Snaith to suggest that the condition is not a true phobia and that a more appropriate label for it would be 'non-specific insecurity fear'. In keeping with Snaith's perspective is the criterion that Roberts (1964) laid down for inclusion in his series, namely a patient's inability to leave his house without a companion.

Not only do these workers find that fear of leaving home when unaccompanied is the principal feature of agoraphobia, but each of them reports also that most patients have been anxious individuals all their lives: some for decades have been uneasy about going out alone (Marks 1969). Between 50 and 70 per cent of patients are reported to have suffered from fears and phobias during their childhood (Roth 1960; Roberts 1964; Snaith 1968). In a recent survey of 786 cases in which information was obtained by means of a questionnaire, 22 per cent described themselves as having been 'school phobic' (Berg, Marks, McGuire and Lipsedge 1974).

Again, although psychoanalysts working in the classical tradition have an approach to the problem entirely different from that of any of the workers so far cited, and different also from that adopted in this work, they report almost exactly the same findings. For example, in an early paper describing the case of a small boy, Abraham (1913) notes that the boy 'does not speak of fear, but of his desire to be with his mother'. This leads Abraham to conclude that the basic problem in patients suffering from agoraphobia is that their 'unconscious . . . does not permit them to be away from those on whom their libido is fixated'.

Both Deutsch (1929) and, in recent years, Weiss (1964) endorse Abraham's view. Weiss notes especially that a patient's anxiety is apt to increase the further from home he goes, which leads him to define agoraphobia as 'an anxiety reaction to abandoning a fixed point of support'.

Thus, despite great variation in the approach and outlook of these many workers, the findings they report are impressively consistent. Only when attempts are made to accommodate the findings within a theoretical framework do differences and difficulties arise.

Three Types of Theorizing

Here, as so often elsewhere, the two rival types of theory that dominate the field are psychoanalytic theory and learning theory. In the case of agoraphobia, however, a third type of theory has also been advanced, namely Roth's psychosomatic theory which invokes psychological and neurophysiological processes (Roth 1960). Strikingly enough, despite all the tell-tale hints that a major part is played by relationships within the patient's family of origin, a fourth type of theory, namely one that invokes pathogenic patterns of family interaction as major aetiological agents, is conspicuous by its absence.

1. *Psychoanalytic theories* of agoraphobia come in two main variants according to whether they focus on fear of being in the street or fear of leaving home.

Freud tends to concentrate on fear of being in the street, which he sees as a displacement outward of the patient's fear of his own libido. Even though in 1926 Freud began a major revision of his views and reached the conclusion that 'the key to an understanding of anxiety' is 'missing someone who is loved and longed for' (see Chapter 2 of this volume), he never applied his new theory to agoraphobia.[2] As a result, his original hypothesis continues to be invoked by a number of psychoanalysts who still see sexual temptation, of one kind or another, as the principal situation that an agoraphobic patient fears (e.g. Katan 1951; Friedman 1959; Weiss 1964).

Other psychoanalysts in their theorizing take as their focus a patient's fear of leaving home and, in doing so, advance theories very similar to those their colleagues advance to account for the similar fear found in children diagnosed as suffering from school

---

2. In one of his last works, *New Introductory Lectures* (1933), Freud writes: 'the agoraphobic patient is . . . afraid of feelings of temptation that are aroused in him by meeting people in the street. In his phobia he brings about a displacement and henceforward is afraid of an external situation' (*SE* 22: 84).

phobia. Thus Deutsch (1929) notes that the reason an agoraphobic patient feels compelled to remain near his mother (or other loved person) is that he entertains unconscious hostile wishes against her and so has to remain with her to ensure that his wishes are not enacted. For Weiss (1964) the patient's urge to remain at home is to be understood as due to a 'regression to unresolved dependency needs'. This is also the view of Fairbairn (1952), although in his case histories he attributes a causal role to the very insecure childhoods his patients had experienced.

In none of the psychoanalytic formulations, apart perhaps from Fairbairn's, is there any suggestion that a patient's refusal to leave home is a response to the behaviour of one of his parents, not only behaviour that may have occurred at some time during the past but behaviour that may be occurring still in the present.
2. During the past decade or so a new approach to a theoretical understanding of phobic conditions of all sorts has been made, this time by *learning theorists*; and formulations that attempt to account for each of the various situations feared have been advanced. Whereas this approach may well help us to understand some of the discrete animal phobias, how much it can contribute to an understanding of agoraphobia remains in doubt. Describing the present position as he sees it Marks (1969), who has made a special study of agoraphobia and draws extensively on learning theory, writes as follows:

Certain phobias, especially agoraphobia, are commonly found together with multiple other symptoms such as diffuse anxiety, panic attacks, depression, depersonalization, obsessions and frigidity. Learning theory does not explain why these symptoms develop, why they occur together, nor why they are associated more often with agoraphobia than with any other type of phobia.

Furthermore, in Marks's view, 'the origin of the panics, depression and other symptoms is not indicated by learning theory' (p. 93).

How the panics and depressions do originate is, for Marks, the most puzzling aspect of the condition. For, in his opinion, not only is learning theory unable to account for them but no other theory can do so either (p. 93). Admitting the quandary, Marks leaves the matter open; but he tends to the view that anxiety attacks probably have an unknown physiological origin. Nowhere does he consider the possibility that they may originate in family situations that create psychological distress.

Having recognized frankly the difficulties in accounting for agoraphobic symptoms entirely in terms of learning theory, Marks believes nevertheless that the theory has much to offer. The hypothesis he advances is based on the idea, suggested by learning theory, 'that panic attacks and depression [may] act as super-reinforcers which facilitate phobic conditioning' whenever a patient who happens to be experiencing such affects goes out of his home. This line of thought leads Marks to propose that, in the development of agoraphobia, the anxiety attack comes first and the situations that the patient reports he fears come to be feared only later, either as a result of a secondary conditioning effect or as a result of rationalization. In that context both fear of going out of the house and fear of becoming separated from a companion, the two symptoms most characteristic of agoraphobic patients, are held to develop through a process of secondary conditioning.

In keeping with his hypothesis, Marks expresses much scepticism regarding the causal role of precipitating factors, holding that they probably act simply as 'non-specific stressors in a patient already liable to the disorder . . . or that the disorder was already present, but hidden until the stressor elicited or exacerbated it'. In support of his position he lays much emphasis on his claim that 'not a few phobias start suddenly without any obvious change in the life-situation of the patient' (p. 128).

Both the sequence of events that Marks postulates and the weakness of his position are illustrated in his description of the case of a woman who sought treatment at the age of thirty-three on account of depression with suicidal ideas. The account she then gave was that, ten years earlier when she was aged twenty-three, she had developed anxiety, sweating, and shaking of the legs while travelling to work by train. Subsequently she had discovered that she felt better if her husband was present and so had taken a job in the firm in which he worked. After a few months, however, she had become afraid of separation from him, had to know exactly where he was and had telephoned him frequently. If for any reason she could not contact him immediately she would panic, feel completely lost and want to scream.

The only information Marks gives regarding this patient's childhood is that 'as a small child [she] used to be frightened when her parents were out and once sent out her younger brother to find them. She had infrequent desires to scream which were hard to stifle. These disappeared in her late teens.'

Despite the uncertain validity of the retrospective data, Marks seems confident about the sequence of symptoms: 'First came the travel phobia and depersonalization, then came the discovery of relief in the presence of her husband and after this he became indispensable. Finally the patient presented for treatment of separation anxiety.' In accounting for the symptoms Marks proposes two distinct pathologies. On the one hand is the agoraphobia and on the other is the anxiety about separation, to which he believes the patient had been sensitized as a child. Originating independently, the two pathologies are held subsequently to have interacted.

There are several flaws in Marks's position. First, in the light of the childhood history of this patient, it is difficult to accept his confident assertion that agoraphobia came first and separation anxiety afterwards. Second, in his ready acceptance of this and other patients' accounts that the initial anxiety attack came 'out of the blue', he makes no allowance for a patient's witting or unwitting suppression of information, a process we know to be extremely common and often to hide clues vital for understanding the condition. Third, to postulate two distinct psychopathologies for a pair of symptoms that habitually go together[3] is far from parsimonious. Finally, as Marks himself admits, he can give no explanation of how or why this patient (or any other) first started to experience anxiety and panic attacks.

An alternative hypothesis to account for this patient's symp-

3. Marks rests his argument on his finding that about 5 per cent of agoraphobic patients are not helped by company and prefer to be alone while travelling (Marks 1969: 98). In most syndromes, however, cases occur that lack one or more typical symptoms; an example is measles without a rash. Such atypical cases require special study.

toms is that, during her childhood, she had been subjected to repeated and realistic threats of being abandoned, so that even after reaching adult life she had continued to be acutely sensitive to any such danger.

As regards the part played by a patient's parents in the genesis of agoraphobia, learning theorists share with traditional psychoanalysts the same shadowy picture. Whereas neither group attributes much importance to parental behaviour, in so far as they do so both invoke the theory of spoiling. As Andrews (1966) points out, Wolpe (1958) and Lazarus (1960), two leading learning theorists, both regard a patient's tendencies to withdraw to and to remain at home as responses he has learnt during interaction with over-protective parents. Marks (1969) in his discussion of prevention implies the same process. Some years earlier Terhune (1949), a psychiatrist whose outlook is in many ways similar to that of present-day learning theorists, wrote confidently: 'The phobic person is one who has been over-protected, brought up "soft".'

3. The third main type of theorizing about agoraphobia, initiated by Roth (1959; 1960), regards the condition as being truly *psychosomatic*. In presenting his theory, Roth lays much emphasis on the vulnerable personalities of his patients, on the precipitating role of stressful events, and on depersonalization, which he regards as a core symptom of the syndrome. The psychological factors to which he points include both situations that, acting perhaps from early childhood, are thought to have contributed to the development of an anxious dependent personality, and stressful events, such as bereavement and illness, that appear to act as precipitants. The somatic factor he postulates is a specific cerebral mechanism that, once triggered, is difficult to inactivate. After considering certain disturbances of perception and consciousness that he finds in these patients, together with symptoms that he attributes to temporal lobe dysfunction, Roth concludes that the somatic pathology is probably to be understood as arising in the mechanisms regulating awareness, which he postulates to have become chronically deranged. Although he gives little detail of how he believes a difficult childhood and stressful situations of later life interact to produce an agoraphobic syn-

drome, Roth's approach is not incompatible with that presented here.

We turn now to consider a fourth type of theory, namely the one that results when the problem of agoraphobia is looked at in the theoretical perspective developed in this work.

Throughout out further discussion it is important to bear in mind that, as all workers now agree, the central symptom of the condition under scrutiny is fear of leaving home.

Pathogenic patterns of family interaction

Whether the theory of anxious attachment, applied already to problems of school phobia, can help to solve problems of agoraphobia also must remain in doubt. For, apart from some limited and mostly rather crude observations, there are few data yet available on patterns of interaction within an agoraphobic patient's family of origin. Almost all the data yet published come either from the patient himself or from a single interview with a relative, with the many distortions and omissions that we know such clinical procedures entail. What is missing, but so necessary to have, is first-hand observations of how a patient and his parents are currently behaving towards one another. In the absence of such data all that is possible here is to draw attention to certain reasonably well-attested findings that are at least consonant with the view that many, if not all, cases of agora-phobia can be understood as products of pathogenic patterns of family interaction.

There is much evidence of a rather general kind which, although it gives little information about specific patterns of interaction, points to a high incidence of disturbance in the families from which agoraphobic patients come. Before considering specific patterns, therefore, we consider this general evidence.

Most reports agree that a majority of agoraphobic patients come from homes that are intact, in the sense that there are two parents living continuously together. Yet there is also substantial evidence that, within these homes, relationships are often far from harmonious; and it is repeatedly indicated that the parents of patients are neurotic or disturbed in some other way. Taking as a criterion clear-cut neurotic breakdown in first-degree relatives, Roth (1959) finds an incidence of 21 per cent. Nor should it be overlooked that a minority of patients, in one study as high as 25 per cent, come from homes broken by death, divorce, or other cause.

In a recent study of eighty-seven consecutive London patients by M. S. Lipsedge (unpublished), a high incidence of disturbance in the families of origin is reported. The patients ranged in age from twenty-two to sixty-four years; fourteen were men and seventy-three women. Almost all the information was obtained from the patients themselves during an initial interview, though occasionally it was supplemented by information from a general practitioner. Inadequate though this method is for obtaining the information required, it is unlikely to exaggerate the degree of disturbance in the families from which the patients came.

On the basis of this information, the patients' families can be divided very roughly into three categories:

I. intact and reasonably stable families

II. intact families in which there was much quarrelling, violence, and alcoholism, and/or almost complete absence of affection

III. families broken by death or divorce, or in which a parent was chronically ill, and/or the patient had had prolonged separations from or changes of parent figure.

The number and proportion of patients from families in each category are shown in the following table.

Category of family	No. of patients	% of patients
I	37	42
II	26	30
III	24	28
Total	87	100

Category I: There were thirty-seven patients who described their home life as having been happy or who gave no particularly adverse information about it. Nevertheless, two of these patients described a parent as having been agoraphobic (one father and one mother), and two others described themselves as having been 'over-protected'. Ten of the patients referred to themselves as having been notably fearful as children; of these, two had been school refusers and one agoraphobic. Thus neurotic trouble of one kind or another is reported in members of about one-third of these not overtly disturbed families.

Category II: There were twenty-six patients whose homes appear to have been intact but who described themselves as having had an extremely unhappy family life when children. Eighteen patients described their parents as having engaged in perpetual quarrels, including violence, and often made worse by alcohol. Another eight complained of having received no affection and/or of having been rejected. In three of these twenty-six cases the patient's mother had been agoraphobic. Two of the patients had themselves been school refusers as children.

Category III: Of the remaining twenty-four patients, there were twenty-one whose family life had been disrupted by death, divorce, or desertion and/or who had experienced many changes of mother figure. Of these, ten had lost one or both parents by death before their tenth birthday (six a father, three a mother, and one both). In five cases mother had deserted and in at least one other father. Two patients when young children had been evacuated for several years from wartime London, starting in one case at the age of three years and in the other at four. A number of children had been brought up by relatives. In addition to the twenty-one patients who had experienced disruption of affectional ties, three had been brought up by chronically sick mothers: in one case mother had had multiple sclerosis from the time the patient was aged seven.

Of this total of twenty-four patients three had had a parent figure who had been agoraphobic: one a father, one a mother, and one the grandmother with whom she lived. Eight patients described themselves as having suffered from anxiety as children; of these two were school refusers and one was agoraphobic.

Despite the manifest limitations of this evidence there is good reason to believe that in over half the cases (namely those from families in categories II and III) there was extensive disturbance of family life during the patient's childhood. Of the minority who were said to have come from stable homes there is clear evidence of covert disturbance in about a third of them.

Some Specific Patterns

Since, as already noted, there is a striking resemblance between cases of agoraphobia in adults and school refusal in children, there are strong prima facie grounds for suspecting that the particular patterns of interaction present in the families of agoraphobic patients may be the same as, or similar to, those found in families of school-refusing children. Despite the very poor quality of the evidence available, such evidence as there is supports this expectation.

The following three patterns of interaction found commonly in the families of school-refusing children are probably to be found fairly frequently also in the families of agoraphobic patients:

Pattern A – mother, or more rarely father, is a sufferer from chronic anxiety regarding attachment figures and either did in the past or still does retain the patient at home to be a companion

Pattern B – the patient fears that something dreadful may happen to mother, or possibly father, while he (the patient) is away from her; he therefore either remains at home with her or else insists that she accompany him whenever he leaves the house

Pattern C – the patient fears that something dreadful may happen to himself if he is away from home and so remains at home to prevent that happening.

As in the case of families with a school-refusing child, these differing patterns of interaction are not incompatible; mixed cases are probably common.

The fourth pattern of interaction found in the families of school-refusing children – pattern D, in which a parent fears for the safety of the child and therefore keeps him at home – is not directly recorded in the families of agoraphobic patients, but indirect evidence suggests that it probably does occur.

Family Interaction of Pattern A

Much evidence suggests that pattern A, in which a parent is retaining a son or daughter at home to be a companion, is common in these families. Thus the dominant and controlling role that parents, usually mothers, have played and may still be playing in the lives of their children is emphasized in almost every study. Roth (1959) describes the relationship of his women patients with mother as tending to be 'close and intense' and as excluding often any contacts outside the immediate family circle. An 'emotionally immature' young woman, whom Roth presents as typical of his series of cases, is reported to have been prevailed upon by her 'masterful domineering mother' to break off her engagement with a quiet clergyman and so to remain at home. Snaith (1968) reports that in at least seven of his twenty-seven cases there was clear evidence of 'over-protection'. Webster (1953), who studied twenty-five cases, reports all but one of the patients' mothers to have been dominant and over-protective. Terhune (1949), reviewing eighty-six cases, concludes that the phobic syndrome arises 'when an apprehensive, dependent, emotionally immature person is trying to realize his ambitions to become an independent member of society'.

Despite these consistent findings, no student of the syndrome seems yet to have given thought to the question why a mother should treat her daughter (or son) in this dominating and possessive way, or by what techniques she succeeds in maintaining her hold over her offspring. In a case reported in the psychoanalytic literature by Deutsch (1929), however, we find evidence to the effect that the patient's mother was making insistent demands upon her daughter to act as companion and caretaker to her. But Deutsch does not discuss why the mother should have behaved in this way.

In presenting the case, that of a twenty-year-old girl who suffered from typical and severe agoraphobic symptoms, Deutsch describes the patient's mother as being 'highly neurotic' and as having from the first 'concentrated all her unsatisfied libido on the child', her only one. By contrast, the patient's father is said to have been treated by mother as a nonentity. Although mother claimed that 'ever since her daughter's birth she had been a slave to her' and that her daughter could never bear her to be away, the evidence suggests strongly that, as in similar cases of school refusal, the account given by mother was the inverse of what the relationship had really been and still was. In other words, it seems likely that, while claiming that her daughter was making great demands upon her, mother was herself making great demands upon her daughter. Support for this interpretation comes from the unpublished study by Lipsedge already referred to. Of the eighty-seven patients in his series, no fewer than eight reported that one or other parent figure was agoraphobic.

Admittedly the findings referred to amount to no more than presumptive evidence for the presence of pattern A in a number of the families from which agoraphobic patients come. At the least they point to the need for systematic research, not only into the relations between a patient and his parents but also into the relations between parents and grandparents. For, if a proper understanding of the psychodynamics of the condition as it passes from one generation to another is to be obtained, it is vital that the neurotic difficulties of the parents of patients should be looked at sympathetically in the context of their own experiences as children. It is also necessary to examine the relationship between an agoraphobic patient and his (or her) spouse. Fry (1962) reports seven patients whose husbands were also agoraphobic, though covertly so. In some of these cases the husband was most insistent that his wife needed to have him with her, though on examination it turned out that the pressure for the other's company was more his than hers.

Family Interaction of Pattern B

A patient's fear that something dreadful may happen to one of his parents is only rarely reported in the literature on agoraphobia. Whereas that might mean that fear of such an eventuality is truly uncommon, it may mean no more than that it goes unreported, either because patients find themselves unable to talk about the situations they fear or else because psychiatrists, ignorant of the significance of family interaction, fail to inquire.[4]

4. Another reason might be that a psychiatrist without training in the recognition of pathogenic patterns of family interaction fails to report the

The picture, given by Lipsedge, of disturbed interaction in many of the families of agoraphobic patients is such that it would hardly be surprising had some of his patients been living during their childhood in chronic fear of what might happen to one or both of their parents. Eleven of his eighty-seven patients reported that one or both parents had shown violent behaviour, and another seven described perpetual quarrels between them. Anyone with experience of children or adults who have grown up in such homes knows how terrifying to a child the violent and quarrelsome behaviour of parents can be. In the first place, violent acts may seem to be of literally murderous intent. In the second, the mere threats uttered may fill a child with horror; for, in quarrels between parents, threats to desert the family or to commit suicide are probably extremely common. The constant apprehension of losing one or both parents by murder or suicide that pervaded Mrs Q's life as a child is described in Chapter 15.

In addition to the threats that are aimed principally at a spouse are the threats that may be used by a parent as a means of controlling the children. And it must be remembered that threats, for example that if a child does not behave mother will get ill or die or commit suicide, can be continued not only throughout adolescence but into adult life as well, and, if applied consistently, can result in an adult's being reduced to a state of permanent intimidation.

A family situation of this kind, it is plausible to believe, may have lain behind one of the cases of agoraphobia already alluded to (p. 346), that of the girl of twenty on whom, in Deutsch's words, mother 'had concentrated all her libido'. Let us consider the case material further.

In this young woman a principal symptom was fear that something dreadful might happen to mother. When her mother left the house she was afraid lest she be run over; each day she waited

---

situations a patient says he fears and, instead, describes the patient simply as suffering from 'irrational fears', a category to which are too often consigned clues that are among the most illuminating for understanding a patient's condition. Of thirty agoraphobic patients described by Harper and Roth (1962) nineteen are reported by them to have suffered from irrational fears.

anxiously at the window and heaved a sigh of relief when she saw her mother return safe and sound. Alternatively, the patient was afraid lest, while she herself was away from the house, something dreadful should happen to mother before she got back.

In commenting on the origin of this patient's anxiety, Deutsch adopts, without discussion, the hypothesis that she claims would be adopted by anyone versed in analytic work: that the patient's 'exaggeratedly affectionate anxiety' is an over-compensation for unconscious hostile wishes directed against mother; and that these hostile wishes have arisen as a result of the patient's oedipus complex. Although there are many psychoanalysts who would still adopt that hypothesis (though they might attribute the hostility to a pre-oedipal rather than an oedipal phase), others, through their experience in family psychiatry, would be aware of several other possibilities. One is that this 'highly neurotic' mother was given to threatening suicide. Another, which assumes Deutsch to be right in thinking that the patient was afraid mainly that her own hostile impulses might be enacted, is that the patient's mother had evoked such wishes by the insistent yet unacknowledged demands she had made upon her daughter over many years. Furthermore, prone as offspring are to adopt patterns of behaviour observed in a parent, it should be borne in mind that this patient, in developing a wish to push her mother under a tram (as Deutsch reports she did wish), might have taken her cue for such an action from a perhaps oft-repeated threat of her mother to throw herself under one.

In view of what we know can happen in families, though we are hardly ever told that it does, none of these ideas is fanciful. Yet all too often such possibilities are not even dreamed of by a clinician because the theory he is applying has no place for them. Only if every case is explored anew with knowledge of the part that can be played by family influences of these kinds are we likely to make progress in understanding and helping our patients.

Family Interaction of Pattern C

Fear that something dreadful may happen to themselves while they are out of the house is an extremely common symptom in agoraphobic patients. The principal situations mentioned as feared are of dying and of becoming helpless. Not infrequently such fear is linked to the various physical symptoms the patients experience – palpitations, dizziness, weakness of legs – which are interpreted by them as signs of imminent disability or death. By other patients again their fear is described as an overwhelming feeling of insecurity.

Although the situations a patient says he fears are frequently dismissed without further ado as irrational, knowledge of what can sometimes lie behind fear of similar happenings in children who refuse to go to school should alert us to the possibility that an agoraphobic patient is being, or at least has been, subjected to threats either of being abandoned or of being ejected from the family. As in the case of school-refusing children, information about such threats is hard to come by, but there is enough in the literature to make it clear that systematic investigation is required.

In most of the studies that have been referred to it is apparent that the possibility has never occurred to the researchers that the symptoms from which their patients suffered may have been a response to threats of being abandoned to which they may have been exposed during many years of childhood and adolescence. An example of the type of case that should clearly be considered in this light is the agoraphobic patient described by Marks (1969), and referred to earlier in this chapter, who recalled how as a child she had often been frightened when her parents left the house and how once she had sent her younger brother to find them.

Among the many studies of agoraphobia published, there appears to be but one in which threats are mentioned and are, moreover, considered to have played a causal role in the patients' condition. This is a study by Webster (1953) who reports findings on twenty-five married women suffering from agoraphobia, all of whom had been in psychotherapy for a minimum of three months. Using as his data the clinicians' notes, Webster rated the attitude of the mothers of these patients towards their daughters. Of twenty-five mothers, twenty-four were rated as being dominant and over-protective. In making these ratings Webster adopted as his main criterion that the mother 'be most solicitous of the daughter's welfare, rewarding her often without good reason and rejecting or threatening to reject her or actually telling her she would not love her any more if she did not behave'. The patients' feelings of insecurity, Webster suggests, were probably a direct result of their having been treated in this kind of way.[5]

As it happens, some years ago I treated a patient in her mid-twenties whose symptoms were typical of severe agoraphobia. Although for a year or more she insisted with great emphasis that nothing too good could be said of her mother, later she described her mother as 'a tartar' who had always used the most dreadful and violent threats, including outright rejection, to get her own way and still used them. Her father, she said, was frightened of his wife and occupied himself as much as possible outside the home; the patient said she was fond of her father and felt sorry for him. The consistency of the story, and especially the coercive and threatening way in which the patient often treated her analyst, suggested that the picture she painted of her mother was probably not exaggerated. Were I to be treating this patient today I should give far greater attention than I did then to the part I now believe her mother's threats to have played both in the aetiology and in the maintenance of her condition.

Support for the view that a substantial proportion of agoraphobic patients have been subjected to harsh treatment in their homes comes, as we have seen, from the unpublished study by Lipsedge. In addition, Snaith (1968) presents evidence that, whereas the mothers of some agoraphobic patients are indeed over-protective, others are rejecting: in his series of twenty-seven patients, seven are reported to have been over-protected and eight others to have been rejected.[6]

Nevertheless, these simple categories are likely to be far too crude to do justice to the facts. Not infrequently a parent who gives the impression of being consistently over-protective is found on occasion to be exactly the reverse; while a parent who appears to be consistently rejecting can on occasion be affectionate. The behaviour of the parents of many agoraphobics, like that

5. Webster does not discuss the possibility that some of these mothers may have threatened to abandon or eject their daughters.

6. In the remaining twelve cases evidence either was inconclusive or suggested that relationships were 'normal'; though in view of other findings it seems open to question that this was so.

of the parents of many school refusers, is probably very often intensely ambivalent. In both types of case the parental behaviour is usually, no doubt, a direct legacy of similar behaviour that the parents in their turn have suffered from one or other grandparent.

Family Interaction of Pattern D

In pattern D a parent is afraid that harm will come to the child and so, in the interests of the child's safety, keeps him at home. In the case of school-refusing children a main reason for a parent's fear of such happenings is the memory of some tragic event that has occurred earlier in his own life.

No direct evidence of this pattern in the families of agoraphobic patients seems to be on record, though repeated references to the over-protectiveness of parents make it likely that the pattern does occur.

This completes our attempt to discover to what extent the clinical features of agoraphobia can be understood in terms of one or other of the four patterns of disturbed family interaction that emerge so clearly in our study of cases of school refusal. With the quality of the data available on agoraphobic patients and their families so ill fitted for the task, the verdict must remain open. It is hoped, nevertheless, that our examination is such as to ensure that, in future studies of the syndrome, skilled attention will be given to interaction within the patients' families of origin, extending, whenever possible, over at least two generations. Only if data are specially gathered for the purpose will it be possible to explore further the set of hypotheses sketched and, in due course, to subject them to systematic test.

'Agoraphobia', bereavement, and depression

There is at least one other respect in which a close resemblance is found between agoraphobic adults and school-refusing children. This is that, in a high proportion of cases of both conditions, acute symptoms are found to have been precipitated by a bereavement, a serious illness (of relative or of patient), or some other major change in family circumstances. In most clinical accounts such events are mentioned only in passing. In the study by Roth (1959; 1960), however, statistics of precipitating events are given.

In Roth's series of 135 cases of agoraphobia, a bereavement, or a sudden illness in a close relative, 'usually a parent, upon whom the patient had been extremely dependent', is reported in 37 per cent. In a further 15 per cent there had been a severance of family ties or some other domestic crisis. Illness of the patient or some other acute danger to him had occurred in yet a further 31 per cent. That gives a total of 83 per cent of cases in which a precipitating event could be identified. Beyond noting the similarity of these findings to those found in cases of school refusal, however, little can be said until cases are reported in far more clinical detail than hitherto. In particular, Roth's material casts no light on the possible mode of action of the events he records.

Nevertheless, there is already evidence that in the psychopathology of agoraphobia bereavement plays a specific part, and not just, as Marks is inclined to argue (see above, p. 339), an incidental one. Using a specially designed projection test consisting of seven poorly structured diffused faces, each of which, the tester suggests, represents a person who has 'experienced trouble' at one time or another in his life, Evans and Liggett (1971) found that a sample of ten agoraphobic patients tended to identify the 'trouble' as a bereavement significantly more often than did matched patients suffering from some other form of phobia, and also more often to identify the bereaved person in the picture as themselves.

To pursue further the relation of anxiety to bereavement would take us beyond the bounds of this volume. It can, however, be noted that studies of bereaved people, for example those of Parkes (1969; 1970), show that it is very common for them to suffer panic attacks and other symptoms of anxiety. Reflection on these findings suggests that there is a spectrum of cases towards one end of which are patients diagnosed by psychiatrists as agoraphobic and towards the other end of which are the much larger proportion of people whose symptoms are either less severe or less long-lasting and who are, therefore, never seen by psychiatrists.

Relevant also to the overall argument of this work is the close link that exists between agoraphobia and depression. First, symptoms of agoraphobia and of depression tend to change simultaneously and in the same direction, either both getting worse or both getting better (Roth 1959; Snaith 1968). Second, agoraphobic patients stand a higher risk of developing depressive illnesses than do other people (Schapira, Kerr and Roth 1970). In the third volume it is hoped to explore these relationships and their implications in greater detail.

A note on response to treatment

In a thoughtful review, Andrews (1966) has pointed out that, in their ways of treating agoraphobic patients, therapists of quite different schools often have more in common than they suppose. In both the behaviour therapy tradition and in some psychoanalytic traditions (e.g. Freud 1919; Fenichel 1945; Alexander and French 1946) it is believed desirable for the patient's relationship with the therapist to develop through two phases. During the first the patient comes to look to the therapist for support. During the second the therapist uses this relationship to urge the patient to confront the situations he most fears.[7] Since the technique of confrontation has been carried furthest by behaviour therapists, who claim some measure of success with it, it may be useful to consider what implications for theory that may have.

During recent years a series of trials of the efficacy of different forms of psychological treatment has been conducted by Marks and Gelder at the Maudsley Hospital, London. Behaviour therapy has been given in two forms: (a) graded retraining together with systematic desensitization in imagination; and (b) flooding, a technique in which a patient is encouraged to visualize his most frightening phobic images continuously and without relief for a fifty-minute session, while the therapist talks constantly about the phobias and endeavours to maintain anxiety at maximum pitch.

7. In a paper on technique, Freud (1919) expressly advises that in the treatment of agoraphobic patients an analyst should 'induce them by the influence of the analysis ... to go into the street and to struggle with their anxiety while they make the attempt' (*SE* 17: 166).

After the fifth and sixth sessions, moreover, the patient, accompanied by the therapist, spends a further hour exposing himself to all the situations that he believes frighten him most.

In a recent report of the results of a crossover trial of the two treatments (Marks, Boulougouris and Marset 1971), improvements in the patients' condition, seen immediately after treatment and maintained twelve months later, are described. In the case of nine agoraphobic patients a combination of both treatments reduced symptom level from severe or very severe to moderate or mild. Of the two techniques flooding proved the more effective. A question that can properly be raised is whether these results are compatible with the hypotheses advanced in this chapter or incompatible with them.

When treatment started the patients were of an average age of thirty-three years and had had their symptoms for about twelve years. They were all highly motivated towards treatment. Many of them regarded the flooding method as a challenge to prove that they could face the phobic situation, and for some it was the first time in years that they had exposed themselves to it. That they benefited from the experience might be attributable, on the basis of the present theory, to two circumstances:

(a) The phobic situations, e.g. being out alone or travelling by public transport, were not the core situations of which the patients were or had been afraid but complementary situations on which a patient's attention, with that of his family, had become focused. Thus although the patient was genuinely afraid of these situations, once he confronted them he found that they were not so frightening after all.

(b) The agoraphobic symptoms in these cases had developed an average of twelve years earlier when the patients were in their early twenties. Whatever the family situation to which a patient was responding may have been then, it is likely to have changed materially during the interval. Thus for some of the patients, and perhaps for all, the family situation that it is postulated had produced the symptoms may have ceased to exist. Once resolutely tackled, therefore, many of the symptoms might be expected to diminish.

Individual Differences in Susceptibility to Fear

Were the latter explanation to prove valid, it would imply that phobic symptoms, once fully developed, may in some cases persist long after the situation that has produced them has changed. That contingency is in keeping with the present theory. Nevertheless, because the theory posits that childhood models of attachment figures persist, it would predict that these patients would continue to be especially sensitive both to loss of an attachment figure and to any situation that they construed as presaging loss. They would thus remain prone to develop anxiety symptoms. Whether this is so is unclear.

The conclusion appears to be, therefore, that there is little in the results of treatment reported so far that is incompatible with the theory advanced. At the same time no claim is made that the results support the theory. In any case to argue from results of treatment to theories of aetiology is notoriously dangerous.

Chapter 20
Omission, Suppression, and Falsification of Family Context

Suppressio veri suggestio falsi

Those who support the view advanced here, that school refusal, agoraphobia, and some forms of animal phobia are best understood in terms of anxious attachment arising from disturbed family interaction, have an obligation to answer two questions that their theory poses. First, how comes it that a phobic patient is afraid, or at least is thought to be afraid, of so many situations, such as schools, crowds, or animals, that have nothing to do with his relationships with parents? Second, and conversely, if the basic problem of a phobic patient lies in his relationships with parents, how comes it that that fact so often goes unrecognized and that his problem is thought to lie elsewhere?

Answers to these questions are not difficult to sketch. Several processes seem to be at work through which the situations truly responsible become obscured and distorted and other situations are picked upon instead.

When an insecure individual, uncertain whether his attachment figures are going to be accessible and responsive, or even alive, is faced with a potentially fear-arousing situation, he is more likely to respond to it with fear, and also more likely to respond with intense fear, than is an individual who feels secure and confident in his attachment figures. Thus the increased propensity of an insecure individual to fear any and all of the myriad of potentially fear-arousing situations present in his life outside his family is readily explained. What then remains unexplained is why concern is commonly so narrowly focused on his fear of those extra-familial situations while his fear of what may be happening to his attachment figures is overlooked.

In Chapter 11 it is noted that, in any one instance, it may be far from easy to identify the nature of the stimulus situations that are arousing fear in a person. Several reasons for the difficulty are discussed. One stems from the properties of compound situations. Whenever fear is aroused by a compound situation, there is a marked tendency to single out one of its components as the one that is arousing fear and to ignore the other(s). An example given there is of a person who is afraid when, alone and in the dark, he hears strange noises. Whereas the intensity of fear aroused in such a situation is likely to be a result of the fact that all three conditions are present simultaneously, there is a strong likelihood that attention will be focused on only one of them, while the other two are regarded as merely incidental or else are overlooked entirely. Which of the components is singled out and which are ignored is likely to be determined by the various biases of the person himself and of those around him.

In Western cultures, at least, there is a bias to give attention to that component in the situation that is most readily taken to spell real danger, in the example given the strange noises, and to disregard the others. By contrast, little weight is given to the component 'being alone'. Indeed in our culture for someone to confess himself afraid when alone is often regarded as shameful or merely silly. Hence there exists a pervasive bias to overlook the very component of fear-arousing situations that a study of anxious patients suggests is usually the most important.

Nevertheless, it is most unlikely that cultural biases alone account for the strong tendency, not only for patients and their relatives but for clinicians also, to misidentify the situations that are giving rise to a patient's fears. In many cases other far more specific factors are at work as well. Those that require attention include: omission of the family context in which a patient's symptoms have developed and are being exhibited; suppression of the family context; and falsification of the family context.

Much emphasis has already been placed on the marked tendency of the parents of patients (both young and old) to keep silent about the part they themselves are or have been playing. Information about their quarrels, or about their threats to separate, to abandon or eject their children, or to commit suicide, is very rarely volunteered to clinicians trying to help. Sometimes such information is not given because a parent genuinely fails to recognize its relevance, or because the clinician seems uninterested. At other times, it is clear, omission is motivated. For example, during the practice of family psychiatry it happens frequently that, when the confidence of parents has been gained, they admit frankly that in the account of events they gave during initial interviews they either suppressed or deliberately falsified key information. Often they did so, they say, because of fear of being criticized; and this is certainly true in many cases. But in a number of others suppression and falsification have much deeper roots.

In certain families it becomes plain, as work proceeds, that the parents are concerned, sometimes at almost any cost, to present the patient's behaviour as unreasonable and incomprehensible and themselves as reasonable people who have done all in their power to help. A perceptive clinician can see how acutely sensitive such parents often are to any sign of criticism of themselves, especially when it comes from the patient, and with what determination they seek to clear themselves of having played any part in creating the problem. The patient's behaviour, they claim, is to be understood solely in terms of the patient: he is emotionally disturbed, ill, mad, or bad.[1]

Alternatively, whenever the patient's problems can plausibly be ascribed to some extra-familial situation, the parents seize eagerly upon it. Unsympathetic teachers, bullying boys, barking dogs, the risk of a traffic accident – each is caught at hopefully in order to explain the patient's condition. Thus are phobias born: and, because so often they provide a convenient family scapegoat, they grow to have a life of their own.

If this analysis is correct, we conclude that both in determining the birth of a condition plausibly diagnosed as phobic and in fostering it parental influence is likely to be dominant.[2] Yet there

1. Scott presents evidence that in some cases a parent adopts this attitude because he is alarmed lest he be regarded as mentally ill himself (Scott, Ashworth and Casson 1970). In other cases a parent's perception of, and behaviour towards, the patient is shot through with fear lest he (the patient) should take after a relative who became psychotic during the parent's childhood (Scott and Ashworth 1969).

2. To this generalization certain restricted animal phobias may be exceptions.

are two other parties active on the scene, the patient himself and the clinician. Both, it is evident, often play strongly supportive roles.

Patients, it seems, vary enormously in the degree to which they accept their parents' definition of their situation. Not a few rebut it, either wholly or in part. Thus, as described in the preceding chapters, only a minority of children diagnosed as school phobic are likely to make any complaint about either teacher or school-mates. Similarly, studies of agoraphobic patients show repeatedly that the principal fear of which many complain is of leaving home and not of what will happen outside it. Given understanding and encouragement, and sometimes without it, many of these patients, whether child or adult, will describe accurately the situations that they really most fear. All too often, unfortunately, a clinician does not grasp the import of what the patient is saying and his story is dismissed or ignored.

Nevertheless, it must be recognized, there are many other patients who seem genuinely to believe that the root of their trouble lies in an unreasonable fear of some extra-familial situation, and who may even go to great lengths to discredit any suggestion that there may be difficulties at home. How, we may ask, does that come about? Here again several potentially inter-acting processes seem to be at work.

In the first place, no child cares to admit that his parent is gravely at fault. To recognize frankly that a mother is exploiting you for her own ends, or that a father is unjust and tyrannical, or that neither parent ever wanted you, is intensely painful. More-over it is very frightening. Given any loophole, therefore, most children will seek to see their parents' behaviour in some more favourable light. This natural bias of children is easy to exploit.

Not only are most children unwilling to see their parents in too bad a light but there are parents who themselves do all in their power to ensure that their child does not do so or at least that he does not communicate an adverse picture to others. When Mrs Q was a girl, it will be remembered, her mother was adamant that on no account should she reveal the appalling quarrels that raged between her parents. As a result Mrs Q told nothing to friendly neighbours, to teachers, or to school-friends; and she also had the greatest difficulty in revealing anything to the therapist who treated her after she was grown up; for to disobey a dominant and ruthless parent, even for an adult, is by no means easy.

Thus, threatened by sanctions against telling the truth as he sees it, a patient may habitually connive to present the family scene in a falsely favourable light. Yet in his heart he may know well enough what is true and, given support, may pluck up courage to describe it.

Such a state of mind is very different from another and related one, in which a patient gives a misleading picture of the family because he hardly knows where truth lies. The latter condition develops, it seems likely, when a person is plied from childhood onwards with systematically false information about family figures, their motives and relationships. This requires expansion.

In Chapter 14 an account is given of how during the course of development a child constructs for himself working models of his attachment figures and of himself in relation to them. The data used for model construction are derived from multiple sources: from his day-to-day experiences, from statements made to him by his parents, and from information coming from others. Usually the data reaching him from these diverse sources are reasonably compatible. For example, not only may a child experience his parents as accessible, considerate, and responsive but information coming from other sources may amply endorse that view. Others tell him how lucky he is to have loving parents; and his parents tell him how much they love him and how lovable they find him. Alternatively, both the experience a child has of his parents and the information he receives from them and from others about them may point consistently to their being unloving. Many more complex relationships can be imagined; but, provided in each case the information reaching the child from the different sources is reasonably compatible, the working models that he builds of parents and of self will be internally consistent in themselves and also complementary to one another. As such the models are able to reflect with a fair degree of accuracy the sort of people the child's parents are, how they see him and how they are likely to treat him. Thus, whether relationships are happy or the reverse, the child is able to make firm and accurate predictions and, on that basis, to construct plans of action likely to prove effective.

For a minority of children, by contrast, the data reaching them from the different sources may be regularly and persistently incompatible. To take a real, though by no means extreme, example: a child may experience his mother as unresponsive to him and unloving and he may infer, correctly, that she had never wanted him and never loved him. Yet this mother may insist, in season and out, that she does love him. Furthermore, if there is friction between them, as there inevitably is, she may claim that it results from his having been born with a contrary temperament. When he seeks her attention, she dubs him insufferably demanding; when he interrupts her, he is intolerably selfish; when he becomes angry at her neglect, he is held possessed of a bad temper or even an evil spirit. In some way, she claims, he was born bad. Nevertheless, thanks to a good fortune he does not deserve, he has been blessed with a loving mother who, despite all, cares devotedly for him.

In such a case, the information reaching the child from his parent not only is systematically distorted but is in sharp conflict with what he infers from his first-hand experience. If he were to accept his mother's view as correct, the model he would build of her, reflecting her behaviour and motives, and the model he would build of himself, reflecting his own behaviour and motives, would be such-and-such; whereas, if he were to accept the view he derives from his own experience as correct, the models he would build would be just the opposite. In such a situation the child is faced with a most grave dilemma. Is he to accept the picture as he sees it himself? Or is he to accept the one his parent insists is true?

To this dilemma there are several possible outcomes. One is that the child adheres to his own viewpoint, even at the risk of breaking with his parent(s). That is far from easy, especially if the parent should back the demand that the child accept the parental version by threatening to abandon or eject him, or else to become ill or commit suicide. Whenever a child or a young adult does take that course the rupture between him and his parent(s) is bound to be serious and may well prove unbridgeable.

A second and opposite outcome is complete compliance with the parent's version at the cost of disowning his own. Both parties will then construe his behaviour and how he feels as due to his disturbed condition and as being altogether unintelligible in terms of the family context as they see it and present it. A third, and perhaps common, outcome is an uneasy compromise whereby a child tries to give credence to both viewpoints and oscillates uneasily between them. A fourth is when he attempts desperately to integrate the two pictures, an attempt that, because they are inherently incompatible, is doomed to failure and may lead to cognitive breakdown. If Schatzman's formulation of the case of Schreber is correct (see Chapter 11), Schreber's condition would be an example of the fourth outcome.

There are many psychiatrists today, including the present writer, who believe that a number of very serious disorders can be understood as developing from cognitive conflict of this kind.[3] Here, however, only two of the possible outcomes need be considered. These are the second and third, in which the maturing child continues to accept his parent's version of the family scene, either without apparent reservations or else with them. When this is so, the child, even though fully adult, is still accepting his mother's picture of herself as a devoted and self-sacrificing woman when to an outsider she may appear demanding and possessive, and is still accepting her picture of himself as selfish and given to unreasonable tempers when to an outsider he may appear pathetically compliant. Should he at any time show signs of questioning her version of their relationship, moreover, she may use threats to insist he maintains it. Should he then be frightened

3. Most of the research stemming from this viewpoint deals with inter-action in the families of schizophrenic patients. In this tradition are the works of Bateson *et al.* (1956), Lidz *et al.* (1958), Wynne *et al.* (1958), Laing and Esterson (1964), and Scott, Ashworth and Casson (1970). The conclusions to which the findings of these and other studies point are, first, that the pathogenic potential of suppression and falsification as they occur within a family is fully as great as the pathogenic potential of repression and splitting as they occur within an individual, and, second, that processes of the two types interact. This is a field to which we shall return in the third volume. Well-planned research designed to explore this interaction is likely to yield insights of the greatest value to psychopathology.

that she will carry out her threats, she may disclaim ever having made them. And should it then be plausible to attribute his anxiety to some extra-familial situation, she will be quick to seize on it. Exposed to all these pressures, it is not surprising that he despairs of establishing his own construction of events and instead complies weakly with his mother's, or even assertively endorses it.

For parents systematically to suppress or falsify the roles they are playing in family life is, of course, gravely pathological. Yet the way in which they tell their story may be so convincing that anyone not alive to the possibility of systematic distortion may be deceived; and this is especially likely whenever the patient endorses the parents' account. Many a clinician, unfortunately, imbued with irrelevant theory and untrained in the field of family psychiatry, finds himself sadly ill equipped to see what is happening. In consequence the family's phobic scapegoat attains the status of psychiatric diagnosis.

Not only are most clinicians untrained in these matters but all too often they show bias. Sometimes the bias is pro-children and anti-parents. More often it is the other way about. Clinicians are often themselves parents, and so are likely unwittingly to identify over-readily with another parent's viewpoint. Parents may be thought of as experienced and sensible; the patients, by contrast, are young, and seen, perhaps, as inclined to exaggerate or even fabricate. In telling their stories parents may seem more lucid and coherent than their children. Furthermore, parents may be respected citizens, perhaps acquaintances or even friends whose account the clinician is reluctant to question. It may be no coincidence that Little Hans's parents were among Freud's 'closest adherents' (SE 10: 6). Pervading the scene, moreover, and influencing all parties is the time-honoured commandment 'Honour thy father and thy mother'.

Yet another factor tipping the balance in the same direction is the tendency, as notable in clinicians as it is in laymen, to reify emotions, especially the more uncomfortable ones. Instead of describing the situation in which a person experiences fear, the person is said to 'have' a fear. Instead of describing the situation in which a person becomes angry, he is said to 'have' a bad temper. Similarly, someone 'has' a phobia, or is 'filled with' anxiety or aggression.[4] Once emotions are reified the speaker is spared the task of tracing what is making the person in question afraid or angry, and will hardly notice when family context is omitted or suppressed. Thus any clinician who thinks in these ways is all too apt to fall in with a parent's claim that the behaviour of a child is altogether baffling and unintelligible, and thence to attribute it to some psychological or physiological anomaly inherent in the child. Preoccupation with nosological entities or biochemical anomalies has the same effect. Much present-day theorizing, both psychoanalytic and non-analytic, is of these kinds.

As a result of all these influences, which, as Scott (1973a and b) argues, converge to form the cultural image of mental illness as it is today, the dominant bias in psychoanalysis and psychiatry is to give credence to a parent's constructions and to throw doubt on a child's. Discrepancies are attributed with great readiness to the distorting effects of a child's feelings and phantasies, and only reluctantly to the distorting effects of those of a parent.

Nevertheless in certain quarters the boot is put firmly on the other foot. By those espousing anti-psychiatry the patient is deemed right and well and the parent is wrong or ill. Unfortunately, so strident and condemnatory of parents have some of these claims been that a family perspective becomes discredited and valid points are lost to sight.

The position adopted here is that, while parents are held to play a major role in causing a child to develop a heightened susceptibility to fear, their behaviour is seen not in terms of moral condemnation but as having been determined by the experiences they themselves had as children. Once that perspective is attained and rigorously adhered to, parental behaviour that has the gravest consequences for children can be understood and treated without moral censure. That way lies hope of breaking the generational succession.

4. The tendency to reify emotions is discussed further in Appendix III.

Chapter 21
Secure Attachment and the Growth of Self-reliance

People are much greater and much stronger than we imagine, and when unexpected tragedy comes ... we see them so often grow to a stature that is far beyond anything we imagined. We must remember that people are capable of greatness, of courage, but not in isolation. ... They need the conditions of a solidly linked human unit in which everyone is prepared to bear the burden of others.
— ARCHBISHOP ANTHONY BLOOM[1]

Personality development and family experience

Throughout the last half-dozen chapters attention is concentrated on conditions within a family that lead a developing child to grow up more than usually prone to be anxious and fearful. Here, in the penultimate chapter, we examine conditions that lead to an opposite and happier outcome. And just as we found that there is a strong case for believing that gnawing uncertainty about the accessibility and responsiveness of attachment figures is a principal condition for the development of unstable and anxious personality so is there a strong case for believing that an unthinking confidence in the unfailing accessibility and support of attachment figures is the bedrock on which stable and self-reliant personality is built.

Naturally any simple statement of that kind needs elaboration. Thus the family experience of those who grow up anxious and fearful is found to be characterized not only by uncertainty about parental support but often also by covert yet strongly distorting parental pressures: pressure on the child, for example, to act as caretaker for a parent; or to adopt, and thereby to confirm, a parent's false models – of self, of child, and of their relationship. Similarly, the family experience of those who grow up to become relatively stable and self-reliant is characterized not only by unfailing parental support when called upon but also by a steady

1. The David Kissen Memorial Lecture, 26 March 1969.

yet timely encouragement towards increasing autonomy, and by the frank communication by parents of working models – of themselves, of child, and of others – that are not only tolerably valid but are open to be questioned and revised.

Because in all these respects children tend unwittingly to identify with parents and therefore to adopt, when they become parents, the same patterns of behaviour towards children that they themselves have experienced during their own childhood, patterns of interaction are transmitted, more or less faithfully, from one generation to another. Thus the inheritance of mental health and of mental ill health through the medium of family microculture is certainly no less important, and may well be far more important, than is their inheritance through the medium of genes.

Evidence to support these propositions fully is, inevitably, insufficient. In the studies available the criteria adopted for deciding who are and who are not stable and self-reliant individuals can be challenged; the adequacy of methods used in collecting information about parental behaviour can be faulted; the assumptions made regarding continuity of personality organization over time can be questioned; and the restriction of samples to Western cultures casts doubt on how far findings can be generalized. Even so, the consistency of findings so far reported remains impressive. This means that those who are inclined to challenge either the evidence or the conclusions to which it leads have a case to answer. Only if they present such data as in their judgement point in a different direction can their objections be taken seriously.

In what follows the results of about a dozen studies, all reported since 1960, are drawn upon. It is not an exhaustive list and is, unfortunately, confined to studies undertaken in the United States. So far as is known, however, the findings are not contradicted by the results of any other study. Certainly, such knowledge of how personality development is related to family experience as has been acquired by those who work professionally with families in the United Kingdom does nothing to call in question the American findings.

Sector Studies of the Life-cycle

Since with present facilities it is not possible to study human beings in the course of their development from the cradle to the grave, it is necessary to consider sectors of the life-cycle piecemeal. Once a sufficient number of such studies is recorded it is reasonable to hope that, by fitting their findings together as a mosaic, a picture will emerge of a range of personality patterns, each of which will be seen developing along its own typical pathway within that version of family environment that, for good or ill, tends inexorably to promote it. In this chapter a sketch map of such a mosaic is attempted.

The sector of the life-cycle most studied is that lying between ten years of age and the early twenties. Typically the sample chosen is representative either of children in certain specified schools or of students in a specified college. Whereas in most studies, e.g. those of Bronfenbrenner (1961), Grinker (1962), Rosenberg (1965), Coopersmith (1967), Megargee, Parker and Levine (1971), information regarding personality and family is obtained at a single point in the individual's life-history, in a few the subjects are followed during a number of years. Examples of such studies are one by Peck and Havighurst (1960) in which subjects were followed from the age of ten to seventeen, one by Offer (1969) in which they were followed from fourteen to eighteen, and one by Murphey *et al.* (1963) in which they were followed from their last year at high school through their first year at college. Samples range in size from a few dozen to several hundred, with an occasional sample running into thousands. The amount of information available on each individual differs enormously and, as might be expected, varies inversely with size of sample. Whereas most samples include both boys and girls, a few are confined to males.

The findings of the batch of studies that focus on the sector running from pre-adolescence to early adult life provide us with an invaluable vantage-point from which to look both at earlier and at later sectors of the life-cycle. Looking in one direction we can consider the results of three studies of personality development and family experience that cover, respectively, the fourth and fifth years (Baumrind 1967; Heinicke *et al.* 1973) and the first two (Ainsworth and her colleagues). Looking in the other we can consider the findings of a study of unusually effective and self-reliant men in their early and middle thirties (Korchin and Ruff 1964). Finally, there are the results, not considered further here, of a study of almost a hundred adults in their early thirties who, since early childhood, have been the subjects of a longitudinal survey (Siegelman *et al.* 1970).

Among the varied aims of these many studies one that all have in common is to relate different degrees and forms of healthy personality organization, and/or of effective performance, to different types of experience within the family. Since in most studies interest focuses mainly on the nature of and conditions for favourable development, many of the samples are deliberately biased so that individuals who are emotionally disturbed or delinquent are under-represented or even excluded. In this way the far more common bias, typical of clinical studies, which leads a sample to be composed mainly or wholly of disturbed or delinquent subjects, is counterbalanced.

Sources of Information

In regard to personality development and its present organization and performance, information can be obtained from at least four main sources:
- from the subject himself, either during interview or in reply to questionnaires and self-rating scales
- from informants who know the subject well, notably parents, teachers, and peers
- from inferences derived from the subject's responses given either during interview or during projective testing
- from first-hand observation of behaviour either in a natural setting, e.g. at home or in school, or in a laboratory.

Similarly, in regard to family experience, information can be obtained from at least four main sources:
- from the subject's parents, or siblings, either during the course of interview or in reply to questionnaires or self-rating scales
- from the subject himself

- from inferences derived from the parents' responses given either during interview or during projective testing
- from first-hand observation of families in interaction, either at home or in a clinical or laboratory setting.

For their information in regard to either or both of these fields, a few researchers rely on only a single source, and by so doing are able to study a large sample. A majority of researchers, however, draw on information derived from several sources but by so doing are limited to studying only a small sample. That findings from these two very different types of study confirm one another gives added confidence to the findings of each.

Criteria of Evaluation

A difficulty intrinsic to every study of the kind we are concerned with is that of deciding the criteria to be used in evaluating personality structure. By what criteria, it may be asked, are we categorizing certain persons as well integrated, secure, and mentally healthy, and others as not so? How valid are these criteria? Are we, perhaps, in judging certain personality characteristics favourably doing no more than apply middle-class standards in an area in which they have no relevance? Is there danger therefore that our results are at the best of no more than limited application and at the worst positively misleading? Since criticisms of this type are often voiced (e.g. Spiegel 1958; Miller 1970; Bronfenbrenner 1970), an answer is necessary.

In the first place the criteria used are far from uniform. In some studies the principal criterion is *competent performance* in the social setting of home, or school, or college, or work. Examples are those by Bronfenbrenner (1961) of high-school students rated by their teachers, by Megargee *et al.* (1971) of college students rated by the researchers on the basis of information given by the students themselves, and by Korchin and Ruff (1964) of astronauts in training. In other studies the principal criterion is the subject's *self-esteem*, measured mainly in terms of how he says he feels about himself in relation to others. Examples are that by Coopersmith (1967) of schoolboys aged ten to twelve, and that by Rosenberg (1965) of high-school children aged sixteen to eighteen. In other studies, for example of college students by Grinker (1962), the criteria applied are complex and *derive from psychiatric experience*. In several studies, moreover, including those of Grinker (1962), Peck and Havighurst (1960), and Offer (1969), criteria of several sorts are used together. In the multiplicity of criteria used by the different researchers lies some safeguard against unwitting prejudice.

A second reason for having confidence in the criteria is that in several studies evidence is given that the criteria used for healthy development correlate negatively with independent measures of mental ill health. For example, Rosenberg (1965) shows that his measure of self-esteem is negatively correlated with a tendency to depression, with a tendency to feel isolated and lonely, and with proneness to psychosomatic symptoms. Similarly, a rather similar measure of self-esteem used by Coopersmith (1967) is shown to be negatively correlated with anxiety, as measured by clinical tests, and also with emotional problems and destructive behaviour, as reported by the subject's mother.

A third reason for having confidence in the criteria is that, when they are applied to a sample of subjects, the grading of personalities that results is only weakly correlated with the social class from which the subjects come, e.g. Peck and Havighurst (1960), Rosenberg (1965), Coopersmith (1967). This means that, because certain values in respect of personality and family relationships have come to be associated especially with the middle classes, it is mistaken to assume that they are not held also by members of the working classes, though admittedly by a rather smaller proportion of them. Nor, conversely, can it be assumed, as seems often to be done, that these so-called middle-class values are unrelated to mental health. On the contrary, it is very plausible to suppose that certain, though not all, of the psychosocial values and practices of a family that make for a modest degree of educational, social, and economic success in a child are the same as some of those that make for his better than average mental health. The plausibility of this view is much strengthened when it is expressed in its complementary form, namely that certain of the psychosocial values and practices of a family that make for below average mental health in a child are the same as some of those that make for his educational, social, and economic failure. Indeed, those studying the causes of intractable poverty no less than those studying the causes of mental ill health find themselves confronted by certain adverse and self-perpetuating patterns of family microculture that there is reason to believe are causal agents common to both conditions.

These are complex and difficult questions some of which are referred to again later in the chapter. Meanwhile enough has been said to show why in what follows the objection that the findings presented are invalidated because suffused with un-witting middle-class prejudice is not accepted.

All the criteria used in these studies are, it is believed, closely related to each other and all are measures, albeit crude, of a characteristic that might be termed 'adaptability'. By this is meant the capacity to adapt successfully to, and therefore to survive for long periods in, any and all of a wide range of physical and social environments, especially when survival turns on cooperation with others. Although this capacity could in principle be subjected to empirical test, in practice it would be far from easy to do. To illustrate the concept, however, an imaginary experiment can be described. In it the experimenter would select several groups of individuals, unfamiliar with each other, and transport each group to a succession of strange and difficult environments – some strange and difficult for reasons of social structure and custom, and others so because of geographical features. The prediction would then be that a group of individuals rated highly on a measure of adaptability would be more likely to succeed and survive over a long period in each one of these environments than would a group of individuals matched in other relevant respects, but rated lower on adaptability.

Thus the criterion of adaptability is distinct from a criterion such as 'adjustment to the *status quo*', to the use of which in this context there would be strong objection. It is distinct also from the criterion of whether a person tends to accept, to criticize, or to reject the *status quo*. Indeed, the ways in which personalities rated highly on the criterion of adaptability may contribute, positively or negatively, to the political life of the societies in which they live are little known; and to elucidate them is a task for which psychiatrists are not qualified.

It is thus clearly recognized that the interrelated criteria with which this chapter is concerned are a few only of the many that are applicable to personality. Some of the others, for example, degree of originality, of creative spirit, or of capacity for innovation, are certainly distinct from criteria of mental health and adaptability, and may, perhaps, be correlated with them in only slight degree. It must therefore be strongly emphasized that, in concentrating on the one set of criteria to the exclusion of others, no claim is made that the criteria selected are the only ones of importance. The reason for so concentrating is that in the practice of psychiatry the issues that must be our first concern are those of mental health and ill health. In so far as in our actions we may apply other criteria we are doing so simply as adherents of a professional ethic or as private persons.

The reader interested in considering problems of criteria further is referred to discussions by Grinker (1962), Heath (1965), and Douvan and Adelson (1966), and to a comprehensive review by Offer and Sabshin (1966).

Studies of adolescents and young adults

The Peck and Havighurst Study

Because clinicians are traditionally sceptical of the results of large samples studied by what they believe to be inadequate methods, we start with an extremely detailed and careful study of thirty-four children, seventeen boys and seventeen girls, growing up in a small town of the American mid-west, code-named Prairie City. This study by Peck and Havighurst, published in 1960, is part of a more extensive study begun during the 1940s of social and psychological life in the town. When selected for study the town had a population of about 10,000, 90 per cent of whom were native born and mainly of Norwegian and Polish extraction. The men were engaged either in agriculture or in local industry. Areas of residence were little segregated by social class and there was no socially disorganized area.

The sample of children studied was a sub-sample of all those born in the town during 1933. All children in the cohort, which numbered 120, were first examined in 1943 when they were ten years old. At that time they were given a number of tests of intelligence and personality and were also rated in regard to personality characteristics both by their teachers and by their peers. As a result of this preliminary screening a sub-sample of thirty-four children was chosen as representative (a) of all ranges of moral character and (b) of the social-class structure of the town. Thenceforward the development of these thirty-four children and of the families in which they lived became the subject of intensive study until 1950 when the children had all turned seventeen.

Since both the criteria used, namely 'moral character' and 'social class', can, as we have seen, give rise to controversy, a word about the place that each holds in this study is necessary.

Although in selecting the sub-sample Peck and Havighurst used a criterion defined in terms of moral character, a reading of their case material makes it plain that there is a high correlation between judgements based on that criterion and judgements based on the degree to which an individual is a well-organized personality, capable of effective performance in fields both of work and of human relationships, and in good standing with peers. In effect, therefore, the scale used is almost equivalent to scales that might be designed to measure, say, 'integration of personality', or 'ego strength', or 'emotional security', or 'mental health', or adaptability as defined here.[2]

As regards the issue of class, it is of advantage that in this study, in contrast to many others, the sample selected is roughly representative of the whole Prairie City population and, as such, comes mainly from the lower half of the socio-economic scale. This is shown in the table below. The criticism that findings are misleading because tangled with middle-class values would, therefore, be of little relevance in this context.

On each of the thirty-four children in the study a great quantity

2. Fairly early in their study Peck and Havighurst, in fact, replace the criterion 'moral character' by that of 'maturity of character'. Reasons why in the present work the latter concept is not employed are already mentioned briefly at the end of Chapter 14, and they are elaborated further in the final one.

| Socio-economic class | Sample studied | | | Population of city |
	Boys No.	Girls No.	All children %	All ages %
Upper	0	0	0	3
Upper-middle	1	0	3	11
Lower-middle	4	5	26	31
Upper-lower	9	10	56	41
Lower-lower	3	2	15	14
	17	17	100	100

of data were amassed. Many data came from the child himself, for example, from interviews with him, from standardized tests and questionnaires, and from projection tests. Other data came from sociometric measures given to the whole cohort of 120 children and from teachers' ratings. Data were analysed and evaluated in several steps. First, data from each source were analysed separately. Next, a clinical conference was called in which data from all sources were drawn upon to arrive at a picture of personality structure. A third step was for each research worker in the project to rate each personality on a series of scales aimed at measuring different aspects of character structure; as a result each child became designated by a personality profile. Finally, on the basis of these profiles the children were grouped into what proved empirically to be eight categories arranged according to their degree of maturity, a dimension equivalent to what in this work is termed adaptability. Brief descriptions of these eight character types are quoted below, starting with the 'least mature', and indicating the number of children assigned to each.

I. *The amoral:* These five children were characterized by

inaccurate perception of social situations, of other people, and of self; poor ability to set clear, realistic, attainable goals of any kind, behavior which is ill-adapted to achieve whatever ends the person does have in mind; and poor control over impulses which will interfere with successful adaptation to the social world, even in the sense of achieving purely personal, selfish gratification.

They show hostile, immature emotionality. There is, moreover, a pattern of childishly inappropriate emotional lability which mobilizes excessive energy and imposes a severe strain on the individual's already weak self-control. The usual nature of these emotions is that of negativism and hostility. These subjects are unwilling to accept the self-restraints and positive precepts their society suggests. . . .

They suffer from punitive but ineffectual guilt feelings, which are of little use in controlling their behavior. This in itself indicates sharp inner conflict and lack of positive, healthy self-regard or self-respect. . . .

The consequence is that they are no more at peace with themselves than they are with the world, though they might defiantly deny it to any representative of the culture they so strongly reject.

II. *A type intermediate between the amoral and the expedient:* Three children (not described in detail).

III. *The expedient:* These four children were characterized by 'taking the easy way out':

Their almost exclusive expediency is . . . not so much an active attempt to manipulate the people and events around them for personal gain as it is an effort to get as much personal gratification as possible by fitting in with their world when they have to, and avoiding as many social demands as possible which would require them to act in a positively socialized way.

Their constriction and relinquishment of direction to the social forces around them leads only to the absence of active immorality . . . it requires them to suppress enough of their selfish spontaneous impulses to make them tense, restless, and uncomfortable with themselves. . . .

They are would-be hedonists . . . but it seems that the inescapable facts of social living make real happiness dependent on actively friendly, mutually warm relationships with other people. Since they have little conception of such relatedness, their efforts to grasp hedonistic pleasure result in empty satisfactions. They seek but do not find, for they are unable to recognize the human warmth and approval they vaguely but intensely want.

IV. *The impulsive yet guilt-ridden:*[3] These two boys were characterized by a 'primitive, harsh conscience' which they disowned:

Thus, they are not 'masters in their own houses'. They react to

3. Peck and Havighurst designate this personality type by letters only, and the title given here is provided by the present author.

impulse or to internalized, irrationally held moral principles in which they do not personally believe ... They don't care much for other people, and feel themselves to be quite bad. They are not conscious of much of their guilt, for they protect themselves against recognizing their basically low self-regard by consciously picturing themselves in more favourable but not very realistic terms. Even so, their inner conflict is too severe to be successfully ignored. They try hard, but don't find much real pleasure in life.

V. *The conforming:* These eight children were characterized by a good deal of hostility that was controlled fairly effectively by a punitive conscience.

Two of them, both girls, are described as being unable to express their wishes spontaneously and to derive little satisfaction from life:

They feel strong, chronic guilt about their 'bad impulses', even though they seldom actively express them. Their superegos are almost entirely composed of negative 'Don'ts' which they have incorporated unquestioningly. They feel themselves to be a bad kind of person, just as they see little to like in others. They are unable to check the punitive voices of their conscience (almost a direct echo of harsh parental strictures, it seems) against the reality of daily life, in any rational, self-directing way. They are, in short, depressed, dull, unhappy, and quite unable to stand up to the world even to express their antagonism toward it.

Some of the other children categorized as 'conforming' are described as being 'friendly in their outlook and relatively at ease with themselves'. They were thought, however, to lack inner direction and to conform rather passively to the demands of those around them.

VI. *The irrational–conscientious:* These three children are described as

walking examples of the 'Puritan conscience'. . . . they have an appreciable degree of generalized hostility. This produces some guilt, but it is not intense since they are so utterly guided by their superego directives. They automatically behave in responsible, 'loyal', honest, 'kind' ways; but it is more by rote than by personal intent. They demand as much of others as of themselves in the way of conventional morality.

Nevertheless, their lack of any strong, positive concern for others as individuals, not to mention their repressed but definite hostility, makes them far too literal minded and rigid in their righteousness to be very easy to live with. . . .

They take some cold satisfaction from rigorously observing the letter of the law. That is about the extent of their joy in living . . . Their peers respect them, but they don't like them.

VII. *A type with good integration but less so than in type VIII:* These five children show 'a high degree of rationality, friendliness, and altruistic impulse . . . high autonomy and good integration of most major drives'. They are 'thoroughly spontaneous', like other people, and are liked in return. Although by no means lacking in moral principles, they are judged as rather too apt to put their own enjoyment first to be placed in category VIII. Even so, they are often very considerate of others.

VIII. *The rational–altruistic:* Finally, there were four children who are described as 'well-integrated' and 'emotionally mature' and who possessed 'firm, internalized moral principles' which they applied in an insightful manner:

They enjoy life thoroughly and actively, having as healthy a respect for themselves as they do for other people. There is no false pride in this. They simply are well and accurately aware of their own natures and capacities. Since they are free from serious conflict, free from any irrational need to follow convention blindly for the sake of 'security', they are free to use almost all their emotional energy.

These judgements of the children made by the researchers in terms of 'moral development', and later equated with level of 'maturity', were closely matched by independent judgements of the children made by their peers in terms of altogether more humdrum criteria. Thus it is found that all nine of the children placed in the highest two categories by level of maturity are almost uniformly well thought of by their peers in terms of their being friendly and cheerful, good participants in joint enterprises, and capable of self-control and leadership. By contrast, the eight children placed in the lowest two categories by level of maturity are uniformly poorly thought of by their peers. The seventeen children placed in the middle four categories by the researchers occupy intermediate positions also in the eyes of peers. The only disagreements centre on three children, of whom one was categorized as 'expedient' and two were categorized as 'conformers' by the researchers, but who were rated more highly by their peers. It is an open issue which group of judges was the more discerning.

Critical readers will doubtless disagree with the raters in respect of some issues and some children; for example, objection can be brought to rating moral development (or 'maturity' of development) along a single dimension. Nevertheless, a majority of readers will recognize that the overall estimates of the children's 'maturity' conform fairly closely to estimates of their mental health that most clinicians would be likely to reach. Moreover, the substantive findings of the study in which personality development is related to family experience do not turn on details of method.

To turn now to the families from which these children come: by a stroke of good fortune detailed information on the families had been collected when the children were aged between thirteen and fourteen by an independent research group working in the Prairie City study and had been stored away untouched. That made it possible to examine how personality structure is, or is not, related to patterns of family interaction by comparing two sets of data gathered entirely independently of one another. The results show significant correlations in the directions our theory would lead us to predict.

Each of the thirty-four families had been rated by the independent team on a number of scales which, when subjected to factor analysis, yielded four dimensions of family interaction. Two of these dimensions were found to be positively correlated with each other and to be strongly correlated also with the ratings of the children in terms of their level of maturity, as agreed by the main team.[4] These two family dimensions and the components that contribute to them are as follows:

4. The other two dimensions of family interaction, namely 'democracy versus autocracy' and 'severity of parental discipline', were not significantly related to the level of maturity of the children's characters.

Mutual trust and approval between the child and his parents:
- parents accept the child as he is and give him much affection and praise
- parents trust their child's judgement and do not insist on close supervision
- child feels free to discuss issues with his parents
- parents encourage the child to make friends and also make his friends welcome
- relations between parents are congenial and compatible.

Consistency of family life:
- regularity of daily routine
- predictability, in nature and timing, of parents' methods of control
- frequent participation by family members in shared activities.

When we consider the family experience of the nine children rated most highly in terms of maturity we find that the families of all but one were rated highly on both these dimensions. Conversely, of the eight children rated lowest in terms of maturity the families of all but one were rated low on both dimensions.

The family patterns found to be characteristic of children in the five most distinctive groups are described below.

Families of the amoral children: 'The most striking feature of these families is that, without exception, they are markedly inconsistent; and [except for one child] they are highly mistrustful and disapproving of their children. These boys and girls have grown up knowing very little love, little emotional security, and little if any consistent discipline.' It is no surprise, therefore, to learn that a child of this type is found to express 'an active hate for his family and for almost anyone else'.

Families of the expedient children: These children come from 'a *laissez-faire* home, where the parents give the child indiscriminate freedom to make his own decisions, approve of him, and are lenient in their discipline, but also are inconsistent . . .' Although these children receive 'a good deal of general parental support . . . it is combined with inconsistency, irregularity, and leniency, [and so] does not contain much real recognition or concern for the child as an individual'.

Again, it is no surprise to learn that a child of this type is found to have little feeling for his parents and to be ready to reject them whenever it suits his purpose.

Families of the conforming children: Most of these children come from severely autocratic punitive homes in which there is also much mistrust. When the parents are also inconsistent the resulting character structure of the child comes close to that of the 'amoral' children. When there is higher consistency and less distrust it comes closer to the 'irrational–conscientious' type.

Families of the irrational–conscientious children: These three children, all girls, had parents who were either severe or very severe in their discipline. In no case was mutual trust in the family rated high and in one it was rated very low. Consistency varied from average to high.

Families of the rational–altruistic children: Features that distinguish the parents of children in this most highly rated group are that they are strongly approving of their child and of his activities and friends, that they engage in many activities with him and have a harmonious relationship with each other. Home routine is regular without being rigidly so. Parents trust their child. In matters of discipline they are consistent in what they demand but 'leniency prevails over severity'. The children are found to have strong positive feelings towards both parents, sentiments that they later extend to others. Standards of behaviour, never having been enforced harshly, are open to discussion; they can then be applied later in ways adapted to the special features of a situation.

In the relationship between 'maturity' of character and family experience one case proves a notable exception to what is found otherwise to be an almost perfect correlation. This is the case of a boy rated very highly by the researchers in terms of his maturity, and also highly regarded by his peers, but whose family had been rated very poorly on the various family scales. When the home was first visited it was described as 'a physically unkempt working-class home, in which little regularity or consistency was seen by the interviewer'. Nevertheless, it is of interest that a few years later another visitor noted that the boy's 'relationships with his family and his extended kin are mutually acceptant and supportive' although, it was thought, lacking in warm affection. A possible explanation of this apparently anomalous case, an explanation which Peck and Havighurst tend to adopt, is that the original worker had been over-impressed by the obvious material untidiness of the home and too little aware of the less evident but far more relevant strong ties that existed within the family and the mutual support that members gave each other.

Since these thirty-four adolescents and the homes from which they came were studied and observed over a period of seven years, it was possible for the researchers to gauge how much, or little, change occurred during that time in the personalities of the children and in their families. In the event what struck the researchers was the very high degree of consistency that was apparent in the development of both of the parties. Thus '. . . the ratings and the actual case histories both suggest that whatever pattern of moral behaviour and character structure a child shows at ten years of age, he is far more likely than not to display into late adolescence'. Moreover, in so far as data were available also on earlier development, they were found to be of a piece with later development. Similarly, it was found that 'the parents tended to be just as consistently what they were, through the years, as did their children – particularly in their relationship with a given child'.

This consistency of development over seven years of early and late adolescence is of importance to our thesis for two reasons. First, it lends credence to the research strategy of building up pictures of personality structures as they develop during the whole life-cycle by fitting together, in a mosaic, findings from studies of different sectors of it. Second, it supports the view, discussed further in the final chapter, that different adult personality types are better accounted for in terms of development having taken place along one or other of a number of distinct and divergent developmental pathways than in terms of development having become fixated at one or another of a set of points thought of as occurring at intervals along a single pathway.

Studies of Large Representative Samples

In the much briefer presentation in this section of some findings from the many other studies available on adolescents and young adults, emphasis is placed on the regularity with which the findings reported are either similar to or compatible with those of Peck and Havighurst, despite the fact that each of these other researchers studied a differently structured sample, and used a different criterion of character development and also different indices of the pattern of family life.

Because Peck and Havighurst studied so small a sample there is advantage in proceeding next to studies which, because they draw on large representative samples, are able to examine rather different aspects of family life. In considering the findings of these large-sample studies, however, it must be remembered that in most of them information about the families comes entirely from the subjects themselves and must therefore be treated with caution.

In two of the large-sample studies a clear relationship emerges between patterns of personality development and certain basic features of the homes from which the subjects come.

One such study is that by Rosenberg (1965) whose sample consisted of no fewer than 5,024 boys and girls; they were aged from sixteen to eighteen years and were attending ten public high schools in New York State, selected to ensure that communities of every sort were represented. The criterion of personality used was a measure of self-esteem, which is best described as a measure of how a person feels towards himself, and especially of how he feels he compares with other people. This Rosenberg measured by means of a checklist of ten questions, each of which was to be answered on a five-point scale, ranging from 'strongly agree' to 'strongly disagree'.

The checklist for the assessment of self-esteem was given as part of a much larger questionnaire. One part inquired about a teenager's family and the other part about his view of himself, his feelings, and any psychosomatic symptoms to which he might be prone. The questionnaire was presented by teachers and completed during school time. From the information available two types of correlation are possible: (a) correlations of a subject's self-esteem with other statements he might make about himself; (b) correlations of a subject's self-esteem with the structure of his family.

As regards correlations of the first type, Rosenberg found that low self-esteem correlates significantly with several measures related to potential psychiatric disability, for example feelings of loneliness, sensitivity to criticism, anxiety, depression, and psychosomatic symptoms. By contrast, high self-esteem is correlated with trust in other people, active social participation, and a likelihood of being chosen as leader.

As regards correlations of the second type, Rosenberg found that, in level of self-esteem, children of divorced parents tend to compare unfavourably with children living in intact families. These lowered levels of self-esteem occur mainly in children of mothers who married young, had children soon after marriage, and were divorced before their twenty-fourth birthday. In a similar way the children of women who married and were widowed young also show a tendency to lowered self-esteem. By contrast, these ill effects are not seen in the children of women who were older when their child was born and when they lost their husband, whether by death or by divorce. Rosenberg explains his findings by postulating, very plausibly, that early divorce or widowhood leaves a mother of young children in a difficult and vulnerable position, which often results in her feeling insecure, anxious, and irritable, which in turn affects the personality development of her child. Another contingency, not mentioned by Rosenberg, is that the young children of young single-handed mothers are very apt to be subjected to periods of unstable substitute care.

In another study with a large sample, comprising 488 university students (280 men and 208 women) of a mean age of nineteen years, Megargee, Parker and Levine (1971) report that a systematic relationship is found between a measure of socialization and the state of the parents' marriage. The measure of socialization used, the California Personality Inventory Socialization Scale, is claimed to be a well-validated and standardized instrument that permits the selection of male and female groups characterized as either superior or inferior in regard to socialization by reference to national norms. On this scale groups of disturbed and delinquent adolescents yield low scores.

When the 488 students are divided into four groups according

to their scores, it is found that the gradient of scores correlates positively with the following features of family life:
– living with both natural parents
– parents' marriage rated by student as excellent
– student's childhood rated by him as having been happy.
By contrast, the gradient correlates negatively with parents being divorced.

In the following table, results are given only for students placed in the highest- and the lowest-scoring of the four groups. In every case the findings for the two intermediate groups lie on the gradient between the extremes. When findings for each sex are considered separately, no differences of consequence emerge. Results are expressed as percentages of the students in each group who report that they come from families with the characteristics shown.

Family experience	% of high-scoring group N = 51	% of low-scoring group N = 110
Living with both natural parents	95	78
Rating parents' marriage as excellent	85	29
Rating own childhood as happy	85	42
Parents are divorced	2	19

In this study no correlation was found between death of a parent and socialization score. Since only about 7 per cent of the whole sample had lost a parent, it is possible that the absence of correlation is in part because a smaller proportion of bereaved adolescents than of non-bereaved ones had reached college.

A third large-sample study is reported by Bronfenbrenner (1961). His aim was to investigate the family background of sixteen-year-old boys and girls rated by teachers in regard to each of two criteria: (a) the extent to which they proved to be leaders or followers at school, and (b) the extent to which they could or could not be relied on to fulfil obligations. Information regarding their families came from a questionnaire, designed to measure twenty different aspects of parent–child relations, which was completed by the subjects themselves.

The sample studied numbered 192, made up of equal numbers of boys and girls and also of equal numbers from each of four socio-economic classes, determined in a rough-and-ready way by the amount of education father is reported to have received.

Results are given separately for boys and girls and for each of the two criteria. Boys tend to be rated higher on leadership than do girls and the reverse is true of responsibility. On each criterion children whose fathers are more educated tend to be rated higher than children whose fathers are less educated. Other principal findings are that an adolescent who shows leadership is likely to come from a home in which he is given much time, affection, and support from his parents; and that one who shows a sense of responsibility is likely to come from a home in which parents exercise a good deal of authority, usually by means of reason and reward rather than punishment. Leadership and responsibility in children and affection and authority in homes are all positively correlated with one another.

At the higher ends of the rating-scales in respect of both criteria certain differences in family experience were found between boys and girls. Whereas boys seemed to thrive on high levels of parental support and control, there seemed to be some danger of girls receiving an overdose of one or both from their parents.

At the lower ends of the rating-scales, by contrast, no differences of consequence in family background were found between boys and girls. Moreover, whether the adolescent was rated low on leadership or on responsibility the picture of the home that emerged was much the same: in either case parental indifference or rejection was the rule. The boy (or girl) concerned was likely to describe his parents as inclined to complain about him, to ridicule him and compare him unfavourably with other children, and to spend little time with him and perhaps to avoid his company. Discipline was likely either to be lacking or else to be administered by means of arbitrary and excessive punishment. In respect of a few children whose leadership was rated low, however, a very different picture emerged: so far from being neglected, they had parents who were markedly over-protective of them.

In a fourth study, which draws on a fairly large sample and is reported by Coopersmith (1967), information about the family was obtained first-hand, although only from mother. The sample was confined to boys from intact white families.

Coopersmith's sample comprised eighty-five boys, aged from ten to twelve years, who were attending schools in two middle-sized towns in New England. The socio-economic classes from which most came were neither high nor low. The sample, which was drawn from a much larger number of children initially assessed, was stratified according to two criteria: (a) the boys' self-assessment on a test designed to measure self-esteem, and (b) the teachers' assessments of the boys in terms of their behaviour. As in the Rosenberg study, low self-esteem was found to be strongly correlated with anxiety as measured by clinical tests; it was also, though less strongly, correlated with emotional problems as reported by mother.

Information regarding the boys' families came from: (i) a questionnaire completed by mother, (ii) a two-and-a-half-hour interview with mother by an interviewer uninformed regarding the boy's rating on self-esteem, and (iii) the boy's answers to a series of questions on his parents' attitudes and practices. Fathers were not seen.

In reviewing his findings Coopersmith stresses, above all, the high level of maternal acceptance found in the families of boys with high self-esteem: 'The findings are all consistent, regardless of the instrument or source of information. They reveal that the mothers of children with high self-esteem are more loving and have closer relationships with their children than do mothers of children with low self-esteem.' Furthermore, as regards the strongly contrasting forms of discipline that were used by the parents of boys in the high and low self-esteem groups respectively, Coopersmith's findings are remarkably similar to those of Peck and Havighurst and to those of Bronfenbrenner, although the criteria of favourable personality development were quite different in the three studies. In the Coopersmith study not only were the boys of high self-esteem expected by their parents to meet high standards but parental control was exercised with care, respect, and firmness, and by the use of reward rather than punishment. By contrast, it was found that the boys of low self-esteem were not only given little care or guidance by their parents but often subjected to harsh and disrespectful punishment, which included loss of love.

Personality Development, Modes of Discipline, and Social Class

The consistency with which differences are reported in the modes of discipline and care to which children who show favourable or unfavourable development respectively are subjected is very striking. Equally striking is the consistency with which some of these same differences are reported to be associated with social class. Thus it is found that less-educated and working-class parents are more likely to use severe and arbitrary punishment, and to ignore or reject a child, than are better-educated and middle-class parents; and working-class fathers are less likely to spend time in joint activities with their adolescent children than are middle-class fathers (see review by Bronfenbrenner 1958). Taken together, these findings regarding (a) modes of discipline and personality development and (b) modes of discipline and social class support the hypothesis proposed earlier that the positive, if weak, correlation found between healthy personality development and higher social class may be explained, in part, by the differences in the ways in which parents belonging to different social classes tend to treat their children.

The findings of Bronfenbrenner's empirical study (1961) can be taken to illustrate a set of correlations that appear to be typical:
- low ratings for leadership and responsibility in children are associated with parents who show little interest in their children and who either adopt arbitrary and punitive methods of discipline or else give them little guidance;
- arbitrary methods of discipline, including physical punishment and ridicule, are more likely to be used by less-educated parents than by better-educated ones;
- the children of less-educated parents are likely to be rated lower

on leadership and responsibility than are those of better-educated parents.

Rosenberg reports a similar set of correlations between level of self-esteem, the amount of attention and concern fathers give their children, and social class. Further evidence compatible with the hypothesis is already given in Chapter 15 in which the relationship between symptoms of anxiety in a child and parental threats to abandon him or to commit suicide is discussed. These threats, it is found, are used by a larger proportion of parents in the working and lower-middle classes than of parents in the higher social classes. It would be inappropriate to pursue these complex and sensitive matters further in this work.

Another large and difficult area which again it is not proposed to pursue here is the differential influence of father and mother on the development of their children, with special reference to the influence of each on boys and on girls. Those interested are referred to the study by Bronfenbrenner (1961) and to one by Douvan and Adelson (1966) who discuss in much detail the difference in developmental patterns shown by boys and girls between the ages of twelve and eighteen.

Further Studies of Small Samples

Next we revert to more intensive studies by considering the findings of three projects in each of which small samples of men or youths, selected especially for their apparently healthy and well-integrated development, were subjected to intensive clinical examination and observation over a period of at least a year. Presented in descending order of the subjects' age, the first study is of astronauts in training, the second of youths attending college, and the third of high-school students bound for college.

In respect both of the developmental pathways that these personalities are following and of the family life they have experienced or are still experiencing, the findings of these three studies are in agreement; they are in agreement also with those of Peck & Havighurst. First, these well-adapted personalities are found to show a smoothly working balance of, on the one hand, initiative and self-reliance and, on the other, a capacity both to seek help and to make use of help when occasion demands. Second, an examination of their development shows that they have grown up in closely knit families with parents who, it seems, have never failed to provide them with support and encouragement.

So far as it goes, each study gives the same picture, that of a stable family base from which first the child, then the adolescent, and finally the young adult moves out in a series of ever-lengthening excursions. While autonomy is evidently encouraged in such families, it is not forced. Each step follows the previous one in a series of easy stages. Though home ties may attenuate, they are never broken.

Astronauts rank high as self-reliant men capable of living and working effectively in conditions of great potential danger and stress. Their performance, personalities, and histories have been studied by Korchin and Ruff. In two articles (Korchin and Ruff 1964; Ruff and Korchin 1967) they publish preliminary findings on a small sample of seven men.

Although these men tend to be individualists who show a high degree of self-reliance and a clear preference for independent action, all are reported to be 'comfortable when dependence on others is required' and to have a 'capacity to maintain *trust*, in what might seem conditions of *distrust*'. The performance of the crew of Apollo 13, which met with a mishap en route to the moon, is testimony to their capacity to sustain trust. Not only did they maintain their own efficiency in conditions of great danger but they continued to cooperate trustingly and effectively with their companions at the base on earth.

Turning to their life-histories we find that they:

grew up in relatively small well-organized communities, with considerable family solidarity and strong identification with the father. . . . a common theme in many of the interviews is the happy memory of outdoor activities shared with the father. . . . Their environments did not challenge them beyond their capacities. They went to schools and colleges in which they could do well. . . . We saw a relatively smooth growth pattern in which they could meet available challenges, increase levels of aspiration, succeed and gain further confidence, and in this way grow in competence. . . . [They] had stable self-concepts in which professional values were clearly and sharply defined.

In evaluating these findings and the conclusions to which they point, it is necessary to consider to what extent the men's history of family solidarity, identification with father, and smooth growth patterns may themselves have been criteria in the procedures that led them to be selected for astronaut training. Since, no doubt, these factors played some part there is danger of circular argument. Yet it must be remembered that, before selection, these men had already proved outstandingly successful test pilots.[5] At the least, therefore, the study demonstrates that the family background and experience described by Korchin is highly compatible with the development of a stable personality in which high self-reliance is combined with a capacity for trustful reliance on others.

The second study, this time of young men at college who appeared to their teachers to be of good general mental health and stability and to promise well as youth leaders and community workers, is reported by Grinker (1962). The sample studied comprised over a hundred students. Though in the drawing of conclusions the danger of circular reasoning remains, in this study it is reduced by its being possible to compare the family backgrounds of the members of three sub-samples which differed in the degree of integration and mental health shown by their members.

The study was initiated when Grinker and his colleagues were seeking healthy subjects on whom to conduct psychosomatic research. During initial interviews at a particular college Grinker was so deeply impressed by how free these young men seemed to be of neurotic difficulties that he decided to make a study of the entire male intake of the college in the following year. The main findings derive from the results of a very extensive questionnaire administered personally to all eighty students. They are much amplified by psychiatric interviews of thirty-four volunteers from that sample and also of another thirty-one students who had been

5. Though it gives less detail than the papers by Korchin & Ruff, a study by Reinhardt (1970) of 105 outstanding US Navy jet pilots suggests that the much larger population of successful pilots from which astronauts are drawn have, in regard to personality and home background and especially in their relation to father, much in common with the astronauts themselves.

seen the previous year. Findings from the interview study are presented first; those from the questionnaire study second.

The college in question is sponsored by the Young Men's Christian Association and has as its aim the training of young men and women to undertake work in keeping with the Association's objectives. Students come from all parts of the United States and Canada, with a preponderance from the middle-west and from rural communities and small towns. Many enter the college 'with strong convictions and motivations for YMCA work or that of settlement houses, community playgrounds etc.'. Entry standards are not as high as at many colleges and the curriculum tends to be less academic. Most of the students tend to be practical and good at games; IQs range from 100 to 130. For a great majority there is a close match between their own values and goals, those of their parents, and those of the college staff. Graduates have an excellent reputation and are much sought after to fill posts.

Among the sixty-five students interviewed Grinker reported only a handful as showing neurotic character structure. The large majority seemed straightforward youths, honest and accurate in their self-evaluation, with a 'capacity for close and deep human relationships . . . to members of their families, peers, teachers and to the interviewer'. Their reports of experiencing anxiety or sadness suggested that such feelings arose in appropriate situations and were neither severe nor prolonged. Grinker notes especially that a majority described how, on the one hand, they liked and sought responsibility and, on the other, would still seek advice on matters of importance. Thus there is nothing incompatible, Grinker concludes, between being prepared to seek aid from others in appropriate circumstances and the development of independence.

As regards their experience of home life, the overall picture reported by the students is remarkably similar to that reported by the astronauts. In almost every case both parents were reported to be still alive. The typical picture presented was of a happy peaceful home in which the parents shared responsibilities and interests, and were regarded by the children as loving and giving. Mother was seen as somewhat more encouraging, warmer, and closer than father. Discipline, mainly from father, was held to have been consistent and fair; it was said to have comprised mainly scolding, physical punishment of a moderate sort, and deprivation of privileges. Only rarely was a parent said to have used a threat to withhold love.

These students described how during childhood they had felt above everything else secure with mother. At the same time they had identified strongly with father. So impressed indeed was Grinker by these youths' strong identifications with father and father figures that he is tempted to conclude that in males such identification is 'an extremely significant factor in the process of becoming and remaining [mentally] healthy'.

These conclusions are strongly supported by the findings from the questionnaire study of the total intake of eighty students, for which a within-group comparison was possible. On the basis of their answers to the questionnaire, students were placed in one of three subgroups according to the degree to which personality development seemed free of neurotic features. Students placed in the most healthy subgroup reported the closest and most rewarding of relationships with both parents, whereas those in the least healthy of the subgroups were more likely to report family relationships that were somewhat distant or strained; and they were also more likely to report episodes of stress, anxiety, and conflict during adolescence. Again, in summing up his findings about the best integrated and most healthy of his students Grinker uses words very similar to those that Korchin uses to describe the astronauts. He is impressed by the simple directness of the developmental pathways they have followed, by the gradualness of the changes that have taken place both in the growth of the personalities and in the environments in which they have grown, and by the almost complete absence in these students' lives of stress, conflict, and disappointment.

Grinker discusses some of the objections that can be made to his study and his conclusions. He is aware, for example, that critics might allege that these young men are merely dull conformists lacking creative spirit and capacity for innovation. Even were that to be true, however, and it is debatable, the criticism would not be relevant. For, as was remarked earlier, as psychiatrists we are concerned with the development of personalities rated highly in respect of mental health and self-reliance, and not in respect of any of the other criteria applicable in evaluating personality. And, as Grinker observes in defending his students against the easy criticisms that might be made by professional people who are committed to innovation and to competitive careers, constant innovation and intense competition may themselves be both symptoms of neurosis and agents in its production. The healthy population, by contrast, may perhaps provide that steady core of stability without which all would be chaos.

Grinker is also aware that the validity of the historical information he uses can be challenged, since all of it is derived from the subjects' own reports. Furthermore, he knows that he is in no position to estimate the extent to which the healthily developing subjects had themselves contributed to the stability and harmony of their homes. These deficiencies are in some measure offset, however, when we find that Grinker's data and conclusions are little different from those of studies in which information regarding parents is obtained first-hand, as it was in the studies of Peck and Havighurst (1960) and of Coopersmith (1967), and as it was also in the study next to be reported.

This is a study of students during their transition from high school to college, undertaken in Washington D.C. by Hamburg and his colleagues (see Murphey *et al.* 1963). The nineteen college-bound students, of both sexes, were selected during their last year at high school, on the basis of school record and a screening interview, as showing a high degree of competence; this was assessed in terms of their academic effectiveness, their satisfying and close peer relationships, and their ability to participate in social groups. The students were interviewed no fewer than seven times during the six months before going to college and four times during their freshman year. Parents were interviewed three times, once before the student went to college, once during the Christmas vacation, and once, jointly with the student, at the end of the year.

At the end of the study each student was assessed on two criteria: (i) the degree of autonomy he showed, defined in terms of his ability to make his own choices and to assume responsibility for his own decisions, and (ii) the extent to which he was able to maintain, or increase, mutually rewarding relationships with his parents. On the basis of these two criteria, the students could be assigned to one of four subgroups:

(a) those high in both autonomy and family relatedness: nine students

(b) those high in autonomy but low in family relatedness: six students

(c) those low in autonomy but high in family relatedness: one student

(d) those low in both autonomy and family relatedness: three students.

The nine students in subgroup (a) were plainly having the best of both worlds, being self-reliant and effective in college yet enjoying increasing intimacy with parents during the vacations. They resemble Grinker's very well-adjusted group. Those in subgroup (b) were also making good use of their opportunities at college, but relations with parents were growing distant or even hostile. The four students in subgroups (c) and (d) combined were showing little ability to stand on their own feet or to organize their own lives. It thus turned out that, on the basis of evidence collected during the course of the year, only half the students in the sample succeeded in living up to the high expectations of those who had originally selected them.

Interviews with parents, including one joint interview with parents and student together, showed considerable differences in the ways in which the students in the different subgroups were treated by their parents.

Parents of students placed in subgroup (a) were found to have clearly defined values and standards, which they were able to communicate to their offspring. At the same time they placed high value on the student's developing his own autonomy and encouraged it. Should their son (or daughter) require help or advice they were ready to respond, but they avoided giving it unless asked. They treated him with respect and kept him informed of both good and bad news, believing him adult enough to carry the responsibility. In a word, they encouraged their child to develop a life and a personality of his own, enjoyed his company during vacations, and were ready to give help when called upon.

The parents of the six students placed in subgroup (b), who showed high autonomy but low family relatedness, were able to provide many of the conditions provided by the parents of those in subgroup (a). The main difference was that the subgroup (b) parents were found to assign a role to their offspring that was more in keeping with their (the parents') interests than the interests of the son or daughter concerned. As a result, given the chance of an independent life, these students broke away from home and went their own way. Whether the resulting conflicts would persist was uncertain; it seemed likely to depend on whether or not the parents could reconcile themselves to the way of life their child had decided upon.

Finally, the three students placed in subgroup (d), who were characterized by low autonomy and low family relatedness, had parents who, it was found, were often unclear who they were and what they stood for. Communication in these families was poor and conflicts of opinion, when present, remained latent and obscure. After making a choice a student might be uncertain whether he had made it himself or been manipulated into making it by one of his parents.

Thus, as in Grinker's study, a within-sample comparison shows that the students who best meet the initial criteria are those who come from homes in which children receive the most support, in which communication between parents and children is most clear, and in which children are most trusted and are given most responsibility. The conclusion seems clear. When a student feels confident that relationships at home are secure, supportive, and encouraging he finds no difficulty in making the most of the new opportunities that college offers.

This same pattern of growing self-reliance resting on a secure attachment to a trusted figure and developing from it, found in each of the studies so far reviewed, is to be found also during the earliest years of life.

Studies of young children

Though there are other studies of adolescents and their families, notably that of Offer (1969), the findings of which support the thesis, it is time to turn to another sector of the life-cycle. What evidence is there, we may ask, that the kind of family experience that is associated with well-integrated and adaptable adolescents is found also to be the kind of family experience that is associated with young children who, so far as can be told, promise to develop along the same or similar pathways? A cross-sectional study by Baumrind (1967) of children attending a nursery school and a short-longitudinal study by Ainsworth and her colleagues of children developing during their first year (Ainsworth, Bell and Stayton 1971), and in some cases to the age of twenty-one months (Main 1973), are steps to answering this question.

Nursery-school Children

To obtain her sample for systematic study Baumrind screened all the 110 children who were attending one of the four sections of a university nursery school. They were aged three or four years and were mainly from middle-class homes. To ensure that the children selected for study fell into three distinctive groups, each containing subjects with clear-cut and consistent patterns of interpersonal behaviour, screening was done in two steps. First, at the end of fourteen weeks of observation, teachers and psychologists ranked the children on five dimensions of behaviour. The second step was carried out immediately afterwards: fifty-two children ranked consistently either high or low on these dimensions were studied in an experimental situation in which each child was given three puzzles, graded in difficulty, to see how he responded in situations of easy success, probable success, and certain failure. As a result of these two screenings three groups of children, numbering thirty-two in all, were selected.

Children in group I, comprising seven boys and six girls, were ranked and rated highly, in nursery class and in the laboratory, in regard to such characteristics as vigorous and cheerful participation in school activities; willingness to tackle new and difficult tasks; active exploration of the environment; ability to sustain effort, to take turns, and to obey school rules; ability to stand up for themselves; and willingness to seek help from adults when necessary.

Children in group II, comprising four boys and seven girls, had low rankings in these regards. In particular, they were poor at exploring, tackling new and difficult tasks, and cooperating with other children; they were also liable to moods, in which they were either aggressive and obstructive or fearful, bored, or subdued.

Children in group III, comprising five boys and three girls, were also poorly thought of. In particular, they were rated low in regard to participation in activities and exploration; ability to sustain effort, to take turns, and to obey school rules; and also in regard to capacity to stand up for themselves and make their own way.

While children in group I can be regarded as well integrated and adaptable for their age, the development of those in groups II and III is clearly suboptimal by almost any standard.

Information regarding the family experience of each child came from three sources: (a) two home visits, each lasting about three hours, one of which was during the evening at a time of maximum domestic stress; (b) a structured observation of mother and child in the laboratory; (c) interview of each parent separately.

During a home visit an observer recorded every occasion of parent–child interaction in which one member of the pair attempted to influence the behaviour of the other. To gauge reliability of observation, eight families were observed by two observers. Records were coded. Subsequently the father and mother of each child were rated on four rating-scales which can be summarized as follows:

nurturance: the extent to which the parent is concerned about the child's physical and emotional wellbeing, is attentive to him, and expresses affection, and pride and pleasure in his achievements;

maturity demands: the extent to which the parent expects the child to be self-reliant and to perform up to his abilities;

control: the extent to which the parent seeks to modify the way the child behaves, either by exerting pressure or by resisting pressure;

mode of communication: the extent to which the parent consults the child's opinions and feelings, and uses reason, and open and clear techniques of control in contrast to manipulative ones.

The second source of information about a child's family experience came from observation of mother and child in a laboratory setting. Their interaction was observed and recorded by two psychologists. The session was divided into two phases: first, mother was asked to teach her child elementary concepts using rods of different lengths and colours; second, she was asked to be with him while he played. Mother was free to play with him or not as she wished, but in any case she was asked to ensure that during play he kept within certain limits set by the experimenters. In this setting it was possible to note how a mother assisted and supported her child, what expectations of him she appeared to have, her use of praise and disapproval, her way of enforcing rules, her modes of teaching, and her ability to secure his collaboration. Subsequently, mothers were rated on the same four rating-scales that were used to rate parents following the home visits.

The consistency of findings for the behaviour of each mother in the two settings, home and laboratory, was such as to suggest that each observation gave a valid picture (though it must be recognized that the two sets of ratings were not made entirely independently of each other).

When the behaviour of parents is compared in relation to the three groups in which their children were initially placed, differences are of exactly the kind that the studies of adolescents and their parents have led us to expect. The fathers and mothers of children in group I are found to be rated highly on each of the four rating-scales described above. The parents of children in both groups II and III are rated consistently lower on these scales than are those of children in group I. Parents of children in group II score especially low on nurturance; those of children in group III score especially low on control and on maturity demands.

Typical pictures of family experience for children in each of the three groups, based on information derived from all three sources, i.e. including interviews, are as follows:

Family experience of children in group I: In the home setting, parents of these active, controlled, and self-reliant children were consistent in handling their child and also loving and conscientious in their care. They respected his wishes but could also stick to their own decisions. They gave their reasons for going against a child's wishes and encouraged plenty of verbal give-and-take. In the laboratory they showed firm control and expected a good deal of the child but were also supportive. They made their wishes clearly known.

Family experience of children in group II: In both the home and the laboratory the parents of these rather anxious and aggressive children were found to give their child relatively little affection, attention, or support. Though they exerted firm control, they gave no reasons for their action. Moreover, they gave their child little encouragement or approval. In interview, mother reported using disciplinary measures that entailed frightening the child.

Family experience of children in group III: The parents of these unassertive and rather inactive children were found to be self-effacing and insecure themselves, and not very effective in managing their homes. Neither parent demanded much of the child, and they were apt to baby him. In interview it emerged that mothers were inclined to use withdrawal of love and ridicule as methods of discipline.

Another study aimed at throwing light on the relationship between family experience and the behaviour of young children in a nursery school is being conducted in Los Angeles by Heinicke. Children are being studied longitudinally, starting when they enter nursery school at the age of three and continuing for the next four years. In addition to regular assessments of performance on educational tasks, a child's day-to-day social and emotional behaviour is recorded in much detail with special reference to the behaviour he experiences from his teachers and from his parents. When the different patterns of behaviour shown in school are correlated with the different ways a mother may treat her child, the same kinds of association that Baumrind reports are found. In a preliminary communication Heinicke and his colleagues (1973) illustrate their results by describing the contrasting development of two children and their families. The extent to which behaviour in school is found to be reactive to experience at home, especially to the availability or non-availability of the child's attachment figures, strongly supports the present thesis. So too do the findings of the rather similar study reported by van Leeuwen and Tuma (1972) (see above, p. 78 n).

Nevertheless, it must be remembered, the children studied by these different workers were already three or four years old, by which age several years of very complex interactions between child and parents have taken place and considerable developments have occurred in a child's personality. What, we may therefore ask, do we know of patterns of personality and the conditions in which they develop during an even earlier sector of the life-cycle? For light on this we turn to the study by Ainsworth and her colleagues of twenty-three infants and their mothers, observed during the first year of the infants' life.

One-year-olds

In Chapter 3 a description is given of Ainsworth's method of observing the interaction of a mother and her twelve-month-old child, first, when they are together in a benign but strange situation and, later, after mother has left the room briefly and has then returned. Of the total of fifty-six infants from white middle-class homes whom Ainsworth studied at twelve months, a sub-sample of twenty-three were observed in their own home with mother throughout their first year.

The home of each child in this sub-sample was visited every three weeks by an observer, who stayed for a long session lasting about four hours during which mother was encouraged to carry on her activities in her usual way. Detailed notes were made during the visits, from which was subsequently dictated and transcribed a narrative report of the infant's behaviour and of the interactions that had occurred between mother and infant. From all the data that are available on this sub-sample it is necessary for our purpose to concentrate on only three sets:

- behaviour of infant as observed at twelve months when with his mother in the experimental situation
- behaviour of infant as observed at eleven and twelve months when with his mother at home
- behaviour of mother towards her infant as observed during visits to the home during the whole of the infant's first year.

An examination of the findings, reported by Ainsworth, Bell and Stayton (1971), shows that, with only few exceptions, the way an infant of twelve months behaves with and without his mother in his own home and the way he behaves with and without her in a slightly strange test situation have much in common. By drawing on observations of behaviour in both types of situation it becomes possible to classify the infants into five main groups, using two criteria: (a) how much or how little an infant explores when in different situations; and (b) how he treats his mother – when she is present, when she departs, and when she returns.[6]

The five groups, with the number of infants classifiable into each, are as follows:

Group P: The exploratory behaviour of an infant in this group varies with the situation and is most evident in mother's presence. He uses mother as a base, keeps note of her whereabouts, and exchanges glances with her. From time to time he returns to her and enjoys contact with her. When she returns after a brief absence he greets her warmly. No ambivalence towards her is evident. $N = 8$.

Group Q: The behaviour of these infants is much like that of infants in group P. Where it differs is in that, first, infants in this group tend to explore more actively in the strange situation and, second, they tend to be somewhat ambivalent towards mother. On the one hand, if ignored by her, an infant may become intensely demanding; on the other, he may ignore or avoid her in return. Yet at other times the pair are capable of happy exchanges together. $N = 4$.

6. The classification presented here, based on behaviour in *both* types of situation, is a slightly modified version of the one presented by Ainsworth *et al.* (1971) in which a child's behaviour in his own home is the *sole* source of data. Infants classified here into groups P, Q, and R are identical with the infants classified into Ainsworth's groups I, II, and III. Those classified here into group T are the same as those classified into Ainsworth's group V, less one infant who, although passive at home, proved markedly independent in the strange test situation and is therefore transferred to group S. The infants in group S are the same as those in Ainsworth's group IV, plus the one infant transferred. The reclassification presented here has Professor Salter Ainsworth's approval.

Group R: An infant in this group explores very actively whether mother is present or absent and whether the situation is familiar or strange. He tends, moreover, to have little to do with his mother and is often not interested in being picked up by her. At other times, especially after his mother has left him alone in the strange situation, he behaves in a very contrary way, alternately seeking proximity to her and then avoiding it, or seeking contact and then wriggling away. $N = 3$.

Group S: The behaviour of infants in this group is inconsistent. Sometimes they appear very independent, though usually for brief periods only; at other times they seem markedly anxious regarding mother's whereabouts. They are distinctly ambivalent about contact with her, seeking it frequently yet not seeming to enjoy it when given, or even strongly resisting it. Oddly enough, in the strange situation they tend to ignore mother's presence and to avoid both proximity to and contact with her. $N = 5$.

Group T: These infants tend to be passive both at home and in the strange situation. They show relatively little exploratory behaviour but much autoerotic behaviour. They are conspicuously anxious about mother's whereabouts and cry much in her absence; yet when she returns they can be markedly ambivalent towards her. $N = 3$.

When an attempt is made to evaluate these different patterns of behaviour as forerunners of future personality development the eight children in groups S and T seem the *least* likely to develop a well-integrated personality in which self-reliance is combined with trust in others. Some are passive in both situations; others explore but only briefly. Most of them seem anxious about mother's whereabouts, and relations with her tend to be extremely ambivalent.

The three children in group R are most active in exploration and appear strongly independent. Yet their relations with mother are cautious, even slightly detached. To a clinician they give the impression of being unable to trust others, and of having developed a premature independence.

The four children in group Q are more difficult to assess. They seem to lie half-way between those in group R and those in group P.

If the perspective adopted in this work proves correct, it would be the eight children in group P who would be most likely in due course to develop a well-integrated personality, both self-reliant and trustful of others; for they move freely and confidently between a busy interest in exploring their environment and the people and things in it, and keeping in intimate touch with mother. It is true that they often show less self-reliance than the children in groups Q and R, and that in the strange situation they are more affected than those children are by mother's brief absences. Yet their relations with mother seem always to be cheerful and confident, whether expressed in affectionate embraces or in the exchanging of glances and vocalizations at a distance, and this seems to promise well for their future.

When we turn now to the type of mothering that was received by infants in each of the five groups, on the basis of data obtained during the long visits observers paid to the homes, the differences and correlations found are, once again, of the same kinds as those found in studies of older children and adolescents.

In assessing a mother's behaviour towards her child Ainsworth uses four distinct nine-point rating-scales. These are: an acceptance–rejection scale, a cooperation–interference scale, an accessibility–ignoring scale, and a scale measuring the degree of sensitivity a mother shows to her baby's signals. Since ratings on all these scales intercorrelate highly, detailed results are given for the last scale only, that of sensitivity or insensitivity to the baby's signals and communications. Whereas a sensitive mother seems constantly to be 'tuned in' to receive her baby's signals, is likely to interpret them correctly, and to respond to them both promptly and appropriately, an insensitive mother will often not notice her baby's signals, will misinterpret them when she does notice them, and will then respond tardily, inappropriately, or not at all.

When the ratings on this scale for the mothers of infants in each of the five groups are examined, it is found that the mothers of the eight infants in group P are rated uniformly highly (range 5·5 to 9·0), those of the eleven infants in groups R, S, and T are rated uniformly low (range 1·0 to 3·5), and those of the four in group Q are in the middle (range 4·5 to 5·5). Differences are statistically significant. Furthermore, when mothers are rated on the other three scales, differences between groups, in the same direction and or roughly the same order of magnitude, are found.

In further analyses of the date (Bell and Ainsworth 1972; Stayton and Ainsworth 1973) it was found that the more responsive a mother was in tending her baby when he cried during the early months of his life the less frequently he cried during the later months of the first year and the more likely he was to greet her cheerfully when she returned after a short absence.

In discussing their findings, Ainsworth and her colleagues (1974) emphasize that

mothers who give relatively much physical contact to their infants in their earliest months ... have infants who by the end of the first year not only enjoy active affectional interaction when in contact but are also content to be put down and turn cheerfully to exploration and play. ... [Such contact] does not make [an infant] into a clingy and dependent one-year-old; on the contrary it facilitates the gradual growth of independence. It is infants who have had relatively brief episodes of being held who tend to protest being put down, and also do not turn readily to independent play ...

Very recently Main (1973) has carried these studies a step further by following up children who had been observed in the strange situation at the age of twelve months and observing them again in a different but comparable situation nine months later. Of forty children so followed up, twenty-five had been classified as secure at twelve months and fifteen as insecure.[7] When observed again at the age of twenty-one months in a free-play session, the children earlier classified as secure were found to concentrate on an activity both more intensely and for longer periods, and to smile and laugh more frequently, than those earlier classified as insecure. When joined by an adult playmate they were far more likely to approach and play with her. When given Bayley developmental tests they proved more cooperative

7. Main's secure infants are those classified here in groups P and Q; her insecure infants are those classified in groups R, S, and T.

and achieved a mean score of 111·2 in comparison with a mean of 96·1 for the insecure. None of these differences could be attributed to variables such as mother's education, the number of siblings a child had, or his previous experience or inexperience of toys. While the gross behaviour of mothers of the two groups of toddlers did not differ appreciably during the observation session, mothers of the secure toddlers showed more interest in the proceedings, watched the child's activities more closely, and expressed more feeling. Thus the pattern of child–mother interaction established at twelve months was found to have had considerable stability during the succeeding nine-month period; and the findings strongly support the earlier conclusion that infants whose mothers are sensitive and responsive to them are those who later turn cheerfully to exploration and play. Their willingness to cooperate, their capacity to concentrate, and their good scores on developmental tests at twenty-one months bode well for their futures.

Plainly a very great deal of further work will be required before it is possible to draw conclusions with any high degree of confidence. Nevertheless the overall patterns of personality development and mother–child interaction visible during these early months are sufficiently similar to what is seen of personality development and parent–child interaction in later years for it to be plausible to believe that the one is the forerunner of the other. At the least, Ainsworth's findings show that an infant whose mother is sensitive, accessible, and responsive to him, and accepts his behaviour and is cooperative in dealing with him, is far from becoming the demanding and unhappy child that some theories might suggest. Instead, mothering of this sort is evidently compatible with a child who is developing a limited measure of self-reliance during his second year combined with a high degree of trust in his mother and enjoyment of her company.

Self-reliance and reliance on others

In Chapter 14 three propositions regarding personality functioning and development are introduced. The first is that, whenever an individual is confident that an attachment figure will be available to him when he desires it, that person will be much less prone to either intense or chronic fear than will an individual who for any reason has no such confidence. The second postulates that confidence in the accessibility and responsiveness of attachment figures, or a lack of it, is built up slowly during all the years of immaturity and that, once developed, expectations tend to persist relatively unchanged throughout the rest of life. The third postulates that expectations regarding the availability of attachment figures that different individuals build up are tolerably accurate reflections of the experiences those individuals have actually had. It is only because each proposition is, or at least has been, so controversial that it has seemed necessary to display the evidence on which they rest in so much detail.

Although each proposition was derived initially from attempts to understand and treat disturbed children, especially those whose disturbance had developed after a separation, the propositions are seen to have a wider application. For not only young children, it is now clear, but human beings of all ages are found to be at their happiest and to be able to deploy their talents to best advantage when they are confident that, standing behind them, there are one or more trusted persons who will come to their aid should difficulties arise. The person trusted provides a secure base from which his (or her) companion can operate. And the more trustworthy the base the more it is taken for granted; and the more it is taken for granted, unfortunately, the more likely is its importance to be overlooked and forgotten.

Paradoxically, the truly self-reliant person when viewed in this light proves to be by no means as independent as cultural stereotypes suppose. An essential ingredient is a capacity to rely trustingly on others when occasion demands and to know on whom it is appropriate to rely. A healthily self-reliant person is thus capable of exchanging roles when the situation changes: at one time he is providing a secure base from which his companion(s) can operate; at another he is glad to rely on one or another of his companions to provide him with just such a base in return.

A capacity to adopt either role as circumstances change is well illustrated by a healthily self-reliant woman during the successive phases of her life running from pregnancy through childbirth and on into motherhood. A woman capable of coping successfully with these shifts is found by Wenner (1966)[8] well able, during her pregnancy and puerperium, both to express her desire for support and help and to do so in a direct and effective fashion to an appropriate figure. Her relationship with her husband is close and she is eager and content to rely on his support. In her turn she is able to give spontaneously to others, including her baby. By contrast, Wenner reports, a woman who experiences major emotional difficulties during pregnancy and puerperium is found to have great difficulty in relying on others. Either she is unable to express her desire for support or else she does so in a demanding and aggressive way; in either case her behaviour reflects her lack of confidence that support will be forthcoming. Commonly she is both dissatisfied with what she is given and is herself unable to give spontaneously to others. A study by Melges (1968) shows that women with these problems almost always have a deeply ambivalent relationship with their own mother.

Agreement on Some Basic Principles

The theoretical position adopted here has much in common with positions adopted by a number of other psychoanalysts, especially those who give substantial weight to the influence of the environment on development.

In the United Kingdom, for example, Fairbairn (1952), insisting that 'any theory of ego-development that is to be satisfactory must be conceived in terms of relationships with objects', postulates that during an individual's development 'an original state of infantile dependence ... is abandoned in favour of a state of adult or mature dependence ...' In Winnicott's view :

8. Wenner (1966) reports preliminary findings from a study of fifty-two married women during and after a pregnancy. The subjects were middle-class, middle-income Americans, aged from twenty years upwards, and included both primiparas and multiparas. They had been referred to a psychiatrist during pregnancy because of possible emotional problems, and were seen in weekly therapeutic interviews until at least three months postpartum. Some of them showed major emotional difficulties during the period of study, but the majority did not.

Maturity and the capacity to be alone implies that the individual has had the chance through good-enough mothering to build up a belief in a benign environment. . . . Gradually the ego-supportive environment is introjected and built into the individual's personality, so that there comes about a capacity actually to be alone. Even so, theoretically, there is always someone present, someone who is equated ultimately and unconsciously with the mother . . . (Winnicott 1958).

In the United States a similar tradition of theorizing has been influential for many years, and is well described in a recent paper by Fleming (1972). Benedek (1938; 1956) emphasizes how a person's confidence in the existence of helping figures derives from repeated gratifying experiences in his relationship with his mother during infancy and childhood and how, as a result, a strong ego develops, capable of maintaining integration and self-regulation during periods when no support is available. Mahler (1968), basing her views on studies of severely disturbed and psychotic children, reaches a similar conclusion. Self-confidence, self-esteem, and pleasure in independence, she concludes, develop out of trust and confidence in others. This trust is built up during infancy and childhood through a child's experience of a mothering person who acts as a 'reference point' for his activities while at the same time giving him sufficient freedom to enable him to pass through the developmental phase that Mahler terms 'separation–individuation'. Fleming (1972), after spending many years studying the problems of adult patients who have suffered bereavement during childhood or adolescence, endorses these views and insists that, even in adult life, 'we are never completely independent of the need that a trusted helpful person exists and could be called if necessary'.

Thus, though the sources of the observations on which different clinicians base their conclusions and the theoretical frameworks within which they describe them are often very different, and different again both from the sources of observation and from the theoretical model used in this work, on certain basic principles there is strong agreement. A well-founded self-reliance, it is clear, not only is compatible with a capacity to rely on others but grows out of and is complementary to it. Both, moreover, are alike products of a family that provides strong support for its offspring combined with respect for their personal aspirations, their sense of responsibility, and their ability to deal with the world. So far from sapping a child's self-reliance, then, a secure base and strong family support greatly encourage it.

Chapter 22
Pathways for the Growth of Personality

Organism and environment are not two separate things, each having its own character in its own right, which come together with as little essential inter-relation as a sieve and a shovelful of pebbles thrown on to it. The fundamental characteristics of the organism are time-extended properties, which can be envisaged as a set of alternative pathways of development ...

– C. H. WADDINGTON (1957)

The nature of individual variation: alternative models

For most of the present century the model of personality development most favoured has regarded a personality as progressing through a series of stages on a single track towards maturity. The various forms of disturbed personality are then attributed to an arrest having occurred at one or another of these stages. Such an arrest, it is thought, can be either more or less complete. Most often, it is supposed, it is only partial. In such an instance development is conceived as continuing in an apparently fairly satisfactory way except that, in conditions of stress, it is liable to breakdown, in which case the personality is thought to regress to whatever stage in development the partial arrest, or fixation, is deemed to have occurred at. In some of the best-known theoretical systems based on that model, for example that of Abraham (1924), each form of personality disorder, of neurosis and of psychosis is held to be traceable to some measure of fixation that has occurred at one or another particular stage of development. It is from this model that application of the terms mature and immature to healthy and disturbed personalities, respectively, derives (see Chapter 14).

A theoretical system more recently outlined by Anna Freud (1965), although more elaborate than Abraham's, none the less retains the same essential features: individual differences are still measured in terms of the degrees of progression, fixation, and regression that are thought to be shown. The main new feature is that, whereas Abraham's model takes account only of stages in libido development, Anna Freud's model takes account of stages of development that are postulated to occur in each of a number of different areas of personality functioning, e.g. in the development of modes of eating or of object relationships. Thus the concept is introduced of a set of 'developmental lines' along all of which a healthy personality is expected to progress relatively evenly and harmoniously, and at a rate appropriate to chronological age. The different forms of psychological disturbance are then explained in terms of a profile in which some degree of fixation and regression is held to have occurred during development along one or more of these lines.

Alternative models of personality development have been little discussed in clinical circles. One alternative, that it is now maintained fits presently available evidence far closer than does the traditional one, conceives of personality as a structure that develops unceasingly along one or another of an array of possible and discrete developmental pathways. All pathways are thought to start close together so that, initially, an individual has access to a large range of pathways along any one of which he might travel. The one chosen, it is held, turns at each and every stage of the journey on an interaction between the organism as it has developed up to that moment and the environment in which it then finds itself. Thus at conception development turns on interaction between the newly formed genome and the intra-uterine environment; at birth it turns on interaction between the physiological constitution, including germinal mental structure, of the neonate and the family, or non-family, into which he is born; and at each age successively it turns on the personality structure then present and the family and, later, the wider social environments then current.

At conception the total array of pathways potentially open to an individual is determined by the make-up of the genome. As development proceeds and structures progressively differentiate, the number of pathways that remain open diminishes.

These two, alternative, theoretical models can be likened to two types of railway system. The traditional model resembles a single main line on which are set a series of stations. At any one of them, we may imagine, a train can be halted, either temporarily or permanently; and the longer it halts the more prone it becomes to return to that station whenever it meets with difficulty further down the line.

The alternative model resembles a system that starts as a single main route which leaves a central metropolis in a certain direction but soon forks into a range of distinct routes. Although each of these routes diverges in some degree, initially most of them continue in a direction not very different from the original one. The further each route goes from the metropolis, however, the more branches it throws off and the greater the degree of divergence of direction that can occur. Nevertheless, although many of these sub-branches do diverge further, and yet further, from the original direction, others may take a course convergent with the original; so that ultimately they may even come to run in a direction close to, or even parallel with, routes that have maintained the original direction from the start. In terms of this model the critical points are the junctions at which the lines fork, for once a train is on any particular line, pressures are present that keep it on that line; although, provided divergence does not become too great, there remains an opportunity for a train to take a convergent track when the next junction is reached.

The implications of these different models for research and practice are far-reaching. In regard to research the traditional model postulates that every form of personality disorder found in adults is patterned on a form of personality structure that is normal and healthy at some (appropriate) phase of life, usually thought to occur during the early years, or even months. In keeping with this assumption, a scheme is advanced that attributes to successive phases of healthy childhood features of a kind that are characteristic of one or another form of disordered personality of later life. Thus a developmental psychology is constructed that takes as its primary data for each phase of early development observations of how one or another form of disturbed personality is found to perform at some point later in the life-cycle.

The implications for research of the alternative model, which postulates a range of diverging developmental pathways, are very different. As was argued at the end of Chapter 14, this model disputes the notion that disordered states of adult personality are reflections of early states of healthy development and it regards as seriously mistaken any attempts to build a developmental psychology on that basis. What is required instead, it holds, is that the many and often divergent developmental pathways potentially available to humans should each be mapped, together with those organismic and environmental variables that constrain an individual to take one pathway rather than another. Such mapping, it insists, can be done only by studying personalities as they develop in the particular environment in which they happen to be developing. Only in this way is it possible to gain understanding of the interactional sequences of personality and environment that result in that personality growing along that particular pathway.

Developmental pathways and homeorhesis

This alternative model, which sees differences in personality structure as being a result of growth having proceeded along different and divergent developmental pathways, is patterned on the theory of epigenesis proposed by Waddington (1957) and now widely adopted by developmental biologists. In this theory the processes that determine an organism's development, and in particular the extent to which each feature of development is sensitive or insensitive to environmental variation, are seen as governed by the genome. Any feature of development that is relatively insensitive to changes of environment can be termed 'environmentally stable'; any feature that is relatively sensitive can be termed 'environmentally labile' (see Chapters 3 and 10 of Volume I).

The advantages and disadvantages, in terms of survival, that ensue for a species according to the greater or lesser degree of sensitivity to environmental change during development with which its members are endowed are discussed by Waddington. On the one hand, a low degree of sensitivity to environmental change may ensure adaptive development within a great variety of environments but at the price of a total inability to adapt should the environment change beyond certain limits. On the other, a high degree of sensitivity enables an organism to vary its development according to the particular environment in which development happens to be taking place, with a good prospect of the adult's being better adapted to that environment than it would otherwise be. It also ensures a reserve of adaptability within the species' gene pool so that, should there be great fluctuations in the environment, there are likely always to be some members of the population capable of adapting and surviving. Such flexibility, however, is bought at the risk that in a number of environments the development of many individuals may go badly astray and the resulting forms may be seriously maladapted to any or perhaps all environments. Because of this danger no species can afford its members more than a limited degree of sensitivity to environmental fluctuation during their development.

In their evolution different species have adopted very different strategies in regard to the degree of sensitivity to environment that is permitted during development. Because either extreme, whether of sensitivity or of insensitivity, has serious dangers for survival every species comes to have some balance of the two properties. Probably in all species such epigenetic sensitivity as is present is greatest during early life and then diminishes.

In order to limit epigenetic sensitivity and so ensure consistent development despite fluctuations of environment, physiological and behavioural processes are evolved that buffer the developing individual against the impact of the environment. Acting in concert, these processes tend to maintain an individual on whatever developmental pathway he is already on, irrespective of most of the fluctuations that might occur in the environment in which further development will be taking place. The strong self-regulative property of which these processes are agents Waddington terms 'homeorhesis'.

When Waddington's concepts are applied to the development of human personality, the model proposed postulates that the psychological processes that result in personality structure are endowed with a fair degree of sensitivity to environment, especially to family environment, during the early years of life, but a sensitivity that diminishes throughout childhood and is already very limited by the end of adolescence. Thus the developmental process is conceived as able to vary its course, more or less adaptively, during the early years, according to the environment in which development is occurring; and subsequently, with the reduction of environmental sensitivity, as becoming increasingly constrained to the particular pathway already chosen.

Ordinary experience suggests that the sensitivity to environment present during the early phases of personality development commonly results in an adaptive outcome, in the sense that the resultant adult personality is able to perform well in any of the culturally determined range of family and social environments in which he is likely to find himself. Nevertheless, as we have seen, such early sensitivity provides no guarantee of an adaptive outcome; for, when the environment of development lies outside certain limits, an organism's sensitivity to environment may result in a developing personality's not only taking a maladaptive pathway but, because of increasing homeorhesis, becoming confined more or less permanently to that pathway. Psychopathic personality, a consequence of development having occurred in a severely atypical family environment during the first three or so years of life, can be regarded as an example of this mode of personality maldevelopment.

Another mode by which personality development can take a course that leads to a maladapted outcome in adult life is when development takes a pathway that results in a growing personality that is reasonably well adapted to the environment in which development is actually taking place but that ceases to be so in the range of environments in which the adult is likely to find himself. A strongly conforming obsessive personality who flourishes in a well-structured social environment but is unable to adapt to change is an example of this other mode of maldevelopment.

Homeorhetic Pressures on Personality Development

We turn next to consider briefly the nature of the processes that tend to keep a developing personality on whatever pathway it is already on. Pressures are of two kinds, those that derive from the environment and those that derive from within the organism. Because of their constant interaction the combined effect of these pressures is immense.

Environmental pressures are due largely to the fact that the family environment in which a child lives and grows tends to remain relatively unchanged, as Peck and Havighurst, among others, report. This means that whatever family pressures led the development of a child to take the pathway he is now on are likely to persist and so to maintain development on that same pathway. This is why attempts to change a child's personality structure by means of psychotherapy without attempts simultaneously to change the family environment by means of family therapy tend to be unavailing.

Yet it is not only environmental pressures that tend to maintain development on a particular pathway. Structural features of personality, once developed, have their own means of self-regulation that tend also to maintain the current direction of development. For example, present cognitive and behavioural structures determine what is perceived and what ignored, how a new situation is construed, and what plan of action is likely to be constructed to deal with it. Current structures, moreover, determine what sorts of person and situation are sought after and what sorts are shunned. In this way an individual comes to influence the selection of his own environment; and so the wheel comes full circle. Because these strong self-regulative processes are present in every individual, therapeutic measures aimed at changing the family or social environment of a patient, whether schoolchild, adolescent, or adult, without attempts simultaneously to change the personality structure of the patient himself, tend also to be unavailing.

Thus, because homeorhetic pressures of the two kinds, environmental and organismic, are constantly reinforcing one another, and thereby maintaining development on its present pathway, the therapeutic measures most likely to effect a change are those designed to deal with both kinds of pressure simultaneously. It is in fact to the improvement of combined therapeutic techniques of this kind that many dynamically oriented psychiatrists are today devoting attention.

The psychological processes and the forms of behaviour that constitute the organism's contribution to homeorhesis are, of course, among those long known in the psychoanalytic tradition of theorizing as 'defensive'. In the third volume it is planned to examine defensive processes and defensive behaviour from this point of view.

One person's pathway: some determinants

The fundamental characteristics of personality, we may say, adapting Waddington, are time-extended properties that can be envisaged as a set of alternative pathways of development. Which one of that great and private set initially open to each one of us is taken turns on a near infinity of variables. Yet among those many variables some are more easily discerned than others because their effects are so far-reaching. And no variables, it is held, have more far-reaching effects on personality development than have a child's experiences within his family: for, starting during his first months in his relations with his mother figure, and extending through the years of childhood and adolescence in his relations with both parents, he builds up working models of how attachment figures are likely to behave towards him in any of a variety of situations; and on those models are based all his expectations, and therefore all his plans, for the rest of his life.

Experiences of separation from attachment figures, whether of short or long duration, and experiences of loss or of being threatened with separation or abandonment – all act, we can now see, to divert development from a pathway that is within optimum limits to one that may lie outside them. In terms of the railway analogy, those experiences so act that the points at a junction are shifted and the train is diverted from a main line to a branch. Often, fortunately, the diversion is neither great nor lengthy so that return to the main line remains fairly easy. At other times, by contrast, a diversion is both greater and lasts longer or else is repeated; then a return to the main line becomes far more difficult, and it may prove impossible.

It must not be supposed, however, that separations, threats of separation, and losses are the only agents that divert development from an optimum pathway to a suboptimum one. If the thesis presented here is correct, very many other limitations and short-comings of parenting can do the same. Furthermore, diversions can follow any life-event that is classifiable as a stress or crisis, especially when it strikes an immature individual or one already on a suboptimum pathway. Thus, as events capable of diverting development along one pathway rather than another, experiences of separation and loss, and of threats of being abandoned, are only a few of a much larger class of events that are usefully described as major changes in the life-space (Parkes 1971). Included in that category also are events that in certain conditions may influence development for the better.

Reasons for concentrating attention on experiences of separation and loss, and of threats of being abandoned, to the exclusion of other events are manifold. In the first place, they are easily defined events that have easily observable effects in the short term and can also, when development continues on a seriously divergent pathway, have easily observable long-term effects. Thus they provide research workers with a valuable point of entry from which to plan projects aimed at casting light on the immensely complex and still deeply shadowed field of personality development and the conditions that determine it.

In the second place, and partly because the effects of these events are not confined to man but are seen also in other species, opportunity is offered for attempting a reformulation of the theory of personality development and its deviations in which are incorporated ideas stemming both from the psychoanalytic tradition and from ethology and developmental biology.

In the third place, these events occur so commonly in the lives of children, adolescents, and adults, and constitute so large a proportion of the major stressors about which we know, that a clear understanding of their effects is of immediate help to clinicians whose task it is to understand psychiatric disability, to treat it and, whenever possible, to prevent it.

Yet, however useful this enterprise may prove, it is only a beginning. Human personality is perhaps the most complex of all complex systems here on earth. To describe the principal components of its construction, to understand and predict the ways in which it works and, above all, to map the multitude of intricate pathways along any of which one person may develop, these are all tasks for the future.

Appendices

Appendix 1
Separation Anxiety: Review of Literature[1]

A study of the literature shows that there have been six main approaches to the problem of separation anxiety: three of them are the counterparts, though not always the necessary counterparts, of theories regarding the nature of the child's attachment to his mother. In the order in which they have received attention by psychoanalysts, they are as follows.

1. The first, advanced by Freud in *Three Essays* (1905b), is a special case of the general theory of anxiety which he held until 1926. As a result of his study of anxiety neurosis (1895) Freud had advanced the view that morbid anxiety is due to the transformation into anxiety of sexual excitation of somatic origin that cannot be discharged. The anxiety observed when an infant is separated from the person he loves, Freud holds, is an example of this, since in these circumstances a child's libido remains unsatisfied and undergoes transformation. This theory may be called the theory of 'transformed libido'.

2. The anxiety shown by young children on separation from mother is a reproduction of the trauma of birth, so that birth anxiety is the prototype of all the separation anxiety subsequently experienced. Following Rank (1924) it can be termed the 'birth-trauma' theory. It is the counterpart of the theory of return-to-womb craving to account for the child's tie.

3. In the absence of his mother an infant or young child is subject to the risk of a traumatic psychic experience, and he therefore develops a safety device which leads to his exhibiting anxiety behaviour whenever she leaves him. Such behaviour has a function: it may be expected to ensure that he is not parted from her for too long. This is usually referred to as the 'signal' theory, a term introduced by Freud in 1926. It is held in many variants

1. A version of this review was published in the *Journal of Child Psychology and Psychiatry*, Vol. I, 1961. Only a few changes have been made; papers published since 1960 are not as systematically considered as those published earlier.

according to how the traumatic situation to be avoided is conceived.

Principal variants are: (a) the traumatic situation is an economic disturbance that is caused when there develops an excessive accumulation of stimulation arising from unsatisfied bodily needs (Freud 1926a); (b) it is the imminence of a total and permanent extinction of the capacity for sexual enjoyment, namely aphanisis (Jones 1927) (when first advanced by Jones as an explanation of anxiety, the theory of aphanisis was not related to the anxiety of separation; two years later, however, he sought to adapt it to fit in with Freud's latest ideas); (c) a variant proposed by Spitz (1950) and presented within a new theoretical model by Joffe and Sandler (1965) is that the traumatic situation to be avoided is one of narcissistic injury. In the history of Freud's thought the signal theory stems from, and is in certain respects the counterpart of, the theory that explains the child's tie to his mother in terms of secondary drive. The variant that regards narcissistic injury as the trauma threatened also stems from the secondary-drive tradition.

4. Separation anxiety results from a young child's believing when his mother disappears that he has eaten her up or otherwise destroyed her, and that in consequence he has lost her for ever. That belief, it is held, arises from the ambivalent feelings a child has for his mother, an ambivalence made inevitable by the existence within him of a death instinct. Advanced by Melanie Klein (1935), the theory can be called, following her terminology, that of 'depressive anxiety'.

5. As a result of projecting his aggression, a young child perceives his mother as persecutory, and this leads him to interpret her departure as due to her being angry with him or wishing to punish him. For this reason, whenever his mother leaves him he believes she will either never return or do so only in a hostile mood, and he therefore experiences anxiety. Again following Melanie Klein (1934), this can be termed the theory of 'persecutory anxiety'.

6. Initially the anxiety is a primary response not reducible to other terms and due simply to the rupture of a child's attachment to his mother. This can be called the theory of 'frustrated attachment'. It is the counterpart of theories that regard a child's

pleasure in his mother's presence as being as primary as his pleasure in food and warmth. A theory of this sort has been advanced by James (1890), Suttie (1935), and Hermann (1936), but has never been given much attention in psychoanalytic circles. It is a theory of this type that I advanced in an earlier paper (Bowlby 1960a) linked to yet another variant of the signal theory. The theory advanced in this work (Chapter 12) is also a combination of the sixth and the third types. It regards separation of a young child from an attachment figure as in itself distressing and also as providing a condition in which intense fear is readily aroused. As a result, when a child senses any further prospect of separation some measure of anxiety is aroused in him.

In Chapter 5 of this volume attention is drawn to the fact that almost all psychoanalytic theorizing about anxiety and fear is conceived in terms of a biological paradigm that antedates modern evolution theory. This accounts, it is believed, for the numerous competing, complex, and contradictory theories to be found in the literature.

Views of main contributors

Sigmund Freud

We have seen that it was not until 1926, when Freud was seventy, that in *Inhibitions, Symptoms and Anxiety* he gave systematic attention to separation anxiety. Prior to this, having paid insufficient attention to the child's attachment to his mother, as he himself affirms (Freud 1931), he had paid correspondingly little to the anxiety exhibited on separation from her. Nevertheless, he had been far from blind to it. In both the *Three Essays* (1905b) and the *Introductory Lectures* (1917b) he had drawn attention to it and in both had treated it as of much importance.[2]

In *Three Essays*, after a section concerned with early object relations, he gives a paragraph to 'infantile anxiety' (*SE* 7: 224).

2. Separation of child from mother as a central and recurrent theme in Freud's thinking about anxiety is clearly brought out in Strachey's valuable introduction to the Standard Edition of *Inhibitions, Symptoms and Anxiety* (Strachey 1959).

Appendix I

In it he advances the view that 'anxiety in children is originally nothing other than an expression of the fact that they are feeling the loss of the person they love'. This view he readily aligns with his hypothesis regarding neurotic anxiety in adults. At that time Freud still held the view that, when a powerful sexual excitation is insufficiently discharged, libido is transformed directly into anxiety. It is the same in children, he believes. Because 'children . . . behave from an early age as though their dependence on the people looking after them were in the nature of sexual love', and because in a separation situation the child's libido goes unsatisfied, Freud concludes that a child deals with the situation just as an adult would, namely 'by turning his libido into anxiety'. Four years later this is also his explanation of the separation anxiety that was Little Hans's first symptom: 'It was this increased affection for his mother which turned suddenly into anxiety . . .' (*SE* 10: 25).

He follows the same reasoning in the *Introductory Lectures* (1917b). After once again drawing attention to the anxiety exhibited when mother is missing, he concludes that 'infantile anxiety has very little to do with realistic anxiety, but, on the other hand, is closely related to the neurotic anxiety of adults. Like the latter, it is derived from unemployed libido . . .' (*SE* 16: 408). This, it will be observed, is tantamount to identifying neurotic anxiety of adults with separation anxiety of infants, a resemblance on which he had already remarked in 1905.[3]

Although in the *Introductory Lectures*, for reasons which appear inadequate, Freud complicates his theory by postulating that the core of anxiety is a repetition of the affect experienced at birth (*SE* 16: 396), it is none the less anxiety arising on separation from mother, as observed empirically, which throughout his writings on infantile anxiety from 1905 onwards holds the centre of the theoretical stage. Anxiety arising at birth, which had first been postulated some years earlier (1910, *SE* 11: 173), starts by being only a rather speculative addition to his theory. Although it

3. '. . . an adult who has become neurotic owing to his libido being unsatisfied behaves in his anxiety like a child: he begins to be frightened when he is alone . . . and he seeks to assuage this fear by the most childish measures' (*SE* 7: 224).

gradually acquires an equal status, it never usurps the place of anxiety arising on separation from mother. This is important since more than one analyst has tended to give it precedence in his theorizing.[4]

The next reference to separation anxiety occurs in *Beyond the Pleasure Principle* (1920) where Freud relates the well-known cotton-reel incident which Jones (1957: 288) tells us he had witnessed five years previously in Hamburg. His eighteen-month-old grandson took all sorts of small objects and threw them away into corners and under the bed with an expression which seemed to signify 'gone'. This appeared to be confirmed when later the boy had a cotton reel on the end of a string and played the double game of throwing it away with an expression of 'gone' and pulling it back again with a joyful 'da'. This simple game, coupled with the fact that the boy 'was greatly attached to his mother', led Freud to an

interpretation of the game . . . it was related to the child's great cultural achievement – the instinctual renunciation (that is, the renunciation of instinctual satisfaction) which he had made in allowing his mother to go away without protesting. He compensated himself for this, as it were, by himself staging the disappearance and return of the objects within his reach (*SE* 18: 14–15).

4. In *Introductory Lectures* Freud describes a child missing 'the sight of a familiar and beloved figure – ultimately of his mother' as the 'situation which is the prototype of the anxiety of children' (*SE* 16: 407). However, he thinks that in this situation there may be in addition a reproduction of birth anxiety. In *Inhibitions, Symptoms and Anxiety*, on the other hand, it is birth anxiety that is described as the prototype. Nevertheless, in one of the addenda to this work he explains how he could make no headway with Rank's ideas on the primary role of birth trauma and, referring to his own conclusions, remarks that the significance of birth is 'reduced to this prototypic relationship to danger' (*SE* 20: 162). This is also the position he takes in the *New Introductory Lectures* (1933) where he repeats his view that 'a particular determinant of anxiety (that is, situation of danger) is allotted to every age of development as being appropriate to it' (*SE* 22: 88). The danger situation of birth and the danger of loss of object or of love seem here to be assigned equal status. See also the discussions by Jones (1957: 274–6) and by Strachey (1959: 83–6). Strachey points out that, in Freud's later work, it is only the *form* taken by anxiety that is to be understood as stemming from the experience of birth.

How well established this cultural achievement was we shall never know, but if Freud's grandson followed a common course of development it is unlikely to have been maintained. There are many infants who are able to permit their mother to leave them for an hour or so without crying when they are eighteen months old, but who in the succeeding months find this less tolerable and may make a great fuss. However that may be, the observation of the incident, and no doubt of others like it, seems to have clarified Freud's perception of the child's tie to his mother and to have led him to reflect further on the theory of anxiety – an early example of the value of direct observation.

It was the publication of Rank's *Trauma of Birth* in 1924, Freud relates in an addendum to *Inhibitions, Symptoms and Anxiety* (1926a), that 'obliged me to review the problem of anxiety once more'. In this work Rank had taken up the suggestion which, as we have seen, had first been thrown out by Freud, 'that the affect of anxiety is a consequence of the event of birth and a repetition of the situation then experienced . . . But', Freud continues, 'I could make no headway with his idea that birth is a trauma, states of anxiety a reaction of discharge to it and all subsequent affects of anxiety an attempt to "abreact" it more and more completely' (*SE* **20**: 161). Instead, what Freud does in his courageous re-examination of theory is to return to the safe ground of empirical observation – which brings him back once more to separation anxiety.

In reading *Inhibitions, Symptoms and Anxiety* we find that Freud wrestled with the theoretical problems of anxiety through seven chapters, in the course of which he abandons a favourite hypothesis, namely that anxiety represents a direct transformation of libido. His reason for doing so lies in his recognition that, whereas formerly he had supposed anxiety to be the product of repression, an examination of clinical material suggests that, on the contrary, repression is a consequence of anxiety (*SE* **20**: 109). As a result of this, at the beginning of the eighth chapter he concludes ruefully: 'Up till now we have arrived at nothing but contradictory views about it [anxiety]. . . . I therefore propose to adopt a different procedure. I propose to assemble, quite impartially, all the facts that we do know about anxiety without expecting to arrive at a fresh synthesis' (p. 132). After a brief diversion he proceeds:

Only a few of the manifestations of anxiety in children are comprehensible to us, and we must confine our attention to them. They occur, for instance, when a child is alone, or in the dark, or when it finds itself with an unknown person instead of one to whom it is used – such as its mother. These three instances can be reduced to a single condition, namely that of missing someone who is loved and longed for. But here, I think, we have the key to an understanding of anxiety ... anxiety appears as a reaction to the felt loss of the object (pp. 136–7).

Up to this point Freud is working from empirical data, data moreover which are now amply confirmed. Nevertheless he still remains puzzled, as others have also been, as to how to explain his observations. Why should there be this reaction of anxiety? It 'has all the appearance', he remarks, 'of being an expression of the child's feeling at its wits' end, as though in its still very undeveloped state it did not know how better to cope with its cathexis of longing' (p. 137). Today we can draw on a more sophisticated theory of instinctive behaviour to frame a hypothesis which regards the 'cathexis of longing' as the essence of the problem. Fifty years ago, however, such ideas on instinctive behaviour were unknown; instead, Freud was under the impression that the child's attachment could be understood only in terms of secondary drive and that the only primary needs are those of the body.

Freud therefore proceeds:

The reason why the infant in arms wants to perceive the presence of its mother is only because it already knows by experience that she satisfies all its needs without delay. The situation then, which it regards as a 'danger' and against which it wants to be safeguarded is that of non-satisfaction, of a *growing tension due to need*, against which it is helpless.

This, he continues, is 'analogous to the experience of being born ... What both situations have in common is an economic disturbance caused by an accumulation of amounts of stimulation which require to be disposed of. It is this factor, then, which is the real essence of the "danger"...' and which he terms the 'traumatic situation'. To avoid this, an infant, by a process of learning, displaces 'the danger it fears ... from the economic situation on to the condition which determined that situation, viz. the loss of object. It is the absence of the mother that is now the danger; and as soon as that danger arises the infant gives the signal of anxiety, before the dreaded economic situation has set in' (pp. 137–8).

In considering Freud's every approach to the problem of anxiety it is necessary constantly to bear in mind that, from the earliest days of his psychoanalytic theorizing onwards, he adopts as his basic postulate that the nervous system has the function of getting rid of stimuli and that the greatest catastrophe that can befall it is that of being overwhelmed by stimuli (see this volume, Chapter 5). Such theorizing constitutes what Freud describes as the economic viewpoint, and is cast sometimes in terms of a psychical energy that builds up and is either discharged in action or else becomes dammed up, and sometimes in terms of excitation or stimulation that similarly varies in quantity. The 'dreaded economic situation' that Freud believes threatens an infant who is separated from his mother is none other than the damming up of psychical energy that cannot be discharged.

As a consequence of his re-examination of the problem, Freud concludes that anxiety has two sources. Anxiety from the first source arises as 'an automatic phenomenon', with physiological features that he believes may well be part of a response appropriate to the situation of birth. Such anxiety occurs whenever a traumatic situation 'is established in the id', that is in 'situation[s] of non-satisfaction in which the amounts of stimulation rise to an unpleasurable height without its being possible for them to be mastered psychically or discharged ...' (*SE* **20**: 137–41). Such traumatic situations are always characterized by helplessness. In Freud's formulation of this source of anxiety we see a direct descendant of his earliest theory, that advanced in his paper on the 'Anxiety Neurosis' (1895), in which he postulated that anxiety is developed when the nervous system is incapable of dealing with a mass of excitation.

Anxiety from the second source, Freud suggests, constitutes 'a rescue signal' designed to indicate that danger is impending. Since it requires foresight, such anxiety can 'only be felt by the ego' (*SE* **20**: 140). It is indeed the task of the ego so to imagine the danger situation in advance that it can restrict 'that distressing experience to a mere indication, a signal' (p. 162). Freud proceeds to list a number of danger situations, each corresponding to a particular developmental phase, which, if allowed to develop, would result in a traumatic situation: among these are birth, loss of object (namely mother), fear of father, and fear of superego (pp. 146–7).

In his account of this second source of anxiety Freud lays much emphasis on the elements of foresight and expectation: 'The individual will have made an important advance in his capacity for self-preservation if he can foresee and expect a traumatic situation . . . which entails helplessness, instead of simply waiting for it to happen' (p. 166). Before anxiety can arise from this source, therefore, a fair degree of cognitive development is necessary.

Although, as has been indicated, Freud conceives of separation anxiety itself as no more than a signal and as being developed through a process of learning, as indeed is necessary if it is based on foresight, it is evident that he is not entirely satisfied with that conclusion. At the end of the book (*SE* **20**: 168) he returns yet again to 'the puzzling phobias of early childhood' and hazards that perhaps, as in other species, the fear of loss of object may be a built-in response: thus he refers to an 'archaic heritage' and 'vestigial traces of the congenital preparedness to meet real dangers'. These reflections, and also the similar ones in regard to the child's tie that are found in the *Outline* (1940), which were noted in the appendix to the first volume of the present work, suggest that towards the end of his life Freud was moving towards a formulation not very different from that advanced here.

It is far more important, however, that in this late work Freud finally clarifies what is held here to be the true relatedness of separation anxiety to mourning and defence. Previously, as he candidly admits, he had been confused. Not only had he supposed that repression is antecedent to anxiety, but he had also found it difficult to believe that anxiety as well as grief can be a response to loss of object. Now he sees that sequence clearly: anxiety is the reaction to the danger of loss of object, the pain of mourning is the reaction to the actual loss of object, and defences protect the ego against instinctual demands which threaten to overwhelm it and which can occur all too readily in the absence of the object (*SE* **20**: 164–72). This formula has not commonly been adopted by later theorists.

Ernest Jones

When Jones (1927) first advanced his theory of aphanisis it is evident, from the absence of references to *Inhibitions, Symptoms and Anxiety*, that he was unaware of Freud's latest train of thought. Furthermore, there is evidence also that he was still unaware of the importance of the attachment to mother (irrespective of the child's sex). It must therefore be noted that Jones's theory of aphanisis – that 'the fundamental fear is [of] the total and of course permanent extinction of the capacity (including opportunity) for sexual enjoyment' – was advanced without any reference to the present topic. The only mention of separation anxiety is in reference to weaning as a pregenital precursor of castration and to a girl's fear of separation from her father.

Two years later, however, Jones (1929) strives to integrate his own theory of aphanisis with Freud's theory of signal anxiety. The union is uneasy and the resulting theory appreciably more complex than either taken singly. One of several difficulties is that Jones is still not aware of the tie to the mother irrespective of the child's sex.[5] Since the combined theory has been little called upon, to delineate it is unnecessary. As a broad generalization, it may be said that Jones accepts Freud's view regarding signal anxiety, believing it to be 'purposely provoked by the ego so as to warn the personality' of the possible approach of serious dangers, and then, in describing these serious dangers, adds to Freud's conception of what constitutes the 'traumatic situation' his own notion of aphanisis.

5. See, for instance, his reference to the external danger arising from withdrawal of object, 'e.g. the mother in the *boy's* case' (p. 311, my italics).

Melanie Klein

Whereas Jones developed his theory of anxiety independently of Freud's and later attempted to marry the two, Melanie Klein not only developed hers independently of Freud's but has frequently underlined the differences between them. Anxiety, in her judgement, is to be understood in terms of the death instinct, to which Freud never referred in this connection, and therefore in terms of aggression. Her views in regard to anxiety in general, which were taking shape between 1924 and 1934, and to separation anxiety in particular, are set out fully in her paper 'On the Theory of Anxiety and Guilt' (1948b, in Klein *et al.* 1952). They represent the only formulation made by a psychoanalyst which is both substantially different from the formulations discussed by Freud and has had significant influence on theory and practice.

In *Inhibitions, Symptoms and Anxiety*, following a line of argument already advanced in *Introductory Lectures* (*SE* **16**: 407–8), Freud explicitly rejected the notion that fear of death is a primary anxiety and concluded instead that it is a later and learnt fear.[6] Melanie Klein differs: 'I do not share this view because my analytic observations show that there is in the unconscious a fear of annihilation of life.' This she assumes must be the response to the death instinct: 'Thus in my view the danger arising from the inner working of the death instinct is the first cause of anxiety' (Klein *et al.* 1952: 276). This, she suggests, is felt by an infant 'as an overwhelming attack, as persecution', and a persecution, moreover, which is first experienced at birth: 'We may assume that the struggle between life and death instincts already operates during birth and accentuates the persecutory anxiety aroused by this painful experience.' From this argument she draws an important conclusion regarding the infant's first object relations: 'It would seem', she says, 'that this experience [i.e. birth] has the effect of making the external world, including the first external

6. It is interesting to note that Sylvia Anthony (1940) in her study of the genesis of children's ideas of death reached a similar conclusion. Furthermore, she believes that it is through its equation with separation that death acquires its emotional significance: 'Death is equated with departure. . . . To the young child death means, in the departure context, its mother's death – not its own.'

object, the mother's breast, appear hostile' (1952: 278). In another paper (1946) she summarizes her view in a sentence: 'I hold that anxiety arises from the operation of the death instinct within the organism, is felt as fear of annihilation (death) and takes the form of fear of persecution' (Klein *et al.* 1952: 296). It is against this backcloth – that anxiety is the result of the perpetual activity of the death instinct and that the newborn infant is already burdened with persecutory anxiety – that Klein presents her views on separation anxiety.

Starting from Freud's distinction between objective anxiety (arising in connection with a known external danger) and neurotic anxiety (arising in connection with an unknown and internal one) (Freud 1926a, *SE* 20: 165 and 167), Klein (1948b) sees both as contributing to the infant's fear of loss. She describes their nature as follows: objective anxiety arises from 'the child's complete dependence on the mother for the satisfaction of his needs and the relief of tension'; neurotic anxiety 'derives from the infant's apprehension that the loved mother has been destroyed by his sadistic impulses or is in danger of being destroyed, and this fear . . . contributes to the infant's feeling that she will never return'. Were Klein to postulate that this depressive anxiety only developed in later infancy, she would not be diverging materially from Freud's view but only expanding it at an important point. This, however, is not her position. She emphasizes that in her view both sources of anxiety are present from the beginning and are constantly interacting. Because of this, 'no danger-situation arising from external sources could ever be experienced by the young child as a purely external and known danger' (Klein *et al.* 1952: 288). On this her own statements and those of her colleagues are consistent. In discussing the cotton-reel incident Klein dissociates herself explicitly from Freud's view and concludes, 'when [an infant] misses [his mother], and his needs are not satisfied her absence is felt to be the result of his destructive impulses' (pp. 269–70). In the same volume it is claimed by Susan Isaacs that always 'mental pain has a content, a meaning, and implies phantasy. On the view presented here, "he behaves as if he were never going to see her again"[7] means

7. Isaacs's quotation, from *Inhibitions, Symptoms and Anxiety*, is from the 1936 English translation (London: Hogarth, p. 167).

his phantasy is that his mother has been destroyed by his own hate or greed and altogether lost' (Klein *et al.* 1952: 87).

These passages seem to make it clear that in their explanations of separation anxiety Melanie Klein and her colleagues see depressive anxiety as virtually its sole component. This, however, is not so since elsewhere they emphasize that the relationship to the mother is itself 'a first measure of defence ... The dependence on the mother and fear of loss of her, which Freud regards as the deepest source of anxiety, is from our point of view (the self-preservative) already a defence against a greater danger (that of helplessness against destruction within)' (Joan Riviere in Klein *et al.* 1952: 46-7). 'From the very beginning,' she writes, 'the internal forces of the death instinct and of aggression are felt to be the cardinal danger threatening the organism' (p. 44). Since these forces are let loose during a separation experience, in the final analysis separation anxiety is seen as a response to the threat of destruction within. Clearly, this theory is very different from that of Freud and also from that advanced here. Whereas Freud gives primacy to anxiety that arises from 'an accumulation of amounts of stimulation' that he conceives as resulting from separation, Melanie Klein and her colleagues give primacy to persecutory anxiety.

It should, however, be added that in various passages Klein refers also to birth as constituting an anxiety-provoking trauma, and seems at times to subscribe to the birth-trauma theory of separation anxiety. Thus, following a passage already quoted above (1952: 296), she writes: 'Other important sources of primary anxiety are the trauma of birth (separation anxiety) and frustration of bodily needs.' Nevertheless, although postulating these additional sources of anxiety, she quickly brings them within the ambit of persecutory anxiety by attributing to an infant a tendency always to suppose fear to be aroused by an object. After having earlier expressed the opinion that 'the fear of the destructive impulse seems to attach itself at once to an object', she completes her statement regarding the trauma of birth and the frustration of bodily needs thus: 'and these experiences too are from the beginning felt as being caused by objects.[8]

8. Freud is not favourable to this type of theory. He writes: 'A child who is mistrustful in this way and terrified of the aggressive instinct which

Even if these objects are felt to be external, they become through introjection internal persecutors and thus reinforce the fear of the destructive impulse within' (p. 296).

In evaluating Melanie Klein's views it is essential to realize that her main theoretical outlook was formed in the years preceding the publication of Freud's *Inhibitions, Symptoms and Anxiety*, and that, unlike Freud, who in the final formulation of his theory took anxiety arising from separation experiences as his point of departure, Klein had already developed her theory of anxiety before she gave any attention to separation from mother as a situation that provokes anxiety. The first occasion she discusses it is in 1935 in her paper on 'The Psychogenesis of Manic-depressive States'.

When we look back on the early papers of Melanie Klein we remain impressed by her observation that anxiety and unconscious aggression often coexist, particularly when there is an unusually anxious and intense attachment of one person to another. In my judgement, however, she assumed too readily that aggression both precedes and causes anxiety so that, instead of recognizing conscious and unconscious aggression as a common response to separation and as constituting an important and frequent condition for the *exacerbation* of separation anxiety, she came to see aggression as the single source of anxiety; and furthermore, by identifying the child's tie to his mother with orality, was led into making implausible assumptions about the mental life of infants during their early months and thence into creating a theoretical superstructure that is far from convincing. This has had two unfortunate results. On the one hand, some of her critics have failed to appreciate the value of certain parts of her contribution; on the other, her followers have been slow to recognize that, significant though depressive and persecutory anxieties may sometimes be, the origin of separation anxiety cannot be understood in such terms, and, more important, that disturbances of the mother–child relationship that arise during the second and many subsequent years can have a far-reaching potential for pathological development.

---

dominates the world is a theoretical construction that has quite miscarried' (*SE* **16**: 407).

Anna Freud

Whereas Melanie Klein has written much about separation anxiety but has recounted few observations of how infants and young children actually behave in situations of separation, Anna Freud was one of the first to record such observations but until recent years has discussed their theoretical implications singularly little. As in the case of Klein, it looks as though a main reason was that her theoretical orientation was already set before Freud's fresh appraisal of the nature and genesis of anxiety appeared. *Inhibitions, Symptoms and Anxiety* is not referred to in her book *The Psycho-analytical Treatment of Children* (1946), which dates from 1926, 1927, and 1945; and, though a chapter is given to processes of defence in relation to the source of anxiety or to danger, there is no reference in *The Ego and Mechanisms of Defence* (1936) either to separation anxiety or to loss of object. Until her experiences with babies and young children in the Hampstead Nurseries during the war, Anna Freud seems to have given little attention to these problems.

In the two modest volumes published with Dorothy Burlingham (Burlingham and Freud 1942; 1944), observation is sharp and description telling. Of children aged between one and three years they write: 'Reactions to parting at this time of life are particularly violent . . . This new ability to love finds itself deprived of the accustomed objects and his greed for affection remains unsatisfied. His longing for his mother becomes intolerable and throws him into states of despair' (1942: 51). Yet, despite this clear understanding of the distress that is implicit in these responses, neither in these two volumes nor in the papers published by Anna Freud during the subsequent decade are such manifestations related in any systematic way to anxiety in general or to separation anxiety in particular.

Instead, one has the impression that Burlingham and Freud were unprepared for the intensity of the responses they saw in the Nurseries and puzzled how to explain them. For instance, there is a passage (1942: 75–7) where they express the belief that perhaps if separations could be arranged more gradually all would be well: 'It is not so much the fact of separation to which the child reacts as the form in which the separation has taken place.' In another passage (p. 57) the distress of a child between three years and five years seems to be attributed, entirely, to his belief that separation is a punishment – 'To overcome this guilt he overstresses all the love which he has ever felt for his parents' – a comment which suggests that in their view there would be no distress at this age were there not guilt and persecutory anxiety. Perhaps they get nearer the truth when in these same passages they refer to 'the natural pain of separation' and to the fact that 'unsatisfied longing produces in him a state of tension which is felt as shock'.

Whenever during that period Anna Freud broaches a theoretical interpretation of these responses or of the long-term results of separation (e.g. 1952; 1953), she takes for granted that the child's tie to his mother is to be accounted for by the theory of secondary drive. Since the infant has no needs but those of his body, his interest is at first confined to anyone who meets those needs; in so far as there is anxiety at separation from mother, it is a result of the fear that bodily needs will go unmet. Her views are perhaps most clearly expressed in an address to medical students (1953). After describing her conception of how attachment grows in the well-cared-for child she proceeds:

> On the other hand, in cases where the mother has carried out her job as provider indifferently, or has allowed too many other people to substitute for herself, the transformation from greedy stomach-love to a truly constant love attachment is slow to come. *The infant may remain too insecure and too worried about the fulfilment of his needs* to have sufficient feeling to spare for the person or persons who provided for them [my italics].

This conclusion is a logical outcome of the secondary-drive theory of the child's tie and of Freud's version of the signal-anxiety theory of separation anxiety.

More recently, in books published in 1965 and 1972, Anna Freud describes several 'forms' taken by anxiety during the early years, each of which she believes to be characteristic of a particular stage in the development of object relations. The sequence of forms runs as follows: 'archaic fears of annihilation, . . . separation anxiety, castration anxiety, fear of loss of love, guilt . . .' Separation anxiety (and also fear of annihilation, starvation, loneliness, and helplessness) is held to be characteristic of, and confined to, the first stage in the development of object relations; that is described as the symbiotic stage, which is one of 'biological unity between the mother–infant couple, with the mother's narcissism extending to the child, and the child including the mother in his internal "narcissistic milieu"'. During subsequent stages, forms of anxiety other than separation anxiety are thought to occur. For example, the third stage, described as that of object constancy, is believed to be characterized by fear of the loss of the object's love. Unusually intense separation anxiety in later years is attributed to fixation at the symbiotic stage; excessive fear of loss of love may result from parental errors in discipline or from a child's over-sensitive ego during the stage of object constancy. The possible effects of events of later childhood are not discussed.

Contributions by Other Exponents of Ego Psychology

The theories advanced by Anna Freud during earlier years are subscribed to also by Nunberg (1932), Fenichel (1945), and Schur (1953; 1958). In his two carefully reasoned studies of anxiety, Schur makes the commonly held assumption that in man the biologically given components of behaviour are strictly limited. In the later paper, in which he draws extensively on ethological data and concepts, he details what he believes they comprise. On the one hand, he postulates the presence of fight and flight reactions characteristic of the phase of development which begins with the ability to perceive external objects. On the other, he postulates an earlier phase ('the undifferentiated phase') during which 'all danger is, due to the infantile development specific for man, "economical", inner danger', namely danger arising from an accumulation of excitation that springs from unmet bodily needs. It is from this, specifically human, source of anxiety that he regards separation anxiety as developing as a learnt derivative: 'The realization that an external object can initiate or end a traumatic situation displaces the danger from the economic situation to the condition which determines that situation. Then it is no longer hunger that constitutes danger for the child but it is the absence of the mother.' Although he discusses various dangers which he thinks 'may be based on innate givens', nowhere does he consider the possibility that loss of mother may be one of them.

Appendix I

After he has come to recognize the importance of separation anxiety Kris (1950) makes a serious effort to incorporate it in his theorizing. But his views are based more on inference from previous theory than on a reassessment of the data; in particular he is concerned, like Schur, to cast them in a form compatible with Hartmann's ego psychology. This leads him to place great emphasis on a distinction between the danger of losing the love object and the danger of losing the object's love. Although this distinction was referred to briefly by Freud (1926a), the way that Kris elaborates it is his own. On theoretical grounds he postulates that the danger of losing the love object is concerned solely with anaclitic (namely bodily) needs and is not concerned with a particular love object. Conversely, the development of a 'relationship to a permanent personalized love object that can no longer easily be replaced' he postulates to occur synchronously with the development of responsiveness to the danger of losing the object's love; it represents, in his opinion, 'a decisive step in ego development'.

This hypothetical association is not, however, borne out by observation. Anxiety reactions to the loss of a particular love object are to be seen some months before it is reasonable to credit a human infant with awareness of the danger of losing the object's love and before the twelve-month age-limit suggested by Kris (1950). As is emphasized in the previous volume (Chapter 15), the responses mediating attachment behaviour both in man and in lower species tend quickly to focus on a particular figure; and there can be no reason to suppose that their doing so represents an important step in ego development. In the event, therefore, the theoretical distinction advanced by Kris must be regarded as mistaken.

The crucial connection between anxiety as the reaction to the danger of losing the object and the pain of mourning as the reaction to its actual loss, which Freud arrives at in the final pages of *Inhibitions, Symptoms and Anxiety*, has been little recognized. Only in the work of Melanie Klein and Therese Benedek is it given much place. Helene Deutsch (1937) explicitly divorces the two: anxiety is an infantile response, she holds, grief and mourning more mature ones. 'The early infantile anxiety', she writes, 'we know as the small child's reaction to separation from the protecting and loving person.' When the child is older, on the other hand, 'suffering and grief [are] to be expected *in place of* anxiety' (p. 14, my italics). Moreover, separation anxiety in the older individual is to be understood always as a regression to infancy, and occurs in situations where 'grief . . . threaten[s] the integrity of the ego, or, in other words, if the ego [is] too weak to undertake . . . mourning' (p. 14). This differentiation by maturity does not stand examination, however. In the responses of infants and young children to loss of mother, elements of grief are undoubtedly present. Conversely, as Therese Benedek among others has recorded, anxiety is the rule even in adults when they are separated for any length of time from someone they love.

For many years Therese Benedek has been concerned with problems of separation from, and reunion with, loved persons, and with responses to loss and bereavement; and as a result of her clinical work she has had a lively awareness of the far-reaching significance of separation anxiety and of its close relatedness to anxiety and mourning. In describing responses to separations, reunions, and bereavements occurring during wartime, she frequently speaks of separation as a trauma in itself and she generalizes boldly: 'The universal response to separation is anxiety' (Benedek 1946: 146). She also recognizes that the experience of being separated, or the expectation of being separated, from a loved person leads to a sharp increase in longing for his company. In a later paper (1956) she notes that a crying fit in an infant is by no means always caused 'by a commanding physiologic need such as hunger and pain, but by the thwarting of an attempt at emotional (psychologic) communication and satisfaction'.

All these observations can be parsimoniously explained in terms of the theories regarding attachment, separation anxiety, grief and mourning that are advanced in the present work. Nevertheless, although her original training took place in Budapest (see Appendix to Volume I), Benedek does not accept these simpler hypotheses. Instead, in all her theorizing she is committed to a secondary-drive theory of the child's tie to his mother with all its complications and disadvantages. Thus the increase in longing evident in adults at separation, which can hardly be considered other than a natural and normal response, is explained as due to a regression to oral dependency. Indeed, as in so much theorizing deriving from the concept of dependence, Therese Benedek tends at times to theorize as though all attachments to loved persons were undesirable regressions to an infantile state.

Nowhere in Benedek's writings is there any systematic discussion of separation anxiety; but, in the later paper (1956) referred to above, two separate theories appear to be adumbrated. The first is similar to Freud's signal-anxiety theory; the second is concerned with the danger of ego disorganization.

Still struggling with the same problem that Freud was wrestling with thirty years earlier, she asks why an infant should respond to 'the frustration of a "dependent" wish' by crying. Reverting to the belief that crying is related intrinsically only to the experiences of hunger and pain, she concludes that 'he responds to the lack of participation from the adult as to a complete interruption of the symbiosis, as if he were abandoned and *hungry*' (p. 402, my italics).

Since, however, she is not altogether confident that crying is to be understood as anxiety, and believes that anxiety proper is a response to the danger of ego disintegration, Benedek advances another view. This is that the young child has to turn to his mother to preserve his ego integration when faced with the 'anxiety, humiliation and shame of failure'. In the case of the older child, 'his ego can maintain itself by its own resources' (pp. 408–9). Thus, although the clinical data she presents are consistent with the theory advanced here, Benedek's interpretations remain firmly embedded within the traditional paradigm.

In much of her theorizing, especially in her use of the concept of symbiosis, Margaret Mahler (1968) follows Therese Benedek; and in attributing a distinct form of anxiety to each stage of the development of object relations she follows Anna Freud. Nevertheless, despite the similarity of their postulated stages, the stage of development to which Mahler attributes separation anxiety is not the same as the one to which Anna Freud attributes it. Whereas Anna Freud regards separation anxiety as a response specific to 'infringements of the biological mother–infant tie' during the first stage of development, Mahler holds that separation anxiety is attributable properly only to a later stage, namely the stage 'after the beginning of object constancy has been achieved'. This she puts in the third and fourth years. The form of anxiety that Mahler attributes to the first stage of development, the symbiotic stage, is a fear of self-annihilation, the reasoning being that at that stage 'loss of the symbiotic object' is thought to amount 'to loss of an integral part of the ego itself'. This mode of theorizing is close to that of Spitz.

Although, like most other analysts, Spitz is an adherent of the secondary-drive theory to account for the child's tie to his mother and endorses Freud's version of the signal-anxiety theory of separation anxiety (1950), he advances, in addition, a variant of that theory. This is a theory of 'narcissistic trauma'. After outlining his views on the development of object relations from a phase of narcissism (first three months) through a phase of pre-objectal relations (second three months) to a phase of true object relations (third three months), he proceeds:

It is in the third quarter that true objects appear for the first time. They now have a face, but they still retain their function of a constituent part of the child's recently established Ego. The loss of the object is therefore a diminution of the Ego at this age and is as severe a narcissistic trauma as a loss of a large part of the body. The reaction to it is just as severe.

From other passages, in which he insists on the warning function of anxiety and its dependence on learning and foresight, it is clear that in Spitz's view anxiety is a signal to warn against the danger of a narcissistic trauma. This is a fresh variant of the signal-anxiety theory: the traumatic situation to be avoided is, this time, one in which narcissism is threatened.

It should be noted that much of Spitz's theorizing about anxiety turns around his concern to explain the anxiety exhibited by an infant of seven or eight months when confronted by a stranger, which he was the first to term eight-months' anxiety; the anxiety exhibited at separation from a loved object is less in his mind. In view of his empirical work this may seem surprising, until we realize that his observations of deprived infants were not concerned with the immediate responses to separation, namely protest, distress, and anxiety, or with responses after reunion, but were largely concentrated on responses seen during the later phases of separation, namely grief and depression. As a result he had no opportunity to observe the continuum of response from separation anxiety to grief and mourning.

The approach of Sandler and Joffe to these problems follows fairly closely the approaches of Kris and Spitz. The traditional theory of secondary drive is adopted to account for the child's tie to his mother, together with the concept of dependency. In keeping with their basic model, moreover, they place almost exclusive emphasis on the feeling states produced in a child by the presence or absence of his mother and make little attempt to relate these feeling states either to instinctive behaviour or to the survival value of mother's presence and the increased risk attendant on her absence. Thus they describe 'the role of the object' in a child's life as 'that of a vehicle for the attainment of the ideal state of well-being'. Conversely, 'loss of the object signifies the loss of an aspect of the self', i.e. that 'part of the self-presentation which . . . *reflects the relation to the object*' (Joffe and Sandler 1965, their italics).

For Sandler and Joffe, therefore, as for Freud, the situation at all costs to be avoided is not so much the actual loss as the traumatic overwhelming of the ego to which loss leads. In terms of the Sandler and Joffe model, the traumatic situation to be avoided is described as a 'disruption of the individual's feeling state' (Sandler and Joffe 1969).

Summing up the differences they see between their theoretical interpretation and my own, Joffe and Sandler (1965) conclude:

Object loss may bring about acute mental pain through creating a wound in the self. This view coincides with what Abraham and others have described as the 'severe injury to infantile narcissism' which object loss entails. And although Bowlby has maintained (1960b) that such a statement misses the true significance of object loss, we take the view that it contains its essence.

Such contrasting positions are, of course, a simple consequence of our having adopted different paradigms.

Other Contributors

In view of Sullivan's insistence that psychiatry is the study of interpersonal relationships, it is not unexpected that he sees all anxiety as a function of the child's relationship to his mother and other significant people. Nevertheless his position is different from that advanced here, especially in the primacy that he gives to the role of learning; for he regards anxiety as being exclusively a product of the mother's attitude. When mother is approving, her child is content; when she is disapproving, her child is anxious. Despite his great emphasis on 'need for contact' and 'need for tenderness' and the strong terms in which he refers to the experience of loneliness – 'really intimidating' and 'terrible' (1953: 261) – that separation from a loved object can of itself induce anxiety appears to be explicitly ruled out. Thus, in a final chapter, he indicates features that man has in common with other species, namely bodily needs and 'even our recurrent need for contact with others'. These he contrasts with features 'restricted to man and some of the creatures he has domesticated', which include 'the experience of anxiety' (p. 370). His assumption that anxiety is confined to domesticated species follows from his assumption that it results from processes of training and learning: 'there is nothing I can conceive in the way of interpersonal action about which one could not be trained to be anxious' (pp. 370–71). Even 'the experience of intense anxiety' which gives rise to repression is conceived as resulting from ill-conceived educational methods (p. 163).[9]

Although in Sullivan's view the induction of anxiety remains something of a mystery – 'the character of situations which provoke anxiety is never completely to be grasped' (p. 190) – it is nevertheless evident that in effect he sees it as always connected with processes of child-training. Since he believes that a main anxiety-inducing sanction used by a mother is restriction or denial of tenderness (p. 162), he comes at times near to my own

9. Dr Mabel Blake Cohen has emphasized that Sullivan did not regard such 'training' as a product only of conscious parental attitudes: 'Sullivan recognized that unconscious attitudes or tensions in the parents' interactions with the child were of considerably more importance than conscious planned behaviour' (personal communication).

concept of separation anxiety and its exacerbation by threats of abandonment. What seems to escape Sullivan, however, is that distress and anxiety can be and often are direct consequences of lack of tenderness and of separation *per se*; and that threats to restrict tenderness would be ineffective were that not so. While aware that loneliness can be a devastating experience for adolescents and adults, Sullivan seems unaware that it is even more distressing for infants and young children; indeed, there are passages in which he seems specifically to exclude that that is so: 'Loneliness, as an experience which has been so terrible that it practically baffles clear recall, is a phenomenon ordinarily encountered *only in pre-adolescence and afterwards*' (p. 261, my italics).

Reading Sullivan's work one gets the impression that he had never observed young children and that he was only partially aware of the close attachment they form to particular people and of the sense of security that mere proximity to a loved figure brings. The 'need for contact with others, often felt as loneliness', is identified, *not* with need for a genital or a parent–child relationship, but with gregariousness in animals (p. 370); his conviction that 'no action of the infant is consistently and frequently associated with the relief of anxiety' (p. 42), which overlooks the relief an infant commonly exhibits when clutching his mother, is a main plank in his theorizing. Because of this, he seems never to have grasped the reality of separation anxiety and, therefore, despite his close attention to the problems to which it gives rise, it remains almost impossible to attribute to him any particular theory of its nature and origin. It is probably for the same reasons that neither grief nor mourning plays any significant part in his system of psychopathology.

In the theorizing of Phyllis Greenacre (1952) separation anxiety, and grief and mourning seem also to be omitted. Instead, experiences during the birth process and the first weeks of postnatal life are advanced as major variables to account for a later differential liability to neurosis (see Chapter 16 of this volume).

Rank's views regarding birth trauma have already been referred to. In his early papers Fairbairn, who sees separation anxiety as the mainspring of all psychopathology, follows Rank closely in regard to its origins: Fairbairn's postulate (1943) that birth anxiety is 'the prototype of all the separation anxiety which is subsequently experienced' is the counterpart of his postulate that a return-to-womb craving accounts for the child's tie. It should be added, however, that these views are peripheral to Fairbairn's main theoretical position (Fairbairn 1952), which is in all other respects consistent with the theory of frustrated attachment advanced here. In a late paper (1963) in which he gives a synopsis of his views he writes: 'The earliest and original form of anxiety, as experienced by the child, is separation anxiety.'

Others have also founded their psychopathology on the central role of separation anxiety and some have adopted a frustrated attachment theory to account for it. For instance, as long ago as 1935, Suttie, holding the view that the child's attachment to his mother is the result of a primary 'need for company', saw anxiety as 'an expression of apprehension of discomfort at the frustration, or threatened frustration, of this all-important motive'. A year later Hermann (1936) expressed an almost identical view. He relates anxiety to the urge to seek and cling to mother: 'Anxiety is basically the feeling of being left on one's own in the face of danger. Its expression is a seeking for help and at the same time a seeking for mother. . . . Anxiety develops in the sense of an urge to cling. . . .'

Odier (1948) appears to adopt the same position. Taking *Inhibitions, Symptoms and Anxiety* as his starting-point, he criticizes Freud's view on the ground that the infant in the second year cannot conceptualize danger. As an alternative he postulates that 'during the second year this affect [i.e. anxiety] indicates that a particular state has become differentiated: the state of subjective insecurity', and concludes, 'originally the cause of the insecurity of the infant is, above all else, the absence of the mother (or her substitute) or separation from her at the time when the infant most needs her care and protection. This state is the basic theory of anxiety as it relates to insecurity' (pp. 44–6). In most respects Odier's view is consistent with that advanced in the present work. Where it differs is in his holding that separation anxiety starts only in the second year, a view that may have arisen because its obtrusive exhibition after the first birthday had misled him into supposing that it does not begin until then.

Winnicott makes no such mistake. Although in several papers (e.g. 1941; 1945; 1955b) he might be thought to favour the Kleinian view that separation anxiety is nothing but depressive anxiety, in his brief contribution 'Anxiety Associated with Insecurity' (1952) he takes a line consistent with that favoured here. He refers to 'the well-known observation that the earliest anxiety is related to being insecurely held', and to anxiety that is caused by 'failure in the technique of infant care, as for instance failure to give the continuous live support that belongs to mothering'. In his judgement 'it is normal for the infant to feel anxiety if there is a failure of infant care technique'.

This is also the view of William James who many years ago wrote simply: 'The great source of terror in infancy is solitude' (James 1890).

Appendix II
Psychoanalysis and Evolution Theory

Since it is not always realized that the paradigm Freud employed throughout in his metapsychology is pre-Darwinian in its assumptions, it is of interest to consider how that should have been so.

During the latter part of last century two separate debates were being held, the first about the historical reality of evolution and the second about how evolution, should it prove to have occurred, comes about. Not infrequently the adjective 'Darwinian' is used to refer to a belief in the historical reality of evolution. That, of course, is mistaken. Many others besides Charles Darwin advocated the historical reality of evolution, though it is true that none organized and displayed the evidence so cogently as he. Nevertheless the adjective Darwinian should not be applied in a general way to the occurrence of evolution but must be kept strictly for the theory that it has been brought about by a particular biological process, the one Darwin named 'natural selection', which is best described in terms of the differential breeding success, or failure, of naturally occurring variants that transmit their characteristics to their offspring.

Freud was certainly an evolutionist, but there is no evidence that he was ever a Darwinian. No doubt it is largely because a belief in evolution is so often regarded as Darwinian that it is easy to overlook how deeply Freud was committed to a pre-Darwinian standpoint. In his *Autobiographical Study* (1925) Freud describes how, as a student in the 1870s, 'the theories of Darwin, which were then of topical interest, strongly attracted me' (*SE* 20: 8); and we learn from Jones (1953) that in his first year at the University of Vienna (1872–3) Freud took a course on 'Biology and Darwinism'. Such references, combined with Freud's enthusiasm for evolution in general and his occasional and always favourable references to some others of Darwin's ideas, e.g. the primal horde and the expression of emotions, are deceptive and lead easily to the supposition that Freud adopted Darwin's theory of the evolutionary process, even though he did not always apply it. Such a view, however, is incompatible with the historical record, as a reading of Ernest Jones's biography clearly shows (see especially Volume 3, 1957, Chapter 10).

Now that the explanatory powers of the principle of natural selection proposed by Darwin are become firmly established and universally accepted by biologists, it is easy to forget that this was far from the case during the formative years of psychoanalysis. Eiseley (1958) has described the scientific climate of the final quarter of last century, by which time belief in the historical reality of evolution was becoming well established whereas ideas on the means by which it is brought about remained in the hottest dispute. In particular, he describes how the authoritative yet mistaken criticism of Darwin's theory by Lord Kelvin had given great encouragement to Darwin's critics and to advocates of Lamarckian ideas.[1] So much so, in fact, that in later editions of the *Origin* Darwin modified his position by incorporating Lamarck's theory of the inheritance of acquired characters into his own theory of evolution by means of natural selection. The to and fro of heated controversy as it reached Freud in Vienna during the 'seventies and 'eighties, mainly through the professor of zoology, Claus, is described by Ritvo (1972). In 1909, the centenary year of Darwin's birth, the status of his theory of natural selection was still so doubtful that the celebrations to mark the event were little more than perfunctory. Throughout the first quarter of the present century, indeed, theories of evolution continued to be in 'a state of chaos and confusion' (De Beer 1963); and it was not until 1942, with the publication of Julian

1. De Beer (1963) points out that history has treated Lamarck unfairly. As one of the first, in 1809, to advance a systematic theory of the evolution of living species from earlier ones, Lamarck made a substantial contribution; but because his account was eclipsed by Darwin's definitive work it has been forgotten, except perhaps in his native France. By contrast, Lamarck's unproductive ideas regarding the processes whereby evolution has come about – he attributed it not only to the inheritance of acquired characters but to the powers of a 'tendency to perfection' and of 'an inner feeling of need' – remain identified with his name. This is because they have been so identified throughout the debate on the nature of the processes causing evolution, a debate that began after the *Origin* was published (in 1859), continued into the early decades of this century, and is occasionally revived even today.

Huxley's volume *Evolution: The Modern Synthesis*, that a definitive account of the theory established during the preceding decade became readily available. It is significant that the turning-point came, during the 1920s, as soon as genetic analysis was applied not only to specimens in a laboratory but to wild populations living and propagating in their natural environment.[2]

Once the key dates in the historical development of Freud's psychoanalytic ideas are set beside those of evolutionary theory, the absence in psychoanalysis (as in most other schools of psychology) of a Darwinian perspective ceases to surprise. On the contrary, it is clear that, not only as a young man but on into his middle and later years, Freud would certainly not have been alone among his generation had he been cautious and non-committal in his approach to theories of the evolutionary process, including Darwin's theory of natural selection.

Yet to be non-committal was hardly in Freud's character. Although he never explicitly rejected Darwinian principles, it is evident that his early, deep, and continuing commitment to pre-Darwinian concepts in theoretical biology left no room for them. Nowhere throughout Freud's writings is Darwin's theory of natural selection debated; instead it is passed by as though it had never been proposed (Jones 1957: 332).

In Chapter 1 of the first volume of this work it is emphasized that the psychical energy model that Freud brought to psychoanalysis came, not from his clinical work with patients, but from ideas he had learnt many years earlier, especially when he was working in the laboratory of his admired professor of physiology, Brücke. Now these ideas long antedate Darwin's *Origin*, published in 1859. During the 1840s, Brücke had been one of a group of dedicated young scientists, of whom Helmholtz was the leader, who were determined to show that all real causes are symbolized in science by the word 'force'. Since the achievements of the Helmholtz school soon became famous, it was natural that Freud, working under one of their number, should have adopted their assumptions. As Jones (1953: 46) points out, the spirit and content of Brücke's lectures of the 1870s correspond closely to the

2. For an account of present-day theories of the evolutionary process see Maynard Smith (1966) and Alland (1967).

words Freud always used to characterize psychoanalysis in its dynamic aspect: '. . . psycho-analysis derives all mental processes (apart from the reception of external stimuli) from the interplay of forces, which assist or inhibit one another, combine with one another, enter into compromises with one another, etc.' (Freud 1926b, *SE* **20**: 265).

The limitations of that model for organizing the clinical phenomena to which Freud drew attention are already discussed in the first volume. The point now being emphasized is that the model is not only pre-Darwinian in origin but also remote from the biological concepts introduced by Darwin. For Freud and his colleagues, deep in Helmholtzian assumptions, the Darwinian perspective would, therefore, have been extremely difficult to reach. As Freud grew older, moreover, his increasing commitment to vitalist theories of the kind advocated by Lamarck made reaching it impossible. In his third volume Jones (1957) gives half a chapter to Freud's life-long adherence to Lamarckian explanations of the process of evolution, starting with the postulated heritability of acquired characters and progressing to a belief in the powers of a postulated 'inner feeling of need'.

During his early professional years Freud followed his colleagues of the Helmholtzian school in espousing what may now seem a rather naïve determinism. But at some time during the years before 1915 his views seem to have undergone radical change, since in 1917 he is expressing the greatest interest in Lamarck's ideas about the effects that an animal's 'inner feeling of need' is thought to have on its structure. During that year, Freud was in a mood of boundless enthusiasm for the whole of Lamarck's work and was in correspondence with Ferenczi and Abraham about an ambitious project to integrate psycho-analysis with Lamarck's theories of evolution. 'Our intention is to base Lamarck's ideas completely on our own theories and to show that the concept of "need", which creates and modifies organs, is nothing else than the power unconscious ideas have over the body . . . in short the "omnipotence of thoughts". Fitness would then be really explained psycho-analytically. . . .'[3] This amounts,

3. Extract from Freud's letter to Abraham of November 1917, quoted by Jones (1957: 335). Although in his first volume Jones (1953: 50) claims that

as Jones remarks, to the belief that 'need' enables an animal to bring about changes not only in its environment but in its own body. Moreover, causation is inextricably confused with function. Thus Freud's position in theoretical biology had by that date become wholly at variance with the biology that was about to dominate the twentieth century.

On reflection it becomes clear that Freud's increasingly deep commitment to a Lamarckian perspective, to the exclusion of Darwinian ideas about differential survival rates and the distinction between causation and function, has suffused the whole structure of psychoanalytic thought and theory.[4] With the remainder of biology resting firmly on a developed version of Darwinian principles and psychoanalysis continuing Lamarckian, the gulf between the two has steadily and inevitably grown wider. There are thus only three conceivable outcomes. The first, which is barely imaginable, is for biology to renounce its Darwinian perspective. The second, advocated here, is for psychoanalysis to be recast in terms of modern evolution theory. The third is for the present divorce to continue indefinitely with psychoanalysis remaining permanently beyond the fringe of the scientific world.

Freud 'never abandoned determinism for teleology', it is plain that that claim cannot be sustained.

4. Even Hartmann's influential book, *Ego Psychology and the Problem of Adaptation* (1939), was conceived and written before knowledge of modern evolution theory had become disseminated.

Appendix III
Problems of Terminology

Early in this volume it is remarked that in discussions of fear and anxiety problems of terminology abound. In Chapters 6, 12, 18, and 20 some of them are discussed. Here we consider some others.

During this century countless efforts have been made to clarify terminology, and a number of writers have proposed specific usages for words in common currency. No solution will satisfy everyone; or at least no solution will do so unless everyone shares a common theory. For as often as not the terms adopted are a reflection of theory.

Danger of Reification

First, it is vital to note that the words 'fear', 'alarm', 'anxiety', and others like them can be used legitimately only with reference to the state of an individual organism. In this work they are used only in their adjectival forms to refer to the way an organism may be appraising a situation, the way it may be behaving, or the way it may be feeling, all of which are closely linked. Conversely, it is never legitimate to refer to 'a fear' or 'an anxiety', as though each were a thing in its own right. The pitfalls into which it is easy to stumble when feelings are reified are discussed in Chapter 7 of the previous volume and in Chapter 20 of this one.

Unfortunately there is a very pronounced tendency not only in common parlance but in psychological, psychiatric, and psychoanalytic literature to reify both fear and anxiety. Thus we find Jersild, whose empirical work is so valuable, not infrequently tabulating the number of fears a sample of children are reported to show – 'fear of three specifically named groups of animals, such as dogs, horses, cats, received a tally of three' (Jersild 1943) – and expressing his results as percentages of the total fears counted. Fortunately, however, in others of his tables, his results are expressed as percentages of children who show fear in particular situations; those are the figures drawn upon in this volume.

In the psychoanalytic tradition it was not until 1926 that Freud treated anxiety as the reaction of an organism to a situation. Prior to that anxiety had been regarded by him as a transformation of libido, and as such was explicitly reified. As Strachey points out in one of his editorial introductions, as late as 1920 Freud added the following in a footnote to the fourth edition of the *Three Essays*: 'One of the most important results of psychoanalytic research is this discovery that neurotic anxiety arises out of libido, that it is the product of a transformation of it, and that it is thus related to it in the same kind of way as vinegar is to wine' (*SE* 7: 224n).

Even today this type of thinking is not dead; and, as I well know, it is very easy to slip into it.

'*Anxiety*', '*Alarm*', '*Fear*', '*Phobia*'

Because the English word 'anxiety' and its German cousin *Angst* play such a great part in psychoanalysis and psychiatry let us begin by considering those two.

In this work the usage already adopted for the word anxiety is that it denotes (a) how we feel when our attachment behaviour is activated and we are seeking an attachment figure but without success (Chapter 6), and (b) how we feel when for any reason we are uncertain whether our attachment figure(s) will be available should we want one (Chapter 15). It may be asked, how does that usage fit into other usages and with the etymological origins of the words? There is no lack of authorities to help to answer these questions.

Freud's use of the German term *Angst* and the difficulties of translation into English to which it gives rise are discussed by Strachey (1959; 1962). The usage of the term anxiety by English-speaking psychoanalysts is discussed by Rycroft (1968b). And the uses in the fields of psychiatry and psychopathology not only of the English 'anxiety' but of its many relatives in other languages are discussed by Lewis (1967), who also examines their etymology. Certain trends in usage, far from consistent, emerge.

A feature of usage to which all three writers point is that, in technical works, both 'anxiety' and *Angst* tend to indicate fear the origins of which are not identified. For example, on the final occasion on which he discusses the problem, Freud (1926a) remarks that *Angst* 'has a quality of *indefiniteness and lack of object*. In precise speech we use the word "fear" [*Furcht*] rather than "anxiety" [*Angst*] if it has found an object' (*SE* **20**: 165). Rycroft (1968b) recommends that anxiety be defined as 'the response to some yet unrecognized factor either in the environment or in the self' and reflects that psychoanalysis is mainly concerned with anxiety evoked by 'the stirrings of unconscious, repressed forces in the self'. Lewis (1967) refers to anxiety as an emotional state akin to fear that is experienced when 'there is either no recognizable threat, or the threat is, by reasonable standards, quite out of proportion to the emotion it seemingly evokes'.

There are a number of difficulties about this type of usage. Thus, it is unclear to whom the situation arousing fear is held to be 'indefinite', or by whom it is 'unrecognized'. Is it the anxious individual himself (as suggested by Freud and Rycroft) or is it the clinician treating him (as in Lewis's formulation)? The answer might be either or both. For, on the one hand, a patient is sometimes aware of what he is afraid of but for some reason does not divulge what he knows; or he may do so and not be believed by the clinician. On the other, a patient may be unaware of what is troubling him, but the clinician may believe, rightly or wrongly, that he can identify it. A further difficulty in this type of usage would arise should either patient or clinician, or both, later come to identify what the patient is afraid of. In that case are we to say that the patient's anxiety is no longer anxiety but fear? And, if so, what is to be done should either or both misidentify what the patient is afraid of? These are not trivial difficulties.

Two other features of the historical usage, in the technical field, of 'anxiety' and *Angst* to which one or another of these authorities refers are: (a) the words are sometimes used to indicate fear that is considered inappropriately intense for the situation that seems to arouse it; and (b) they are sometimes used to indicate fear of a situation foreseen as more or less likely to occur in the future rather than fear of a situation actually present. Neither criterion is satisfactory, however. In Chapters 9 and 10 it is emphasized how misleading it is to apply notions of reasonableness or appropriateness to fear and fear behaviour. In Chapter 10 it is argued that, more often than not, fear is aroused by situations that are forecast and not actually present, and that the time-scale of the forecast can vary on a continuum from the immediate to the remote future. How far distant in the future does the situation forecast have to be for an individual to be described as feeling anxious rather than feeling afraid? Does the future prospect of hell-fire make a believer afraid or anxious?

The convention adopted in this work, which is to use anxiety to refer especially to what is felt when separation is threatened, is, of course, a reflection of the theory advanced. Nevertheless, it remains in keeping with the etymological origins of anxiety (and related words) and also with the way in which Freud came to use the German *Angst* in his later writings.

According to Lewis (1967), the English anxiety and the German *Angst* have cousins in ancient Greek and Latin with meanings that centre on grief and sadness, a German cousin that in the seventeenth century could also mean longing, as well as two cousins in contemporary English: 'anguish' and 'anger'. Since separation from an attachment figure is accompanied by longing and often also by anger, and loss by anguish and despair, it is entirely appropriate to use the word anxiety to denote what is felt either when an attachment figure cannot be found or when there is no confidence that an attachment figure will be available and responsive when desired. Such usage is compatible also with Freud's thinking when he wrote that 'missing someone who is loved and longed for ... [is] the key to an understanding of anxiety' (1926a, *SE* **20**: 136–7).

The usage of 'alarm' in this work, where it is employed as complementary to anxiety and applied to what is felt when we try to withdraw or escape from a frightening situation, is again in keeping with the word's origins. 'Alarm' derives from sixteenth-century Italian meaning 'to arms!' and implies, therefore, surprise attack (Onions 1966).

Although the usages adopted for both anxiety and alarm are well suited to their origins, it cannot be said that there is any etymological justification for using the word 'fear' in the general-purpose way proposed here. 'Fear' (French *peur* and German

Furcht) has cousins in Old High German and Old Norse with meanings that include ambush and plague (Onions 1966); as such fear is close to alarm. In defence of using it as a general-purpose term, however, it can perhaps be argued that in modern English fear is very commonly so used.

On the usage of the term 'phobia' there is widespread agreement, though in this work the term is not favoured. Marks (1969) discusses its history and defines a phobia 'as a special form of fear which 1. is out of proportion to demands of the situation, 2. cannot be explained or reasoned away, 3. is beyond voluntary control, and 4. leads to avoidance of the feared situation'. Rycroft (1968b) defines phobia as: 'The symptom of experiencing unnecessary or excessive anxiety in some specific situation or in the presence of some specific object.' The term always smacks of pathology (*OED*).

The disadvantages of the term are as follows:
– it tends to reify fear, as in the title of Marks's book *Fears and Phobias*;
– a principle criterion in the definition is the unreasonableness of fearing so intensely the situation in question; on this definition fear of the dark or of loud noises or of any other natural clue would qualify as phobic, and thence would become tarred with pathology;
– when a clinician introduces the concept of phobia in trying to understand what a patient is afraid of, he is focusing attention (i) on a particular aspect of the situation to the neglect of others which may be more important, and (ii) on the escape component of fear behaviour to the neglect of the attachment component (see Chapters 18 and 19) because the meaning of the Greek word *phobos* centres on flight and escape;
– when used today by psychoanalysts phobia always implies the result of a particular pathological process, namely that the object or situation is feared 'not on its own account but because it has become a symbol of something else, i.e. because it represents some impulse, wish, internal object, or part of the self which the patient has been unable to face' (Rycroft 1968b); in Chapters 11, 18, and 19 reasons are given for believing that the process in question is implicated far too readily.

Once the term phobia is abandoned it becomes easier to consider how the person concerned may have developed so that he has become more frightened and anxious in certain situations than are his fellows.

References

Abraham, K. (1913). 'On the Psychogenesis of Agoraphobia in Children.' In Abraham, *Clinical Papers and Essays on Psycho-analysis*. London: Hogarth; New York: Basic Books, 1955.

Abraham, K. (1924). 'A Short Study of the Development of the Libido.' In Abraham, *Selected Papers on Psycho-analysis*. London: Hogarth, 1927. New edition, London: Hogarth, 1949; New York: Basic Books, 1953.

Ainsworth, M. D. S. (1972). 'Attachment and Dependency: A Comparison.' In J. L. Gewirtz (ed.), *Attachment and Dependence*. Washington, D.C.: Winston (distributed by Wiley, New York).

Ainsworth, M. D. S. & Bell, S. M. (1970). 'Attachment, Exploration, and Separation: Illustrated by the Behaviour of One-year-olds in a Strange Situation.' *Child Dev.* **41**: 49–67.

Ainsworth, M. D. S., Bell, S. M. & Stayton, D. J. (1971). 'Individual Differences in Strange-situation Behaviour of One-year-olds.' In H. R. Schaffer (ed.), *The Origins of Human Social Relations*. London & New York: Academic Press.

Ainsworth, M. D. S., Bell, S. M. & Stayton, D. J. (in press). 'Infant–Mother Attachment and Social Development: Socialization as a Product of Reciprocal Responsiveness to Signals.' In M. Richards (ed.), *The Integration of a Child into a Social World*. Cambridge: Cambridge University Press.

Ainsworth, M. D. S., Blehar, M. C., Waters, E. & Wall, S. (in prep.). 'Strange-situation Behaviour of One-year-olds: Its Relation to Mother–Infant Interaction in the First Year and to Qualitative Differences in the Infant–Mother Attachment Relationship.' (Monograph.)

Ainsworth, M. D. & Boston, M. (1952). 'Psychodiagnostic Assessments of a Child after Prolonged Separation in Early Childhood.' *Brit. J. med. Psychol.* **25**: 169–201.

Ainsworth, M. D. S. & Wittig, B. A. (1969). 'Attachment and Exploratory Behaviour of One-year-olds in a Strange Situation.' In B. M. Foss (ed.), *Determinants of Infant Behaviour*, Vol. 4. London: Methuen.

Alexander, F. & French, T. M. (1946). *Psychoanalytic Therapy*. New York: Ronald Press.

Alland, A. (1967). *Evolution of Human Behavior*. New York: Doubleday; London: Tavistock, 1969.

References

Anderson, J. W. (1972a). 'An Empirical Study of the Psychosocial Attachment of Infants to their Mothers.' Thesis presented for the degree of Ph.D., University of London.

Anderson, J. W. (1972b). 'Attachment Behaviour Out of Doors.' In N. Blurton Jones (ed.), *Ethological Studies of Child Behaviour*. Cambridge: Cambridge University Press.

Anderson, J. W. (1972c). 'On the Psychological Attachment of Infants to their Mothers.' *J. biosoc. Sci.* 4: 197–225.

Andrews, J. W. D. (1966). 'Psychotherapy of Phobias.' *Psychol. Bull.* 66: 455–80.

Anthony, S. (1940). *The Child's Discovery of Death*. London: Kegan Paul.

Argles, P. & Mackenzie, M. (1970). 'Crisis Intervention with a Multi-problem Family: A Case Study.' *J. Child Psychol. Psychiat.* 11: 187–95.

Arnold, M. B. (1960). *Emotion and Personality*. Vol. 1, *Psychological Aspects*; Vol. 2, *Neurological and Physiological Aspects*. New York: Columbia University Press; London: Cassell, 1961.

Arsenian, J. M. (1943). 'Young Children in an Insecure Situation.' *J. abnorm. soc. Psychol.* 38: 225–49.

Backett, E. M. & Johnston, A. M. (1959). 'Social Patterns of Road Accidents to Children: Some Characteristics of Vulnerable Children.' *Brit. med. J.* (*1*): 409.

Baker, G. W. & Chapman, D. W. (eds.) (1962). *Man and Society in Disaster*. New York: Basic Books.

Bandura, A. (1968). 'Modelling Approaches to the Modification of Phobic Disorders.' In R. Porter (ed.), *The Role of Learning in Psychotherapy*. London: J. & A. Churchill.

Bandura, A. & Menlove, F. L. (1968). 'Factors Determining Vicarious Extinction of Avoidance Behavior through Symbolic Modeling.' *J. Pers. soc. Psychol.* 8: 99–108.

Bandura, A. & Rosenthal, T. L. (1966). 'Vicarious Classical Conditioning as a Function of Arousal Level.' *J. Pers. soc. Psychol.* 3: 54–62.

Barker, R. G., Kounin, J. S. & Wright, H. F. (eds.) (1943). *Child Behavior and Development*. New York & London: McGraw-Hill.

Bateson, G., Jackson, D. D., Haley, J. & Weakland, J. (1956). 'Toward a Theory of Schizophrenia.' *Behav. Sci.* 1: 251–64.

Baumeyer, F. (1956). 'The Schreber Case.' *Int. J. Psycho-Anal.* 37: 61–74.

Baumrind, D. (1967). 'Child Care Practices Anteceding Three Patterns of Preschool Behavior.' *Genet. Psychol. Monogr.* 75: 43–88.

Bell, S. M. (1970). 'The Development of the Concept of Object as related to Infant–Mother Attachment.' *Child. Dev.* **41**: 291–311.

Bell, S. M. & Ainsworth, M. D. S. (1972). 'Infant Crying and Maternal Responsiveness.' *Child. Dev.* **43**: 1171–90.

Bender, L. & Yarnell, H. (1941). 'An Observation Nursery: A Study of 250 Children on the Psychiatric Division of Bellevue Hospital.' *Amer. J. Psychiat.* **97**: 1158–72.

Benedek, T. (1938). 'Adaptation to Reality in Early Infancy.' *Psychoanal. Quart.* **7**: 200–15.

Benedek, T. (1946). *Insight and Personality Adjustment: A Study of the Psychological Effects of War.* New York: Ronald Press.

Benedek, T. (1956). 'Toward the Biology of the Depressive Constellation.' *J. Amer. psychoanal. Ass.* **4**: 389–427.

Berecz, J. M. (1968). 'Phobias of Childhood: Aetiology and Treatment.' *Psychol. Bull.* **70**: 694–720.

Berg, I., Marks, I., McGuire, R. & Lipsedge, M. (1974). 'School Phobia and Agoraphobia.' *Psychol. Med.* **4**: 428–34.

Berger, S. M. (1962). 'Conditioning through Vicarious Instigation.' *Psychol. Rev.* **69**: 450–66.

Bernfeld, S. (1925, Eng. trans. 1929). *The Psychology of the Infant.* London: Kegan Paul.

Blehar, M. C. (1974). 'Anxious Attachment and Defensive Reactions associated with Day Care.' *Child Dev.* **45**: 683–92.

Bloch, D. A., Silber, E. & Perry, S. E. (1956). 'Some Factors in the Emotional Reaction of Children to Disaster.' *Amer. J. Psychiat.* **113**: 416–22.

Bolwig, N. (1963). 'Bringing up a Young Monkey.' *Behaviour* **21**: 300–30.

Bower, T. G. R., Broughton, J. M. & Moore, M. K. (1970). 'Infant Responses to Approaching Objects: An Indicator of Responses to Distal Variables.' *Percept. Psychophysics* **9**(2B): 193–6.

Bowlby, J. (1940). 'The Influence of Early Environment in the Development of Neurosis and Neurotic Character.' *Int. J. Psycho-Anal.* **21**: 154–78.

Bowlby, J. (1944). 'Forty-four Juvenile Thieves: Their Characters and Home Life.' *Int. J. Psycho-Anal.* **25**: 19–52 and 107–27.

Bowlby, J. (1951). *Maternal Care and Mental Health.* Geneva: WHO; London: HMSO; New York: Columbia University Press. Abridged version, *Child Care and the Growth of Love.* Harmondsworth, Middx: Penguin Books, second edition, 1965.

Bowlby, J. (1953). 'Some Pathological Processes Set in Train by Early Mother–Child Separation.' *J. ment. Sci.* **99**: 265–72.

Bowlby, J. (1958a). 'Psycho-analysis and Child Care.' In J. D. Suther-

References

land (ed.), *Psycho-analysis and Contemporary Thought*. London: Hogarth. Reprinted in P. Halmos & A. Iliffe (eds.), *Readings in General Psychology*. London: Routledge, 1958.

Bowlby, J. (1958b). 'The Nature of the Child's Tie to his Mother.' *Int. J. Psycho-Anal*. **39**: 350–73.

Bowlby, J. (1960a). 'Separation Anxiety.' *Int. J. Psycho-Anal*. **41**: 89–113.

Bowlby, J. (1960b). 'Grief and Mourning in Infancy and Early Childhood.' *Psychoanal. Study Child* **15**: 9–52.

Bowlby, J. (1961a). 'Separation Anxiety: A Critical Review of the Literature.' *J. Child Psychol. Psychiat*. **1**: 251–69.

Bowlby, J. (1961b). 'Processes of Mourning.' *Int. J. Psycho-Anal*. **42**: 317–40.

Bowlby, J. (1963). 'Pathological Mourning and Childhood Mourning.' *J. Amer. psychoanal. Ass*. **11**: 500–41.

Brain, C. K. (1970). 'New Finds at the Swartkrans Australopithecine Site.' *Nature* **225**: 1112–19.

Britton, R. S. (1969). 'Psychiatric Disorders in the Mothers of Disturbed Children.' *J. Child Psychol. Psychiat*. **10**: 245–58.

Broadbent, D. E. (1973). *In Defence of Empirical Psychology*. London: Methuen.

Broadwin, I. T. (1932). 'A Contribution to the Study of Truancy.' *Amer. J. Orthopsychiat*. **2**: 253–9.

Bronfenbrenner, U. (1958). 'Socialization and Social Class through Time and Space.' In E. E. Maccoby, T. M. Newcomb & E. L. Hartley (eds.), *Readings in Social Psychology*. New York: Holt, Rinehart & Winston.

Bronfenbrenner, U. (1961). 'Some Familial Antecedents of Responsibility and Leadership.' In L. Petrullo & B. M. Bass (eds.), *Leadership and Interpersonal Behavior*. New York: Holt, Rinehart & Winston.

Bronfenbrenner, U. (1970). 'Some Reflections on "Antecedents of Optimal Psychological Adjustment".' *J. consult. clin. Psychol*. **35**: 296–7.

Bronson, G. W. (1968). 'The Development of Fear in Man and Other Animals.' *Child Dev*. **39**: 409–31.

Bronson, G. W. (1972). 'Infants' Reactions to Unfamiliar Persons and Novel Objects.' *Monogr. Soc. Res. Child Dev*. **37** (3).

Brun, R. (1946). *A General Theory of Neurosis*. New York: International Universities Press.

Burlingham, D. & Freud, A. (1942). *Young Children in War-time*. London: Allen & Unwin. Reprinted in Freud, A., *Infants without Families: Report on the Hampstead Nurseries 1939–1945*. New York: International Universities Press, 1973.

Burlingham, D. & Freud, A. (1944). *Infants without Families*. London:

Allen & Unwin. Reprinted in Freud, A., *Infants without Families: Reports on the Hampstead Nurseries 1939–1945*. New York: International Universities Press, 1973.

Burnham, D. L. (1965). 'Separation Anxiety.' *Archs gen. Psychiat.* **13**: 346–58.

Burton, L. (1968). *Vulnerable Children*. London: Routledge; New York: Schocken Books.

Caplan, G. (1964). *Principles of Preventive Psychiatry*. New York: Basic Books; London: Tavistock.

Choi, E. H. (1961). 'Father–Daughter Relationships in School Phobia.' *Smith Coll. Stud. soc. Wk* **31**: 152–78.

Clancy, H. & McBride, G. (1969). 'The Autistic Process and its Treatment.' *J. Child Psychol. Psychiat.* **10**: 233–44.

Clyne, M. B. (1966). *Absent: School Refusal as an Expression of Disturbed Family Relationships*. London: Tavistock.

Cole, S. (1963). *Races of Man*. London: British Museum (Natural History).

Colm, H. N. (1959). 'Phobias in Children.' *Psychoanal. psychoanal. Rev.* **46**(3): 65–84.

Coolidge, J. C., Hahn, P. B. & Peck, A. L. (1957). 'School Phobia: Neurotic Crisis or Way of Life.' *Amer. J. Orthopsychiat.* **27**: 296–306.

Coolidge, J. C., Tessman, E., Waldfogel, S. & Willer, M. L. (1962). 'Patterns of Aggression in School Phobia.' *Psychoanal. Study Child* **17**: 319–33.

Coopersmith, S. (1967). *The Antecedents of Self-esteem*. San Francisco: W. H. Freeman.

Cox, F. N. & Campbell, D. (1968). 'Young Children in a New Situation with and without their Mothers.' *Child Dev.* **39**: 123–32.

Croake, J. W. (1969). 'Fears of Children.' *Human Dev.* **12**: 239–47.

Crook, J. H. (1968). 'The Nature and Function of Territorial Aggression.' In M. Ashley Montagu (ed.), *Man and Aggression*. New York: Oxford University Press.

Darwin, C. (1859). *On the Origin of Species by means of Natural Selection*. London: Murray.

Darwin, C. (1871). *The Descent of Man*. London: Murray.

Davidson, S. (1961). 'School Phobia as a Manifestation of Family Disturbance: Its Structure and Treatment.' *J. Child Psychol. Psychiat.* **1**: 270–87.

De Beer, G. (1963). *Charles Darwin: Evolution by Natural Selection*. Edinburgh: Nelson; New York: Doubleday, 1964.

Deutsch, H. (1929). 'The Genesis of Agoraphobia.' *Int. J. Psycho-Anal.* **10**: 51–69.

Deutsch, H. (1937). 'Absence of Grief.' *Psychoanal. Quart.* **6**: 12–22.

References

DeVore, I. & Hall, K. R. L. (1965). 'Baboon Ecology.' In I. DeVore (ed.), *Primate Behavior*. New York & London: Holt, Rinehart & Winston.

Douglas, J. W. B. (in press). 'Early Hospital Admissions and Later Disturbances of Behaviour and Learning.' *Devl. Med. Child. Neurol.* **17**.

Douvan, E. & Adelson, J. (1966). *The Adolescence Experience*. New York: Wiley.

Edelston, H. (1943). 'Separation Anxiety in Young Children: A Study of Hospital Cases.' *Genet. Psychol. Monogr.* **28**: 3–95.

Eiseley, L. (1958). *Darwin's Century*. New York: Doubleday.

Eisenberg, L. (1958). 'School Phobia: A Study in the Communication of Anxiety.' *Amer. J. Psychiat.* **114**: 712–18.

English, H. B. (1929). 'Three Cases of the "Conditioned Fear Response".' *J. abnorm. soc. Psychol.* **34**: 221–5.

Estes, H. R., Haylett, C. H. & Johnson, A. (1956). 'Separation Anxiety.' *Amer. J. Psychother.* **10**: 682–95.

Evans, P. & Liggett, J. (1971). 'Loss and Bereavement as Factors in Agoraphobia: Implications for Therapy.' *Brit. J. med. Psychol.* **44**: 149–54.

Fagin, C. M. R. N. (1966). *The Effects of Maternal Attendance during Hospitalization on the Post-hospital Behavior of Young Children: A Comparative Study*. Philadelphia: F. A. Davis.

Fairbairn, W. R. D. (1941). 'A Revised Psychopathology of the Psychoses and Psychoneuroses.' *Int. J. Psycho-Anal.* **22**. Reprinted in Fairbairn, *Psychoanalytic Studies of the Personality*. London: Tavistock/Routledge, 1952; New York: Basic Books, 1954 (US edition entitled *Object-relations Theory of the Personality*).

Fairbairn, W. R. D. (1943). 'The War Neuroses: Their Nature and Significance.' In Fairbairn, *Psychoanalytic Studies of the Personality*. London: Tavistock/Routledge, 1952; New York: Basic Books, 1954 (US edition entitled *Object-relations Theory of the Personality*).

Fairbairn, W. R. D. (1952). *Psychoanalytic Studies of the Personality*. London: Tavistock/Routledge. Published in the USA under the title *Object-relations Theory of the Personality*. New York: Basic Books, 1954.

Fairbairn, W. R. D. (1963). 'Synopsis of an Object-relations Theory of the Personality.' *Int. J. Psycho-Anal.* **44**: 224–5.

Fantz, R. L. (1965). 'Ontogeny of Perception.' In A. M. Schrier, H. F. Harlow & F. Stollnitz (eds.), *Behavior of Nonhuman Primates*, Vol. 2. New York & London: Academic Press.

Fenichel, O. (1945). *The Psychoanalytic Theory of Neurosis*. New York: Norton.

Flavell, J. H. (1963). *The Developmental Psychology of Jean Piaget.* Princeton, N. J. & London: Van Nostrand.

Fleming, J. (1972). 'Early Object Deprivation and Transference Phenomena.' *Psychoanal. Quart.* **41**: 23–49.

Fraiberg, S. (1971). 'Separation Crisis in Two Blind Children.' *Psychoanal. Study Child* **26**: 355–71.

Freud, A. (1936). *The Ego and Mechanisms of Defence.* London: Hogarth.

Freud, A. (1946). *The Psycho-analytical Treatment of Children.* London: Imago; New York: International Universities Press, 1959.

Freud, A. (1952). 'The Mutual Influences in the Development of Ego and Id.' *Psychoanal. Study Child* **7**: 42–50.

Freud, A. (1953). 'Some Remarks on Infant Observation.' *Psychoanal. Study Child* **8**: 9–19.

Freud, A. (1965). *Normality and Pathology in Childhood: Assessments of Development.* New York: International Universities Press; London: Hogarth, 1966.

Freud, A. (1972). *Problems of Psycho-analytic Technique and Therapy 1966–1970.* London: Hogarth.

Freud, S. (1894). 'The Neuro-psychoses of Defence (1).' *SE* **3**: 45–61.[1]

Freud, S. (1895). 'Anxiety Neurosis.' *SE* **3**: 90–115.

Freud, S. (1905a). 'Fragment of an Analysis of a Case of Hysteria.' *SE* **7**: 7–122.

Freud, S. (1905b). *Three Essays on the Theory of Sexuality. SE* **7**: 135–243.

Freud, S. (1909). 'Analysis of a Phobia in a Five-year-old Boy.' *SE* **10**: 5–149.

Freud, S. (1910). 'A Special Type of Choice of Object Made by Men.' (Contributions to the Psychology of Love I.) *SE* **11**: 165–75.

Freud, S. (1911). 'Psycho-analytic Notes on an Autobiographical Account of a Case of Paranoia.' *SE* **12**: 9–82.

Freud, S. (1915a). 'Instincts and their Vicissitudes.' *SE* **14**: 117–40.

Freud, S. (1915b). 'The Unconscious.' *SE* **14**: 166–204.

Freud, S. (1917a). 'Mourning and Melancholia.' *SE* **14**: 243–58.

Freud, S. (1917b). *Introductory Lectures on Psycho-analysis.* Part III. *SE* **16**.

Freud, S. (1919). 'Lines of Advance in Psycho-analytic Therapy.' *SE* **17**:159–68.

Freud, S. (1920). *Beyond the Pleasure Principle. SE* **18**: 7–64.

[1] The abbreviation *SE* denotes the Standard Edition of *The Complete Psychological Works of Sigmund Freud,* published in 24 volumes by the Hogarth Press Ltd, London.

References

Freud, S. (1925). *An Autobiographical Study*. *SE* **20**: 7–70.

Freud, S. (1926a). *Inhibitions, Symptoms and Anxiety*. *SE* **20**: 87–172.

Freud, S. (1926b). 'Psycho-analysis.' *SE* **20**: 263–70.

Freud, S. (1931). 'Female Sexuality.' *SE* **21**: 225–43.

Freud, S. (1933). *New Introductory Lectures on Psycho-analysis*. *SE* **22**: 7–182.

Freud, S. (1937). 'Constructions in Analysis.' *SE* **23**: 257–69.

Freud, S. (1940). *An Outline of Psycho-analysis*. *SE* **23**: 144–207.

Frick, W. B. (1964). 'School Phobia: A Critical Review of the Literature.' *Merrill-Palmer Quart.* **10**: 361–74.

Friedman, J. H. (1950). 'Short-term Psychotherapy of "Phobia of Travel".' *Amer. J. Psychother.* **4**: 259–78.

Friedman, P. (1959). 'The Phobias.' In S. Arieti (ed.), *American Handbook of Psychiatry*. New York: Basic Books.

Fry, W. F. (1962). 'The Marital Context of an Anxiety Syndrome.' *Family Process* **1**: 245–52.

Goldberg, T. B. (1953). 'Factors in the Development of School Phobia.' *Smith Coll. Stud. soc. Wk* **23**: 227–48.

Goldfarb, W. (1943). 'Infant Rearing and Problem Behavior.' *Amer. J. Orthopsychiat.* **13**: 249–65.

Greenacre, P. (1941). 'The Predisposition to Anxiety.' In Greenacre, *Trauma, Growth and Personality*. New York: Norton, 1952.

Greenacre, P. (1945). 'The Biological Economy of Birth.' In Greenacre, *Trauma, Growth and Personality*. New York: Norton, 1952.

Greenacre, P. (1952). *Trauma, Growth and Personality*. New York: Norton.

Grinker, R. R. (1962). ' "Mentally Healthy" Young Males (Homoclites).' *Archs gen. Psychiat.* **6**: 405–53.

Hagman, E. (1932). 'A Study of Fears of Children of Pre-school Age.' *J. exp. Educ.* **1**: 110–30.

Hall, K. R. L. & DeVore, I. (1965). 'Baboon Social Behavior.' In I. DeVore (ed.), *Primate Behavior*. New York & London: Holt, Rinehart & Winston.

Hansburg, H. G. (1972). *Adolescent Separation Anxiety: A Method for the Study of Adolescent Separation Problems*. Springfield, Ill.: C. C. Thomas.

Hare, E. H. & Shaw, G. K. (1965). *Mental Health on a New Housing Estate*. London: Oxford University Press.

Harlow, H. F. (1961). 'The Development of Affectional Patterns in Infant Monkeys.' In B. M. Foss (ed.), *Determinants of Infant Behaviour*, Vol. 1. London: Methuen; New York: Wiley.

Harlow, H. F. & Harlow, M. K. (1965). 'The Affectional Systems.'

In A. M. Schrier, H. F. Harlow & F. Stollnitz (eds.), *Behavior of Nonhuman Primates*, Vol. 2. New York & London: Academic Press.

Harlow, H. F. & Zimmermann, R. R. (1959). 'Affectional Responses in the Infant Monkey.' *Science* **130**: 421.

Harper, M. & Roth, M. (1962). 'Temporal Lobe Epilepsy and the Phobic Anxiety–Depersonalization Syndrome.' *Compreh. Psychiat.* **3**: 129–51.

Hartmann, H. (1939, Eng. trans. 1958). *Ego Psychology and the Problem of Adaptation*. London: Imago; New York: International Universities Press.

Hayes, C. (1951). *The Ape in our House*. New York: Harper; London: Gollancz, 1952.

Heard, D. H. (1973). 'Unresponsive Silence and Intra-familial Hostility.' In R. Gosling (ed.), *Support, Innovation, and Autonomy*, London: Tavistock.

Heath, D. H. (1965). *Explorations of Maturity*. New York: Appleton-Century-Crofts.

Heathers, G. (1954). 'The Adjustment of Two-year-olds in a Novel Social Situation.' *Child Dev.* **25**: 147–58.

Hebb, D. O. (1949). *The Organization of Behavior*. New York: Wiley.

Heinicke, C. (1956). 'Some Effects of Separating Two-year-old Children from their Parents: A Comparative Study.' *Hum. Relat.* **9**: 105–76.

Heinicke, C. M., Busch, F., Click, P. & Kramer, E. (1973). 'Parent–Child Relations, Adaptation to Nursery School and the Child's Task Orientation: A Contrast in the Development of Two Girls.' In J. C. Westman (ed.), *Individual Differences in Children*. New York: Wiley.

Heinicke, C. & Westheimer, I. (1966). *Brief Separations*. New York: International Universities Press; London: Longmans.

Hermann, I. (1936). 'Sich-Anklammern–Auf-Suche-Gehen.' *Int.Z. Psychoanal.* **22**: 349–70.

Hersov, L. A. (1960a). 'Persistent Non-attendance at School.' *J. Child Psychol. Psychiat.* **1**: 130–6.

Hersov, L. A. (1960b). 'Refusal to Go to School.' *J. Child Psychol. Psychiat.* **1**: 137–45.

Hill, R. & Hansen, D. A. (1962). 'Families in Disaster.' In G. W. Baker & D. W. Chapman (eds.), *Man and Society in Disaster*. New York: Basic Books.

Hinde, R. A. (1970). *Animal Behaviour: A Synthesis of Ethology and Comparative Psychology*. Second edition. New York: McGraw-Hill.

Hinde, R. A. & Davies, L. (1972). 'Removing Infant Rhesus from

Mother for 13 Days compared with Removing Mother from Infant.' *J. Child Psychol. Psychiat.* **13**: 227–37.

Hinde, R. A., Spencer-Booth, Y. & Bruce, M. (1966). 'Effects of Six-day Maternal Deprivation on Rhesus Monkey Infants.' *Nature* **210**: 1021–3.

Hinde, R. A. & Spencer-Booth, Y. (1968). 'The Study of Mother–Infant Interaction in Captive Group-living Rhesus Monkeys.' *Proc. R. Soc. B.* **169**: 177–201.

Hinde, R. A. & Spencer-Booth, Y. (1970). 'Individual Differences in the Responses of Rhesus Monkeys to a Period of Separation from their Mothers.' *J. Child Psychol. Psychiat.* **11**: 159–76.

Hinde, R. A. & Spencer-Booth, Y. (1971). 'Effects of Brief Separation from Mother on Rhesus Monkeys.' *Science* **173**: 111–18.

Hug-Hellmuth, H. von (1913, Eng. trans. 1919). *A Study of the Mental Life of the Child.* Washington: Nervous & Mental Disease Pub. Co.

Huxley, J. (1942). *Evolution: The Modern Synthesis.* London: Allen & Unwin; New York: Harper.

James, W. (1890). *Principles of Psychology.* New York: Holt.

Janis, M. G. (1964). *A Two-year-old Goes to Nursery School.* London: Tavistock.

Jay, P. (1965). 'The Common Langur of North India.' In I. DeVore (ed.), *Primate Behavior.* New York & London: Holt, Rinehart & Winston.

Jensen, G. D. & Tolman, C. W. (1962). 'Mother–Infant Relationship in the Monkey, *Macaca nemestrina*: The Effect of Brief Separation and Mother–Infant Specificity.' *J. comp. physiol. Psychol.* **55**: 131–6.

Jersild, A. T. (1943). 'Studies of Children's Fears.' In R. G. Barker, J. S. Kounin & H. F. Wright (eds.), *Child Behavior and Development.* New York & London: McGraw-Hill.

Jersild, A. T. (1947). *Child Psychology.* Third edition. London: Staples Press.

Jersild, A. T. & Holmes, F. B. (1935a). *Children's Fears.* Child Dev. Monogr. no. 20. New York: Teachers College, Columbia University.

Jersild, A. T. & Holmes, F. B. (1935b). 'Some Factors in the Development of Children's Fears.' *J. exp. Educ.* **4**: 133–41.

Jersild, A. T., Markey, F. V. & Jersild, C. L. (1933). *Children's Fears, Dreams, Wishes, Day Dreams, Likes, Dislikes, Pleasant and Unpleasant Memories.* Child Dev. Monogr. no. 12. New York: Teachers College, Columbia University.

Jewell, P. A. & Loizos, C. (eds.) (1966). *Play, Exploration and Territory in Mammals.* London & New York: Academic Press.

Joffe, W. G. & Sandler, J. (1965). 'Notes on Pain, Depression, and Individuation.' *Psychoanal. Study Child* 20: 394–424.

John, E. (1941). 'A Study of the Effects of Evacuation and Air-raids on Pre-school Children.' *Brit. J. educ. Psychol.* 11: 173–82.

Johnson, A. M., Falstein, E. I., Szurek, S. A. & Svendsen, M. (1941). 'School Phobia.' *Amer. J. Orthopsychiat.* 11: 702–11.

Jolly, A. (1972). *The Evolution of Primate Behavior.* New York: Macmillan.

Jones, E. (1927). 'The Early Development of Female Sexuality.' In Jones, *Papers on Psycho-analysis.* Fifth edition. London: Ballière, Tindall & Cox, 1948.

Jones, E. (1929). 'Fear, Guilt and Hate.' In Jones, *Papers on Psycho-analysis.* Fifth edition. London: Ballière, Tindall & Cox, 1948.

Jones, E. (1953). *Sigmund Freud: Life and Work,* Vol. 1. London: Hogarth; New York: Basic Books.

Jones, E. (1955). *Sigmund Freud: Life and Work,* Vol. 2. London: Hogarth; New York: Basic Books.

Jones, E. (1957). *Sigmund Freud: Life and Work,* Vol. 3. London: Hogarth; New York: Basic Books.

Jones, M. C. (1924a). 'The Elimination of Children's Fears.' *J. exp. Psychol.* 7: 383–90. Reprinted in H. J. Eysenck (ed.), *Behaviour Therapy and the Neuroses.* Oxford: Pergamon, 1960.

Jones, M. C. (1924b). 'A Laboratory Study of Fear: The Case of Peter.' *Pedag. Semin.* 31: 308–15. Reprinted in H. J. Eysenck (ed.), *Behaviour Therapy and the Neuroses.* Oxford: Pergamon, 1960.

Kahn, J. H. & Nursten, J. P. (1968). *Unwillingly to School.* Second edition. Oxford: Pergamon.

Katan, A. (1951). 'The Role of "Displacement" in Agoraphobia.' *Int. J. Psycho-Anal.* 32: 41–50.

Kaufman, I. C. & Rosenblum, L. A. (1967). 'Depression in Infant Monkeys Separated from their Mothers.' *Science* 155: 1030–1.

Kaufman, I. C. & Rosenblum, L. A. (1969). 'Effects of Separation from Mother on the Emotional Behavior of Infant Monkeys.' *Ann. N.Y. Acad. Sci.* 159: 681–95.

Kawamura, S. (1963). 'The Process of Subculture Propagation among Japanese Macaques.' In C. H. Southwick (ed.), *Primate Social Behavior.* Princeton, N. J. & London: Van Nostrand.

Kellogg, W. N. & Kellogg, L. (1933). *The Ape and the Child: A Study of Environmental Influence upon Early Behavior.* New York: McGraw-Hill (Whittlesey House Publications).

Kennedy, W. A. (1965). 'School Phobia: Rapid Treatment of Fifty Cases.' *J. abnorm. Psychol.* 70: 285–9.

References

Kessen, W. & Mandler, G. (1961). 'Anxiety, Pain, and the Inhibition of Distress.' *Psychol. Rev.* **68**: 396–404.

Kestenberg, J. S. (1943). 'Separation from Parents.' *Nerv. Child* **3**: 20–35.

Klein, E. (1945). 'The Reluctance to go to School.' *Psychoanal. Study Child* **1**: 263–79.

Klein, M. (1932). *The Psycho-analysis of Children.* London: Hogarth.

Klein, M. (1934). 'On Criminality.' In Klein, *Contributions to Psychoanalysis 1921–1945.* London: Hogarth, 1948.

Klein, M. (1935). 'A Contribution to the Psychogenesis of Manicdepressive States.' In Klein, *Contributions to Psycho-analysis 1921–1945.* London: Hogarth, 1948.

Klein, M. (1946). 'Notes on Some Schizoid Mechanisms.' In Klein *et al.*, *Developments in Psycho-analysis.* London: Hogarth, 1952.

Klein, M. (1948a). *Contributions to Psycho-analysis 1921–1945.* London: Hogarth.

Klein, M. (1948b). 'On the Theory of Anxiety and Guilt.' *Int. J. Psycho-Anal.* **29**. Reprinted in Klein *et al.*, *Developments in Psycho-analysis.* London: Hogarth, 1952.

Klein, M., Heimann, P., Isaacs, S. & Riviere, J. (1952). *Developments in Psycho-analysis.* London: Hogarth.

Korchin, S. J. & Ruff, G. E. (1964). 'Personality Characteristics of the Mercury Astronauts.' In G. H. Grosser, H. Wechsler & M. Greenblatt (eds.), *The Threat of Impending Disaster: Contributions to the Psychology of Stress.* Cambridge, Mass.: MIT Press.

Kreitman, N., Philip, A. E., Greer, S. & Bagley, C. R. (1969). Parasuicide. Letter in *Brit. J. Psychiat.* **115**: 746–7.

Kreitman, N., Smith, P. & Tan, E. S. (1970). 'Attempted Suicide as Language: An Empirical Study.' *Brit. J. Psychiat.* **116**: 465–73.

Kris, E. (1950). 'Notes on the Development and on Some Current Problems of Psychoanalytic Child Psychology.' *Psychoanal. Study Child* **5**: 24–46.

Kris, E. (1956). 'The Recovery of Childhood Memories in Psychoanalysis.' *Psychoanal. Study Child* **11**: 54–88.

Kuhn, T. S. (1962). *The Structure of Scientific Revolutions.* Chicago & London: University of Chicago Press.

Kummer, H. (1967). 'Tripartite Relations in Hamadryas Baboons.' In S. A. Altmann (ed.), *Social Communication among Primates.* Chicago: University of Chicago Press.

Laing, R. D. & Esterson, A. (1964). *Sanity, Madness, and the Family.* London: Tavistock; New York: Basic Books. Second edition, 1970.

Lapouse, R. & Monk, M. A. (1959). 'Fears and Worries in a Representative Sample of Children.' *Amer. J. Orthopsychiat.* 29: 803–18.

Laughlin, H. P. (1956). *The Neuroses in Clinical Practice.* London: Saunders.

Lawick-Goodall, J. van (1968). 'The Behaviour of Free-living Chimpanzees in the Gombe Stream Reserve.' *Anim. Behav. Monogr.* 1: 161–311.

Lazarus, A. A. (1960). 'The Elimination of Children's Phobias by Deconditioning.' In H. J. Eysenck (ed.), *Behaviour Therapy and the Neuroses.* Oxford: Pergamon.

Lee, S. G. M., Wright, D. S. & Herbert, M. (in preparation). 'Aspects of the Development of Social Responsiveness in Young Children.'

Leeuwen, K. van & Tuma, J. M. (1972). 'Attachment and Exploration: A Systematic Approach to the Study of Separation–Adaptation Phenomena in response to Nursery School Entry.' *J. Amer. Acad. Child Psychiat.* 11: 314–40.

Leighton, D. C., Harding, J. S., Macklin, D. B., Macmillan, A. M. & Leighton, A. H. (1963). *The Character of Danger.* New York: Basic Books.

Levy, D. (1937). 'Primary Affect Hunger.' *Amer. J. Psychiat.* 94: 643–52.

Levy, D. (1951). 'Observations of Attitudes and Behavior in the Child Health Center.' *Amer. J. publ. Hlth* 41: 182–90.

Lewis, A. (1967). 'Problems presented by the Ambiguous Word "Anxiety" as used in Psychopathology.' *Israel Ann. Psychiat. & related Disciplines* 5: 105–21.

Lidz, T., Cornelison, A., Fleck, S. & Terry, D. (1958). 'The Intrafamilial Environment of the Schizophrenic Patient: The Transmission of Irrationality.' *Archs Neurol. Psychiat.* 79: 305–16.

Lorenz, K. (1937). 'Über die Bildung des Instinktbegriffes.' *Naturwissenschaften* 25. Eng. trans. 'The Establishment of the Instinct Concept.' In Lorenz, *Studies in Animal and Human Behaviour*, Vol. 1. Trans. by R. Martin. London: Methuen, 1970.

Lynch, J. J. (1970). 'Psychophysiology and the Development of Social Attachment.' *J. nerv. ment. Dis.* 151: 231–44.

MacCarthy, D., Lindsay, M. & Morris, I. (1962). 'Children in Hospital with Mothers.' *Lancet* (*I*): 603–8.

Maccoby, E. E. & Feldman, S. S. (1972). 'Mother-attachment and Stranger-reactions in the Third Year of Life.' *Monogr. Soc. Res. Child. Dev.* 37 (1).

Maccoby, E. E. & Masters, J. C. (1970). 'Attachment and Dependency.' In P. H. Mussen (ed.), *Carmichael's Manual of Child Psychology.* Third edition. New York & London: Wiley.

References

McCord, W., McCord, J. & Verden, P. (1962). 'Familial and Behavioral Correlates of Dependency in Male Children.' *Child Dev.* **33**: 313–26.

McDougall, W. (1923). *An Outline of Psychology.* London: Methuen.

Macfarlane, J. W., Allen, L. & Honzik, M. P. (1954). *A Developmental Study of the Behavior Problems of Normal Children between 21 Months and 14 Years.* Berkeley: University of California Press.

Mahler, M. D. (1968). *On Human Symbiosis and the Vicissitudes of Individuation.* Vol. 1, *Infantile Psychosis.* New York: International Universities Press; London: Hogarth, 1969.

Main, M. (1973). 'Exploration, Play and Cognitive Functioning as related to Child–Mother Attachment.' Thesis submitted for the degree of Ph.D., Johns Hopkins University.

Malmquist, C. P. (1965). 'School Phobia: A Problem in Family Neurosis.' *J. Amer. Acad. Child Psychiat.* **4**: 293–319.

Marks, I. M. (1969). *Fears and Phobias.* London: Heinemann Medical.

Marks, I. M. (1971). 'Phobic Disorders Four Years after Treatment: A Prospective Follow-up.' *Brit. J. Psychiat.* **118**: 683–8.

Marks, I. M., Boulougouris, J. & Marset, P. (1971). 'Flooding versus Desensitisation in the Treatment of Phobic Patients: A Crossover Study.' *Brit. J. Psychiat.* **119**: 353–75.

Marler, P. R. & Hamilton, W. J. (1966). *Mechanisms of Animal Behavior.* New York: Wiley.

Marris, P. (1974). *Loss and Change.* London: Routledge.

Martin, H. L. (1970). 'Antecedents of Burns and Scalds in Children.' *Brit. J. med. Psychol.* **43**: 39–47.

Marvin, R. S. (1972). 'Attachment and Communicative Behavior in Two-, Three- and Four-year-old Children.' Doctoral Dissertation submitted to the University of Chicago.

Mason, W. A. (1965). 'Determinants of Social Behavior in Young Chimpanzees.' In A. M. Schrier, H. F. Harlow & F. Stollnitz (eds.), *Behavior of Nonhuman Primates*, Vol. 2. New York & London: Academic Press.

Megargee, E. I., Parker, G. V. C. & Levine, R. V. (1971). 'Relationship of Familial and Social Factors to Socialization in Middle-class College Students.' *J. abnorm. Psychol.* **77**: 76–89.

Meili, R. (1959). 'A Longitudinal Study of Personality Development.' In L. Jessner & E. Pavenstedt (eds.), *Dynamic Psychopathology in Childhood.* New York: Grune & Stratton; London: Heinemann.

Melges, F. T. (1968). 'Postpartum Psychiatric Syndromes.' *Psychosom. Med.* **30**: 95–108.

Meng, H. & Freud, E. L. (eds.) (1963). *Psycho-analysis and Faith: The*

Letters of Sigmund Freud and Oskar Pfister. Trans. by E. Mosbacher. London: Hogarth.

Miller, D. R. (1970). 'Optimal Psychological Adjustment: A Relativistic Interpretation.' *J. consult. clin. Psychol.* **35**: 290–5.

Mitchell, G. (1970). 'Abnormal Behavior in Primates.' In L. A. Rosenblum (ed.), *Primate Behavior: Developments in Field and Laboratory Research*, Vol. 1. New York & London: Academic Press.

Montenegro, H. (1968). 'Severe Separation Anxiety in Two Pre-school Children: Successfully Treated by Reciprocal Inhibition.' *J. Child Psychol. Psychiat.* **9**: 93–103.

Moore, T. W. (1964). 'Children of Full-time and Part-time Mothers.' *Int. J. soc. Psychiat.*, Special Congress Issue no. 2.

Moore, T. W. (1969a). 'Effects on the Children.' In S. Yudkin & A. Holme (eds.), *Working Mothers and their Children.* Second edition. London: Sphere Books.

Moore, T. W. (1969b). 'Stress in Normal Childhood.' *Hum. Relat.* **22**: 235–50.

Moore, T. W. (1971). 'The Later Outcome of Early Care by the Mother and Substitute Daily Régimes.' Summary of paper given to the International Society for the Study of Behavioral Development, Nijmegen, July.

Morgan, G. A. & Ricciuti, H. N. (1969). 'Infants' Responses to Strangers during the First Year.' In B. M. Foss (ed.), *Determinants of Infant Behaviour*, Vol. 4. London: Methuen.

Morris, R. & Morris, D. (1965). *Men and Snakes.* London: Hutchinson.

Moss, C. S. (1960). 'Brief Successful Psychotherapy of a Chronic Phobic Reaction.' *J. abnorm. soc. Psychol.* **60**: 266–70.

Murphey, E. B., Silber, E., Coelho, G. V., Hamburg, D. A. & Greenberg, I. (1963). 'Development of Autonomy and Parent–Child Interaction in Late Adolescence.' *Amer. J. Orthopsychiat.* **33**: 643–52.

Murphree, O. D., Dykman, R. A. & Peters, J. E. (1967). 'Genetically Determined Abnormal Behavior in Dogs: Results of Behavioral Tests.' *Conditional Reflex* **2**: 199–205.

Murphy, L. B. (1962). *The Widening World of Childhood.* New York: Basic Books.

Nagera, H. & Colonna, A. B. (1965). 'Aspects of the Contribution of Sight to Ego and Drive Development: A Comparison of the Development of Some Blind and Sighted Children.' *Psychoanal. Study Child* **20**: 267–87.

Newson, J. & Newson, E. (1968). *Four Years Old in an Urban Community.* London: Allen & Unwin; Chicago: Aldine.

References

Niederland, W. G. (1959a). 'The "Miracled-up" World of Schreber's Childhood.' *Psychoanal. Study Child.* **14**: 383–413.

Niederland, W. G. (1959b). 'Schreber: Father and Son.' *Psychoanal. Quart.* **28**: 151–69.

Nunberg, H. (1932, Eng. trans. 1955). *Principles of Psychoanalysis.* New York: International Universities Press.

Odier, C. (1948, Eng. trans. 1956). *Anxiety and Magic Thinking.* New York: International Universities Press.

Offer, D. (1969). *The Psychological World of the Teenager: A Study of Normal Adolescent Boys.* New York: Basic Books.

Offer, D. & Sabshin, M. (1966). *Normality: Theoretical and Clinical Concepts of Mental Health.* New York: Basic Books.

Onions, C. T. (ed.) (1966) *The Oxford Dictionary of English Etymology.* Oxford: Clarendon Press.

Parkes, C. M. (1969). 'Separation Anxiety: An Aspect of the Search for a Lost Object.' In M. H. Lader (ed.), *Studies of Anxiety.* Brit. J. Psychiat. Special Publication no. 3. Published by authority of the World Psychiatric Association and the Royal Medico-Psychological Association.

Parkes, C. M. (1970). 'The First Year of Bereavement: A Longitudinal Study of the Reaction of London Widows to the Death of their Husbands.' *Psychiatry* **33**: 444–67.

Parkes, C. M. (1971). 'Psycho-social Transitions: A Field of Study.' *Soc. Sci. Med.* **5**: 101–15.

Parkes, C. M. (1972). *Bereavement: Studies of Grief in Adult Life.* London: Tavistock; New York: International Universities Press.

Peck, R. F. & Havighurst, R. J. (1960). *The Psychology of Character Development.* New York: Wiley.

Piaget, J. (1937, Eng. trans. 1954). *The Construction of Reality in the Child.* New York: Basic Books. Published in the UK under the title *The Child's Construction of Reality.* London: Routledge, 1955.

Preston, D. G., Baker, R. P. & Seay, B. (1970). 'Mother–Infant Separation in the Patas Monkey.' *Devl. Psychol.* **3**: 298–306.

Rank, O. (1924, Eng. trans. 1929). *The Trauma of Birth.* London: Kegan Paul.

Reinhardt, R. F. (1970). 'The Outstanding Jet Pilot.' *Amer. J. Psychiat.* **127**: 732–6.

Rheingold, H. L. (1969). 'The Effect of a Strange Environment on the Behaviour of Infants.' In B. M. Foss (ed.), *Determinants of Infant Behaviour*, Vol. 4. London: Methuen.

Rheingold, H. L. & Eckerman, C. O. (1970). 'The Infant Separates Himself from his Mother.' *Science* **168**: 78–83.

Ritvo, L. B. (1972). 'Carl Claus as Freud's Professor of the New Darwinian Biology.' *Int. J. Psycho-Anal.* **53**: 277–83.

Roberts, A. H. (1964). 'Housebound Housewives: A Follow-up Study of a Phobic Anxiety State.' *Brit. J. Psychiat.* **110**: 191–7.

Robertson, J. (1952). Film: *A Two-year-old Goes to Hospital* (16 mm., 45 mins.; guidebook supplied; also abridged version, 30 mins.). London: Tavistock Child Development Research Unit; New York: New York University Film Library.

Robertson, J. (1953). 'Some Responses of Young Children to the Loss of Maternal Care.' *Nurs. Times* **49**: 382–6.

Robertson, J. (1958a). Film: *Going to Hospital with Mother* (16 mm., 40 mins.; guidebook supplied). London: Tavistock Child Development Research Unit; New York: New York University Film Library.

Robertson, J. (1958b). *Young Children in Hospital*. London: Tavistock. Second edition, 1970.

Robertson, J. & Bowlby, J. (1952). 'Responses of Young Children to Separation from their Mothers.' *Courr. Cent. int. Enf.* **2**: 131–42.

Robertson, J. & Robertson, J. (1967–73). Film series, *Young Children in Brief Separation*:

No. 1 (1967). Kate, 2 years 5 months; in fostercare for 27 days.

No. 2 (1968). Jane, 17 months; in fostercare for 10 days.

No. 3. (1969). John, 17 months; 9 days in a residential nursery.

No. 4 (1971). Thomas, 2 years 4 months; in fostercare for 10 days.

No. 5 (1973). Lucy, 21 months; in fostercare for 19 days.

London: Tavistock Institute of Human Relations (Films available from Concord Films Council, Ipswich, Suffolk; and from New York University Film Library). Guides to the film series are available from the Tavistock Institute of Human Relations and New York University Film Library.

Robertson, J. & Robertson, J. (1971). 'Young Children in Brief Separation: A Fresh Look.' *Psychoanal. Study Child* **26**: 264–315.

Rosenberg, M. (1965). *Society and the Adolescent Self-image*. Princeton, N.J.: Princeton University Press.

Rosenblum, L. A. & Kaufman, I. C. (1968). 'Variations in Infant Development and Response to Maternal Loss in Monkeys.' *Amer. J. Orthopsychiat.* **38**: 418–26.

Roth, M. (1959). 'The Phobic Anxiety–Depersonalization Syndrome.' *Proc. R. Soc. Med.* **52**: 587–95.

Roth, M. (1960). 'The Phobic Anxiety–Depersonalization Syndrome and Some General Aetiological Problems in Psychiatry.' *J. Neuropsychiat.* **1**: 293.

Roth, M., Garside, R. S. & Gurney, C. (1965). 'Clinical–Statistical

References

Enquiries into the Classification of Anxiety States and Depressive Disorders.' In F. A. Jenner (ed.), *Proceedings of Leeds Symposium on Behavioural Disorders*. Dagenham, Essex: May & Baker.

Rowell, T. E. & Hinde, R. A. (1963). 'Responses of Rhesus Monkeys to Mildly Stressful Situations.' *Anim. Behav.* **11**: 235–43.

Ruff, G. E. & Korchin, S. J. (1967). 'Adaptive Stress Behavior.' In M. H. Appley & R. Trumbull (eds.), *Psychological Stress*. New York: Appleton-Century-Crofts.

Rycroft, C. (1968a). *Anxiety and Neurosis*. London: Allen Lane The Penguin Press.

Rycroft, C. (1968b). *A Critical Dictionary of Psychoanalysis*. London: Nelson.

Sandels, S. (1971). *The Skandia Report: A Report on Children in Traffic* (English summary). Stockholm: Skandia Insurance Co.

Sandler, J. (1960). 'The Background of Safety.' *Int. J. Psycho-Anal.* **41**: 352–6.

Sandler, J. & Joffe, W. G. (1969). 'Towards a Basic Psychoanalytic Model.' *Int. J. Psycho-Anal.* **50**: 79–90.

Scarr, S. & Salapatek, P. (1970). 'Patterns of Fear Development during Infancy.' *Merrill-Palmer Quart.* **16**: 59–90.

Schaffer, H. R. (1958). 'Objective Observations of Personality Development in Early Infancy.' *Brit. J. med. Psychol.* **31**: 174–83.

Schaffer, H. R. (1971). 'Cognitive Structure and Early Social Behaviour.' In H. R. Schaffer (ed.), *The Origins of Human Social Relations*. London & New York: Academic Press.

Schaffer, H. R. & Callender, W. M. (1959). 'Psychological Effects of Hospitalization in Infancy.' *Paediatrics* **24**: 528–39.

Schaffer, H. R. & Parry, M. H. (1969). 'Perceptual–Motor Behaviour in Infancy as a Function of Age and Stimulus Familiarity.' *Brit. J. Psychol.* **60**: 1–9.

Schaffer, H. R. & Parry, M. H. (1970). 'The Effects of Short-term Familiarization on Infants' Perceptual–Motor Co-ordination in a Simultaneous Discrimination Situation.' *Brit. J. Psychol.* **61**: 559–69.

Schapira, K., Kerr, T. A. & Roth, M. (1970). 'Phobias and Affective Illness.' *Brit. J. Psychiat.* **117**: 25–32.

Schatzman, M. (1971). 'Paranoia or Persecution: The Case of Schreber.' *Family Process* **10**: 177–207.

Schiff, W., Caviness, J. A. & Gibson, J. J. (1962). 'Persistent Fear Responses in Rhesus Monkeys to the Optical Stimulus of "Looming".' *Science* **136**: 982–3.

Schnurmann, A. (1949). 'Observation of a Phobia.' *Psychoanal. Study Child* 3/4: 253–70.

478

Schur, M. (1953). 'The Ego in Anxiety.' In R. D. Loewenstein (ed.), *Drives, Affects, Behavior*. New York: International Universities Press.

Schur, M. (1958). 'The Ego and the Id in Anxiety.' *Psychoanal. Study Child* 13: 190–220.

Schur, M. (1967). *The Id and the Regulatory Principles of Mental Functioning*. London: Hogarth.

Scott, J. P. & Fuller, J. L. (1965). *Genetics and the Social Behavior of the Dog*. Chicago: University of Chicago Press.

Scott, R. D. (1973a). 'The Treatment Barrier: 1.' *Brit. J. med. Psychol.* 46: 45–55.

Scott, R. D. (1973b). 'The Treatment Barrier: 2, The Patient as an Unrecognized Agent.' *Brit. J. med. Psychol.* 46: 57–67.

Scott, R. D. & Ashworth, P. L. (1969). 'The Shadow of the Ancestor: A Historical Factor in the Transmission of Schizophrenia.' *Brit. J. med. Psychol.* 42: 13–32.

Scott, R. D., Ashworth, P. L. & Casson, P. D. (1970). 'Violation of Parental Role Structure and Outcome in Schizophrenia: A Scored Analysis of Features in the Patient–Parent Relationship.' *Soc. Sci. Med.* 4: 41–64.

Sears, R. R., Maccoby, E. E. & Levin, H. (1957). *Patterns of Child Rearing*. Evanston, Ill.: Row, Peterson.

Seay, B., Hansen, E. & Harlow, H. F. (1962). 'Mother–Infant Separation in Monkeys.' *J. Child Psychol. Psychiat.* 3: 123–32.

Seay, B. & Harlow, H. F. (1965). 'Maternal Separation in the Rhesus Monkey.' *J. nerv. ment. Dis.* 140: 434–41.

Shand, A. F. (1920). *The Foundations of Character*. Second edition. London: Macmillan.

Shirley, M. M. (1942). 'Children's Adjustments to a Strange Situation.' *J. abnorm. soc. Psychol.* 37: 201–17.

Shirley, M. & Poyntz, L. (1941). 'Influence of Separation from the Mother on Children's Emotional Responses.' *J. Psychol.* 12: 251–82.

Shoben, E. J. & Borland, L. (1954). 'An Empirical Study of the Etiology of Dental Fears.' *J. clin. Psychol.* 10: 171–4.

Siegelman, E., Block, J., Block, J. & Lippe, A. von der (1970). 'Antecedents of Optimal Psychological Development.' *J. consult. clin. Psychol.* 35: 283–9.

Smith, J. Maynard (1966). *The Theory of Evolution*. Second edition. Harmondsworth, Middx: Penguin Books.

Snaith, R. P. (1968). 'A Clinical Investigation of Phobias.' *Brit. J. Psychiat.* 114: 673–98.

Spencer-Booth, Y. & Hinde, R. A. (1967). 'The Effects of Separating

References

Rhesus Monkey Infants from their Mothers for Six Days.' *J. Child Psychol. Psychiat.* **7**: 179–97.

Spencer-Booth, Y. & Hinde, R. A. (1971a). 'Effects of Six Days Separation from Mother on 18- to 32-week-old Rhesus Monkeys.' *Anim. Behav.* **19**: 174–91.

Spencer-Booth, Y. & Hinde, R. A. (1971b). 'The Effects of 13 Days Maternal Separation on Infant Rhesus Monkeys compared with those of Shorter and Repeated Separations.' *Anim. Behav.* **19**: 595–605.

Spencer-Booth, Y. & Hinde, R. A. (1971c). 'Effects of Brief Separations from Mothers during Infancy on Behaviour of Rhesus Monkeys 6–24 Months Later.' *J. Child Psychol. Psychiat.* **12**: 157–72.

Sperling, M. (1961). 'Analytic First-aid to School Phobias.' *Psychoanal. Quart.* **30**: 504–18.

Sperling, M. (1967). 'School Phobias: Classification, Dynamics, and Treatment.' *Psychoanal. Study Child* **22**: 375–401.

Spiegel, J. P. (1958). 'Homeostatic Mechanisms within the Family.' In I. Galdston (ed.), *The Family in Contemporary Society.* New York: International Universities Press.

Spitz, R. A. (1946). 'Anaclitic Depression.' *Psychoanal. Study Child* **2**: 313–42.

Spitz, R. A. (1950). 'Anxiety in Infancy: A Study of its Manifestations in the First Year of Life.' *Int. J. Psycho-Anal.* **31**: 138–43.

Stayton, D. J. & Ainsworth, M. D. S. (1973). 'Individual Differences in Infant Responses to Brief Everyday Separations as related to Other Infant and Maternal Behaviors.' *Devl. Psychol.* **9**: 226–35.

Stendler, C. B. (1954). 'Possible Causes of Overdependency in Young Children.' *Child Devl.* **25**: 125–46.

Stott, D. H. (1950). *Delinquency and Human Nature.* Dunfermline, Fife: Carnegie UK Trust.

Strachey, J. (1958). Editor's Note to the Standard Edition of Freud's 'Psycho-analytic Notes on an Autobiographical Account of a Case of Paranoia.' *SE* **12**: 3–8.

Strachey, J. (1959). Editor's Introduction to the Standard Edition of Freud's *Inhibitions, Symptoms and Anxiety. SE* **20**: 77–86.

Strachey, J. (1962). 'The Term *Angst* and its English Translation.' Editor's Appendix to the Standard Edition of Freud's paper on Anxiety Neurosis. *SE* **3**: 116–17.

Sullivan, H. S. (1953). *The Interpersonal Theory of Psychiatry.* New York: Norton; London: Tavistock, 1955.

Suttie, I. D. (1935). *The Origins of Love and Hate.* London: Kegan Paul.

Talbot, M. (1957). 'Panic in School Phobia.' *Amer. J. Orthopsychiat.* **27**: 286–95.

Terhune, W. B. (1949). 'The Phobic Syndrome.' *Archs Neurol. Psychiat.* **62**: 162–72.

Thorpe, W. H. (1956). *Learning and Instinct in Animals.* Cambridge Mass.: Harvard University Press; London: Methuen. Second edition, 1963.

Tinbergen, E. A. & Tinbergen, N. (1972). 'Early Childhood Autism: An Ethological Approach.' Zugleich Beiheft 10 zur *Zeitsch. für Tierspsychologie.* Reprinted in Tinbergen, N., *The Animal in its World,* Vol. 2. London: Methuen, 1973.

Tinbergen, N. (1957). 'On Anti-predator Responses in Certain Birds – A Reply.' *J. comp. physiol. Psychol.* **50**: 412–14.

Tizard, B., Joseph, A., Cooperman, O. & Tizard, J. (1972). 'Environmental Effects on Language Development: A Study of Young Children in Long-stay Residential Nurseries.' *Child. Dev.* **43**: 337–58.

Tizard, J. & Tizard, B. (1971). 'The Social Development of Two-year-old Children in Residential Nurseries.' In H. R. Schaffer (ed.), *The Origins of Human Social Relations.* London & New York: Academic Press.

Tyerman, M. J. (1968). *Truancy.* London: University of London Press.

Ucko, L. E. (1965). 'A Comparative Study of Asphyxiated and Non-asphyxiated Boys from Birth to Five Years.' *Devl. Med. Child Neurol.* **7**: 643–57.

Valentine, C. W. (1930). 'The Innate Bases of Fear.' *J. genet. Psychol.* **37**: 394–419.

Waddington, C. H. (1957). *The Strategy of the Genes.* London: Allen & Unwin.

Waldfogel, S., Coolidge, J. C. & Hahn, P. (1957). 'The Development, Meaning and Management of School Phobia.' *Amer. J. Orthopsychiat.* **27**: 754–80.

Walk, A. (1972). An Objection to 'Parasuicide'. Letter in *Brit. J. Psychiat.* **120**: 128.

Walk, R. D. & Gibson, E. J. (1961). *A Comparative and Analytical Study of Visual Depth Perception.* Psychol. Monogr. 75, no. 519.

Walker, N. (1956). 'Freud and Homeostasis.' *Brit. J. Phil. Sci.* **7**: 61–27.

Warren, W. (1948). 'Acute Neurotic Breakdown in Children with Refusal to go to School.' *Archs. Dis. Childh.* **23**: 266–72.

Washburn, S. (1966). Statement quoted (p. 139) by William Dement in his comment on a paper by Frederick Snyder entitled 'Toward an Evolutionary Theory of Dreaming'. *Amer. J. Psychiat.* **123**: 121–42.

Washburn, S. L. & Hamburg, D. A. (1965). 'The Study of Primate Behavior.' In I. DeVore (ed.), *Primate Behavior.* New York & London: Holt, Rinehart & Winston.

References

Watson, J. B. & Rayner, R. (1920). 'Conditioned Emotional Reactions.' *J. exp. Psychol.* **3**: 1–14.

Webster, A. S. (1953). *The Development of Phobias in Married Women.* Psychol. Monogr. 67, no. 17.

Weiss, E. (1964). *Agoraphobia in the light of Ego Psychology.* New York: Grune & Stratton.

Weiss, M. & Burke, A. (1970). 'A 5- to 10-year Followup of Hospitalized School Phobic Children and Adolescents.' *Amer. J. Orthopsychiat.* **40**: 672–6.

Weiss, M. & Cain, B. (1964). 'The Residential Treatment of Children and Adolescents with School Phobia.' *Amer. J. Orthopsychiat.* **34**: 103–14.

Wenner, N. K. (1966). 'Dependency Patterns in Pregnancy.' In J. H. Masserman (ed.), *Sexuality of Women.* New York: Grune & Stratton.

Westheimer, I. J. (1970). 'Changes in Response of Mother to Child during Periods of Separation.' *Soc. Wk* **27**: 3–10.

Winnicott, D. W. (1941). 'The Observation of Infants in a Set Situation.' *Int. J. Psycho-Anal.* **22**. Reprinted in Winnicott, *Collected Papers.* London: Tavistock, 1958.

Winnicott, D. W. (1945). 'Primitive Emotional Development.' *Int. J. Psycho-Anal.* **26**. Reprinted in Winnicott, *Collected Papers.* London: Tavistock, 1958.

Winnicott, D. W. (1952). 'Anxiety Associated with Insecurity.' In Winnicott, *Collected Papers.* London: Tavistock, 1958.

Winnicott, D. W. (1955a). 'Metapsychological and Clinical Aspects of Regression within the Psycho-analytical Set-up.' *Int. J. Psycho-Anal.* **36**. Reprinted in Winnicott, *Collected Papers.* London: Tavistock, 1958.

Winnicott, D. W. (1955b). 'The Depressive Position in Normal Emotional Development.' *Brit. J. med. Psychol.* **28**. Reprinted in Winnicott, *Collected Papers.* London: Tavistock, 1958.

Winnicott, D. W. (1958). 'The Capacity to be Alone.' *Int. J. Psycho-Anal.* **39**: 416–20. Reprinted in Winnicott, *The Maturational Processes and the Facilitating Environment.* London: Hogarth; New York: International Universities Press, 1965.

Wolfenstein, M. (1955). 'Mad Laughter in a Six-year-old Boy.' *Psychoanal. Study Child* **10**: 381–94.

Wolfenstein, M. (1957). *Disaster.* London: Routledge.

Wolfenstein, M. (1969). 'Loss, Rage, and Repetition.' *Psychoanal. Study Child* **24**: 432–60.

Wolpe, J. (1958). *Psychotherapy by Reciprocal Inhibition.* Stanford, Calif.: Stanford University Press.

Wynne, L. C., Ryckoff, I. M., Day, J. & Hirsch, S. I. (1958). 'Pseudo-mutuality in the Family Relations of Schizophrenics.' *Psychiat.* **21**: 205–20.

Wynne-Edwards, V. C. (1962). *Animal Dispersion in relation to Social Behaviour*. Edinburgh: Oliver & Boyd.

Yarrow, L. J. (1963). 'Research in Dimensions of Early Maternal Care.' *Merrill-Palmer Quart.* **9**: 101–14.

Yerkes, R. M. & Yerkes, A. W. (1936). 'Nature and Conditions of Avoidance (Fear) Response in Chimpanzees.' *J. comp. Psychol.* **21**: 53–66.

Zetzel, E. R. (1955). 'The Concept of Anxiety in relation to the Development of Psychoanalysis.' *J. Amer. psychoanal. Ass.* **3**: 369–88.

Index

By Lilian Rubin, M.A.

(*Note: An asterisk denotes inclusion in the list of references*)

Index

Index

Index

'emotional' absence, of mother, 43

*English, H. B., 147–8

environment of evolutionary adaptedness, 106, 173

Eric, case of, 321–2

escape behaviour, 115, 121

*Estes, H. R., Haylett, C. H. and Johnson, A., 302, 305, 321

ethological approach to fear, behaviour, 101–216

*Evans, P. and Liggett, J., 353

Evolution: The Modern Synthesis (Huxley), 451

evolutionary perspective, 50, 106–7, 109–11, 416, 425, 449–53

experience
  availability of attachment figures, 235–6, 241
  cases of overdependency and spoiling, 283
  cases of school refusal, 312–13
  determination of working models, 241–3
  susceptibility to fear, 214–15, 228
  see also family experience

experimental studies
  fear, 137–41, 160–65
  separation, 60–74, 83–98, 401–4

exploration, 51, 53, 66, 88, 165, 166, 262, 397–8, 402–4, 406

*Fagin, C. M. R. N., 255–6

*Fairbairn, W. R. D.
  on agoraphobia, 338
  on frustration and aggression, 294, 295
  on mature dependence, 408
  on role of experience, 241

on separation anxiety, 49, 52, 276, 446–7

on threats, 249

falsification, of family context, 357–65

familiar companions and siblings, 29, 35–6, 147, 176–9

familiar environment, 87, 94, 127, 166, 176–81

familiar possessions, 28, 35, 147

family context, suppression of, 357–65

family experience
  of adolescents and young adults, 373–96
  and agoraphobia, *see* family interaction patterns
  and animal phobias, 331–2
  and overdependency, 278–83
  and personality development, 242–3, 366–410, 412, 415–16, 418–19
  and school refusal, *see* family interaction patterns
  sector studies of life-cycle, 368–9
  sources of information, 369–70
  and susceptibility to fear, 214–15, 243
  of young children, 396–406
  see also personality development

family interaction patterns
  and agoraphobia, 342–52, 360
  consistency of, 406, 417
  and forecasts of behaviour of attachment figures, 241
  and personality development, 379–82, 383–8, 398–401
  and school refusal, 300, 303–24, 360
  and social class, 388–9

490

Index

Index

Index

Index